Distributed Work

Distributed Work

edited by Pamela Hinds and Sara Kiesler

The MIT Press
Cambridge, Massachusetts
London, England

This book was set in Sabon by SNP Best-set Typesetter Ltd.

Printed and bound in the United States of America.

Library of Congress Cataloging-in-Publication Data

Distributed work / edited by Pamela Hinds and Sara Kiesler.
    p.   cm.
  Includes bibliographical references and index.
  ISBN 0-262-08305-1 (hc. : alk. paper)
  1. Division of labor. 2. International division of labor. 3. Teams in the workplace.
4. Communication in management—Technological innovations. 5. Computer networks.
6. Globalization. I. Hinds, Pamela. II. Kiesler, Sara, 1940–
HD51 .D57 2002
658.4′036—dc21   2001056237

To Herbert A. Simon, 1916–2001

Contents

Foreword

The chapters in this book breathe fresh air into a critical area of research: the increasing geographical distribution of work enabled by shifts in the world economy, increasing investments in new information technologies and changing expectations about how people will use these technologies to carry out their work and engage with their colleagues. Such research is critical if we care about high-quality worklife, organizational productivity, innovation, collaboration, learning, and knowledge generation. Can work be effectively carried out at a distance? If so, how should that work be managed, supported, and carried out? What technologies are useful, and at what point? And what is lost or gained when we embrace these changes in our workplaces? While research on transformations in the workplace related to information technologies has been carried out for several decades, this book represents a significant leap in the development of an overarching multidisciplinary framework for carrying out this work. With this book, the field has a new starting place for understanding how information technologies interact with the various dimensions of work relationships at a distance, for example, with ambiguity, proximity, awareness, know-how, trust, control, knowledge sharing, and leadership.

Over the past fifteen years, the Computation and Social Systems (CSS) Program (formerly called Information Technology and Organizations) at the National Science Foundation has been interested in developing new knowledge about collective phenomenon and social action. This book and the workshop that helped produce it were funded by CSS to bring together researchers from various disciplines— computer science, information systems, communications, industrial relations, social sciences, human-computer interaction, and others—who work on these important topics. Multidisciplinary research is critical to further our understanding of distributed, collective action and how it can be supported by information technologies.

The editors, Pamela Hinds and Sara Kiesler, have produced a book that makes a serious intellectual contribution to this field of inquiry. Their guidance and persistence made this book possible.

C. Suzanne Iacono
Information and Intelligent Systems Division
Computer and Information Sciences and Engineering
National Science Foundation

Preface

Technological advances and changes in the global economy are motivating and enabling an increasing geographic distribution of work. Today, the geographic distance between an average pair of workers is increasing in industries ranging from banking, to wine production, to clothing design. According to Bureau of Labor surveys of workers, more people worked for an employer with more than one location in 1998 (61.8 percent) than in 1979 (52.3 percent). Many workers today communicate regularly with coworkers at a distance; some monitor and manipulate tools and objects at a distance. Work teams are spread across different cities or countries. For example, research and development laboratories are increasingly deploying labs in countries other than the home of their headquarters (Brockhoff 1998), and software development teams increasingly are composed of programmers from around the globe (Carmel 1999). Joint ventures and multiorganizational projects are pervasive and entail work in many places. Complex work arrangements involving long-distance commuting and multiple employers are becoming commonplace. Some spectacular examples—ranging from the Hudson's Bay Company's fur trading empire in the seventeenth century to the recent development of the Linux computer operating system—suggest that distributed work arrangements can be innovative, flexible, and highly successful.

Nonetheless, geographically distributed work has always presented challenges to the conduct of work and personal life. Distributed work can change the way people communicate, how they organize themselves and their work, and the manner in which they live. Research from over thirty years ago to the present suggests that physical proximity can have powerful and positive effects in everyday life as well as in science, government, and business (Sykes, Larntz, and Fox 1976). Moreover, proximity has proven to be hard to simulate through modern technologies such as videoconferencing.

Given the benefits of proximity and collocation, organizations would seem to face some major hurdles when the work is distributed rather than collocated. What are the forces favoring distributed work arrangements? There are many. In mergers of companies or acquisitions of new companies, it may be infeasible to bring all employees to a single site, perhaps because key personnel refuse to move or perhaps because of the expense involved in orchestrating a move. To leverage expertise from these multiple sites, companies often form cross-site project groups and consultations. This is possible when jobs and professions use cognitive and social skills that can be practiced anywhere and the work process can proceed without close supervision.

Some organizations choose to distribute work geographically to acquire otherwise unavailable expertise, perhaps by hiring or contracting with workers who prefer to live in the distant location. Carmel (1999) describes a software development project for which the organization scoured the globe to find a few people with the required expertise. Because workers could not be uprooted, a team was formed with experts working together across four continents. In addition to increasing access to expertise, organizations can reduce costs by tapping into the lower-cost labor supply in developing countries.

Some organizations distribute work purposely as a way to establish a presence in multiple locations and increase the global appeal of their products. For example, LM Ericsson achieves a more global product by having members of product development teams located on multiple continents collaborate on actual designs (Mayer 1998). Organizations also can reduce the time required to bring products to market and the time required to trouble-shoot customer problems by using globally distributed teams. For example, Pape (1997) described a team at Verifone that worked on a customer problem around the clock by handing it off from team members in San Francisco to team members in Singapore and then to team members in Greece, so that they could deliver a solution in twenty-four hours.

Workers themselves may choose distributed work because of external incentives and priorities. For example, to promote innovative science, the National Science Foundation has been offering financial support for multidisciplinary collaborations—scientific or technical groups whose members have diverse skills and disciplinary or professional backgrounds that are applied to their collaboration (see Goodwin 1996). These collaborations can range from dyads or partnerships, to small teams, to huge projects of 100 members or more.

These and many other factors, are motivating the rapid expansion in the amount of distributed work. However, neither the phenomenon of distributed work, nor its causes and effects, are clearly understood. In contrast to the detailed statistics that the U.S. government collects and analyzes about other work conditions, it has no direct measure of the geographic distribution of workers within organizations, the mobility of workers in their jobs, or the reliance of organizations on communications and computer technologies to get work done across distance.

In 1994, a group of scientists and engineers convened to discuss research on distributed work and ways to facilitate basic technologies and applications for distributed work (see Committee on Telecommuting and Technology 1994). This group worked mainly on a research agenda that would encourage appropriate technological support for distributed work in teams and better understanding of the processes of distributed work. In the ensuing years, technological and economic change, as well as new studies of distributed work, suggested that distributed work is even more varied and complex than was envisioned five years ago.

Research on distributed work is being conducted by psychologists, sociologists, anthropologists, historians, computer scientists, economists, and others. These scholars are located with disciplinary programs as well as cross-disciplinary programs in information systems, cognitive science, organizational behavior, human-computer interaction, industrial engineering, and other hybrid fields. Because of their diverse backgrounds and separate venues for publication and research peer groups, there have been few opportunities for these researchers to meet and work together to understand distributed work from a broader perspective. Our objective in this project was to provide a forum for researchers from many fields to exchange ideas and present research on distributed work. A group of the authors met for this purpose at a workshop in Carmel, California, in August 2000 to share papers and ideas.

One can understand distributed work on many levels: at the individual level, as on stress, family life, and careers; at the group and organizational levels, as on communication, innovation, and effectiveness; and at the industry and societal levels, as on regional economies and the maintenance of community. The main topic in this workshop was particularly the group and organizational aspects of distributed work.

This book, based on the papers presented at the workshop, is a compendium of essays and research reports representing a variety of fields and methods. It is intended primarily for researchers and others who seek to understand the nature of distributed work groups and organizations, the challenges inherent in distributed work, and ways of enabling and organizing more effective distributed work. Through this work, we hope to spur more research on this topic and encourage debate on the design of technologies for and policies relating to distributed work. The chapters are organized to begin with a historical perspective on distributed work, starting in ancient times. We then follow with a collection of four chapters on proximity and collocation to provide a basis for comparing distributed work with collocated work. The next six chapters address the group dynamics and social processes involved in distributed work. We then present four chapters that describe factors associated with successful distributed work. Finally, two chapters present research on distributed work in one domain, collaborative scientific research.

Because of space limitations, much excellent research and some entire areas of work are not represented here. We do not include studies of the effects of distributed work on people's personal lives. For example, we do not include a chapter on workers who are required to travel extensively and often work on the road. This choice was partly motivated by a dearth of research on this topic. We also do not include chapters addressing industrial organization—changes in the nature of industries and economies—because that literature is too large a domain of inquiry. Nor do we include chapters on telecommuting or telecommuters. We believe that this work has been reasonably well covered elsewhere. Many chapters discuss technologies to support distributed work, but this is mainly a book designed to foster understanding of what distributed work entails rather than to understand technology itself.

Several cross-cutting questions about distributed work arise in the book and suggest where promising research on distributed work is headed. One question concerns the organization and management of distributed work and distributed workers. Starting with the two historical chapters (1 and 2), many other chapters in the book describe alternative ways that distributed work is organized and managed. Many of the authors discuss divisions of labor, incentives, methods for controlling group members, ways of facilitating interaction among distant workers, and ways of monitoring performance. From these discussions, it seems clear that much remains to be learned, but that research on the organization of distributed work is emerging as an exciting and fruitful domain of inquiry.

Effective strategies for organizing and managing distributed work may depend in part on the type of work being conducted. A question one can draw from the chapters concerns the role that the type of work plays in determining the success of distributed work arrangements. The types of work represented in this book range from soldiering and missionary work (chapter 1) to project management (chapters 2, 7, 13, 16) to field engineering and support (chapter 15), to secretarial work (chapter 10) and scientific collaborations (chapters 6, 17, and 18). The authors report both positive and negative aspects of distributed work. However, to varying degrees, all of these domains are populated by professionals who can operate to a large extent locally and autonomously. Further, few empirical comparisons are made to collocated workers in the same domain, so it is difficult to determine the effect of distribution on different types of work. Some types of work may be more effective when distributed than when collocated. For example, in chapters 17 and 18, we find some evidence that distant scientific collaborations may be more productive than collocated collaborations. The reason for this difference is important to discern. We need to study more kinds of collaborations over time and observe more varieties of distributed work in context to know the answer to this question.

A third question arising from this collection of work is whether social relationships in distributed work are as important as they are in collocated work. Early chapters in the book point to the virtues of collocated work, one of which is that it fosters social ties. To what extent do group activities, such as agreeing on goals and passing along information, depend on people's social contacts and ties to each other or to the group, that is, to their social networks and group identities? Many organizations are successfully distributing workers who never meet face-to-face and have a limited social relationship with their colleagues. For example, the Linux community described by Moon and Sproull (chapter 16) is wonderfully productive, but many members have never met. We can expect advances in theory and practice in distributed work to come from research on the nature of social ties in electronic work groups and organizations, and on their role in the interactions and effectiveness of distributed workers.

Finally, many authors in this book address the question of whether and how technology can support distributed work. The authors are not agreed on this question, and particularly on whether technology can make it possible for all kinds of work to be distributed successfully. However, many authors discuss the requirements of new technology to support distributed work and workers—for example, the kinds of awareness technology should help sustain (chapter 13), the varieties of social interaction that it should promote (chapter 4), and the infrastructure it should provide for social interaction and exchange, not simply instrumental exchanges of information (chapters 14, 16, and others). From the interest of the authors, their many citations to recent conferences and literature and the technologies represented in the studies, research and development of technologies to support distributed work seems to be thriving.

Acknowledgments

Through the support of the Computation and Social Systems Program of the National Science Foundation, 0000566, we were able to host a workshop for most of the authors represented in this book to present their work, review one another's papers, and discuss directions for future work in this field. Suzanne Iacono provided many valuable suggestions and ideas. Lawrence M. Greene drew the cover illustration of picnickers discussing a project over lunch. Mark Mortensen handled workshop logistics. Jonathan Cummings designed and maintained the Web site for the workshop and volume. Mary Scott made all financial arrangements. P. N. wishes to thank Mark Diel for his support during the development of the book. Both of us wish to acknowledge the contributions of Larry, Moe, Pilar, Tai, and Mauser, especially to their persistent reminders of the value of collocation.

References

Brockhoff, K. (1998). *Internationalization of research and development.* New York: Springer.

Carmel, A. (1999). *Global software teams: Collaborating across borders and time zones.* Upper Saddle River, NJ: Prentice Hall.

Committee on Telecommuting and Technology. (1994). *Research recommendations to facilitate distributed work.* Washington, DC: National Academy Press.

Goodwin, Charles (1996). Transparent vision. In E. Ochs, E. A. Schegloff, and S. A. Thompson (eds.), *Interaction and grammar* (370–404). Cambridge: Cambridge University Press.

Mayer, M. (1998). *The virtual edge: Embracing technology for distributed project team success.* Newton Square, PA: Project Management Institute.

Pape, W. (1997). Group insurance. *Inc, 19,* 29–31.

Sykes, R. E., Larntz, K., and Fox, J. C. (1976). Proximity and similarity effects on frequency of interaction in a class of naval recruits. *Sociometry, 39,* 263–269.

Distributed Work

"*Grab some lederhosen, Sutfin. We're about to climb aboard the globalization bandwagon.*"

I
History of Distributed Work

When we embarked on this project, many colleagues reminded us that distributed work is not a new phenomenon. The two chapters in this part provide historical examples of distributed work in centuries when computers and modern transportation and communication technologies did not exist. These examples offer many lessons to us as we try to understand new forms of distributed work enabled and encouraged by technology.

John King and Robert Frost, in chapter 1, argue that people in ancient times invented ways of stabilizing information and agreements—money, written contracts, and so forth—so that exchanges could be made without ongoing negotiation and surveillance. They address a major issue in understanding distributed work: the extent to which it requires clear, precise exchanges of information across distance. The authors present arguments for ambiguity. Institutions, names, and principles can provide a rubric under which local adaptations and flexible behaviors can take place.

Michael O'Leary, Wanda Orlikowski, and JoAnne Yates, in chapter 2, present a fascinating case study of the Hudson Bay Company, which for a century and a half conducted trade across two continents. They show how the management practices and organization of the company created mechanisms for managing work despite the vast distances that stood between the headquarters offices in London and the traders in the New World. This chapter sets the stage for many of the chapters to come, in which issues of trust and control arise in distributed work.

1

Managing Distance over Time: The Evolution of Technologies of Dis/Ambiguation

John Leslie King and Robert L. Frost

The management of distance is as old as work itself. Successful management of distance requires a careful balancing of disambiguation and ambiguation in the construction of meaning among disparate parties in collaboration. We argue that current efforts to develop technology for improved management of distance concentrate almost exclusively on improving means of disambiguation. This strategy overlooks the subtle but crucial role of ambiguation in maintaining shared understanding while allowing local discretion. We explore four successful technologies of dis/ambiguation that have evolved over centuries: writing and money as examples of disambiguating technologies, the doctrinal traditions of the Roman Catholic Church, and the creation of constitutional government as examples of ambiguating technologies.

The management of distance is an ancient art. Hunter-gatherers moved ever outward to forage what nature provided. Herders moved their flocks among pastures. Fixed agriculture eliminated the need to chase after food, and when done successfully, it created sufficient surplus to allow for more complex social orders of specialization. Growing the crops was only part of the necessity; getting them to market was the other. Trade in agricultural commodities and other goods dates back at least four thousand years, and trade hinges on the management of distance. The industrial revolution altered the management of distance yet again, moving people from their households to factories. Some, like the farm girls of New England who labored in the textile mills along the fall lines of rivers, literally moved from home to work. Countless others in cities commuted from their homes to the manufactories that employed them daily. The industrial revolution also spawned advances in transportation that enabled large-scale sourcing of raw materials for mass production and corollary systems of mass distribution. There has never been a time since humans became human when the management of distance was far from a daily concern.

New technologies are changing important aspects of how we live and work and, among them, the ways we manage distance. However, the management of distance has always required far more than technical artifacts. It has required as well techniques, social conventions and norms, folkways and mores, organizational structures, and institutions. All of these are technologies in the broad sense of methods or mechanisms of management. If contemporary efforts to reconceptualize the management of distance in the information age are to be fruitful, it pays to reflect on the underlying nature of past strategies for managing distance.

In this chapter, we argue that approaches to the management of distance have been built largely around the need to handle ambiguity across temporal, geographic and social distance. Handling ambiguity is a complex and nuanced matter. Current research on the social aspects of technology (see, for example, chapters 5, 6, and 10) emphasizes disambiguation, making clear what is meant and intended across distance. Less attention has been paid to ambiguation—the effort to keep meaning and intent vague across distance. We use historical analysis to demonstrate that both facets of ambiguity management have been key challenges to managing distance.

Our argument begins with the discussion of ambiguity—why in some cases it is a problem and why in others it is a solution. We then examine the mechanisms for managing ambiguity that enabled the first true collaborations over long distance— regional trade and empire. These show that careful handling of ambiguity is required to balance the local and the global. To illustrate technologies of disambiguation, we discuss the development of writing and the establishment of money. To illustrate technologies of ambiguation, we examine the doctrinal practices of the evangelical arm of the Roman Catholic Church and the creation of constitutional government. We close with some observations that might be of use to contemporary students of the problem of managing distance.

The Construction of Ambiguity

It is tempting to assume that the primary objective in improving the management of distance is to improve the precision and veracity of communication: to "get it right." We acknowledge the importance getting it right in many cases, as when exchange students going to another country are coached to modify their behavior so as not to give offense in their host culture. Much trouble in work across distance could be avoided if simple mistakes in understanding and interpretation were eliminated by making text and context more precisely coupled across distance. However, the value of precision does not obviate the importance of what we call constructive ambiguity that shows up in all cultures. Perhaps the iconic instance of this is located in seduction rituals that would be crippled without a bit of useful vagueness. The significance of constructive ambiguity can be seen in many other important venues.

Rituals of ceremonial robing that occurred across central Asia in the Middle Ages created a loose set of meanings that served to please all parties in an environment where acts of flattery, degradation, and subservience could be read in divergent ways among very different cultures (Gordon 2001). Giving a robe could be viewed as creating a subservient state on the part of the recipient, or inversely, as proof of the fealty of the giver. This eerily ambiguous ritual facilitated statesmanship, setting a context in which concrete negotiations and alliances could proceed. The purpose of the ritual was to shape a new context and make a new social space in which very different parties could meet and transcend barriers of language, culture, and religion. Less precise information about how to do things sometimes makes it possible to get better results in work across geographic distances that is intended to unite people separated by differences in culture, nationality, gender, race, and so forth.

Technologies of Disambiguation: Writing and Money

Two technologies have played powerful roles in enabling work across distance by disambiguating communication. One is writing, which was essential in facilitating regional trade and establishing robust empires. The other is money, which allowed the normalization and rapid expansion of trade over vast distances. Both provided a fixity to meanings across space, allowing a shorthand that relieved users from having to reframe endlessly the meanings of messages and markets. Each afforded mechanisms whereby meanings separated by space become clearer and spatially separated cognitive commmunities could be reliably built.

Writing and money are broad categories of disambiguating technologies, but for purposes of illustration, we focus on the more precise technologies of texts and coins. Text is the creation of a concrete representation on some medium (e.g., paper) of abstract symbols that refer to something concrete—in the world of things, ideas, feelings, and so forth. Coins made of valuable metals carry value in themselves, in both their metallic content and their inscriptions. Texts and coins act as warranted tokens that carry specific content. Text has an author and often has the more complex authentication of a publisher. A coin is the product of a mint that is a basic institution of almost any state. Such warranting provided by texts and coins implicitly avoids intermediation: the authenticity is not second-hand, but is present in the object.

Another powerful feature of texts and coins is that they allow content to be fixed. Once the seal of the author (e.g., a signature) is imprinted or the face of the coin (e.g., the likeness of the king) is struck, the content remains unambiguously fixed. Forgery and counterfeit are possible only because of this warranting and content fixation power. If the original text or the official coin did not exhibit such power, there would be no payoff in forging or counterfeiting. The warranting process also helps to ensure a shared space of sociocultural meanings on each side of the text or transaction. Even if meanings are never completely fixed and are open to interpretation, there is still value in getting as close as possible. Warranting reduces the skewing of intended meaning (Law 2000). Texts and coins are "immutable mobiles"—objects that can be moved across distance while retaining their content and meaning (Latour 1990).

Writing and Texts

The development of character and phoneme-based writing, the cuneiform, occurred sometime after 3000 B.C.E. in Sumer, at the north end of the Persian Gulf (Diamond 1997, Hobart and Schiffman 1998). Derivatives of Sumerian evolved into Phoenician, Hittite, and Hebrew, among other languages. The purpose of Sumerian was record keeping, which made it possible to keep the religious-bureaucratic hierarchy in line and track resources such as property. Sumerian used a document generation system (preformed, reverse-image characters pressed into damp clay) that produced authenticated or warranted texts. These texts made it possible for those in power in an administrative center to ensure that orders would not get lost or altered in transmission to the periphery.

There is little evidence of the social spread of the written Sumerian, but many assume it to have been restricted to the political and religious elite. This is in keeping with what is known of text production in Asia Minor and the Mediterranean more generally, which was closely tied to religious organization. Texts codified specific belief systems and thereby guaranteed social cohesion and empowered the priestly hierarchy. The abstractions of knowledge inherent in document making could travel far from their origin with minimal misunderstanding, provided the interpretive context at the receiving site was enough like that at the sending site. Restricting the ability to create and read religious texts in cultures that had a strong priestly-political elite proved socially useful. The texts of the Hebrews, Hittites, Minoans, and Sumerians strengthened the ideological and religious foundations of their authority systems. Restricted literacy helped maintain a strict social hierarchy in which dissent was blasphemy, and the literate elite defined the blasphemy.

Text was also instrumental in trade. The Phoenician writing system seems to have been the earliest rendition of an effective information technology for doing business over distances. Phoenician trade enclaves were spread throughout the Mediterranean watershed, from the Black Sea shores to Iberia. Well before the elaborate trade networks of Hellenic Greece or early Rome, Phoenician traders developed extensive agricultural and luxury goods markets, for example, moving amber from the Arabian Peninsula and grain from Sicily and the Black Sea. The Phoenicians were neither ethnically or religiously homogeneous; their identity derived from their shared commercial interests, reinforced by periodic face-to-face contacts and a powerful text-based information system of characters on papyrus. The Phoenicians constructed a large, collective social space in which trade proceeded effectively for centuries. However, written Phoenician did not disambiguate universally. It contained an important though implicit encryption system; the written language lacked vowels, making interpretation impossible to those who did not know the spoken language. This lack of transparency meant that the written language was incommensuable to outsiders. Text thus disambiguated meaning within the widely dispersed trade culture of the Phoenicians, but it was extremely ambiguous (in fact, incomprehensible) to those outside the culture. The Phoenican culture itself stopped at the boundaries of textual understanding. The role of writing in Phoenican trade made the Phoenicians one of the few cultures characterized almost entirely by the work they did.

The Phoenicians worked largely on a barter system; goods were exchanged in kind, and wealth accumulated largely through the accumulation of goods alone. Writing helped the Phoenicians keep track of their exchanges, but those exchanges were limited in a crucial way by the fact that they were entirely reflexive. No deal was possible unless a trader took away from the transaction goods equal in utility to himself as that which he gave in exchange. This system missed the benefits of transitivity, whereby an intermediary object of value could represent the proceeds of any past trade and be used to execute any future trade. Poor transitivity in exchange inhibited both physical and temporal economies. Traders had to burden themselves with goods taken in exchange, and they were eager to execute new trades that would unburden themselves of new cargo. The Phoenician trader lacked the mechanism of intermediary value we call money.

Money and Coinage

Exchange relationships are deeply important to the management of distance. As Jacobs (2000) has shown, exchanges of goods have facilitated specialization in production and helped to enhance economic efficiency through the division of labor. Exchange relationships help to develop social and cross-cultural ties and build alliances and trust. Indeed, these social uses of exchange probably predated economically motivated trades (Mauss 1990). The early social practice of exchanging women across clans and villages provided crucial genetic diversity, deepened cultural practices, and spurred innovation as women brought foreign experiences to their new communities. Gift giving was often accompanied by a rich set of trust-enhancing social rituals that created flatter social relationships while reinforcing social hierarchies. For example, potlatch ceremonies provided a means by which wealth was given away to demonstrate one's socioeconomic status and demand subservience on the part of the recipient. Another key exchange relationship was resource begging, where the recipient pledged fealty to the donor. Oaths of fealty in manorial society developed when a subordinate pledged fidelity, resources, and even the right of the lord to have sex with newly wed wives in return for protection.

These kinds of exchange relationships did not require money and were closely contained within geographically proximate communities. It was more difficult to move across geographic and sociocultural borders. The information context required for trade was lacking, and the terms of commitment among contracting parties were vague.[1] This shortcoming began to change when rare metal began to be used as a medium of exchange. At various moments, gold, a metal of minimal practical utility, came to stand transcendently for value in cultures ranging from the Levantine and Chinese to the Incan and Fulani. But money as we examine it did not really appear until the development of coins containing signifiers impressed on them. The cutting of gold into coins was not merely to aid convenience in carrying and counting, and the stamping of the emperor's likeness on the face of the coin was not merely aesthetic. Coins were powerful state-sponsored mechanisms for disambiguating critical aspects of exchange.

Coinage served to minimize internal incommensurability within the kingdom, thus constructing a polity and a kind of economy. Coins warranted the value of otherwise eminently debasable specie in a period long before chemical assays were possible.[2] The sovereign was the guarantor of exchange media; to debase a coin was to debase the person of the sovereign. Imperial sovereignty reduced errors in translating value among cultures within the realm and implied to traders that a solid basis for personal enrichment could be pursued through imperial expansion and political loyalty.

It is important to note that the underlying value of precious metal in coins is not a sufficient mechanism to ensure stable exchange over a distance. The demise of Classical empires in the Mediterranean saw the West slide into a long period of reliance on unmarked specie or irrelevantly decorated coinage from Byzantium. Unfortunately, the intrinsic value of precious metals was generally unfixed and unfixable. Surpluses and shortages due to the luck of mining efforts, which in themselves usually had little to do with economic activity overall, dictated terms in the marketplace. Low bullion supplies depressed economies, and high supplies inflated them—with neither supply factor being based on productivity. For example, a massive economic upheaval struck Europe in the fifteenth century with the influx of tons of bullion extracted from the New World. The resulting raging inflation dissolved the traditional relations between lords and serfs, guilds and consumers, sovereigns and subjects. The inflation spread across the continent at a dramatic rate. Similarly, a shortage of bullion in the late seventeenth century depressed the growing Atlantic economy and spawned counterfeiting and debasements of coins.

By the 1690s, John Locke had written essays on the value of solid money, arguing that only the value of the precious metal mattered.[3] His argument was strengthened when his friend Robert Boyle developed an innovative hydrometric method for assaying gold.[4] However, another illustrious contemporary, Isaac Newton, understood that coinage was a more complex matter. Newton had become the warden of the Royal Mint in the Tower of London and had instigated a great recoinage to reestablish the lost warrant of the English pound. Under the strictest security measures, Newton's mint produced new coins of sophisticated design, replete with gnurled rims to prevent clipping. This was an important strategy to ensure the consistency of the coinage, but it was not sufficient. Newton also became a terror to counterfeiters, sending many to the gallows. As Newton clearly saw, it was essential for stable money that the warrant of the state not be violated in any manner.

From that point until today, money has evolved from physical tokens of inherent value to symbolic tokens embodying the warrant of the issuer. The eventual consequence was paper money. Paper money began when Venetian traders and financiers on the Piazza San Marco started issuing notes of exchange and circulating IOUs. The "fiat" money was neither made of specie nor endorsed by a sovereign, but its value was a function of public perception of the trustworthiness of the issuer. This was a crucial step in the evolution from bullion-as-commodity to the contemporary lingua franca of the U.S. twenty dollar bill. The intervening historical process in the evolution of money can be characterized as a set of steps: (1) the matching of agreed-on values to various tokens, (2) the squaring up of the image on a coin with the metallic content within, (3) creation of the paper note backed on demand by precious metal (e.g., the U.S. silver certificate), and (4) the freeing of tokens from any reference to metal at all, backed only by the "full faith and credit" of an abstract entity, the sovereign nation (e.g., the Federal Reserve note). Today in the United States, coins have virtually no inherent value, being made of the cheapest metals that can do the job.

The West now enjoys a system of money (and, ultimately, of financial markets) based almost entirely on such trust. It is striking that such a thing was even possible: reputation is a thin reed on which to secure the value of exchange media, particularly outside the range of recognition of personal or organizational reputation. Nevertheless, money emerged as a powerful boundary object—an artifact for translating intentions and goals across disparate operant social groups (Star and Griesemer 1989, Star 1995, Bowker and Star 1999).

Technologies of Ambiguation: Roman Catholic Doctrine and Constitutional Governance

Technologies of disambiguation, such as writing and money, were critical in the development of dispersed societies. However, these technologies were appropriate only when the work to be done or exchanges to be made were rule bound and standardized. For more creative work that had to adjust to local contingencies, technologies of disambiguation proved to be too brittle because they were too precise. They worked when projecting reality onto the tabula rasa of a distant site, but they could not succeed if the task was to embrace and make use of the reality of the distant site. With the rise of great powers—Rome, the Catholic Church, nation-states—technologies of ambiguation developed that allowed for and took advantage of disparities in local practice, even under a centralized and hierarchical general authority. Two examples illustrate this point. One is over two thousand years old: the doctrinal structure of the Roman Catholic Church, which evolved into the world's first genuinely global service enterprise. The other is a little over two centuries old: the technology of constitutional government, which revolutionized the concept of governance following the Enlightenment.

Doctrinal Ambiguity in the Roman Catholic Church

How, in an age when transportation and communication were tediously slow, did the religious enterprise of the Roman Catholic Church create a highly coherent global presence that persists to this day? The Church spread far beyond the boundaries of great historical empires such as Rome and Byzantium, and it outlasted them. It is tempting to ascribe the success of the church to the establishment of a highly rigorous and strictly enforced hierarchy of authority and belief, reaching down from the pope to the most remote parish priest. In this model, the doctrines of the Church were articulated precisely and disseminated down through the hierarchy. A closer look at the history of the Church during its great evangelical expansion reveals that institutional survival was very much the result of a carefully constructed and maintained doctrinal ambiguity.[5]

The Christianity of the Roman Catholic Church proceeds from a base of scripture that itself contains a number of ambiguities. The core books of the New Testament, the gospels attributed to the four apostles Matthew, Mark, Luke, and John, contain numerous differences in accounts of the same events. Some quotations of Jesus, such as that in the Gospel of Matthew (19:24)—"it is easier for a camel to go through a needle's eye, than for a rich man to enter into the kingdom of God"— remain disputed today. The epistles of the New Testament, especially those written by the convert, Paul, contain passages that have confused many readers. Indeed, the Apostle Peter admonished his flock in one of his epistles (II Peter 3:15–16) to be careful with Paul's writings because they can be hard to understand. The last book of the New Testament, the Revelation of John, is filled with allusion and prophecy so obscure and complex that it has inspired argument among the most ardent believers for centuries. Given the history of Christianity, it seems doubtful that it is even possible to disambiguate the scriptures enough to please everyone. The success of the Roman Catholic Church at managing distance did not result from disambiguating the scriptures or other matters of doctrine. It resulted instead from the careful management of ambiguity in the interests of institutional strength and sustainability.

After the fifth century C.E., Rome's great army and its commercial law system vanished. Its most enduring legacy is the Roman Catholic Church, the world's oldest continuing institution. The Church today exemplifies an ornate hierarchy and a canonical set of unifying texts, but it was not always so. The crucial decades of early Christianity were marked by a near-absence of formal organization, and Church doctrine was supported by the circulation of a theologically divergent body of *samizdat*-style texts. Early Christianity was in many ways a strong oppositional subculture, with an emerging set of dissident social views. It called into sharp question existing practices and institutions, including the Judaic rabbinate and its subservient laic support structure, the sexist practices of both Judaic and Roman societies, the elitism of Roman and quisling Jewish authorities, the socioeconomic inequalities of ancient Palestine, and, of course, the imperial authority of an occupying army and political structure.

The adhesive of early Christian unity was a wonderfully ambiguous doctrine that appealed to diverse communities with disparate beliefs. To some communities, Christianity was a theology of social or political liberation; to others, it was an acceptance of the suffering of the world of the living in exchange for the promise of an eternal afterlife; and for a mystical few, it was separation from the world to seek the beauty of God. This multivalent doctrine held a powerful appeal for whoever heard it, for it offered a means of liberation and power regardless of political or social station. God was powerful and terrible yet loving and forgiving enough to have allowed the sacrifice of his only son to redeem the world. Access to God's good grace was literally as simple as accepting the doctrine and joining the fellowship, which explicitly excluded no one, no matter how wretched. Genuine (i.e., unforced) conversion began with the penitent's own experiences and religious beliefs, which were transformed by Christian doctrine into a abandonment of old ways and the acceptance of the new way. The ability of the Church to operate effectively over vast distances rested on the adaptation of doctrine to fit local settings while maintaining institutional loyalties through organizational enforcement and discipline.

Early Christian theology was not fixed and clear, and could not be made so. The epistles of Paul demonstrate that the various communities of Christians needed constant guidance and exhortation. Doctrinal schisms multiplied as the faith spread.

Holding the community of believers together required clarification and direction. At the same time, the fundamental faith of the Church rested on a set of mysteries that were, almost by definition, not amenable to precise description or explication. This apophatic mystical tradition was a powerful counterweight to the kataphatic efforts of the bishops, who had to maintain order and keep the faith together. The tension that resulted was recognized as essential to theology in the Church until at least the seventeenth century.

This recognition of the unresolvable tension was a great source of inspiration for early Church fathers such as Clement of Alexandria and Augustine of Hippo in their efforts to build a lasting institutional structure. Faith in core doctrines and effective working relationships with established secular authorities could be maintained simultaneously. Augustine's Cathoicized neo-Platonism created a strict boundary between affairs of spirit and the decadence of the world, in which the Church stood "above" the declining Roman Empire (and the emergent Europe) while remaining an integral part of it. The Church could enjoy considerable secular power without exposing itself to the dangers of fragile political authority, a legacy that remains to this day in the institutions of Western Europe. The tradition of dualism between secular and religious authority allowed dissenters to operate in the complicated interstices between the two, inviting each to adapt or wither. Berber Islam in medieval Spain followed a similar strategy and remained strong until ethnically cleansed by Ferdinand and Isabella in the late fifteenth century. In contrast, one can argue that Confucian China, Orthodox Russia, and Islamic Ottoman Turkey became brittle precisely because their unified religious-political systems meant that a crisis in either could bring down both. The Church's institutional survival and its amazing ability to get things done over thousands of miles, hundreds of years, and multitudes of sociocultural divides has been due to an inherent mystical bent, doctrinal flexibility, and mastery in negotiating a powerful—yet not entirely dominant—position within local spaces.[6]

This ambiguity was only part of a larger effort to balance consistency with diversity. The Church's uniform ritual practices were consistent, allowing a church member to enjoy fellowship a world away from home. The essence of the main celebration, mass, was and remains the avowed mystery of the Eucharist, in which bread and wine are transformed literally into the body and blood of Jesus. Belief in this transubstantiation requires believers to suspend other beliefs in favor of the mystery of the faith, creating a constructively ambiguous framework for forging partnerships and collective identities. Even today the ritual of mass is largely the same whether in an conservative *Opus Dei* parish or a revolutionary Latin American one. Ritual creates a sense of unity across vastly divergent groups. Similarly, when the Church speaks with one voice, it does so in powerful but broadly interpretable doctrinal catch-phrases. For example, when the Church reaffirms the "sanctity of life," it can unify around a core value while obscuring and sublimating profound and potentially fractious disagreements over the specifics of artificial birth control, abortion, and the death penalty.

The power of ambiguation to manage distance can be emphasized by the instances when disambiguation has resulted directly in challenges to the authority of the Church by believers within. The most graphic illustration of this remains the Reformation, in which increasing adherence by the Church hierarchy to its particular doctrinal views and (often corrupt) prerogatives compelled Martin Luther and a large fraction of the believers of Northern Europe to revolt against the authority of the papacy. The effects of the Reformation are still felt in Europe today, although it began four centuries ago. The Church has been at pains to manage ambiguity effectively since the Reformation. The difficulty of this challenge is illustrated well by the doctrine of papal infallibily, which, we argue, was probably an error on the side of disambiguation. To many who are unfamiliar with Church history, this doctrine seems a relic of the Middle Ages. In fact, it emerged in the 1870s.

The sociopolitical context of the creation of the doctrine offers instructive lessons. The Reformation deeply wounded the Church, and the remaining Church hierarchy took action to stop it in the Counter-Reformation. A key instrument in the Counter-Reformation was the Creed of the Council of Trent (1564), which sacralized the voice of the pontiff and Vatican Council. This doctrine dangerously embrittled the Church, for it could easily permit the pontiff to engage in doctrinal micromanagement of local affairs, annihilating the advantages of ambiguity-based local autonomy. Wiser heads adjusted this doctrine later, attempting to reintroduce some ambiguating nuance. Of special importance in this regard was an 1879 encyclical of Leo XIII (pope from 1878 to 1903), *Aeterni patris* ("On the Restoration of Christian Philosophy"), which adjusted the implications of the Council of Trent by insisting that faith is most reliably based on reason rather than dogma or authority (Pope Leo XIII 1879).[7] Nevertheless, Leo XIII's encyclical could not completely restore the balance because of an action of his immediate predecessor, Pius IX (pope from 1846 to 1878).

In 1870, Pius IX convened the First Vatican Council (Vatican I) to reaffirm the faith. During the council, there arose a major doctrinal dispute regarding the role of Mary, the mother of Jesus. Veneration of Mary had been well established in the church since the thirteenth century, manifesting itself first in the Cult of the Virgin (Warner 1976). Prior to 1870, details regarding Mary's role in the faith were handled largely on a local basis. During Vatican I, Pope Pius IX issued a specific doctrine on Mary that he made binding on all local communities. In doing so, he went far beyond Church traditions regarding the doctrinal role of the pope, declaring that his doctrine on Mary arose from "infallible" revelation. In essence, he declared that he and future popes could, on occasion, declare doctrine that was literally incapable of error. This claim was protested by many of the faithful, including American Catholics, who feared it would excite Protestant claims that Catholics were slavishly loyal to the pope.[8] Liberal theologians from Germany and France saw the measure as dangerous overreaching, but the measure passed the assembly of bishops (Hughes n.d.). Interestingly, and again on the side of ambiguity, popes since Pius IX have seldom used the authority of the infallible pronouncement. Most papal bulls are letters to the community of believers on issues the pope believes important and in need of clarification. They seldom carry the weight of an infallible doctrinal decree.

The Catholic Church has managed to remain institutionally adaptive across vast distances and over a very long time by the successful management of ambiguity. Medieval Catholicism grafted many non-Christian ideas into its doctrine, including geocentrism from Ptolemy, Platonic and (later) Aristotelian epistemology, Persian astrology, and Galenic nutritional theory. On one hand, it preserved its power in the presence of secular authorities by reminding the believers of their duty to defer to such authority. On the other hand, it powerfully shaped secular authority toward Church ends. Catholic dogma has generally been far less rigid than its detractors have claimed, at least over the very long term. The Church has been able to act quickly when core values are threatened and to bide its time with regard to issues that are more peripheral. The fact that the Church was able to wait over four hundred years to admit that Galileo was right suggests that it knew when its long-run interests were threatened and when they were not. Maintaining the balance has not been easy, but it has been done.

Perhaps the most stunning recent act of ambiguation in the Church was John XXIII's convening of the Second Vatican Council in 1962. Vatican II took several steps that reestablished a profound and humbling uncertainty in the Church. It relaxed the long-held doctrine that declared the Roman Catholic Church to be the only path of Christian salvation and brought leaders of other Christian denominations to an ecumenical council at the Vatican. The result was a necessarily ambiguated and therefore mutually acceptable joint declaration of shared faith. The very idea of the resulting ecumenical movement would have been impossible without selective and constructive ambiguation. Vatican II also affected the Church itself in a profound way by shifting the ritual of the mass from the universal Latin liturgy to the vernacular of local communities. This opened the most potent and ubiquitous experience of the faith to local character and charisma. In doing so, John XXXIII reasserted the ambiguity and dynamism that marked the early Church and created a bulwark against the efforts of centrists to control the details of the faith at the periphery.

Constructive ambiguity in Christian movements has not been the sole province of the Roman Catholic Church. What we today call fundamentalist Christianity arose from efforts to both disambiguate and ambiguate doctrine in the interest of Protestant Christian unity. The contemporary fundamentalist movement began in the first decade of the twentieth century among lay Christians who were deeply disturbed by the rise of "modernism" in established churches.[9] Modernism, in their view, substituted nonessential doctrine for essential Christian beliefs. They established a set of five "basic doctrines," adherence to which constituted true Christian belief: the doctrine of the Trinity, Jesus Christ as both God and man, the Second Coming of Jesus as foretold in scripture, salvation through faith in Christ, and the inerrancy of scripture. All other doctrinal issues were, by definition, not basic doctrines and therefore were unworthy of doctrinal dispute to the point of schism. The ambiguating character of these doctrines is arguably an important part of the rapid growth of fundamentalist Christianity in this century.

Constitutional Government

The Enlightenment spawned a deep desire for transparency in social and political relationships, with far-reaching consequences. Perhaps the most interesting was the implementation of its most potent insight—that power corrupts those who hold it—into the architecture of the institutional order that we now call constitutional government. The essence of constitutional government is at once disarmingly simple and deeply complicated. It is rooted in the idea of a social contract between those who govern and those who are governed and incorporates the pragmatic position that those who govern draw their power from the consent of the governed.

A constitution is a formal contract that stipulates the various roles to be played in the execution of governance by both the governors and the governed. The enactment of social contracts is not a new thing; elements of the social contract between governors and governed appear as early as the Code of Hammurabi and are clearly evident in the Hebrew scriptures, the writings of Confucius and Plato, and Roman commercial law. It is furthermore doubtful that any system of governance could long survive without at least implicit contracts in the form of social conventions, folkways, and so forth. However, the idea of a formal, written agreement binding together not just particular individuals but role holders is much more recent. Louis XIV's famous phrase, "*L'état, c'est moi,*" symbolized a relatively recent construction of personal power. The beginnings of such constitutional government are often traced to the signing of the Magna Carta in 1214, in which the feudal aristocracy of England imposed sixty-three specific restrictions on the authority of the English monarchy.[10] However, our purpose in this discussion is served by focusing on the constitutional structure of the United States.

The framers of this structure were deeply influenced by Enlightenment thinkers and took to heart the problematic of balancing the power of individuals against the power of the collective. They recognized that any government structure that would persevere and maintain the protection of individual rights would have to be very explicit in some respects and ambiguous in others. The ingenious solution they created to deal with this challenge rested on the insight that process and outcome could and should be separated, and the social contract created accordingly.

One of the most remarkable features of the U.S. Constitution is that it goes into great detail regarding the process by which decisions will be made, but it says virtually nothing about what those decisions should be. It dictates *how* to decide but says little about *what* to decide. The objectives of the Constitution are a tissue of ambiguous allusion. The Constitution embodies the goal of the Declaration of Independence: to ensure the citizenry, an ambiguous category itself, its "inalienable rights," including "life, liberty, and the pursuit of happiness." The Preamble to the Constitution references equally ambiguous ambitions: "to form a more perfect union, establish justice, insure domestic tranquility, provide for the common defence, promote the general Welfare, and secure the blessings of liberty." These are never defined, nor are any clues provided for how these objectives are to be interpreted. Rather, the Constitution reserves its explicit orders to stating exactly which role holders will make such decisions and exactly how such decisions will be made.

This was a brilliant strategy because it recognized the incontrovertible fact that all important governance decisions are deeply context specific. They cannot be decided in advance because it is impossible to see the future. In order to be effective at guiding the conduct of government, the Constitution had to be scrupulously careful not to infringe on the judgment of those to whom decision authority had been conferred. This opened up a wide space of ambiguity in which constitutionally elected or appointed decision makers could exercise their own discretion and not have to worry about running afoul of the social contract. At the same time, the hard-learned lessons about the corrupting influence of power persuaded the designers of the Constitution to divide power very carefully among constitutional officers in order to make it nearly impossible for any individual or group to gain a decisive advantage over the others.

Taken as a whole, the U.S. Constitution managed ambiguity in three ways. First, it strictly defined the authority and limits of authority of the central government and, with equal strictness, divided that authority among three branches. The executive branch would be responsible for executing all of the functions of the government but would be given no resources to execute them. In addition, the executive would be charged with the execution and enforcement of the laws promulgated by the central government but would have minimal authority to enact such laws. The legislative branch was given the sole authority to appropriate revenues for the execution of government functions, but it had no authority to direct those functions. In addition, the legislature had the ultimate authority to enact laws, even to the point of overriding the objections of the executive. This power included the authority to remove the executive from power if necessary. The legislature itself was divided into two chambers: a smaller chamber of individuals elected for relatively long terms to provide a stable deliberative body and advise the executive on key appointments and a large chamber of individuals elected for short terms to monitor and guide key workings of the overall legislature and to have primary authority over taxation. The judicial branch was given the exclusive authority to interpret the meaning of the law arising in disputes between the executive and the legislature, and to be the final interpreter of all legal texts. The judiciary alone was appointed for life terms, thus greatly reducing the power of the elected executive and legislature to influence judicial decisions.

The second mechanism for the management of ambiguity was the ratification of the circumstances that gave rise to the confederation. The union was created as a compact among separate colonies that had been under the dominion of the sovereign monarch of Great Britain. After gaining independence, the colonies were sovereign in their own right. The question before the framers of the Constitution was whether and in what ways these new states would subordinate themselves to a collective government. The Constitution deliberately and very carefully limited the jurisdiction of this collective government, specifically reserving all duties and powers not covered by the Constitution to the states and the people. This federated concept of government was the first fully elaborated and formalized government system built by design. The design disambiguated many important elements of the government but left deliberately vague others in order to devolve power and decision making as close to the local level as practical. The intent in this design was captured beautifully in Benjamin Franklin's observation that the purpose of the Constitution was to bring together those who fundamentally disagree with one another.

The third mechanism to manage ambiguity was the establishment of a formal and rigorous mechanism for modifying the Constitution. Unique among the other features of the Constitution, the amendment process requires action by both the national and state legislatures. It is instructive that the framers immediately used this process to amend the Constitution and establish the Bill of Rights. These ten rights disambiguated a set of key questions related to the power of the federal government. For the most part, they expressly limited the power of central government lawmaking in the areas of freedom of speech, freedom of the press, the establishment of religion, and so on. In an interesting arabesque, the framers created the Constitution to articulate the process of governing, leaving ambiguous direction as to what decisions should be made. They then reversed course and used the mechanism they had created to establish a set of strict limits on the government with regard to intrusion on individual rights. The first ten amendments were adopted almost upon the creation of the Constitution, but it took nearly 200 years to double the number of amendments. Excepting the perhaps frivolous cases of the eighteenth and twenty-first amendments (prohibiting alcohol and then repealing that prohibition), the history of constitutional amendments reflects a circumspect and sober reluctance to disambiguate further. The amendment process has been used mainly to adjust procedural matters (e.g., the Twenty-Second Amendment limiting the presidency to two consecutive terms and the Sixteenth Amendment enabling the income tax) or to establish a bold departure from past practice (e.g., the Thirteenth and Fifteenth amendments instrumental in abolishing slavery).

The instance of slavery provides a powerful illustration of the efficacy and risk in the constitutional effort to maintain ambiguity and resolve key issues at the local level. Slavery is today acknowledged to be the great tragedy of American history, and one for which the country has paid a dreadful price. But it is precisely the gravity of slavery that illustrates the power of deliberately maintaining ambiguity in the direction of decisions from the central government. Slavery was an established and arguably essential economic practice in a number of the original colonies. It is doubtful the Union could have formed had the colonies opposed to slavery insisted on national abolition in the 1780s. A significant number of the framers of the Constitution and the Bill of Rights were themselves slave owners, guided by the norms and conventions of their era. Some appeared to wrestle mightly with the morality of slavery, while others simply regarded the practice as part of the normal order of things.[11]

Abraham Lincoln expressed abolitionist sentiment, and he eventually became the Great Emancipator. Yet he struggled to preserve the Union prior to the Civil War by assuring the slave states that he had no intention of challenging the institution of slavery. Many of those who had bitterly opposed slavery refused to insist on a national mandate of abolition out of respect for the tradition of ambiguity established by the Constitution that left such matters to the states and to the people. Slavery was abolished only after the defeat of the slave states in terrible civil war. This war was fought in part over the issue of slavery, but many scholars argue that the more fundamental cause of the conflict was the need to determine once and for all whether states, having once joined the Union, were free to secede from it at will, as the southern states had done.[12] The Constitution had left ambiguous the question of whether secession was possible, and that ambiguity was resolved only through the abject defeat of the secessionists. It is hard to imagine what would have happened had the framers provided protocols for states to secede from the Union that were as clear and explicit as those they established for states to join the Union.

Managing Distance through Dis/Ambiguation

The ability to operate effectively across space, time, and divergent sociocultural contexts is one of the great triumphs of humans. This ability did not spring forth like Athena from the brow of Zeus, however. It was painstakingly created over centuries by the invention and deployment of technologies for selective disambiguation and ambiguation of critical issues, tasks, beliefs, values, and so on. Linguistic innovations allowed for a reliable codification of knowledge to be transmitted across distance, solidifying practice and enabling things to be done within and across sociocultural divides. Innovations in organizational structure and legal practice made it possible to perpetuate organizational and institutional efficacy, while at the same time permitting significant individual and group direction finding and task autonomy at the local level. Practices of warranting and legitimation, of ritual and liturgy, constructed social spaces in which people could do business without getting mixed up in disagreements about large issues (religion, metaphysics) or small ones (local politics, office squabbles). Successful management of dis/ambiguation, in short, allowed people to get down to work.

The concept of incommensurability suggests that information is not knowledge—that cultural and social differences result in errors of translation in transmitting knowledge. Context is important even though it is often not translatable, fungible, or movable. The invention of written text greatly facilitated the management of distance, and an even greater breakthrough occurred in the evolution of that dubious global leveler, money. At the same time, work over distance has been greatly facilitated by the establishment and maintenance of constructive ambiguity. The Catholic Church built a set of doctrines that could adapt to many different contexts. In so doing, it brought together diverse social and cultural actors who could communicate useful knowledge across space and time and create a common space in which many meanings did not have to be explained in order to proceed.

As we pursue the application of new information technologies to the management of distance, we should remind ourselves of the need to maintain ambiguity where it is necessary. A cautionary lesson from the modern penchant for disambiguation can be seen in the idealisms of Edward Bellamy and Thorstein Veblen and their predecessors in the royal societies of the eighteenth century. These men advocated the achievement of universalism through the emergence of transcendent systems of technocratic or scientific authority (Bellamy 1894, Veblen 1921). In their view, the laws of science, engineering, and economic modeling were objectively demonstrable and could be seen as such by all. These laws would provide a politically and epistemologically legitimate basis for universal translatability, and thus pave the way for a universally efficient and peaceful world. Despite the tremendous accomplishments of science and the other fruits of advancing knowledge, their cherished universalism remains an elusive dream.

The pitfall is not in the belief that new knowledge can be applied productively; that belief has been amply justified. Rather, it is in the confidence that knowledge per se can readily transcend the inherently ambiguous nature of things as we find them in the world. Much of the recent work in sociology of scientific knowledge and the social construction of technology suggests that claims of objective and universal knowledge—of the facticity of the world—almost always end up as little more than claims to make transcendental truth out of contingent local knowledge.[13] Audacious technical "solutions" to problems of ambiguity work well in some instances but not at all in others. Perhaps the most evident example of this is the crusade for standardization. It is incontestable that business picked up when a *livre* of wheat finally weighed the same in Rennes, Paris, and Aix-la-Chapelle. Standardization around the metric system, the British Thermal Unit, and even the norms of the Society of Automotive Engineers yielded huge dividends. Yet we often forget how tortuous are the routes by which such standardization is achieved. The word *steel* now has a seemingly transparent meaning, but standardizing that meaning was a long and difficult task (Misa 1995).

Standards are a two-edged sword. It is often forgotten that the fundamental purpose of any standard is to stop innovation. Of course, a sensible standard will stop only inefficient innovation around things that are good enough already (e.g., the configuration of a country's electrical outlets and plugs), freeing up resources for more important innovative efforts. But standards that are set too early, too narrowly, or by incomplete agreement among essential parties can direct innovation along less than optimal trajectories. An interesting example of an effort to avoid dysfunctionally preemptive standardization is the ISO 9000 effort to improve manufacturing quality control. The ISO 9000 strategy embodies some aspects of doctrine in the early Catholic Church and the structure of the U.S. Constitution. It sets a frame for making meanings rather than dictating the content of those meanings. Earlier ISO standards for things like film speeds and emulsions dictated what should be done. ISO 9000, by contrast, leaves local producers the discretion over how quality goods are to be manufactured. It makes what would otherwise be local knowledge of production characteristics commensurable by insisting on standards of documentation and transparency, without dictating that knowledge. ISO 9000 thereby facilitates the transfer of local knowledge along transparent vectors, revealing what is being included and excluded. Potential users of that knowledge can then proceed accordingly and on their own discretion. Knowledge does not travel well, but its parameters do. Broad standards of transparency can build cognitive communities that get things done.

Conclusion

The balance of this book focuses on contemporary issues of work at a distance, and especially the implications of emerging information technologies for facilitating such work. Although research into the affordances required to support this work is relatively recent, some telling lesssons have been learned that reinforce the importance of managing dis/ambiguation. A considerable body of work has demonstrated the relative advantages of physical collocation over physical separation in getting work done. Much of this work has concentrated on the role of communications in the coordination of work. Success in work at a distance hinges on communications that are as close as possible to the conditions of physical copresence. Most of this work has identified the crucial elements of communication to be the relative richness of the channel used. It is relatively easy to see how rich channels might facilitate the transmission of disambiguating information. After all, the very role of such information is to be as precise as possible to strike the right chord in the context of the receiver. It is often necessary for the sender to interact iteratively with the receiver to be sure the disambiguating information has been imparted correctly.

We suggest that a fruitful course of action lies in exploring rich channels for their potential in constructive ambiguation in the processes of routine work. Ambiguation is constructive only when the unambiguous and the ambiguous are mixed precisely. It is difficult to imagine seduction and courtship behavior without careful management of ambiguity. The objective cannot succeed unless the message is clear to the intended, but that intention must not be too overtly played, lest the intended break off the communication out of anxiety or disapprobation. In a more businesslike example, Forster and King (1995) show how the selective maintenance of ambiguity in the international air freight industry enables the role of key market-clearing factors such as freight consolidators. They point out that contemporary information technologies developed to improve the coordination of trade among shippers, agents, and carriers have frequently met with disappointment due to lack of facility for selective information hiding essential to the welfare of parties throughout the value chain. Despite many efforts to build information infrastructure in this specialized business, transactions often default to direct personal communications between the parties. One wonders in this context how successful Covisent, the auto industry's effort to implement business-to-business in parts purchasing, will be in supplanting the usually cozy, face-to-face relations among suppliers and purchasers.

We must take seriously the need for the management of ambiguity in efforts to build information infrastructure to support work at a distance. At minimum, we urge that every effort to create such infrastructure incorporate a careful assessment of the role of dis/ambiguation in the work to be supported. In many cases, failure to attend to these needs will cause a failure of the infrastructure to yield desired results. At minimum, the resulting infrastructure is likely to miss many of the benefits that could have been realized.

Notes

We thank Pamela Hinds, Sara Kiesler, Joel Mokyr, John Staudenmaier, and JoAnne Yates for their help.

1. This set of issues echoes the Enlightenment debates over the notion of "contractability" in the social contract theories of Hobbes and Locke. Many Tory supporters of the Hobbesian rendition of contract theory argued that suffrage could never be extended to "servants" (workers) because the latters' dependence on the economic whims of others made them unfree and thus unable to contract reliably. On this score, and for a critique of the "liberal myth" of the possibility of political democracy without economic democracy, see Reddy (1987, chap. 3).

2. Assays became the eventual definitive test of the value of coins, but this was not until centuries after coins became common. Robert Boyle is quoted by Simon Schaffer (2000) to have written that after assaying, "If I find it counterfeit, neither the prince's image or its inscription, nor its date (how ancient soever) nor the multitudes of hands through which it has passed unsuspected will engage me to receive it" (6). Boyle later became the executor of Locke's estate.

3. In his pamphlets on money written in the 1680s, John Locke (n.p.) insisted on the criticality that money's metallic content as a commodity was the source of its value, regardless of the image on the coin.

4. Schaffer (2000) described Boyle's assay method as an almost theatrical ritual—a "choreography of credit and measurement" (27).

5. Some of the ideas explored here can be found in Brytting (1986), although his focus is on organizational hierarchy and centralization.

6. This is a subtle issue and can swing both ways. It has been argued that Pope Pius XII's alleged acquiescence to Nazism was a failure of the Church to stand up for core values related to human dignity, a drift too far in the direction of local discretion (Cornwell 1999). Similarly, it has been argued that Pope John Paul II's opposition to liberation theology has eroded the papacy's institutional legitimacy in regions where poor and often indigenous people have been brutally persecuted which constitutes insufficient local discretion (Barnes 1999). Also, there are occasions when efforts to convert local "knowledge" into transcendent, universal truth have raised questions about the Church's legitimacy, as with Pope John Paul II's use of the 1917 Fatima revelations to claim victimhood of Catholics and especially priests in the twentieth century (Wills 2000).

7. Leo XIII was not moving leftward; see his encyclical "On the Evils of Socialism."

8. Whether this fear was realized, it is worth noting that many outside the Church mistakenly believe that the doctrine covers all of the pope's official doctrinal pronouncements. In fact, the infallible pronouncement, is a relatively rare exception. Nevertheless, the very existence of the power of the pope to declare his view infallible altered the balance of power

between the pope and the pastorate significantly, and in favor of the pope and the Holy See.

9. The original publication was a book called *The Fundamentals*, edited by R. A. Torrey. The real effect of the movement began with its republication as *The King's Business* by the Bible Institute of Los Angeles in 1910. This book was mailed free to over 300,000 ministers.

10. Pundits often contend that the Magna Carta was the origin of Anglo-Saxon democratic "tradition"; in fact, it managed the competition within the elite over the fruits of peasant labor.

11. Jefferson illustrates the complexity of the matter. He abhorred slavery but at the same time believed racial integration to be impossible (cf. his autobiography of 1821).

12. After the institutional centralizations of the New Deal and the Warren Court, many legal scholars are dismayed to see neofederalism reemerging in the Rehnquist Court.

13. For an example of universalist claims of objectivity in economic policymaking that turned out to reflect local knowledge and social contingencies, see Frost (1985). Parallel arguments in science and technology studies are too voluminous to mention.

References

Barnes, J. (1999). *John Paul II: His life and legacy: Solidarity and liberation theology*. PBS. Available at: www.pbs.org/wgbh/pages/frontline/shows/pope/etc/bio2.html.

Bellamy, E. (1894). *Brief summary of the industrial plan of nationalism set forth in "Looking Backward."* New York: Humboldt Publishing Co.

Bowker, G. C., and Star, S. L. (1999). *Sorting things out: Classification and its consequences.* Cambridge, MA: MIT Press.

Brytting, T. (1986). The management of distance in antiquity. *Scandinavian Journal of Management Studies*, 2, 139–155.

Cornwell, J. (1999). *Hitler's pope: The secret history of Pius XII.* New York: Viking.

Diamond, J. M. (1997). *Guns, germs, and steel: The fates of human societies.* New York: Norton.

Forster, P. W. F., and King, J. L. (1995). Information infrastructure standards in heterogeneous sectors: Lessons from the worldwide air cargo community. In B. Kahin and J. Abbate (eds.), *Standards for information infrastructure* (148–177). Cambridge, MA: MIT Press.

Frost, R. L. (1985). Economists as nationalised sector managers: Reforms of the electrical rate structure in France, 1951–1969. *Cambridge Journal of Economics*, 14, 285–300.

Gordon, S. (ed.). (2001). *Robes and honor: The medieval world of investiture.* New York: Palgrave.

Hobart, M. E., and Schiffman, Z. S. (1998). *Information ages: Literacy, numeracy, and the computer revolution.* Baltimore: Johns Hopkins University Press.

Hughes, P. (s.d.). The First General Council of the Vatican, 1869–70. In M. P. Hughes, *The Church in crisis: A history of the twenty great councils.* London: Burns and Oats.

Jacobs, J. (2000). *The nature of economies.* New York: Modern Library.

Kraut, R. E., Fussell, S. R., Brennan, S. E., and Siegel, J. (2002). Understanding effects of proximity on collaboration : Implications for technologies to support remote collaborative work. In P. Hinds and S. Kiesler, *Distributed work* (pp. 137–162). Cambridge, MA: MIT Press.

Latour, B. (1990). Drawing things together. In S. Woolgar and M. Lynch (eds.), *Representation in scientific practice* (19–68). Cambridge, MA: MIT Press.

Law, J. (2000). *Objects, spaces, and others.* Lancaster UK: Centre for Science Studies and Department of Sociology, Lancaster University.

Locke, J. Further considerations concerning raising the value of money. Available at: www.soc-sci.mcmaster.ca/~econ/ugcm/3ll3/locke/furth.txt.

Mauss, M. (1990). *The gift: The form and reason for exchange in archaic societies.* New York: Routledge.

Misa, T. J. (1995). *A nation of steel: The making of modern America, 1865–1925.* Baltimore: Johns Hopkins University Press.

Olson, J. S., Teasley, S., Covi, L., and Olson, G. (2002). The (currently) unique advantages of collocated work. In P. Hinds and S. Kiesler, *Distributed work* (pp. 113–135). Cambridge, MA: MIT Press.

Reddy, W. M. (1987). *Money and liberty in modern Europe: A critique of historical understanding.* Cambridge: Cambridge University Press.

Schaffer, S. (2000). *Golden means: Assay instruments and the geography of precision in the Guinea trade.* Cambridge: Cambridge University Science Studies Group.

Star, S. L. (1995). The politics of formal representations: Wizards, gurus, and organizational complexity. In S. L. Star (ed.), *Ecologies of knowledge: Work and politics in science and technology* (88–118). Albany: State University of New York Press.

Star, S. L., and Griesemer, J. R. (1989). Institutional ecology, "translations" and boundary objects: Amateurs and professionals in Berkeley's Museum of Vertebrate Zoology, 1907–39. *Social Studies of Science*, 19, 387–420.

Veblen, T. (1921). *The engineers and the price system.* New York: B. W. Huebsch.

Walther, J. B. (2002). Time effects in computer-mediated groups: Past, present, and future. In P. Hinds and S. Kiesler, *Distributed work* (pp. 235–257). Cambridge, MA: MIT Press.

Warner, M. (1976). *Alone of her sex: The myth and the cult of the Virgin Mary.* New York: Knopf.

Wills, G. (2000). Fatima: The "third secret." *New York Review of Books*, 47 (13), 51.

2

Distributed Work over the Centuries: Trust and Control in the Hudson's Bay Company, 1670–1826

Michael O'Leary, Wanda Orlikowski, and JoAnne Yates

Trust and control have typically been viewed as opposites or substitutes, and this is especially true in publications regarding distributed work. According to the conventional wisdom, trust is critical in such work because it is impossible to monitor and control geographically distributed employees directly. In this chapter, we use a 150-year-long case study of the Hudson's Bay Company (HBC) to argue that trust and control are closely intertwined and often mutually reinforcing—rather than alternative—approaches to managing distributed work. We make this argument by examining the repertoire of socialization, communication, and participation practices engaged in by the HBC's leaders in London to establish, maintain, and adapt trust in and control over the widely distributed HBC organization. Building on the HBC story, we also present implications for modern distributed organizations and the broad array of potentially trust- and control-enhancing practices in distributed work.

We know it is impossible at this distance to give such orders as shall answer every occurrence and be strictly observed in all points, so that when we have said all, we must leave much to your prudent conduct, having always in your eye the true interest and advantage of the Company, who have chosen and trusted you in the chief command they have to bestow. [Instructions from the London-based Hudson's Bay Company Executive Committee to one of its managers in North America, 1679 (in Rich 1948, 10)[1]]

Distributed work and virtual organizations are currently the object of considerable attention from the academic and popular presses (e.g., DeSanctis and Monge 1999, Maznevski and Chudoba 2000, Haywood 2000), but such organizations are far from modern. In fact, with *virtual* defined in terms of geographic dispersion, virtual organizations are quite ancient, as Frost and King noted in chapter 1. Two millennia ago, the Roman Empire spanned a considerable part of the globe, and distributed work was one of its major challenges (Brytting 1996). Several centuries later, the Catholic Church emerged as another major virtual organization (Harris 1996). Today's distributed work occurs at a considerably faster pace than it did during the days of the Roman Empire and early Catholic Church, but the basic challenges remain quite similar. As exemplified by the special issues of the *Academy of Management Review* (July 1998) and *Administrative Science Quarterly* (June 1998), building trust and maintaining organizational control are two of those challenges. However, the scholarly literature has not considered the role that both trust and control play in distributed work (for an important exception, see Crisp and Jarvenpaa 2000).

Trust and control have typically been viewed as opposites or substitutes (Rousseau et al. 1998, Mishra and Spreitzer 1999), and this is especially true in publications regarding distributed work (e.g., Handy 1995). Trust is described as critical in such work because it is impossible to monitor and control geographically distributed employees (Wiesenfeld et al. 1999). In order to explore this conventional wisdom and modern distributed work more generally, we believe it is necessary to have a better understanding of its historical forms. To develop this understanding, we follow previous work on the historical antecedents of modern management (e.g., Barley and Kunda 1992, Guillén 1994, Yates 1989) and explore the interplay between trust and control in action at the Hudson's Bay Company (HBC or the Company, as it was often called by its employees) between 1670 and 1826.

The HBC was established in 1670 as a highly dispersed organization with headquarters in London and operations thousands of miles away in modern Canada (see figure 2.1). Drawing on the Company's original records from 1670 to 1826, we examine its internal operations and the repertoire of socialization, communication, and participation practices that were especially important bases for trust and control.[2] Based on this examination, we argue that trust and control are closely intertwined and often mutually reinforcing approaches to managing distributed work. We also present implications for modern distributed work and encourage researchers and practitioners to move beyond simple quick-fix remedies (e.g., the commonly prescribed initial face-to-face meetings) to consider the broad array of potentially trust- and control-enhancing practices in distributed work.

The HBC was chartered by a "Company of Adventurers" to trade furs along the shores of Hudson Bay and its large offshoot, James Bay. This group of London-based merchants financed and coordinated the establishment of posts in present-day Canada from which their employees traded guns, knives, blankets, and other European goods for beaver, marten, fox, and other furs trapped by Native Americans. These furs were then shipped back to England each year to be sold at auction and made into hats and dress goods. The HBC survives today as the longest continually operating company in North America. It is also among the few companies in the world that have been in continuous operation for more than three centuries. Today, it is Canada's largest retailer, accounting for approximately 39 percent of Canadian department store sales (Hudson's Bay Company 2000). The Company and its famous point blankets have become widely recognized symbols of the Canadian North (Kyle 2000).

While this size, tremendous staying power, and notoriety are interesting in their own right, it is the Company's considerable geographic dispersion that makes it the focus of this chapter. From its founding until its three hundredth anniversary in 1970, the Company's headquarters were in London, while its fur trading posts and 99 percent of its employees were thousands of miles (and a long sea voyage) away in a territory then called Rupert's Land. This territory was larger than the Roman Empire at its peak and made the HBC the de facto civil and commercial ruler of an area equal to approximately one-twelfth of the earth's land mass.[3]

For the first 104 years, the Company's posts (also known as factories, forts, and houses) numbered seven or fewer and were all concentrated along the shores of Hudson and James Bays. Complements of three to one hundred Company "officers" (including post managers—called "chief factors,"—apprentice managers, post doctors, and others) and "servants" (including laborers, tradesmen, seamen, and other staff) maintained each post throughout the year and conducted the trade. Most of the posts were at least ten days' travel apart by canoe, dog sled, or snowshoe (depending on the season and terrain).

While the organization and number of posts and employees changed from year to year, the annual cycle in London and on the Bay continued essentially unchanged for two centuries. It was dominated by the weather, hunting and trapping seasons, and the annual passage of the Company's ships, whose access was limited to a brief window in late August when the narrow opening to the Bay was not frozen closed.

Given the considerable distance between London and the Bay, and among the Company's North American posts, the HBC operation is a quintessential example of distributed work. It allows us to examine trust and control in an organization that predates today's virtual organizations by three centuries.

Company History

Understanding the context of trust and control in the HBC requires some familiarity with the Company's major players and the broad outlines of its historical evolution. Each of the Company's posts included a contingent of salaried staff and managers (or "servants" and "officers," respectively). Posts ranged in size from

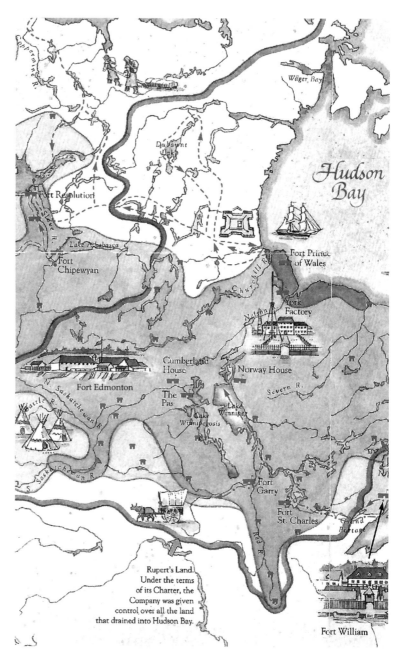

Figure 2.1
Location of key HBC posts.
Modified by Michelle Fiorenza from the original illustration by Jack McMaster © 1989, The
Madison Press Limited from *Empire of the Bay* (pp. 18–19). A Viking Studio/Madison Press
book.

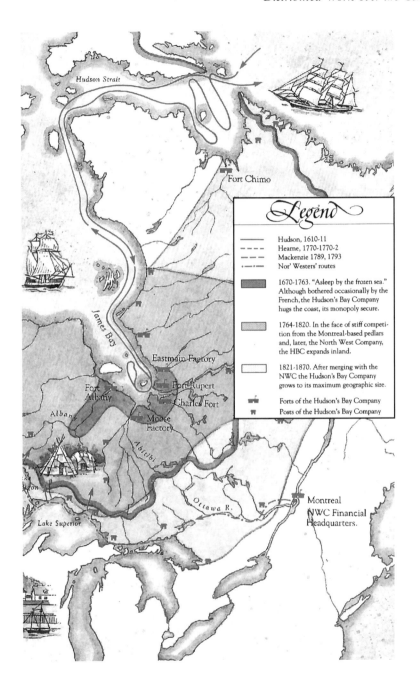

Hudson Strait

Fort Chimo

Legend

———	Hudson, 1610-11
- - - -	Hearne, 1770-1770-2
– – –	Mackenzie 1789, 1793
·—·—·—	Nor' Westers' routes

1670-1763. "Asleep by the frozen sea." Although bothered occasionally by the French, the Hudson's Bay Company hugs the coast, its monopoly secure.

1764-1820. In the face of stiff competition from the Montreal-based pedlars and, later, the North West Company, the HBC expands inland.

1821-1870. After merging with the NWC the Hudson's Bay Company grows to its maximum geographic size.

Forts of the Hudson's Bay Company

Posts of the Hudson's Bay Company

James Bay

Eastmain Factory

Fort Rupert

Fort Albany

Charles Fort

Albany

Moose Factory

Abitibi

Ottawa R.

Lake Superior

Montreal
NWC Financial
Headquarters.

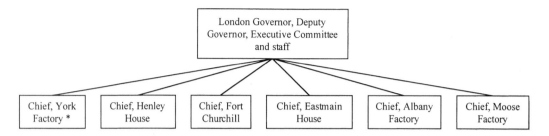

Figure 2.2
High-level HBC organization, prior to the 1810 reorganization.
* Prior to the reorganization in 1810, the chief factors reported directly to the Governor and Committee in London. In addition, one of the chief factors (typically from York Factory) also held the title of "Bayside Governor," which included nominal oversight of his fellow chief factors.

small, temporary, tentlike ones operated by only a few employees to large, permanent ones with upwards of a hundred employees. The larger posts generally had several officers, including the "chief factor," a second in command, clerk (or clerks), surgeon, and sloopmaster. The chief factors were primarily responsible for their posts' trade each year and for managing the men who maintained the posts.[4]

Factors and other officers worked on three- to five-year contracts and were accountable to the Company's Executive Committee in London (see figure 2.2). During the Company's early years, the most senior chief factor also served as "bayside governor," but his power and authority were nominal until after an 1810 reorganization (see figure 2.3).

Most factors and other officers made the Company their career, serving in various capacities for several decades (Brown 1980, Williams 1983, Goldring 1985). Some began their service as officers, and others worked their way up from apprentice clerks. Few had any face-to-face contact with the Committee in London, and virtually no Committeemen visited the Bay. This exacerbated the problem of distance and forced the Committee to fill the information vacuum with extensive record keeping and correspondence between London and the Bay (Brown 1980).

Making up the Company's lower ranks, the "servants" at each post included a wide range of skilled tradesmen, general laborers, and seamen. They typically had no formal education, came to the Bay on Company ships, and served out contracts obligating them for three to five years. In addition to its officers and servants, the Company relied heavily on Indians to supply furs and act as its guides, canoeists, couriers, and messengers.

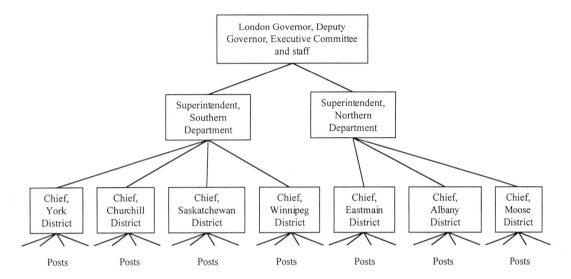

Figure 2.3
High-level HBC organization, following the 1810 reorganization.
The 1810 reorganization added departments and districts to the Company's organizational structure. Each district included one main post (or depot) and several smaller satellite posts. Typically, the factor in charge of the district was also the factor in charge of the district's main post. The shortest lines above symbolize the existence of posts in each district, not the actual number of posts.

In London, the Company was led by a governor, deputy governor, and the seven-member Executive Committee. In some respects, the Committee resembled modern corporate boards, but it met more frequently (at least weekly) and played a more hands-on role in Company operations. In addition to the weekly work of the whole Committee, individual Committee members and subcommittees worked between general meetings on specific issues such as recruitment and auctions. The governor and Committee also contracted with various people outside the Company and depended heavily on a small, dedicated staff in its London office, including a secretary, an accountant, a warehousekeeper, and upto three clerks.

The Company's early years were a "precarious infancy," characterized by heavy competition and military conflict with the French (Davies 1965, p. ix). Consequently, the Committee's attention was focused on establishing regular trading relations with the Indians and defending its operations against French attacks. By 1697, the French had reduced the Company to a single post at Albany (see figure 2.1; ibid.). Its stake in North America remained small and tenuous from then until 1713, when Great Britain and France signed the Treaty of Utrecht.

From 1713 until 1774, the Company reestablished control over the posts it had lost to the French and established several new ones. However, it had no more than seven posts during this period and limited them to the shores of the Bay. For adhering to this strategy of hugging the Bay and not exploring inland, critics in London derided the HBC as having "for eighty years slept at the edge of a frozen sea" (Robson 1752, quoted in Williams 1983).

After the 1713 treaty, the Company's competition shifted from the French to independent traders based in Montreal. By 1774, this competition had become so serious that the Company abandoned its century-old strategy of waiting for Indians to come to its seven bayside posts and began a massive inland expansion. In 1784, the independent traders responded by organizing themselves as the North West Company (NWC). By 1795, the NWC dominated the North American fur trade, with an 80 percent market share (Rich 1961). Nonetheless, the HBC's route through the Bay was considerably faster and more cost-effective than the NWC's overland routes to Montreal. The HBC leveraged this advantage and continued to expand inland, using both temporary and permanent posts. Like modern McDonalds and Burger Kings, the HBC and NWC established dozens of posts within yards of each other.

With the costs of these posts weighing heavily on the Company, the London Committee instituted a series of "radical" organizational changes in 1810 (HBCA, PP 1810–1811, May, 31 1810).[5] This retrenching was intended to rein in costs and energize the HBC men with a new compensation scheme. However, cutting costs and continuing to compete head on with the NWC proved difficult, and tensions between the companies only grew.

Ultimately unable to surmount (or buy rights to) the HBC's route through the Bay, the NWC initiated merger talks in 1819. By 1821, the companies agreed on terms and approved an "amalgamation." The new, merged Company retained the HBC name and governing board in London, but adopted the NWC's partnership model, giving the fifty-three commissioned officers in North America a formal stake in the Company. It also gave them a larger decision-making and coordinating role with the creation of annual, face-to-face councils of chief factors and traders.

After the merger, bayside governors William Williams and George Simpson quickly consolidated the two companies' operations and eliminated its redundant posts. During this process, Simpson demonstrated his considerable (and somewhat imperial) management skills and was given charge of the Company's two main departments in 1826. These departments were geographically based administrative entities which encompassed dozens of posts (see figure 2.3).

Trust and Control in the HBC

In discussions of virtual organizations, trust and control are often presented as opposites or substitutes (e.g., Handy 1995, Lipnack and Stamps 1997). In contrast, our study suggests that trust and control are closely intertwined and interdependent. Specifically, we found that the HBC developed and relied on a repertoire of organizing practices to support both trust and control.

As a working definition, we consider *trust* the confidence in and willingness to rely on another party (where a *party* can be an individual, group, organization, institution, or system) under conditions of risk or vulnerability.[6] While some have studied people's general predispositions to trust, we focus on trust situated within a specific organizational context as it is manifested in the relationship between two parties. In this case, we deal primarily with trust between the HBC Committee in London and its employees on the Bay, and secondarily with trust among managers on the Bay. In so doing, we are treating the employees in Rupert's Land as fairly bounded, uniform groups (despite inevitable diversity among them) and are also leaving treatment of other important trust relationships for later work.

We see control as "the capability that some actors, groups, or types of actors have of influencing the circumstances of action of others" (Giddens 1984, 283). Thus, we define *organizational controls* as the means through which organizational members are influenced to align their actions with organizational goals.[7] In this case, we deal primarily with the HBC's executives' control over their North American employees, and vice versa.

Despite the Company's royal charter, its monopoly was frequently challenged by French and independent traders. This, in combination with the very real potential for HBC employees to switch sides and work for the NWC, other smaller rivals, or themselves, created a centrifugal force that made trust and control important elements in the HBC's continued success. Carlos and colleagues (Carlos and Nicholas 1990, Carlos 1992, 1994, Carlos and Kruse 1996) have written about this force extensively (in principal-agent terms) and have shown how other companies (e.g., the Royal Africa) collapsed as a result of control failures. Our examination of the HBC records suggests that the Company's repertoire of socialization, communication, and participation practices helped it succeed where other companies failed.

Socialization: Creating and Maintaining Culture

The socialization practices of the HBC fostered a very common and consistent cultural perspective (Van Maanen and Schein 1979). This so-called strong culture, which promoted intense devotion to its business, served as the basis for both trust and control. Employees first encountered this when they were recruited to work for the Company.

Recruiting for the Bay   Initially, the Company staffed its lower ranks with young men from the London suburbs, but it soon experienced disciplinary problems with and high levels of dissatisfaction among these "servants." Subsequently, the Committee began seeking employees who would be more obedient and accepting of the isolated life on the Bay. Believing that the young London men would never acclimate to life on Hudson Bay, they began recruiting almost all servants from the similarly isolated and climatically harsh Orkney Islands, north of the Scottish mainland (Rich 1945). During the eighteenth century, the Orkneys supplied 75 percent of the Company's servants on the Bay (Burley 1997). Figuratively, these Scots became the "clan" in the Company's cultural approach to trust and control (Ouchi 1980, O'Reilly and Chatman 1996).

Initial selection of servants was handled largely by independent recruiting agents in the Orkneys, Hebrides, Glasgow, and elsewhere. The agents acted in response to the Committee's requests for a certain number of men in each of the various categories (e.g., craftsman, laborer, mariner). Once the agents had selected new recruits, the Committee sent out contracts assigning each new employee to a post.

Once the Company started expanding inland in 1774, it began to need men with greater expertise in Indian ways and inland travel. The people who had this expertise were the independent (and, later, NWC) traders or trappers working out of Montreal, but the Company was extremely hesitant to hire them. In general, neither the Committeemen in London nor the Company men on the Bay trusted the "Canadian" men affiliated with the NWC, and they feared loss of control over them. They were regarded as "bellicose risk takers unhampered by the discipline of a strict corporate structure" (Newman 1985, 84). Furthermore, the Canadians' perceived focus on short-term gains over long-term trading relationships "precluded them from establishing stable business patterns" (ibid., Greif 1989).

While the majority of servants came from the Orkneys, officers and apprentices were drawn from a broader pool, including London and its charity schools. Their selection was guided more closely by the Committee itself, with little assistance from agents. Frequently, officers were chosen based on connections with individual Committee members, such as familial and professional ties. Apprentices were chosen based on Committee members' connections to the headmasters of several charity schools. Initially, these schools provided young men with some education but uncertain futures and much to gain from a strong commitment to the Company. In the 1770s, the schools also provided boys who had specific technical training in the mathematics and basic surveying required to map the Company's rapidly expanding operations (Brown 1980, Goldring 1985, Cowie 1993, Burley 1997).

By narrowing the field of candidates in this way, it was also selecting men whom it viewed as especially adaptable, hard working, reliable, competent (or at least trainable), and honest. The last three of these characteristics are among the half-dozen most commonly described bases of interpersonal trust (Kramer 1999). Through its active involvement early in the recruiting process and its use of third-party evaluators, such as potential apprentices' headmasters, the Committee began to exert control and establish trust before its men had even signed their contracts.

Getting to the Bay   Building on the perceived qualities of the Orcadians, the in-experience of its young apprentices, and the personal ties with its officers, the Company used a variety of socialization techniques to enhance its control over life on the Bay. Socialization in the HBC differed depending on the level and time at which one entered the firm, but for most, it began with the long voyage across the Atlantic to Hudson Bay. The departure began with an elaborate send-off ritual full of pomp, tears, and Company symbolism, including a farewell breakfast, cannon salute, singing, and hoisting of the "Company's arms" or "house flag" (Cowie 1993).

During the course of this voyage, the new recruits, whether officers, apprentices, or servants, got an intense, face-to-face introduction to some of their future colleagues. For example, a young man who left Stromness as an apprentice clerk described the captain as a "fatherly" man who gave him "good advice . . . for my welfare" (ibid., 80, 85). In addition, the voyage provided direct access to the tales of seamen and captains who traveled back and forth annually and spent at least several weeks on the Bay every year.

In some cases, the ships also included officers and servants returning to the Bay after furloughs in London or other breaks in their service. Such contact provided the greatest opportunity for new recruits to learn what to expect of life working for the Honourable Company. In addition to these experiences, the basic organization of lodging and dining aboard the ship paralleled the distinction between the officer and servant ranks on the Bay (ibid., 75, 79).

Working on the Bay   After the long ocean journey, the next step in the Company's socialization was the carefully crafted ceremony held on the ships' arrival at the Bay. During this ceremony, the Company hoped that a "formal reading of orders, followed by stirring words, would make the men mindful of the 'Duties they owed to the Committee whose servants they are, whose bread they eat and whose wages they take'" (Burley 1997, 25, citing 1688 orders from the Committee). This was followed by the new recruits' introduction and presentation of their papers to the factor in charge of the bayside post.

Once the men had been presented to their new bosses, they were shown to their quarters and given their initial assignments. In all cases, these men's status in the organization became clear by their first meal and day on the Bay, in which officers and servants had different tables, food, drink, lodgings, and furnishings (Rich 1948). The distinction between officers and servants at meals held particular symbolic value for apprentices. In fact, being "in the Mess" was a widely used phrase to describe officers' status. The Committee urged its officers to "observe as a general rule" that apprentices "take meals at the chief's table as it will serve as an excitement to their assiduity and attention and maintain a proper distinction between them and the common men" (HBCA B.135/c/1, May 31, 1797). More generally, the young apprentice officers were set apart from the other employees, given special privileges, and raised as part of the "Company family."

For both servants and officers, the Committee encouraged close identification with the Company by hiring mostly bachelors who had limited family ties in Great Britain, socializing them carefully, and promoting from within. With a staff of relatively unattached bachelors, the Company's "people strategies" created an increasingly familial household environment. After 1713, when armed conflict abated and the men's focus shifted from defense to trade and long-term maintenance of their posts, the emphasis on a more family-oriented model became especially clear. At the same time, men's tenure on the Bay began to increase, with many making the Company their career for life (Brown 1980). These staffing practices furthered the family orientation and combined to enhance the Committee's trust in and control over its distant staff.

The family orientation, the sense of commitment to the Company, and the importance of developing and maintaining reputations were all enhanced by long tenures and extensive internal promotion. With few exceptions (most prominent and strategic among them being George Simpson), the Committee hired its officers from within. To do so, it relied on the apprenticeship program, management training for some servants who had education or other unusual skills, and deliberate rotation of junior officers among posts. In the few instances where it diverged from internal promotion, the externally hired officers suffered from both their lack of local knowledge and the lack of support from career officers (Brown 1980).

In summary, the Committee enhanced its trust in and control over its employees by: (1) recruiting them carefully, (2) hiring them based on a connection (often kinship) to other Company employees or Committee members, (3) hiring apprentice officers (some as orphan boys) and young bachelors with few ties in Britain, (4) rearing those young recruits into the Company family, (5) promoting almost solely from within the Company, and (6) building on these long ties and tenure to develop a sense of family, professionalism, and loyalty.

Communication: Negotiating for Information

From its beginning, the Committee in London depended almost entirely on the records and written communication carried by the annual ships for all information about operations on the Bay. The written communication practices were established during the first half century of the Company's existence.[8] Then, beginning in 1730 and gaining momentum in the 1780s and 1790s, the Committee initiated a series of negotiations with bayside factors about the form and content of those communications—and thus about the bases for trust and control between London and the Bay.

Establishing Communication Norms   The Company's written communication between London and the Bay centered around annual letters in both directions, daily journals kept at the posts and sent to England each year, and financial account books. The Committee relied almost exclusively on a single annual "Letter Outward" to each post to communicate with its bayside officers. These letters often reflected a recognition by the Committee that it had to trust its officers to act in the Company's best interests. For example, in its 1682 instructions to bayside Governor Nixon, the Committee wrote, "We must leave much to yours and the Captain's prudence and conduct, not doubting but [that] you will both do that which in your understanding [is] best for our service" (Rich 1957, 57–58).

The letters also drew on expense figures, returns, and basic profit reckonings as the sources for praise of or complaints to its officers. Finally, the letters contained all notices of appointments and reappointments of officers and servants.

The annual letters from each factor to London ("Letters Inward"), supplemented by daily journals of life at the posts, were the other side of the transatlantic interaction. These letters described each post's operations and results, and the "indents" included with them requested supplies and personnel for the coming year. As the primary vehicle by which factors documented the performance of their men, their posts, and themselves, the letters, journals, and supporting accounts were the foremost means by which factors could demonstrate their competence and earn London's trust. The only other source for London's knowledge of what was happening on the Bay were the ships' captains, returning officers and servants, and occasional travelers. These personal reports back to London were irregular and, according to those who remained on the Bay, unfairly skewed. For example, bayside Governor John Nixon complained that "this advantage all my adversaries have above me, that they come first home [and] by fraud and flattery can have their tale first told and they can be heard [directly] by you, though it proves to your loss" (Rich 1945, 278). However, the Committee was sensitive to the potential for its officers to use such contact to their advantage and dismissed at least one officer for "set[ting] so great a value on himself" during a return trip to London (Rich 1948, 3).

This asynchronous annual communication contained information that was used to establish (and express) trust and simultaneously to control behavior through instructions, admonitions, and evaluations of past actions. The norms and expectations for annual letters and journals were set in the early instructions from London. For example, in 1680, in one of its first references to the annual letters, the Committee instructed bayside Governor Nixon, "You are every year to send us a punctual and particular account of all our servants in the country, and how they are employed in the several factories and vessels" (Rich 1948, 8). In these letters, it required "an exact account of the disposal of our goods and also what quantities of our provisions are expended" so that it might know of any "profuse and extravagant" expenditures and "see your good husbandry and conduct in the management" (ibid., 45, May 15, 1682). Furthermore, outgoing letters from previous years were not intended to be read and forgotten or discarded. The factors were expected to "look them over and observe such things as are still necessary to be done." In these interactions, the Committee demonstrated its first concern for managing the flow and volume of paperwork in the Company, noting that factors need not repeat certain things each year (ibid., 46). While it would become much more explicit about the norms for factors' answers to its concerns, the Committee was already beginning to request "particular answer[s] to the several things we write to you about" (ibid.). It was also clearly beginning to make comparisons of performance and expenditures across posts as early as 1682, requesting annual information in a form such that it could "distinguish whether the benefit of each factory is proportionably [*sic*] equivalent" to its costs (ibid., 48).

The Committee also began to set norms for communications *among* its posts. For example, in 1682, it wrote to its governor at Fort Nelson, "As soon as possible

..., we would have you contrive a way of correspondence with [your fellow governor on the Bay] that you may from time to time understand the condition of each other." This interpostal communication served a vital coordinating and trust-building purpose among officers. Yet, the Committee also requested "copies of such letters" in order to enhance its information about and control over those officers (ibid., 35).

While the Committee demanded details in its reports from the Bay and asked factors to "always giv[e] us the reasons" for departing from its advice, it acknowledged, "We know it is impossible at this distance to give such orders as shall answer every occurrence and be strictly observed in all points, so that when we have said all, we must leave much to your prudent conduct, having always in your eye the true interest and advantage of the Company, who have chosen and trusted you in the chief command they have to bestow" (Rich 1948, 10). Instructions such as these clearly indicate how the Committee was invoking its distant representatives' good judgment and identification with the Company as bases for its current and future trust. Based on this identification and the men's concern for their reputations and careers, the Committee made it clear that men's service should not be limited to what the Committee could capture explicitly in its contracts or sailing instructions (ibid.). At the same time, it noted that it would "not exact from you the strict performance of the letter of our agreement," recognizing that conditions beyond London's control necessitated its reliance on the men's good judgment and commitment to the Company (ibid., 30).

Tightening Communication Norms   The Company initially tightened norms for annual correspondence in the late 1730s. During that time, London's interest in these letters shifted somewhat, from seeing them primarily as a source of general information about bayside operations to seeing them also as a way to monitor events more carefully. This shift resulted in part from an incident at Moose Fort that revealed a gap between London's admonitions and existing practices at the posts. In 1735, drunken Christmas revelry resulted in a fire. Too "stupefied" to contain it, the men watched as the flames consumed their post and provisions in two hours. Subsequently, they nearly died from cold and hunger while awaiting assistance from Albany (Davies 1965, p. xlvi). The man London sent out to inspect the burned post and take charge of a rebuilt one in 1737 found that drunkenness had been to blame and also that Indian women had been living in the post, in direct violation of London's policies. While the offending factor was replaced, this incident made the London leadership more suspicious and less trusting than before. As a result, they requested additional information from the factors, whose letters grew from three to nine transcribed pages (Davies 1965). Over time, this breach of trust was repaired through the information contained in the longer annual letters. Within several years, having satisfied themselves that most factors were not allowing the indiscretions that led to Moose's destruction and were using reasonable standards of trade, their requests for detailed operational information relaxed (ibid.).

Renegotiating Communication Norms   As competition intensified and the HBC grew, London experimented with a series of further changes to its correspondence and record keeping in hopes of improving the quality and comparability of the information from the Bay. While most of the changes were eventually achieved (though not always to the extent London desired), they were the subject of ongoing exchanges negotiating the amount and nature of information sent to London.

In 1774, the company responded to competition by expanding and beginning to move inland. For the past century, the annual letters to London had included several narrative lists (e.g., of supplies requested and of information on personnel) embedded in the text of the annual letters. By the 1780s, the company's growth rendered these narratives increasingly burdensome and ineffective for London, and the Committee attempted to standardize the flow of information from its factors. For example, the Committee complained in 1786 that "much trouble is occasioned in collecting the indents of accounts of stores from want of having them placed in the same order at all our factories" (HBCA B.135/c/1/p. 186, May 26). To alleviate this problem, they "sent out a general list to be followed in the future and direct[ed] that the particular parts be alphabetically arranged under the general heads" (ibid.). Similarly, in 1790, they asked that all information about employees' movements, salaries, disciplinary actions, and so forth be removed from the narrative and handled in list form. Accounts were also made more extensive and more specific in their requirements during this period.

Because London's attempts to secure better-organized information had implications for trust, these changes sometimes became a point of contention between the Executive Committee and the factors, who resisted what they viewed as burdensome and intrusive requirements imposed by distant directors. As the Company began establishing its inland posts, this lack of understanding became more salient and the "disadvantages of rule from London became ever more obvious" (Williams 1970, 35). Even with three excellent surveyors mapping its inland posts and waterways, London struggled to understand the geography, resources, climate, and competition in the same way that the more proximate NWC leaders could. Expressing his frustration with the Committee's "local ignorance," one factor told London that "your rivers never freeze, ours are only for a short while open. . . . I intreat you to dismiss from your minds the sprucely-dressed wherryman with his plush breeches and his silver badge, nor conceive the descent of the solitary bargeman at London Bridge with that thro' the shallow horrors of rocky chasms [here] as at all synonymous" (ibid.). Even the Committee acknowledged at one point that it had "no sort of Clue" about many aspects of trade in Rupert's Land (ibid.).

Partially because of London's avowed cluelessness, factors resisted some of London's directions regarding record keeping. As the Committee's 1794 letter indicates, the factors did win some concessions: "To the complaints [that chief factor John Thomas] makes of prolixity and tediousness in keeping the account book of provisions, in the present mode, all we have to reply is that it matters not how it is kept, provided [that] it be accurately done—the principal intention of it is to furnish . . . a constant check upon those who distribute the provisions and, by sending a transcript of it home, to give us all the necessary information respecting it. We are also of the same opinion with Mr. Thomas that the expenditure for any number of men . . . may be carried out in one line, as well as in separate lines . . . by which much time and writing may be saved" (HBCA B.135/c/1/p. 223, May 29).

A desire to keep "a constant check upon those who distribute the provisions" was the clearly stated goal of the Committee, but it had to balance that desire with the resistance of its factors. Moreover, no matter how much London desired control, the exigencies of the increasingly competitive business required increased trust of factors to make decisions themselves.

In addition, systematic information was a potential basis for increased trust. Indeed, during this period, and probably reflecting increased competitive threat as well as increased trust, London's "annual letter for 1790 gave, for the first time, the chiefs of bayside posts the right to distribute men among their bayside and inland posts" (HBCA B.135/c/1, May 1790; Spraakman and Wilke 2000). This trust in turn created obligations among the bayside factors to both the inland posts and London to make this distribution for the good of all. However, negotiation and renegotiation between London and its officers on the Bay continued well into the 1800s, reflecting the ongoing tensions over information, as well as the trust and control based on it.

Participation: Generating Situated Knowledge and Relationships

While socialization and written communication were sources of trust and control in the HBC, participation in everyday life on the Bay was also particularly important. Only through such direct participation could factors (and later the governors on the Bay) develop the situated knowledge and the network of relationships that allowed effective operations in areas where London lacked the requisite knowledge. Bayside officers generated such knowledge and relationships through at least three means: being there, canoeing around, and staying on.

Being There   Through their presence on the Bay, the factors and officers developed knowledge of local conditions and personnel about which London understood very little. For example, during the period of expansion that began in 1774, London could not have adequate knowledge of the new terrain or the dynamic competitive conditions. Consequently, London gave its factors relative autonomy, entrusting its bayside and inland officers with many of the decisions about when, where, and how to expand. Their success depended less on strategy, direction, or advice from London than it did on their own skills and local knowledge.

The value of being there is illustrated by the expanded role taken on by Humphrey Marten, the chief factor at York, as the inland expansion began. Marten had been in the Company's service since 1750 and had served at Albany and Severn before taking over as factor at York when the previous factor, William Tomison, was moved inland. Thus, he knew Tomison and many of the other officers sent inland. Marten put the needs of the new inland post at Cumberland above those of his own at York by, for example, giving Tomison the unusual privilege "to pick and chuse the goods he liketh best" (Rich 1952, xxv).

York was 700 miles from Cumberland by canoe, and subsequent inland posts were even more isolated. Although ill health kept Marten from traveling to oversee these new posts in person, he worked to increase his own knowledge of the inland officers' situation and build relationships with them by poring over their reports and keeping them at York for days of conversation every time they journeyed to the Bay. Based on what he learned from them, he created "unsparingly blunt" reports to London that "lay the [inland] situation mercilessly bare." Depicting the location and nature of the competition in "meticulous" detail, "season after season Marten pounded into his masters the urgency of [the inland posts'] need for men" (ibid., xxix). In addition, Marten was "too big and wise a man to be jealous of his subordinate's success" and was able to "depute authority and leave his subordinates freedom to use their own initiative" (ibid., xxv). Marten did his best to empower the inland factors. In fact, to convince men to travel inland, he offered them bonuses out of his own account, trusting the men to do a good job and trusting London to support his bonus plan (ibid.). Based on his knowledge of the officers going inland, Marten knew whose judgment to trust and how to interpret the written and oral information he got from these inland factors.

Because of his presence on the Bay, Marten began with the localized knowledge of bayside (if not inland) conditions and the relationships with individuals such as Tomison that enabled him to combine trust and control successfully in his relations with the inland factors. During this period, he made the most out of being at York, continuing to develop new knowledge and relationships useful in his management at a distance.

Canoeing Around   When Marten took on the new role supervising the inland posts, he had the benefit of a quarter-century's experience on the Bay and the resulting local knowledge. In contrast, when George Simpson was made head of the Northern Department right after the 1821 merger with the NWC, he had been an officer on the Bay for only one year and had no experience with the NWC men who were now under his management. In order to gain the situated knowledge of local operations and establish the relationships necessary to act as London's delegated representative, Simpson adopted a strategy that could be called "management by canoeing around." Rather than being in one or two locations for a long time, Simpson attempted to be everywhere for short periods.

Simpson's tireless travel crisscrossing the Company's territory allowed him to observe firsthand the managerial strengths and weaknesses at each post. His initial focus was on consolidating posts and controlling the deficiencies. In his own words, Simpson's travel allowed him to rein in the "abuses which nothing but *my own presence* can effectually stop" (Williams 1983, 52, emphasis added). He saw his role in part as increasing the direct control over what he perceived as lazy and inflexible factors. Simpson's travels also allowed him to discover what conditions were like at each post and which of his factors were competent and trustworthy. Over time, they gave him the benefits in situated knowledge of places and people that Marten had known through his long tenure at the Bay. After Simpson became governor of all Rupert's Land in 1826, he spent winters in London every other year or so. That practice allowed him to share more of the local knowledge he had gained with the Committee in London and to use his personal influence to push his view of how matters on the Bay should be handled.

Simpson also used his "canoeing around" to reinforce company values and spread his own values by example. He stage-managed his arrivals at and departures from each post to produce an air of pomp and circumstance. For example, as he neared a post, he would change from his sweat-soaked canoe gear into dry and dashing clothes befitting his station. A bagpiper who traveled with Simpson would provide a rousing musical announcement of the governor's arrival. These symbols reinforced the hierarchical values of the Company and Simpson's own authority.

Although he took full advantage of (and deliberately emphasized differences in) rank within the Company's hierarchy, Simpson was not impressed by ranks of other sorts. For example, when a Company employee wrote to complain about serving under the direction of a man with lesser British military credentials, Simpson replied with "sovereign contempt" at the man's "impertinent and ridiculous note": "Your honor and rank in his majesty's service are quite immaterial to me and all I require of you is to do your duty faithfully as a clerk in the service of the Honourable Company" (Newman 1985, 173).

Simpson also used his canoeing around to lead by example, displaying his own personal strength and tireless dedication to the Company's goals. His travels sent clear signals about the level of effort that he expected from his men. He was clearly conscious of the symbolic effect of his behavior, writing, "The example I show them of a total disregard for personal ease and comfort does much good" (Williams 1983, 52). Simpson was known for regularly starting his eighteen-hour day at 2 A.M., and tales abounded of his pace reducing "to total exhaustion" a pair of British army officers traveling with him (ibid.). As such tales spread widely throughout the ranks of the Company, Simpson's arduous travels quickly took on epic proportions and served as powerful symbols. Through his travel, direct observation, heavy use of symbols, and personal exertions, Simpson gained knowledge of, demonstrated control over, and established trust in the Company's posts and men.

Staying On   A final way in which participation in life on the Bay contributed to the building of knowledge about locales and people was by officers who chose to stay on well beyond their initial three- to five-year contracts. Despite the isolation of life on Hudson Bay, many Bay men made the Company their career for life, ensuring the development of knowledge about individuals, conditions, and practices. They stayed on at the Bay, playing key and irreplaceable roles, despite the potential to capitalize on their earnings and return to Europe or embark as independent traders (as many employees of the Royal Africa did; Carlos 1992, 1994).

They were rewarded for this in part by the respect that the Committee gave to such loyalty and seniority. As a promotion letter to one such officer noted, "We shall never send new, raw, and unexperienced men to put over the heads of such as have served us long and faithfully" (Rich 1948, 6). On the rare occasions when the Committee violated this policy, the officers were quick to complain. For example, in 1811, chief factor William Auld complained about officers hired from outside the Company, saying that there was a "very considerable time . . . requisite to qualify as an officer to perform with success the duties of his station" (ibid., citing A.11/118, fol. 24). The Company also encouraged this lengthy tenure through the use of pensions and other retirement supports. Like the Royal Navy, which retired men on the "half pay list," the HBC developed a system to house, support, and feed its retirees in North America, as well as to support those elderly employees who returned to Europe.

The value of long tenure is clear in the careers of both Marten and Simpson. At the time of the initial inland expansion, Marten's long tenure—already a quarter-century—had enabled him to build up his knowledge of the Bay and the other officers serving there. Simpson began without that advantage, but he ultimately served forty years on the Bay. As the decades passed, Simpson's lengthening tenure gave him similar advantages in knowledge and relationships, both on the Bay and, because of his frequent winters in London, with the Committee there.

In summary, the HBC benefited from the direct participation of individuals in daily life, primarily on the Bay, through their accumulated knowledge of the situation and their relationships with other people. Bayside officers with special authority from London gained this knowledge by being there, canoeing around, and staying on, either individually or (most often) in combination. Ultimately, these modes of participating strengthened both their ability to control and their bases for trust in those under their charge. Moreover, it gave London the assurance that they could trust officers such as Marten and Simpson who acted on their behalf on the Bay over long periods of time.

Trust and Control Then and Now

In this chapter, we have argued that trust is closely connected to and intertwined with control, and that both are enacted through ongoing organizing practices. Our investigation of the HBC suggests that at least three practices—socialization, communication, and participation—were particularly important sources of trust and control. As a result, our findings provide support for the idea that trust and control are not opposites or subsets of one another, as some have suggested in the literature (Bradach and Eccles 1989). On the contrary, our findings from the HBC indicate that trust and control are highly interdependent aspects of organizing, enacted through a number of different ongoing practices and, thus, are overlapping, interacting, and emergent.

At the HBC, the dispersed operations relied heavily on a combination of explicit information and detailed record keeping, as well as the more tacit and situated knowledge developed through socialization and participation in life on the Bay. Correspondence from London to the Bay in the early years of the HBC contained repeated statements of trust, reflecting both the reality of the distance and a sense that by reinforcing this trust, London could also reinforce the trustworthiness of the actions taken on the Bay. For example, London's letter to one officer noted that it had received a complaint against him from someone returning to London, but that "we have overlooked all, and are resolved to lay such an obligation of kindness and confidence upon you, as shall engage your fidelity as well as utmost industry" (Rich 1948, 7). Here, obligation and commitment are clearly linked, making trust reinforce trustworthiness (and, at the same time, control). At the point of expansion inland, letters from London similarly stated the Committee's faith in Marten and the local officers to decide where to place new posts (Davies 1965).

Contrary to some discussions in the organizational literature that focus on firms' preferences for one form of control (e.g., Ouchi 1980), the HBC did not have a clear preference for one form of control and appeared to engage in a variety of controls both simultaneously and over time, shifting repertoires of control dynamically as appropriate. Our examination of the HBC's dispersed operations suggests that the HBC enacted a variety of control mechanisms—selection techniques, information requirements, and direct local oversight—through its primary practices of socialization, communication, and participation. For example, the elaboration of reporting requirements during the period of the inland expansion did not replace (but was added) to the continued use of the Orkneys as the main source for servants and the use of orphanages and individuals known to Committee members as the source for officers. Both of these were supplemented by the participation of individuals such as Marten, and later Simpson, in positions of heightened authority on the Bay.

Our examination also finds that the HBC's senior management learned early on about the strengths and weaknesses of contracts as a means of controlling distant agents (Carlos 1992, Carlos and Nicholas 1993). As early as 1682, the Committee was surprised to find that "common sense" was not enough to "cause all our servants to comply." In response, it resorted to "all manner of means" to bind its men to the Company's interests. Initially, these means were simple extensions of the contracts, such as bonds and oaths (Rich 1948). Over time, however, the Committee shifted away from contractual controls to a reliance on the types of trust and control we have described here.

Our view of the intertwined nature of trust and control as enacted in organizations suggests that a more complex, practice-oriented view of trust would be beneficial in current research on trust and control in virtual groups and organizations. In particular, our longitudinal examination suggests that researchers and practitioners would do well to consider the broad array of potential trust- and control-enhancing practices and move beyond the single and simplistic quick-fix remedies so widely propounded in the literature, such as the commonly prescribed initial face-to-face meetings. Many authors use trust as a catchall for all things good in teams and communities. We agree that trust is important, but do not view it as the "cure" for the ills of the traditional organization (Handy 1995, 44), or the "elixir" of distributed or virtual work (Davidow and Malone 1992, 264; Lipnack and Stamps 1997, 224–225). Indeed, the story of the HBC suggests that the process and outcome of geographically dispersed work are shaped by the interaction of a number of elements that are more complex, dynamic, and emergent than suggested by the contemporary literature on virtual working. Empirical research that explores and elaborates on these elements and their interaction would be particularly valuable.

We also suggest that in considering the repertoire of practices that virtual organizations may adopt, both researchers and practitioners need to be attentive to how these practices are experienced in different situations. This chapter is based on a particular situation of a trading company operating hundreds of years ago. Not all the practices we have identified, such as the six-week voyages for socialization, will generalize directly to our contemporary context. Moreover, researchers and practitioners need to be alert to the inevitability of unintended consequences. For example, unintended outcomes were evident in the HBC when the Committee attempted to increase the amount of information it obtained about the posts. To the Committee's surprise, the factors resisted, and a renegotiation of norms and expectations was required.

Although it is dangerous to draw too direct a connection between centuries-old organizing practices and those of today's geographically dispersed organizations, the HBC records demonstrate that trust is not solely a twenty-first-century concept applied retrospectively to this seventeenth-century organization; *trust* was a term and concept referred to frequently and explicitly in Company communications (Rich 1948). In addition to these explicit references to trust between the Committee and its factors, London's early letters repeatedly demonstrate this trust through its reliance on the factors' prudence, faithfulness, honesty, diligence, good behavior, integrity, reputation, justice, ability, courage, conduct, fidelity, and local knowledge (Rich 1948, in which at least one of these terms is used in each letter outward). Many of these concepts (especially honesty, integrity, reputation, and competence) are all commonly cited bases for trust in the modern literature (Mayer, Davis, and Schoorman 1995, McAllister 1995, Kramer and Tyler 1996, Kramer 1999).

Furthermore, the story of the HBC suggests several important additional implications for modern virtual organizations. While some of the HBC's practices may seem a bit archaic by today's standards, some of them might usefully be enacted today in slightly modified forms. First, the HBC's emphasis on socialization practices might be especially important for contemporary companies as they try to counter the effect of tight labor markets, frequent job jumping, and low levels of loyalty.

Second, the HBC case clearly highlights the value of retaining and sharing business communications and other records in an accessible manner. The Company's carefully maintained records provided it with an important source of organizational memory and allowed the Committee and its officers to analyze and act on long-term trends in key business indicators (e.g., cyclical fluctuations in beaver populations). Its attention to detail and use of version control numbers, the eighteenth-century equivalent of unique employee IDs, and the strategic use of carbon copy (CC) and blind carbon copy (BCC), all predate many database features that are now considered critical for knowledge management.

Third, some aspects of participation and being there can be facilitated by faster, twenty-first-century communications technology, but other aspects still evade the enabling nature of that technology. In the modern version of Simpson's management by canoeing around, many leaders of virtual organizations may feel little choice but to manage by flying around. However, Simpson did not maintain his aggressive travel schedule indefinitely. After developing his own local knowledge, he began to use alternative approaches to being there. For example, he and the Committee supported a strong sense of identity among key staff groups (e.g., chief factors, clerks, and apprentice officers) and thus strove to develop a sense of esprit de corps and professional community among employees. By explicitly supporting participation in professional and occupational communities, contemporary companies may be able to build on some of the HBC's techniques to counteract the sense of dislocation that is emerging as the downside of frequent travel and telecommuting

Finally, the HBC story illustrates the complex balancing act that geographically dispersed organizations must perform: finding a workable balance between central control and local discretion. The HBC and similarly dispersed companies must maintain reasonable and prudent levels of control, but because they can never have enough information to direct their dispersed operations completely, they must also establish and build trust among their employees to ensure that they respond appropriately and effectively within local circumstances. This is especially challenging when dispersed organizations face tough competition and turbulent environmental conditions, such as those that the HBC confronted in the last quarter of the eighteenth century. Contrary to a number of theories of organizational control, the HBC's story also suggests that unidimensional approaches to trust or control are unlikely to succeed in geographically dispersed organizations. That is, both trust and control need to be generated jointly through a variety of ongoing organizing practices.

Notes

We thank the Hudson's Bay Company Archives (HBCA), Provincial Archives of Manitoba, Winnipeg, Canada, and especially Anne Morton, head of research and reference there. Without the HBCA's rich collections and the expert assistance of Morton and her staff, this research would not have been possible.

1. The volumes by Rich (1939, 1945, 1948, 1952, 1954, 1957), Davies (1965), and Williams (1975) include invaluable transcriptions of full series of letters, minutes, journals, and other HBC records. They are not selections of (or from) these primary source records, but full runs for the years covered.

2. Our longitudinal perspective is possible because the Company's extremely detailed records survive in its archives. The HBCA is one of the world's largest and most comprehensive collections of records for a single company (Simmons 1994). For this chapter, we visited the archives and also obtained microfilmed copies of hundreds of Company documents through interlibrary loan.

3. In 1870, the HBC sold most of this territory back to the government to create 75 percent of modern Canada.

4. We use masculine pronouns because the HBC had an all-male staff until the twentieth century.

5. Citations of the HBCA refer to the original records maintained at the archives. For good descriptions of these records and the syntax of their classification codes, see Burley (1997) and Craig (1970).

6. See McKnight and Chervany (1996) for more on the various general definitions of trust and Bandow (1998) for definitions of trust in an explicitly distributed context.

7. Our focus is on internal trust and controls rather than external and environmental influence.

8. Many of these communication and record-keeping practices (as well as other business practices) predate those of the American railroads and the conventional chronology of big business (Chandler 1977) by more than a century.

References

Bandow, D. (1998). *Behind the mask, across the miles: Defining and using trust in geographically dispersed work groups.* Unpublished Ph.D. dissertation, Fielding Institute.

Barley, S. R., and Kunda, G. (1992). Design and devotion: Surges of rational and normative ideologies of control in managerial discourse. *Administrative Science Quarterly, 37,* 363–399.

Bradach, J. L., and Eccles, R. G. (1989). Price, authority, and trust: From ideal types to plural forms. *Annual Review of Sociology, 15,* 97–118.

Brown, J. S. H. (1980). *Strangers in blood.* Vancouver: University of British Columbia Press.

Brytting, T. (1996, November). The management of distance in antiquity. *Scandinavian Journal of Management Studies, 3,* 139–155.

Burley, S. (1997). *Servants of the Honorable Company: Work, discipline, and conflict in the Hudson's Bay Company, 1770–1870.* Ontario, Canada: Oxford University Press.

Carlos, A. M. (1992). Principal-agent problems in early trading companies: A tale of two firms. *American Economic Review, 82,* 140–145.

Carlos, A. M. (1994). Bonding and the agency problem: Evidence from the Royal African Company, 1672–1691. *Explorations in Economic History, 31,* 313–335.

Carlos, A. M., and Kreuse, J. B. (1996). The decline of the Royal African Company: Fringe firms and the role of the charter. *Economic History Review, 49,* 291–313.

Carlos, A. M., and Nicholas, S. (1990). Agency problems in early chartered companies: The case of the Hudson's Bay Company. *Journal of Economic History, 50,* 853–875.

Chandler, A. D. (1977). *The visible hand: The managerial revolution in American business.* Cambridge, MA: Belknap Press.

Cowie, I. (1993). *Company of adventurers: A narrative of seven years in the service of the Hudson's Bay Company during 1867–1874.* Lincoln: University of Nebraska Press. (Originally pulished 1913.)

Craig, J. (1970). Three hundred years of records. *The Beaver,* 1970 (Outfit 301), 65–70.

Crisp, C. B., and Jarvenpaa, S. L. (2000, August 8). *Trust over time in global virtual teams.* Paper presented at the Academy of Management Annual Meeting, Toronto, Canada.

Davidow, W. H., and Malone, M. S. (1992). *The virtual corporation: Structuring and revitalizing the corporation for the twenty-first century.* New York: Edward Burlingame Books/HarperBusiness.

Davies, K. G. (ed.). (1965). *Letters from Hudson Bay, 1703–1740.* London: Hudson's Bay Record Society.

DeSanctis, G., and Monge, P. (1999). Introduction: Communication processes for virtual organizations. *Organization Science (Special Issue)*, *10*, 693–703.

Giddens, A. (1984). *The constitution of society: Outline of the theory of structuration.* Berkeley: University of California Press.

Goldring, P. (1985). Governor Simpson's elite recruitment in a British overseas enterprise, 1834–1870. *Prairie Forum*, *10*, 251–282.

Greif, A. (1989). Reputation and coalitions in medieval trade: Evidence on the Maghribi traders. *Journal of Economic History*, *49*, 857–882.

Guillén, M. F. (1994). *Models of management: Work, authority, and organization in a comparative perspective.* Chicago: University of Chicago Press.

Handy, C. (1995). Trust and the virtual organization. *Harvard Business Review*, *73*, 40–50.

Harris, S. (1996). Confession-building: Long-distance networks and the organization of Jesuit science. *ESM*, *1*, 284–318.

Haywood, M. (2000). *Managing virtual teams: Practical techniques for high-technology project managers.* Boston: Artech House.

Hudson's Bay Company. (2000). Hudson's Bay Company. www.hbc.com/hbc/overview.

King, J. L., and Frost, R. L. (2002). Managing distance over time: The evolution of technologies of dis/ambiguation. In P. Hinds and S. Kiesler, *Distributed work* (3–26). Cambridge, MA: MIT Press.

Kramer, R. M. (1999). Trust and distrust in organizations: Emerging perspectives, enduring questions. *American Review of Psychology*, *50*, 569–598.

Kramer, R. M., and Tyler, T. R. (1996). *Trust in organizations: Frontiers of theory and research.* Thousand Oaks, CA: Sage.

Kyle, R. (2000, October 12, 2000). Blanket approval. *Washington Post*, pp. G01.

Lipnack, J., and Stamps, J. (1997). *Virtual teams: Reaching across space, time, and organizations with technology.* New York: Wiley.

Mayer, R. C., Davis, J. H., and Schoorman, F. D. (1995). An integrative model of organizational trust. *Academy of Management Review*, *20*(3), 709–734.

Maznevski, M. L., and Chudoba, K. M. (2000). Bridging space over time: Global virtual team dynamics and effectiveness. *Organization Science*, *11*, 473–492.

McAllister, D. J. (1995). Affect- and cognition-based trust as foundations for interpersonal cooperation in organizations. *Academy of Management Journal*, *38*, 24–59.

McKnight, D. H., and Chervany, N. L. (1996). *Meanings of trust.* Management Information Systems Research Center Working Paper Series, No. 96-04. Available at: misrc.umn.edu/wpaper/.

Mishra, A. K., and Spreitzer G. M. (1999). Giving up control without losing control: Trust and its substitutes' effects on managers' involving employees in decision making. *Group and Organization Management, 14*(2), 155–187.

Newman, P. C. (1985). *Company of adventurers.* Markham, Ontario: Viking.

O'Reilly, C. A., and Chatman, J. A. (1996). Culture as social control: Corporations, cults, and commitment. *Research in Organizational Behavior, 18,* 157–200.

Ouchi, W. G. (1980). Markets, bureaucracies, and clans. *Administrative Science Quarterly, 25,* 129–141.

Rich, E. E. (ed.). (1939). *Colin Robertson's correspondence book, September 1817 to September 1922* (Vol. 2). Toronto: Champlain Society.

Rich, E. E. (ed.). (1945). *Minutes of the Hudson's Bay Company, 1679–1684.* London: Hudson's Bay Record Society.

Rich, E. E. (ed.). (1948). *Letters outward, 1679–94.* Toronto: Champlain Society.

Rich, E. E. (ed.). (1952). *Cumberland House journals and inland journals, 1775–82, Second Series, 1779–82* (Vol. 15). London: Hudson's Bay Record Society.

Rich, E. E. (ed.). (1954). *Moose Fort journals, 1783–85* (Vol. 17). London: Hudson's Bay Record Society.

Rich, E. E. (ed.). (1957). *Hudson's Bay Copy Booke of letters and commissions outward, 1688–1696.* London: Hudson's Bay Record Society.

Rich, E. E. (1961). *Hudson's Bay Company, 1670–1870.* New York: Macmillan.

Robson, J. (1752). *An account of six years' residence in Hudson Bay.* London.

Rousseau, D. M., Sitkin, S. B., Burt, R. S., and Camerer, C. (1998). Not so different after all: A cross-discipline view of trust. *Academy of Management Review, 23*(3), 393–404.

Simmons, D. (1994). Annals of the fur trade, "... if it can bee soe soone done": The making of the Hudson's Bay Company archives. *The Beaver, 74,* 4–12.

Spraakman, G., and Wilkie, A. (2000). The development of management accounting at the Hudson's Bay Company, 1670–1820. *Accounting History,* n.s. 5, 59–84.

Van Maanen, J., and Schein, E. H. (1979). Toward a theory of organizational socialization. *Research in Organizational Behavior, 1,* 209–264.

Williams, G. (1970). Highlights in the first two hundred years of the Hudson's Bay Company. *Beaver* (Outfit 301), 4–63.

Williams, G. (ed.). (1975). *Hudson's Bay miscellany, 1670–1870.* Winnipeg, Canada: Hudson's Bay Record Society.

Williams, G. (1983). The Hudson's Bay Company and the fur trade: 1670–1870. *Beaver* (Outfit 314), 4–86.

Wiesenfeld, B. M., Raghuram, S., and Garud, R. (1999). Communication patterns as determinants of organizational identification in a virtual organization. *Organization Science, 10*(6), 777–790.

Yates, J. (1989). *Control through communication: The rise of system in American management.* Baltimore: Johns Hopkins University Press.

II
Lessons from Collocated Work

Collocation and all it implies—face-to-face communication, close proximity, lots of informal social interaction, quick feedback, and so forth—is usually considered the gold standard of work environments. Collocation calls to mind the sociable quilting bee, the tightly coordinated ballet troupe, the cohesive firefighting group, and the cockpit crew. If collocation is superior as a work environment and if we can understand its features in detail, then we can measure distributed work environments by how well they approximate collocated work, and we can develop technologies for virtual collocation.

In chapter 3, Sara Kiesler and Jonathon Cummings review a large body of research on the impact of proximity on social interaction and group dynamics. From work on such phenomena as social facilitation, territoriality, and familiarity effects, they conclude that proximity generally aids work and that distributed work is likely to require more formal management and technology to succeed. Bonnie Nardi and Steve Whittaker, in chapter 4, report their interviews and observations of workers who talked about their face-to-face and long-distance contacts with coworkers and others. Face-to-face collaboration, meetings, dinners, and so on are invaluable in some ways and onerous in others. The authors propose the idea of "media ecologies" as a way of thinking about balancing the benefits and drawbacks of collocated and distributed work. Judy Olson, Stephanie Teasley, Lisa Covi, and Gary Olson describe in chapter 5 their studies of "radically" collocated work, where teams do everything in the same room over an extended period. They document the high productivity of these teams, show the kinds of flexible interaction that collocation can offer, and argue that a technology for distributed work is needed that can recreate these opportunities. In the last chapter in part II, Robert Kraut, Susan Fussell, Susan Brennan, and Jane Siegel examine the role of proximity in the success of collaborative work and parse its different features for creating interaction opportunities and awareness of others. This chapter too addresses the technologies needed to sustain collaborative work environments at a distance.

3

What Do We Know about Proximity and Distance in Work Groups? A Legacy of Research

Sara Kiesler and Jonathon N. Cummings

Significant increases in the geographic distribution of work have been touted widely. Yet a large body of evidence suggests that close proximity is beneficial to relationships and group interaction. We examine these benefits through the lens of research on the mere presence of others, face-to-face communication, shared social settings, and frequency of spontaneous communication. Technological and organizational remedies for the absence of these factors in distributed work groups are popular but often problematic. We propose that communication technology is more likely to be effective when groups are cohesive than when they are not and that structured management (as well as technology) is likely to be needed in groups lacking cohesion.

"Collaboration is a body contact sport." The researcher who said this during an interview believes, as many others do, that physical proximity has a tremendous impact on the ability to work together. There is considerable support for this belief in the academic community as well. Research harking back fifty years has demonstrated that close proximity among people is associated with numerous emotional, cognitive, and behavioral changes that affect the work process for the better. In this chapter, we describe these findings, discuss reasons that proximity has been thought very good for group functioning, and consider how well people adapt to working apart. Our purpose is to stimulate discussion on fundamental problems in the psychology of distributed work and the management of distance.

What Is Proximity?

Proximity refers to the physical distance between people measured in units such as inches, meters, or miles. In the research literature, however, concepts like proximity, physical distance, collocation, and dispersion have been operationalized differently over time (Monge and Kirste 1980). Four and five decades ago, the dominant model of group dynamics was the small group framework of Kurt Lewin and his students (Forsyth 1998). Groups studied within this framework typically were collocated. A social psychologist in the 1960s, when speaking of proximity, might be talking about the seating arrangements at a table of diners, a jury, or a committee (Strodtbeck and Hook 1961, Howells and Becker 1962). During this same decade, the dominant model of organizations was driven by the production framework (Thompson 1967), in which the proximity of workers typically was defined and dictated by work flow, task interdependence, and coordination needs (Kmetz 1984).

Recent views of work groups are more differentiated. Researchers are studying on-line work groups whose members meet rarely or never (see Walther, chapter 10, and Moon and Sproull, chapter 16, both this volume), as well as teams that are collocated, but for reasons of mutual learning and support rather than work flow (Liang, Moreland, and Argote 1995; Olson, Teasley, Covi, and Olson, chapter 5, this volume). Theorists of organization have embraced the idea that work groups can be strategically designed and distributed (or redistributed) to take advantage of changing resources and opportunities, including social network relationships (Eccles and Crane 1988). Today, proximity might be defined in many ways: as the hallways and buildings separating work group members, the number of different locations in which people work over time, or the distance of members, units, or sites from headquarters (see, for example, Finholt, Sproull, and Kiesler, chapter 15, this volume). A technologist developing an application for virtual proximity might not care about users' actual proximity at all but rather about their perceived proximity; There is even a journal on this topic: *Presence: Teleoperators and Virtual Environments* (MIT Press).

Our review of research on proximity is necessarily dominated by researchers' and practitioners' changing perspectives on groups, work, and technology rather than by a fixed definition of proximity. For example, as many organizations have grown in size and complexity, researchers have focused increasingly on how coworkers can collaborate in a distributed work environment (Kraut, Egido, and Galegher 1990).

Despite researchers' changing perspectives on proximity over time, some rules of thumb seem evident. First, it seems clear that closer proximity among people has beneficial, but nonmonotonic, effects on interpersonal relations and group functioning. At nearly zero distance, people in most situations are very uncomfortable. Generally, we only want to be extremely close to people we already like a lot (Freedman 1975). People are most comfortable when they are a few feet from others, the distance varying a bit depending on culture, relationship, and task (Sommer 1969).

The first major response to greater distance occurs when people move or are placed outside the presence of others. Once people are no longer collocated, then direct observation and face-to-face conversation are difficult or impossible. A lack of observation and conversation poses problems for many groups trying to make decisions or work together. Alternatively, the absence of others aids people who want to work autonomously and without interruption, and those who value privacy and personal space. People tend to feel more comfortable in private than public spaces (Baum and Davis 1980).

The second major response to greater distance occurs when people move or are placed sufficiently far away that the costs of getting together are markedly increased. When employees work at locations more than approximately 30 meters apart, they have much-reduced daily contact and less frequent informal communication (Allen 1977, Kraut and Streeter 1995). Physical separation from other employees in daily life and work drastically reduces the likelihood of voluntary work collaboration (Kraut, Fussell, Brennan, and Siegel, chapter 6, this volume).

We turn now to the mechanisms behind these two major responses to changes in proximity. That is, why is it often important to be able to work in the presence of others, face-to-face? Why might we need to share social settings and run into coworkers in the course of a day or week? Are there any clear benefits for group work at a distance? If we are to evaluate the benefits and costs of distributed work, we need to have the answers to these questions. We discuss them below, and provide a summary table of concepts and findings (see table 3.1).

Effects of the Presence of Others

In the earliest studies of groups, researchers noted a "social facilitation" effect (for a review, see Forsyth 1998). That is, when people are in the presence of an audience, coworkers, or even others doing unrelated tasks, their performance changes. When they are working on well-learned or easy tasks, the presence of others increases their alertness, motivation, and speed. However, when people are working on difficult or unlearned tasks, the presence of others can be distracting, reduce accuracy, and increase feelings of stress (Zajonc 1965).

The presence of others seems to increase a person's concern with what others think and increase involvement with the group and the group's activity. When people

Table 3.1
Concepts and research findings related to proximity

Concept	Psychological effects	Behavioral and group effects	Effects on work	Related factors
Mere presence of others	Evaluation apprehension ↑ Sense of privacy ↓	Stress ↑ Distraction ↑ Effort ↑	Performance of automated tasks ↑ Performance of difficult tasks ↓	Work complexity
	Observation of and attention to those present ↑ Social pressure ↑	Involvement ↑ Imitation ↑ Social influence ↑ Conformity ↑	Urgency of proximate task, time spent on proximate group's work ↑	Competing tasks and deadlines
	Familiarity ↑ (mere exposure effect)	Liking, positive responding ↑ Group identity ↑	Contributions to group ↑	Time spent in presence of others
Face-to-face communication	Felt social contract (commitment) ↑	Cooperation ↑ Conflict ↓	Agreements ↑ Contributions to group ↑	
	Interpersonal attraction ↑	Group identity ↑	Agreements ↑ Contributions to group ↑	
	Information exchange, mutual observation, and backchannel and direct feedback ↑	Task adjustments, decisions ↑	Coordination ↑ Learning and overlapping expertise ↑	Type of task
	Perceived participation ↑ Social pressure ↑ Persuasion ↑	Participation ↑ Group identity ↑	Conformity ↑ Consensus ↑ Work satisfaction ↑	Decision rules (e.g., majority)

	Shared expectations and norms ↑	Roles and behaviors matched to situation ↑	Enactment of expected work behavior and roles↑	Cues that demark situations and territories
Shared social setting	Territoriality ↑ Group identity ↑	Demarcation and protection of territory ↑ Interaction ↑	Control of work and access within the territory ↑ Work satisfaction ↑	
Spontaneous communication	Information exchange, mutual observation, and backchannel and direct feedback ↑	Group meetings and decisions ↑ Creation of interdependent tasks ↑ Mutual understanding ↑	Task adjustments ↑ Know-how and overlapping expertise ↑ Social support ↑	Work interdependence
	Interpersonal attraction ↑	Group identity ↑ Close ties ↑ Intentional contact ↑	Likelihood of collaboration ↑	

Note: Adjacent cells along the same row represent relationships shown in the research literature. (See the text for discussion and citations).

Arrows up = more of this quality increases the proximity effect.

Arrows down = more of this quality reduces the proximity effect.

are in others' presence, their heart rate and blood pressure increase, and they breathe more quickly (Walden and Forsyth 1981). Members of the audience at a live performance enliven one another, an effect simulated in the television laugh track. People in face-to-face meetings command one another's attention and feel involved with group tasks. The attention we pay to those present tends to make our interactions with them more memorable than our interactions with those far away (Latane, Liu, Nowak, and Bonevento 1995).

The presence of others increases conformity through its effect on felt surveillance and social pressure. In the famous Milgram experiments (e.g., Milgram 1974), when an experimenter and subject were in the same room, about 65 percent of subjects obeyed the experimenter's command to give 450-volt electronic shocks to a "poor learner" (a confederate). However, when the experimenter left the room and gave his commands by telephone, only 20 percent were obedient to the 450-volt level. Milgram also tried changing the proximity of the subjects to the victim. When the subjects were seated next to the victim, only 40 percent of the subjects were obedient and shocked the victim to the 450-volt level. Thus, if the experimenter was close to the subjects, his authority was strong, but if the victim was close to the subjects, then the victim's protests overrode the demands of the experimenter. Latane and his colleagues developed a theory of social impact that has, as one of its main premises, that people who are proximate have more impact (Latane 1981). Proximity increases social impact, such as obeying someone's request to sing loudly, contribute to a charity, give a large tip, or do a favor or expend effort for the group. In a group, free riding (letting others do the work) is minimized when members are proximate and each member's contribution to the group project can be clearly identified (Hardy and Latane 1986). A similar observation has been made in game-theoretic discussions of cooperation. The ability to observe others directly increases the chance that observers can see people cooperate and learn to cooperate themselves (Macy 1991).

Over time, the continued presence of others improves people's feelings of familiarity with them. This "mere exposure effect" (Zajonc 1968) has been applied to the liking of people, music, art, and food to which we have had repeated exposure. In a simple experiment, women tasted good-tasting or distasteful liquids in the presence of other women. Between each tasting, some of the women were moved from one tasting booth to another, such that each woman spent ten, five, two, one, or no trials with another woman. As predicted, the greater the exposure was to another woman, the more the woman was liked—and the taste of the liquid was irrelevant (Saegert, Swap, and Zajonc 1973).

In sum, research suggests that the presence of others increases attention, social impact, and familiarity. These effects imply support for the dictum, "out of sight, out of mind," with several implications for distributed work. That is, distributed work that causes people to be out of one another's sight may lead also to their comparative inattention to coworkers, a lower level of effort, or an increase in free riding. If getting work done depends on close attention to others—say, to make prompt corrections, help out when work loads are heavy, or receive handoffs—this inattention, lack of effort, or free riding can lead to delays in the work (Herbsleb, Mockus, Finholt, and Grinter 2000). Many people have multiple tasks to do and many roles, with pulls on their attention from many directions. In the absence of coworkers, members are likely to choose tasks with more immediate demands. On the other hand, some distributed work might experience an improvement from the absence of others. For example, if task and reward interdependence are low and the work is complex, working alone should be beneficial to performance, because there would be little distraction from the presence of others and attention to their needs. Journalists authoring articles for their newspapers are an example of such a situation.

Effects of Face-to-Face Communication

In studies of the mere presence of others, researchers prevent research participants from talking with one another because communication always dominates the effects of mere presence. Only a few moments of face-to-face discussion can have huge effects on an interaction. For instance, in one of the earliest studies of competitive games, subjects who were instructed to "win as much as you can for yourself" nevertheless made cooperative choices that helped both players when they could communicate with their partner. They cooperated on 71 percent of trials when they could communicate, whereas they cooperated on only 36 percent of the trials when they could not communicate with their partner (Deutsch 1958). Kerr and Kaufman-Gilliland (1994) showed that group members who were given five minutes to discuss an investment game with one another were far more likely to cooperate with the group than were group members who did not have this opportunity, and the effect was not duplicated when group members heard the group discussion but were not able to participate. Indeed over one hundred studies show the powerful effect of face-to-face discussion on cooperative choices in social dilemmas (Orbell, Dawes, and van de Kragt 1988; see the review by Sally 1995). These effects are thought to derive from both the commitment people feel when they make social contracts face-to-face and increases in group identity that accrue from face-to-face interaction.

Another important role of face-to-face discussion is in coordinating the efforts of a highly interdependent group such as a jury, aircraft crew, coaching staff, or research team (Tushman 1979, Weick and Roberts 1993). Heavy use is made of discussion in research and development teams where work is uncertain (Pelz and Andrews 1966, Adams 1976, Allen 1977, Tushman 1977). For example, a research team will need to decide what is to be done and how different people and subunits will work together. It will need to agree on a common definition of what they are doing, plan how to hand off components of the work expeditiously, decide who will take responsibility for meeting deadlines, and in general mesh the activities of the group. If the group is small and members are physically proximate, effective coordination can occur because the group can talk out problems together, keep all the details of the task in focus, and organize work (Kameda, Stasson, Davis, Parks, and Zimmerman 1992; Weldon, Jehn, and Pradhan 1991). With discussion, group members develop deeper understandings of the task, and they have opportunities to observe and learn from one another, though typically they do not reach theoretically maximum results (Steiner 1972). (Coordination losses result in part from group inefficiency in combining effort and from free riding; Ringelmann 1913; Williams, Harkins, and Latané 1981.)

Face-to-face discussion also is a powerful tool to develop and maintain group culture, authority, and tacit norms (Levitt and March 1988, Nelson and Winter 1982). Discussions improve group commitment, socialization, and control. Discussion can overcome severe conflict among team members, as in the case of one U.S. Olympic rowing team (Lenk 1969). In spite of animosity and disunity among the members, discussion led to the formation of coalitions that decided to cooperate with others, and the team won the Olympic gold medal (see Carron 1982).

In sum, research shows that face-to-face discussion has a strong impact on cooperation through its effects on bonds, social contracts, and group identity. It is the most powerful medium known for coordinating work within an interdependent group. To the degree that a distributed work group lacks chances to talk face-to-face, it also lacks the most direct and easy route to cooperation and coordination.

Effects of Shared Social Settings

Research in the tradition of social ecology (Barker 1968) examines proximity through the template of social settings. Social settings, such as offices, meeting rooms, cars, restaurants, stores, and friends' homes, are associated with behavioral norms, mental schemas, and even scripts that sharply affect the way people act and the expectations they have of others. Mr. Smith's behaviors in a supermarket and in a bar are likely to differ far more across these two social settings than Mr. Smith's behavior in the supermarket as compared with Mr. Brown's behavior in the supermarket. The strong impact of social settings in shaping behavior implies that people with whom we share social settings also share similar expectations, experiences, and perspectives.

Shared social settings promote the tendency to develop proprietary feelings about physical spaces. People use cues from their own and others' locations, such as functional activities associated with the location, artifacts, physical boundary cues, and physical distance signals, to establish territories (Forsyth 1998). Territories associated with social settings help organize people's social and work experiences (Edney 1976).

The "shells" or boundaries that surround territories help groups avoid intrusion and interruption; others tend not to invade these spaces even if they are in a public space or path (Knowles 1973). People start invading group spaces if the boundaries become fuzzy or the distance among group members becomes large (Cheyne and Efran 1972). Marking territory not only keeps others out but also increases feelings of ownership about the people in the territory. Hence, territories contribute to group identity and increase people's satisfaction with their group and their work (Newman 1972, Baum and Valins 1977, Edney and Uhlig 1977). People with contiguous territories tend to interact and to like one another (Moreland 1987). Territories also reinforce feelings of privacy, information sources, and ownership of artifacts within the territory.

In sum, research shows that sharing social settings in physical space affects the similarity of people's expectations and experiences and influences the likelihood of establishing a shared territory. These effects may be important in distributed work for two reasons. First, distance among workers typically means that the shared social setting is at a more abstract or symbolic level than when workers are really in the same geographic location. Abstract similarities may be useful for some purposes (see Frost and King, chapter 1, this volume), but abstractions may present problems in accomplishing collaborative work. Second, the natural tendency to establish local territories may interfere with coworkers' identification with the larger collective, such as the distributed project group. Ambiguity of membership reduces group identity (Brown and Wade 1987; see also Armstrong and Cole, chapter 7, this volume).

Effects of Spontaneous Communication

Distances between offices and work locations possibly have their highest impact on group functioning through their effect on informal, spontaneous communication opportunities (Brockner and Swap 1976; Ebbesen, Kjos, and Konecni 1976; Hays 1985; Kraut and Streeter 1995; Newcomb 1981). That is, people who work in proximate offices run into one another at the water cooler, coffee machine, and copier. They see one another come and go to meetings. They meet in the lunch room. These casual encounters increase the convenience and pleasure of communication, and they allow for unplanned and multipurpose interactions (see Kraut, Fussell, Brennan, and Siegel, chapter 6, and Nardi and Whittaker, chapter 4, both this volume). Ongoing work progresses more seamlessly when people communicate often and spontaneously. With spontaneous casual communication, people can learn informally how one another's work is going, anticipate each other's strengths and failings, monitor group progress, coordinate their actions, do favors for one another, and come to the rescue at the last minute when things go wrong (Allen and Hauptman 1990; Davenport 1994; Trevino, Lengel, and Daft 1987; de Meyer 1991, 1993; Weisband, chapter 13, this volume). When the distance between workplaces increases to about 30 meters or more, the amount of contact declines precipitously (Zipf 1949; Allen 1977; Kraut, Egido, and Galegher 1987).

Casual contact is important to relationships. People tend to like and be influenced most by people they encounter and talk with frequently (Festinger, Schachter, and Back 1950; Insko and Wilson 1977). They receive most of their social support from people who live and work nearby and those with whom they are in most frequent contact (Wellman 1992). Generally, strong personal ties—ties that are frequent, reciprocal, and extending over multiple content domains—are supported by spontaneous communication that occurs when people are in close physical proximity. Once strong ties are established, they can be, and frequently are, sustained using telephones or e-mail (Wellman and Wortley 1990, 1993).

Today, one hears many stories of people forging close work relationships at a distance through electronic communication. Some researchers argue that over time, electronic communication allows for sufficient spontaneous communication to support the development of new close ties (Walther, chapter 10, this volume). However, the evidence thus far suggests that physical proximity, with its many spurs to spontaneous communication, serves this purpose better. Work collaborations are more likely to be created and sustained, and are likely to be more satisfying and productive, than distributed (geographically distant) collaborations (Orlikowski 1992; Smith et al. 1994; Kraut et al., chapter 6, this volume; Shunn, Crowley, and Okada, chapter 17, this volume).

In sum, research shows that the frequency of spontaneous, informal communication has dramatic effects on the strength of social and work ties and on the evolution of activities that people do together and functions they serve for one another. These effects imply that distributed workers will have more difficulty forming close collaborations, dealing flexibly with one another, and expanding the breadth of the relationships through a variety of unplanned mutual experiences. It implies that strong ties will be more difficult to forge and to sustain in the distributed than in the collocated work group. Hansen (1999) found that it was more difficult to transfer complex knowledge from one location to another when ties were weak.

Remedies for Distance

In centuries past, traders, sailors, explorers, and diplomats maintained relationships with distant colleagues, coworkers, sponsors, and supervisors (Frost and King, chapter 1, and O'Leary, Orlikowski, and Yates, chapter 2, both this volume). Today's groups and organizations, however, have far more options to support distributed group work and remedy problems of distance.

Communication Technology

Networked communication technologies, especially e-mail and telephone, seem to offer a substitute for face-to-face communication (Sproull and Kiesler 1991). In this regard, many researchers have examined whether mediated communication differs from face-to-face communication (De Meyer 1991; Kraut, Galegher, and Egido 1988; McGuire, Kiesler, and Siegel 1987; Siegel, Dubrovsky, Kiesler, and McGuire 1986; see Walther, chapter 10, this volume). In laboratory studies during the past two decades, researchers typically compared participants who made decisions or solved problems in the presence of others and face-to-face, or separated, using e-mail or other technology to communicate. In studies outside the laboratory, researchers typically examined the relationship of the amount of mediated communication use with some outcome variable, such as work satisfaction or performance.

Many consistent communication benefits and costs have been demonstrated in the use of mediated communication. Technologies like the wired and cell telephone are awkward for group conversation but facilitate many other work tasks at a distance, such as scheduling, interviewing, talking over a problem, and touching base (Short, Williams, and Christie 1976). E-mail is convenient for including many people in consideration of a plan or document, carrying on multiple discussions asynchronously, staying in touch, and encouraging participation in group decisions (Sproull and Kiesler 1991).

On the negative side, as many of us have discovered, e-mail seems to encourage ever more communication and therefore is time-consuming. Theories such as social presence and media richness posit large costs to mediated communications because of their low bandwidth (Daft and Lengel 1984, 1986; Short, Williams, and Christie 1976). All mediated communications constrain backchannel feedback to promote mutual understanding, and they limit paralinguistic cues to soften or emphasize verbal information (Krauss, Garlock, Bricker, and McMahon 1977). Mediated communications also may discourage effective conversational strategies, such as small talk that precedes and personalizes one person's helping out another, or Socratic questioning in which one person leads another to adopt a new idea, or implicit learning of social conventions (see these points developed in Mark, chapter 11, and Nardi and Whittaker, chapter 4, both this volume). Perhaps as important, mediated communications do not facilitate companionship—people doing things together. It is still hard to attend a conference or have a meal or go on a bike ride with someone by telephone or e-mail.

Nonetheless, people seem able to adapt these technologies to their activities over time. Some distributed groups develop a strong group identity despite the limitations of e-mail (Walther, chapter 10, and Armstrong and Peter chapter 7 addendum, both this volume). We do not know, however, whether long-term collaborations in these instances depend on at least occasional face-to-face contact (see, for example, Schunn et al., chapter 17, this volume). The strongest and most active collaborations seem still to be proximate ones.

In sum, many distributed work groups adapt their interactions well to today's communication technologies. These technologies allow for the exchange of work information without face-to-face communication and for spontaneous communication. However, because of the lack of real and perceived presence of others and lack of shared social setting, these technologies do not necessarily encourage communication. The style of communication in electronically sustained work groups is likely to be somewhat less mutually attentive, less companionable, less frequent, and more effortful than when the team is nearby and talking face-to-face. Computer-based technology today allows distant coworkers to exchange an ever-increasing variety of information: documents, funds, drawings, advice, schedules, votes, and so on. It has been shown that the mediated exchange of information about coworkers' skill can be as effective in promoting joint performance as when the coworkers are actually trained together (Moreland and Myaskovsky 2000). However, it remains unclear how well these technologies can sustain ongoing work that requires close collaboration. One possibility, which we address at the end of this chapter, is that the use of communication technology is likely to be most successful when work groups have already forged close relationships, so that the existing feelings of alliance or commitment sustain motivation.

Structured Management
Practitioners and scholars have argued that work can be designed for the situation (Hackman and Oldham 1980, Wageman 1995). In software development, for example, modularization or task decomposition (Parnas 1972) rationalizes the work, and standard procedures for version control prevent conflicts in code. Task decomposition and version control help people understand their goals and those of others, reduce errors, and reduce the need to redo work.

Structured management approaches have been applied to distributed work as well because they are theoretically an efficient alternative to face-to-face and spontaneous communication under conditions of complexity and uncertainty (Aldrich 1979, Downs 1967, Cyert and March 1963, March and Simon 1958). Instead of having to talk repeatedly about what each person should do, for instance, task decomposition allows a team to divide its work into manageable chunks. The members of the group can then work autonomously and hand over work according to a standard procedure. It should not be surprising, therefore, to find that recent solutions to effective teamwork in distributed software development have emphasized these methods (Moon and Sproull, chapter 16, this volume).

Task decomposition and standard procedures for administration can promote autonomy and independence of decision making, which in turn can reduce role ambiguity and increase local innovativeness (Johnson et al. 1998). Evidence from an extensive comparison of automotive product development teams suggests that one reason that Japanese teams did well is that the managers of these teams had greater authority and independence than American and European managers did (Clark, Chew, and Fujimoto 1987). In distributed software development, each phase of the work cycle, from planning through operation and maintenance, can be done independently, but deliverables are subject to review before they are passed on. Thus, it is specified what is being delivered at each stage and how the deliverables can be tested or scrutinized to ensure that they do what they are supposed to do. All official project documents also may be under review. As well, groups can adopt naming conventions that must be adhered to project-wide. Perhaps they also agree that code cannot be written without design reviews, designs cannot be tested before design walk-throughs, changes cannot be made without issuing a modification request, and no piece of code goes to system test without an integration test.

Structured management is far from a panacea, however. Grinter, Herbsleb, and Perry (1999), in their recent study of distributed research and development, describe problems of coordination, trust, and information exchange in projects that used four different modularization designs: organization around functional areas, products, customers, or process steps. All of these projects experienced problems in coordination, and in each of the projects, workers at distributed sites often lacked the expertise they needed to do their work. For example, when work was distributed by functional area, employees at each site did not have critical knowledge about other functional areas. Another problem was that employees at sites that were distant from the core work site missed much of the spontaneous communication that moved the work forward:

For satellite sites, . . . it is difficult not to be constantly surprised. Not having access to the corridor conversations, people at remote sites may have no clue about what is happening until a decision has formally been made. Potentially serious problems flow from this. For one, decisions that seem relatively unimportant to the central site may affect the satellite in significant ways simply because the issues are not obvious to the center. Even when there is no single killer consequence of a decision, the cumulative effect of many surprises can be substantial. As one manager of a satellite site remarked, it is as if you are "fighting upstream instead of going with the flow." (314)

As this study shows, structured management reduces some of the uncertainty of distributed work but does not solve all the problems of distance. Moreover, formalization itself can place an extra burden on the group by increasing the need for a coordination infrastructure: clerical and management staff, training, reporting, and archiving. The care and feeding of bureaucracy can become more significant to employees than the ultimate goals they are supposed to accomplish. Management sometimes uses standardization and rationalization of tasks to increase control, which can sap motivation. Structured management also might impede innovation by limiting the options explored by a work group.

Another disadvantage of structured management as a coordination strategy is that it can depersonalize interaction. For instance, with task decomposition, team members, or subgroups on the team, have different roles. Team members or subgroups working on their own tasks tend to develop divergent perspectives and habits of work (Brewer and Kramer 1985, Tajfel 1982). They may have little opportunity and eagerness to learn from others on the team, impeding the exchange of expertise and discovery (Newcomb 1961; Faunce 1958; Festinger, Schachter, and Back 1950; Monge and Kirste 1980; Jablin, Putnam, Roberts, and Porter 1986). Task decomposition can exacerbate demographic or skill differences that existed at the start (Jablin 1979; Sykes, Larntz, and Fox 1976; Monge, Rothman, Eisenberg, Miller, and Kirste 1985).

A Hypothesis

Good work group performance often depends on coordination of the individual efforts of members and cohesiveness of the group. Both seem particularly important when the work is complex and disjunctive—where everyone in the group must solve a problem and agree to a single solution—but other work tasks also benefit from coordination and cohesiveness (for example, voting on a decision, in which each person's contribution adds legitimacy to the whole). Distributed work seems prone to both coordination and cohesiveness losses for the reasons we have reviewed and summarized in table 3.1.

Furthermore, many distributed groups at the outset are likely to suffer not just from physical distance but also from social distance—a lack of group identity, or social diversity of the membership (Hinds and Bailey 2000). For example, the decision to create a distributed work group might have been motivated by employees' geographic dispersion. With geographic dispersion often comes social and cultural diversity, which can make it harder for people to form friendships and organize themselves and can increase relationship conflict in groups (Shaw 1982; Orlikowski 1992; Olson and Teasley 1996; Pelled, Eisenhardt, and Xin 1999; Smith et al. 1994); Jackson, May, and Whitney 1995; Moreland et al. 1996; see Mannix, Griffith, and Neale, chapter 9, this volume).

Task or cognitive diversity may result also when people with appropriate expertise, organizational experience, or credentials of people to do the work are geographically dispersed. Diversity in skill or technical background does not always boost performance in groups (Tziner and Eden 1985), but management often believes that a mix of expertise increases creativity and know-how devoted to the task (Pelz and Andrews 1966, Peterson and Nemeth 1996). However, to integrate this diverse expertise, the group must resolve differences of opinion, perspective, and expectations. Distributed work groups might do this poorly (Williams and O'Reilly 1998; Mannix, Griffith, and Neale, chapter 9, this volume). Certainly they are less likely to try when they begin as strangers or with a strong sense of social distance (Gruenfeld, Mannix, Williams, and Neale 1996).

We hypothesize that the effectiveness of remedies for physical distance in work groups will depend on the degree of existing social distance or cohesion in the group. If existing cohesion is high—that is, if the work group members have a strong commitment to the group or to one another—then mediated communication technologies provide a plausible remedy for the lack of close physical proximity. Because the members are committed to the group's work, cohesiveness and motivation to keep in touch are less of a problem than when there is high social distance among members. Members with high commitment can use technology spontaneously to coordinate their work. On the other hand, if cohesion is low and members do not have a commitment to the group, then the distributed work group faces problems not just of coordination but also of cohesiveness. It seems unlikely that e-mail and other communication technologies would provide a sufficient remedy for a lack of cohesiveness and common group identity. Concerted attempts by some group members might increase the closeness of the group if the task had to be accomplished, but delays would be expected as the group worked through conflict.

We propose that structured management, in addition to the use of technology, may be a necessary (but possibly insufficient) remedy to the lack of physical proximity when a group lacks cohesion. The research reported by Moon and Sproull in chapter 16 suggests that if distributed work can be modularized and if standardized procedures for coordination can be imposed, then social distance and a lack of cohesion may matter less to the group. Since the members of the group are comparatively autonomous and working within a clear structure, members do not need to adjust all of their work to the ideas of others. They do not need to be friends. They can use communication technology to chat with any group member with whom they have a common interest, but they need not participate in group decision making.

In short, we propose that technology will help cohesive distributed groups manage distance but that structured management as well will be needed in distributed groups that lack social cohesion. Other factors will need to be considered, of course. For example, Grinter, Herbsleb, and Perry (1999) argue that the selection of the appropriate division of labor should be driven by the hardest coordination problem in the project.

Conclusion

It seems evident that far more research has been done on the ramifications of proximity than on its causes. Distributed work does not drop from the sky on hapless groups. Surely it matters whether the antecedents of collocation or great distance include chance, management decision, personal choice, technology investment, the architecture of the task, or side effects of some other problem such as resource dependence. The absence of an analysis of antecedents in the literature is worrisome and probably leads us to reify and oversimplify the meaning of proximity and distance in distributed groups. A fruitful task for the future would be a better understanding of the factors that bring us to be engaged in proximate or distributed work.

Note

We gratefully acknowledge the support of the National Science Foundation (IIS-9872996) and comments by members of the workshop, especially Pamela Hinds, Janet Fulk, Susan Fussell, and John L. King.

References

Adams, J. S. (1976). The structure and dynamics of behavior in organizational boundary roles. In M. D. Dunnette (ed.), *Handbook of industrial and organizational psychology* (1175–1199). Chicago: Rand-McNally.

Aldrich, H. (1979). *Organizations and environments.* Englewood Cliffs, NJ: Prentice Hall.

Allen, T. (1977). *Managing the flow of technology.* Cambridge, MA: MIT Press.

Allen, T. J., and Hauptman, O. (1990). The substitution of communication technologies for organizational structure in research and development. In J. Fulk and C. Steinfeld (eds.), *Organizations and communication technology* (275–294). Newbury Park, CA: Sage.

Armstrong, D. J., and Cole, P. (2002). Managing distances and differences in geographically distributed work groups. In P. Hinds and S. Kiesler (eds.), *Distributed work* (167–186). Cambridge, MA: MIT Press.

Armstrong, D. J., and Peter, E. B. (2002). Addendum to Managing distances and differences in geographically distributed work groups: Virtual proximity, real teams. In P. Hinds and S. Kiesler (eds.), *Distributed work* (187–189). Cambridge, MA: MIT Press.

Barker, R. G. (1968). *Ecological psychology.* Stanford, CA: Stanford University Press.

Baum, A., and Davis, G. E. (1980). Reducing the stress of high-density living: An architectural intervention. *Journal of Personality and Social Psychology, 38,* 471–481.

Baum, A., and Valins, S. (1977). *Architecture and social behavior: Psychological studies of social density.* Hillsdale, NJ: Erlbaum.

Brewer, M., and Kramer, R. (1985). The psychology of intergroup attitudes and behavior. *Annual Review of Psychology, 36,* 219–243.

Brockner, J., and Swap, W. C. (1976). Effects of repeated exposure and attitudinal similarity on self-disclosure and interpersonal attraction. *Journal of Personality and Social Psychology, 17,* 45–56.

Brown, R., and Wade, G. (1987). Superordinate goals and intergroup behavior: The effect of role ambiguity and status on intergroup attitudes and task performance. *European Journal of Social Psychology, 17,* 131–142.

Carron, A. V. (1982). Cohesiveness in sports groups: Interpretations and considerations. *Journal of Sport Psychology, 4,* 123–128.

Cheyne, J. A., and Efran, M. G. (1972). The effect of spatial and interpersonal variables on the invasion of group controlled territories. *Sociometry, 35,* 477–487.

Clark, K., Chew, B., and Fujimoto, T. (1987). Product development in the world auto industry. *Brookings Papers on Economic Activity, 3,* 729–781.

Cyert, R. M., and March, J. G. (1963). *Behavioral theory of the firm.* Englewood Cliffs, NJ: Prentice Hall.

Daft, R., and Lengel, R. (1984). Information richness: A new approach to managerial behavior and organizational design. *Research in Organizational Behavior, 6,* 191–233.

Daft, R., and Lengel, R. (1986). Organizational information requirements, media richness and structural design. *Management Science, 32,* 554–571.

Davenport, T. (1994). Saving IT's soul: Human centered information management. *Harvard Business Review, 72,* 119–131.

de Meyer, A. (1991). Tech talk: How managers are stimulating global R&D communication. *Sloan Management Review, 37,* 49–58.

Deutsch, M. (1958). Trust and suspicion. *Journal of Conflict Resolution, 2,* 265–279.

Downs, A. (1967). *Inside bureaucracy.* Boston: Little, Brown.

Ebbesen, E., Kjos, G., and Konecni, V. (1976). Spatial ecology: Its effects on the choice of friends and enemies. *Journal of Experimental Social Psychology, 12,* 505–518.

Eccles, R. G., and Crane, D. B. (1988). *Doing deals: Investment banks at work.* Boston: Harvard Business School Press.

Edney, J. J. (1976). Human territories: Comment on functional properties. *Environment and behavior, 8,* 31–48.

Edney, J. J., and Uhlig, S. R. (1977). Individual and small group territories. *Small Group Behavior, 8,* 457–468.

Festinger, L., Schacter, S., and Back, K. (1950). *Social pressures in informal groups.* Palo Alto, CA: Stanford University Press.

Finholt, T. A., Sproull, L., and Kiesler, S. (2002). Outsiders on the inside: Sharing know-how across space and time. In P. Hinds and S. Kiesler (eds.), *Distributed work* (357–378). Cambridge, MA: MIT Press.

Forsyth, D. (1998). *Group dynamics.* Pacific Grove, CA: Brooks/Cole.

Freedman, J. L. (1975). *Crowding and behavior.* San Francisco: Freeman.

Grinter, R. E., Herbsleb, J. D., and Perry, D. W. (1999). The geography of coordination: Dealing with distance in R&D work. In *Proceedings of SIGGROUP Conference on Supporting Group Work* (306–315). New York: ACM Press.

Gruenfeld, D. H., Mannix, E. A., Williams, K. Y., and Neale, M. A. (1996). Group composition and decision making: How member familiarity and information distribution affect process and performance. *Organizational Behavior and Human Decision Processes, 67,* 1–15.

Hackman, J. R., and Oldham, G. R. (1980). *Work redesign.* Reading, MA: Addison-Wesley.

Hansen, M. (1999). The search-transfer problem: The role of weak ties in sharing knowledge across organization subunits. *Administrative Science Quarterly, 44,* 82–111.

Hardy, C., and Latane, B. (1986). Social loafing on a cheering task. *Social Science, 71,* 165–172.

Hays, R. B. (1985). A longitudinal study of friendship development. *Journal of Personality and Social Psychology, 50,* 304–313.

Herbsleb, J. D., Mockus, A., Finholt, T. A., and Grinter, R. E. (2000). Distance, dependencies, and delay in a global collaboration. In *Proceedings of the ACM Conference on Computer-Supported Cooperative Work (CSCW)* (319–328). New York: ACM Press.

Hinds, P. J., and Bailey, D. E. (2000). *Virtual team performance: Modeling the impact of geographic and temporal virtuality.* Paper presented at the Academy of Management annual meeting, August, Toronto.

Howells, L. T., and Becker, S. W. (1962). Seating arrangement and leadership emergence. *Journal of Abnormal and Social Psychology, 64,* 148–150.

Insko, C., and Wilson, M. (1977). Interpersonal attraction as a function of social interaction. *Journal of Personality and Social Psychology, 35,* 903–911.

Jablin, F. M. (1979). Superior-subordinate communication: The state of the art. *Psychological Bulletin, 86,* 1201–1222.

Jablin, F. M., Putnam, L. W., Roberts, K. H., and Porter, L. W. (eds.). (1986). *Handbook of organizational communication: An interdisciplinary perspective.* Thousand Oaks, CA: Sage.

Jackson, S. E., May, K. E., and Whitney, K. (1995). Understanding the dynamics of diversity in decision making teams. (pp. 204–261). In R. Guzzo and E. Salas (eds.), *Team.*

Johnson, J. D., La France, B. H., Meyer, M., Speyer, J. B., and Cox, D. (1998). The impact of formalization, role conflict, role ambiguity, and communication quality on perceived organizational innovativeness in the Cancer Information Service. *Evaluation and the Health Professions, 21,* 27–51.

Kameda, T., Stasson, M. F., Davis, J. H., Parks, C. D., and Zimmerman, S. K. (1992). Social dilemmas, subgroups, and motivation loss in task-oriented groups: In search of an "optimal" team size in division of work. *Social Psychology Quarterly, 55,* 47–56.

Kerr, N. L., and Kaufman-Gilliland, C. M. (1994). Communication, commitment, and cooperation in social dilemmas. *Journal of Personality and Social Psychology, 66,* 513–529.

King, J. L., and Frost, R. L. (2002). Managing distance over time: The evolution of technologies of dis/ambiguation. In P. Hinds and S. Kiesler (eds.), *Distributed work* (3–26). Cambridge, MA: MIT Press.

Kmetz, R. L. (1984). An information processing study of a complex workflow in aircraft electronics repair. *Administrative Science Quarterly, 29,* 255–280.

Knowles, E. S. (1973). Boundaries around group interaction: The effect of group size and member status on boundary permeability. *Journal of Personality and Social Psychology, 26,* 327–331.

Krauss, R., Garlock, C., Bricker, P., and McMahon, L. (1977). The role of audible and visible back-channel responses in interpersonal communication. *Journal of Personality and Social Psychology, 35,* 523–529.

Kraut, R. E., Egido, C., and Galegher, J. (1990). Patterns of contact and communication in scientific research collaboration. In J. Galegher, R. Kraut, and C. Egido (eds.), *Intellectual teamwork: Social and technological bases of cooperative work* (149–171). Hillsdale, NJ: Erlbaum.

Kraut, R. E., Fussell, S. R., Brennan, S. E., and Siegel, J. (2002). Understanding effects of proximity on collaboration: Implications for technologies to support remote collaborative work. In P. Hinds and S. Kiesler (eds.), *Distributed work* (137–162). Cambridge, MA: MIT Press.

Kraut, R., Galegher, J., and Egido, C. (1988). Relationships and tasks in scientific research collaboration. *Human-Computer Interaction, 3,* 31–58.

Kraut, R., and Streeter, L. (1995). Coordination in software development. *Communications of the ACM, 38,* 69–81.

Latane, B. (1981). The psychology of social impact. *American Psychologist, 36,* 343–356.

Latane, B., Liu, J., Nowak, A., and Bonevento, M. (1995). Distance matters: Physical space and social impact. *Personality and Social Psychology Bulletin, 21,* 795–805.

Lenk, H. (1969). Top performance despite internal conflict: An antithesis to a functionalistic proposition. In J. W. Loy and G. S. Kenyon (eds.), *Sport, culture, and society* (393–397). New York: Macmillan.

Levitt, B., and March, J. G. (1988). Organizational learning. *Annual Review of Sociology, 14,* 319–340.

Liang, D., Moreland, R., and Argote, L. (1995). Group versus individual training and group performance: The mediating factor of transactive memory. *Personality and Social Psychology Bulletin, 21,* 384–393.

Mark, G. (2002). Conventions for coordinating electronic distributed work: A longitudinal study of groupware use. In P. Hinds and S. Kiesler (eds.), *Distributed work* (259–282). Cambridge, MA: MIT Press.

Macy, M. W. (1991). Learning to cooperate: Stochastic and tacit collusion in social exchange. *American Journal of Sociology, 97,* 808–843.

Mannix, E. A., Griffith, T., and Neale, M. A. (2002). The phenomenology of conflict in distributed work teams. In P. Hinds and S. Kiesler (eds.), *Distributed work* (213–233). Cambridge, MA: MIT Press.

March, J. G., and Simon, H. (1958). *Organizations.* New York: Wiley.

McGuire, T., Kiesler, S., and Siegel, J. L. (1987). Group and computer-mediated discussion effects in risk decision making. *Journal of Personality and Social Psychology, 52,* 917–930.

Milgram, S. (1974). *Obedience to authority.* New York: Harper & Row.

Monge, P., Rothman, L., Eisenberg, E., Miller, K., and Kirste, K. (1985). The dynamics of organizational proximity. *Management Science, 31*(9), 1129–1141.

Monge, R. R., and Kirste, K. K. (1980). Measuring proximity in human organizations. *Social Psychology Quarterly, 43,* 110–115.

Moon, J. Y., and Sproull, L. (2002). Essence of distributed work: The case of the Linux kernel. In P. Hinds and S. Kiesler (eds.), *Distributed work* (381–404). Cambridge, MA: MIT Press.

Moreland, R. L. (1987). The formation of small groups. *Review of Personaity and Social Psychology, 8,* 80–110.

Moreland, R. L., Argote, L., and Krishnan, R. (1996). Socially shared cognition at work: Transactive memory group performance. In J. L. Nye and A. M. Brower (eds.), *What's social about social cognition? Research on socially shared cognition in small groups* (57–84). Thousand Oaks, CA: Sage.

Moreland, R. L., and Myaskovsky, L. (2000). Exploring the performance benefits of group training: Transactive memory or improved communication? *Organizational Behavior and Human Decision Processes, 82,* 117–133.

Nardi, B. A., and Whittaker, S. (2002). The place of face-to-face communication in distributed work. In P. Hinds and S. Kiesler (eds.), *Distributed work* (83–110). Cambridge, MA: MIT Press.

Nelson, R. R., and Winter, S. G. (1982). *An evolutionary theory of economic change.* Cambridge, MA: Belknap Press.

Newcomb, T. R. (1961). *The acquaintance process.* New York: Holt, Rinehart and Winston.

Newman, O. (1972). *Defensible space.* New York: Macmillan.

O'Leary, M., Orlikowski, W., and Yates, J. (2002). Distributed work over the centuries: Trust and control in the Hudson's Bay Company, 1670–1826. In P. Hinds and S. Kiesler (eds.), *Distributed work* (27–54). Cambridge, MA: MIT Press.

Olson, J., and Teasley, S. (1996). Groupware in the wild: Lessons learned from a year of virtual collaboration. In *Proceedings of the ACM conference on Human Factors in Computing Systems* (419–427). Cambridge, MA: ACM Press.

Olson, J. S., Teasley, S., Covi, L., and Olson, G. (2002). The (currently) unique advantages of collocated work. In P. Hinds and S. Kiesler (eds.), *Distributed work* (113–135). Cambridge, MA: MIT Press.

Orbell, J. M., Dawes, R. M., and van de Kragt, A. J. C. (1988). Explaining discussion-induced cooperation. *Journal of Personality and Social Psychology, 54,* 811–819.

Orlikowski, W. (1992). Learning from notes: Organizational issues in groupware implementation. In *CSCW 92 Proceedings* (362–369). New York: ACM Press.

Ouchi, W. G. (1980). Markets, bureaucracies, and clans. *Administrative Science Quarterly, 25,* 129–140.

Parnas, D. L. (1972). On the criteria to be used in decomposing systems into modules. *Communications of the ACM, 5,* 1053–1058.

Pelled, L., Eisenhardt, K., and Xin, K. (1999). Exploring the black box: An analysis of work group diversity, conflict, and performance. *Administrative Science Quarterly, 44,* 1–28.

Pelz, D. C., and Andrews, F. M. (1966). *Scientists in organizations: Productive climates for research and development.* New York: Wiley.

Peterson, R. S., and Nemeth, C. J. (1996). Focus versus flexibility: Majority and minority influence can both improve performance. *Personality and Social Psychology Bulletin, 22,* 14–23.

Ringelmann, M. (1913). Research on animate sources of power: The work of man. *Annales de l'Institut National Agronomique, 2e série, 12,* 1–40.

Saegert, S. (1978). High-density environments: Their personal and social consequences. In A. Baum and Y. M. Epstein (eds.), *Human response to crowding* (257–281). Hillsdale, NJ: Erlbaum.

Saegert, S., Swap, W., and Zajonc, R. B. (1973). Exposure, context, and interpersonal attraction. *Journal of Personality and Social Psychology, 25,* 234–242.

Sally, D. (1995). Conversation and cooperation in social dilemmas: A meta-analysis of experiments from 1958 to 1992. *Rationality and Society, 7,* 58–92.

Schunn, C., Crowley, K., and Okada, T. (2002). What makes collaborations across a distance succeed? The case of the cognitive science community. In P. Hinds and S. Kiesler (eds.), *Distributed work* (407–430). Cambridge, MA: MIT Press.

Short, J., Williams, E., and Christie, B. (1976). *The social psychology of telecommunications.* New York: Wiley.

Siegel, J. L., Dubrovsky, V., Kiesler, S., and McGuire, T. (1986). Group processes in computer-mediated communication. *Organizational Behavior and Human Decision Processes, 37,* 157–187.

Smith, K. G., et al. (1994). Top management team demography and process: The role of social integration and communication. *Administrative Science Quarterly, 39,* 412–438.

Sommer, R. (1969). *Personal space.* Englewood Cliffs, NJ: Prentice Hall.

Sproull, L., and Kiesler, S. (1991). *Connections: New ways of working in the networked organization.* Cambridge, MA: MIT Press.

Steiner, I. D. (1972). *Group process and productivity.* New York: Academic Press.

Strodtbeck, F. L., and Hook, L. H. (1961). The social dimensions of a twelve-man jury table. *Sociometry, 24,* 397–415.

Sykes, R., Larntz, K., and Fox, J. (1976). Proximity and similarity effects on frequency of interaction in a class of naval recruits. *Sociometry, 39,* 263–269.

Tajfel, H. (1982). Social psychology of intergroup relations. *Annual Review of Psychology, 33,* 1–39.

Thompson, J. D. (1967). *Organizations in action.* New York: McGraw-Hill.

Trevino, L., Lengel, R., and Daft, R. (1987). Media symbolism, media richness, and media choice in organizations: A symbolic interactionist perspective. *Communication Research, 14,* 553–574.

Tushman, M. (1977). Special boundary roles in the innovation process. *Administrative Science Quarterly, 22,* 587–605.

Tushman, M. (1979). Work characteristics and subunit communication structure: A contingency analysis. *Administrative Science Quarterly, 24,* 82–98.

Tziner, A., and Eden, D. (1985). Effects of crew composition on crew performance: Does the whole equal the sum of its parts? *Journal of Applied Psychology, 70,* 85–93.

Wageman, R. (1995). Interdependence and group effectiveness. *Administrative Science Quarterly, 40,* 145–180.

Walden, T. A., and Forsyth, D. R. (1981). Close encounters of the stressful kind: Affective, physiological, and behavioral reactions to the experience of crowding. *Journal of Nonverbal Behavior, 6,* 46–64.

Walther, J. B. (2002). Time effects in computer-mediated groups: Past, present, and future. In P. Hinds and S. Kiesler (eds.), *Distributed work* (235–257). Cambridge, MA: MIT Press.

Weick, K., and Roberts, K. (1993). Collective mind in organizations: Heedful interrelating on flight decks. *Administrative Science Quarterly, 38*(3), 357–382.

Weldon, E., Jehn, K. A., and Pradhan, P. (1991). Processes that mediate the relationship between a group goal and improved group performance. *Journal of Personality and Social Psychology, 61,* 555–569.

Wellman, B. (1992). Which types of ties and networks provide which types of support? (207–235). In E. Lawler, B. Markovsky, C. Ridgeway, and H. Walker (eds.), *Advances in group processes*. Greenwich, CT: JAI Press.

Wellman, B., and Wortley, S. (1990). Different strokes from different folks: Community ties and social support. *American Journal of Sociology, 96,* 558–588.

Williams, K. D., Harkins, S., and Latané, B. (1981). Identifiability as a deterrent to social loafing: Two cheering experiments. *Journal of Personality and Social Psychology, 40,* 303–311.

Williams, K., and O'Reilly, C. (1998). Demography and diversity in organizations: A review of 40 years of research. *Research in Organizational Behavior, 20,* 77–140.

Zajonc, R. B. (1965). Social facilitation. *Science, 149,* 269–274.

Zajonc, R. B. (1968). Attitudinal effect of mere exposure. *Journal of Personality and Social Psychology,* Monograph Supplement, *9,* 2–17.

Zipf, G. (1949). *Human behavior and the principle of least effort.* Reading, MA: Addison-Wesley.

*"Yes, Ted, on this team we take off our jackets,
but we don't loosen our ties."*

4

The Place of Face-to-Face Communication in Distributed Work

Bonnie A. Nardi and Steve Whittaker

Most distributed work requires mediated communication, but the appropriate use of mediated, as compared with face-to-face, communication is not well understood. From our ethnographic research on workplace communication, we characterize unique aspects of face-to-face communication. Face-to-face communication supports touch, shared activities, eating and drinking together, as well as informal interaction and attention management. We argue that these activities are crucial for sustaining the social relationships that make distributed work possible. We contrast these social aspects of communication with the informational aspects emphasized by traditional communication theories, arguing that social linkages are a precondition of information exchange. We document the disadvantages of face-to-face communication—that it can be disruptive, expensive, and effortful—and we describe when mediated communication is preferable. We discuss the design of "media ecologies" that balance the advantages and disadvantages of mediated and face-to-face communication to provide cost-effective solutions for communication in distributed organizations.

Most distributed work requires mediated communication, but the appropriate use of mediated as compared with face-to-face communication is not well understood. Many theorists imply that face-to-face discussion is the gold standard of communication (Clark and Brennan 1990; Kiesler, Siegel, and McGuire 1984; Rutter 1987; Short, Williams, and Christie 1976), and possibly irreplaceable (Nohria and Eccles 1992; Handy 1995; Hallowell 1999; Olson and Olson 2000; Olson, Teasley, Covi, and Olson, chapter 5, this volume). On the other hand, in the distributed situation, face-to-face communication can be costly and disruptive, and mediated communication sometimes may be preferable (Hollan and Stornetta 1992; Sproull and Kiesler 1992; DeSanctis and Gallupe 1987; Jarvenpaa and Leidner 1999; Morley and Stephenson 1969; Nardi, Whittaker, and Bradner 2000; Walther 1994).

From our ethnographic research on workplace communication, we characterize the uniquely valuable aspects of face-to-face communication, especially in sustaining social relationships, but document circumstances when other media are preferable. We discuss ways to design "media ecologies" that provide cost-effective solutions to the problems of distributed organizations.

The Value of Face-to-Face Communication

A variety of new technologies support remote interaction, but business travel has increased so much that airports are nearly in gridlock. Why? An impressive body of research demonstrates that face-to-face communication is the most information-rich medium (Doherty-Sneddon et al. 1997; O'Conaill, Whittaker, and Wilbur 1993; Short, Williams, and Christie 1976; Daft and Lengel 1984; Clark and Brennan 1990; Clark 1996). We will argue another key reason face-to-face communication persists in the workplace is that it is surest way to establish and nurture the human relationships underlying business relationships. These relationships are grounded in social bonding and symbolic expressions of commitment. We contrast social aspects of communication with information aspects—information transfer, finding common ground topically, repairing misunderstandings, and referring to shared objects in the environment. Our focus is not what people communicate about, but how they create a social environment in which they can communicate at all. Social linkages between people are a precondition of information exchange.

Information exchange is a key goal of communication, but by focusing our theories exclusively on information we overlook the social processes that scaffold information exchange. We theorize that people create social "fields" within which communication can take place. We call these fields "communication zones." A *zone* is a potentiality for productive communication between two people. In everyday human activity, the management of communicative zones involves long-term projects of creating appropriate social bonds of connection, which may stretch over years, or even decades, as well as much shorter-term projects of managing attention (Nardi, Whittaker, and Bradner 2000).

We have documented communication zones in our research on instant messaging (Nardi, Whittaker, and Bradner 2000). Here we further our goal of exploring communication zones by analyzing face-to-face communication. Unlike many other aspects of communication that are clearly observable such as turn taking or head nodding, communication zones emerge only in informants' accounts of their communicative activities. These accounts include metaphoric language utilizing spatial metaphors, discussion of the problems of communication, and descriptions of the deliberate staging of communicative events.

Communication zones are like Shakespeare's "local habitations"—mutually constituted, local universes that people construct to communicate. Although Shakespeare was talking about poetic creativity in the following passage from *A Midsummer Night's Dream*, he might well have been addressing the creative work of communicating:

And as the imagination bodies forth
The forms of things unknown, the poet's pen
Turns them to shapes, and gives to airy nothing
A local habitation and a name.

In our empirical data, "airy nothing" constantly threatens communication, as we shall see, and people go to a great deal of trouble to create and maintain local habitations within which communication can take place.

The creation and maintenance of communication zones involve two key processes: establishing social bonds that enable people to feel emotionally connected to one another and managing "attentional contracts" in which people agree (sometimes fleetingly) to pay attention to one another's communications. Most media and communication theories address exchanges that are already underway. By contrast, we are interested in how people get into a state where communication can take place. Processes needed to attain that state are not peripheral to communication but suffuse and shape it.

We report findings from a study of workers collaborating across organizational boundaries (Nardi, Whittaker, and Schwarz 2000). We carried out in-depth interviews and observations in a sample of twenty-two people in twelve organizations. Our sample included public relations specialists, an executive who transfers technology across corporate boundaries, an attorney who appeals life sentence cases, graphic artists, Web designers, a nonprofit consultant, small business owners, Internet company executives, and a secretary. Some in our sample were independent contractors or consultants. Some worked for a very large telecommunications company, "TelCo," some for a medium-size Internet portal company, and some for small companies of fewer than one hundred people, including "CreativePix," an animation and Web company, and "MediaMax," a company that produced Web pages, CD-ROMs, and user interfaces for computer games. About half the sample was male and half female. Most were in their thirties or forties. Most worked in California, and some in New Jersey. All but one had a college degree. Some had been to film school, law school, or graduate school. All were proficient with a variety of communication technologies.

We audiotaped interviews in informants' workplaces and sometimes observed them at work. We asked them about the work they did and how they communicated. We learned about their use of communication media including phone, cell phone, voice mail, conference calls, fax, express mail, e-mail, e-mail attachments, videoconferencing, pagers, the Internet, FTP, the Web, chats, intranets, and extranets, as well as face to face. About fifty hours of interviews generated over a thousand pages of transcripts, which we analyzed for recurring patterns relating to the questions we asked about communication activities. Names attributed to the quotations from the interviews in this chapter are pseudonyms, and details have been changed to provide anonymity.

Face-to-Face Interaction Engenders Social Bonding

Social bonding is effected through two linked processes: engagement of the human body in social interaction and informal conversation. So ubiquitous and ordinary are these arenas of social action that they have often been theoretically invisible. Media theories have considered the body as a source of information about communication and the sense of "presence" of the person with whom one is communicating. Key aspects of presence are signaled by a specific sense of the other's body—physical appearance, body language, facial expressions—as well as accoutrements including clothing, makeup, hair style, and jewelry (Daft and Lengel 1984; Short, Williams, and Christie 1976).

In our interviews, informants had a complementary, more social perspective on the role of the body in communication. They talked about the importance of shared bodily activities in facilitating social bonding and showing commitment: touching, eating and drinking together, engaging in mutually meaningful experiences in a common physical space, and "showing up" in person.

Understanding these activities is key to understanding the uniqueness of face-to-face communication because they are impossible in other media (though they can be simulated in MOOs, MUDS, and virtual worlds). The first three elements of what we might call *"body work"* lead directly to the creation and maintenance of social bonds. The fourth element, "showing up," symbolizes commitment to a particular social bond.

Interleaved with body work is informal, off-the-cuff conversation: jokes, gossip, how-are-the-kids questions, and other kinds of office chat. Such informal talk aids bonding and reinvigorates communicative ties. Previous research has shown that seemingly inconsequential informal interactions serve critical functions such as coordination and learning (Allen 1977; Kraut and Streeter 1996; Whittaker, Frohlich, and Daly-Jones 1994; Nardi and Engeström 1999). Informal communications have also been shown to be extremely difficult to support using mediated communication (Kraut, Galegher, and Egido 1987; Kraut et al. 1990a). Face-to-face communication provides support for such informal interactions.

We now turn to an analysis of the interview data, reporting what informants said about body work and informal conversation.

Touching

Touch helps create social bonds that scaffold communication. The first requirement of managing zones is to create social bonds that make people feel connected to one another. We shake hands or otherwise touch each other upon being introduced. Face-to-face introductions are deeply valued, in part because people have the opportunity to make physical contact. The second requirement of managing communication zones is to keep them going. Communication zones appear to degrade over time. After being "out of touch," initiating communication can be problematic. So when we have not seen each other for some time, we often exchange warm hugs. Communication zones require renewal and "refreshing," as one informant said, of the social bonds. In the following interview segment, touch was used both to create a new bond and to maintain an existing one. Carl, a public relations specialist at TelCo, described how he managed the introduction of a famous journalist to TelCo's CEO at a high-profile invitational gathering for the American media:

Carl: In fact, "Ken Swift" [a well-known journalist], is a very important guy obviously. I am probably a little far down the food chain for him to spend a whole lot of time with. But I can get a[n] [e-mail] reply from him based on—he'll shoot me back an e-mail, but it's based somewhat on the fact that when he walked in here [to the media event], he walks in and says, "Hey, I'm sure there's a line to meet the big guy, right?" [i.e., the CEO]. It's like, "Ken! Didn't I introduce you to the last big guy? Come on!" Actually, I was able to kind of deliver him right into—I looked around, saw where [the CEO] was, and actually, Gail was with him then. She was right at his elbow. So I like—I grabbed her. I said, "Ken wants to meet him. I'm bringing him right over." And Ken and Gail are good friends. I was able to like deliver Ken right into Gail's arms; you know, big hug, right at the elbow of [the CEO]. That's going to make him answer my next e-mail.

Carl mentioned various bodies touching: "I grabbed her," "big hug," "right at the elbow," "into Gail's arms." The bodies belonged to Carl, Gail, the journalist, and the CEO. The leverage from the face-to-face communication stemmed from a richly physical moment of arms, elbows, and hugs involving the four people needed for the crucial introduction. The encounter fostered both the new bond formed between the journalist and the CEO and the intensification of existing social bonds (the journalist and Gail, Carl and Gail). The entire encounter was managed by Carl, who had to act quickly, in a highly unscripted way, to bring the bodies together in the right configuration. This kind of body work is only possible face to face.

A recurrent problem for Carl was the responsiveness of the journalists he dealt with. In our terms, Carl's problem was to maintain active communication zones with the journalists. His satisfaction with the success of the introduction is evident in his cheerful comment that Ken Swift will now "shoot me back an e-mail." Evidence for the fragility of communicative zones—their tendency to degrade—comes from the fact that although Carl had introduced the journalist to a previous CEO (as he did not fail to remind the journalist), getting the journalist to respond was a continuing problem. Carl opportunistically solved the problem—at least temporarily—through the dramatic high-touch introduction. Elsewhere, Carl affirmed the general importance of maintaining bonds, mentioning that the media event was a great way to "refresh my list," as he put it—to make personal contact with many journalists he dealt with, to refresh social bonds.

The ironic, calculating discourse in Carl's description ("a little far down the food chain," "That's going to make him answer my next e-mail") contrasts vividly with his engaged description of getting all those bodies in the right place at the right time. Although the media event was thrilling and Carl was closely attending to its emergent possibilities, he was also anticipating the mundane realities of accommodating familiar journalistic peccadilloes. The detached, objective work of monitoring the state of communication zones was executed simultaneously with the exciting body work in which touch created and reinforced social bonds. Carl's focus (and that of many other informants) was not on the information being communicated in the encounter but on the trajectory and nature of the relationships among the conversational participants. The face-to-face meeting was exploited to develop these relationships.

Working within a mutually constituted communication zone, Carl invoked his history with the journalist in reminding him of the introduction to a previous CEO, and he drew attention to the wider context of the zone, which included the fact that

Ken and Gail were "good friends." A zone seen as a local habitation suggests a "space" with a specific history and context, as well as a staging area for enacted bodily activity. People inhabit communicative zones that extend over time in order to accomplish communicative work embedded in a highly social, contextually nuanced matrix.

Eating and Drinking Together

Eating and drinking together are perhaps the most fundamental way in which people come to feel connected. We all know this from personal experience, but researchers have largely ignored these prosaic activities, missing an important contribution of face-to-face communication (although see Short et al. 1976).

Greg managed a small media firm in San Francisco. In our interview, he explained how "bonding" occurred between him and his clients through shared meals.

Greg: We were talking about the lunch-dinner thing. That's, that's kinda where the bonding happens. Especially if we've had a successful pre-pro [preproduction meeting], everybody feels it's gonna be a good job, the agency feels that they've brought their client into a professional house, we've all had our acts together . . . So then we go out to some fancy restaurant here in San Francisco, which they love—you know, we always try and keep the most trendy, up-to-date kind of thing—and everyone gets a little drunk, and the client generally holds court talking about how hard it is to work for Procter and Gamble, or whatever, you know. It's kind of . . . they're usually pretty high-energy fun.

The dinner was not a forum for exchanging business information; rather, clients used the occasion to share details of the minor miseries of their work lives. It facilitated social bonding after the initial, task-focused preproduction meeting. As far as the work itself was concerned, that was already accomplished. Apparently trust had been established as "everybody feels it's gonna be a good job" and the company's credentials as a "professional house" were in good standing.

Why then did the dinner take place? We believe it took place to deepen and enrich the social bonds shaping the communication zone inhabited by the consultants and clients, to make the zone a more congenial habitation for the future work, following the preproduction meeting. The meal also provided a context for informal conversation where the clients could share personal information in a relaxed setting. The language in this interview again reveals the juxtaposition of terms connoting detached calculation, with words suggesting human connection. Greg revealed the premeditation of identifying a special restaurant as the perfect staging area for the bonding. But then he rapidly shifted to chummy phrases about everyone getting a "little drunk" and having "high-energy fun." It seems that however much we calculatedly manage our relationships at the same time we easily get caught up in the human connections we forge. People deliberately plan to exploit face-to-face communication to create, renew, and deepen social bonds, while still participating fully in the social encounter. Relationship management is then an arena for a constructed set of staged events—hastily improvised in Carl's case, well planned in Greg's case—that may come to be a site of authentic human connection enacted in face-to-face communication through shared bodily activity.

Sharing Experience in a Common Space

Another means of social bonding enabled in face-to-face communication is sharing mutually meaningful experience in a common physical space. Carl explained how he established relationships with the press through the shared experience of attending trade shows and other industry events:

Carl: I think you need to come to know them [new press contacts] as a person at some point and have some physical engagement with them, be at the same place for some reason. You know—whether that's a trade show or some industry event or something like that—it's a chance to meet them in that context—what's going on in the industry. But then, it's nice because there's the physical connection which has been fun for me.

Carl wanted to "be at the same place *for some reason.*" The bond was fostered through an experience that involved shared interest in "what's going on in the industry." Carl emphasized physical connection in context, using the word *physical* twice in this short segment, first speaking of "physical engagement" and then "physical connection." Again the word *fun* is used to characterize face-to-face communication.

Carl's coworkers were located a continent away, on the opposite U.S. coast. Describing informal meetings with coworkers when he traveled to their site, Carl noted the physical engagement needed to renew bonds in communicative zones he had previously established:

Carl: In [one] three-day swoop you can hear an awful lot of what's going on in [the remote office] and physically see a lot of these people which you need to do.

Same as with the press. You can never cultivate these relationships without physically engaging in people as part of it.

Carl observed that "you need to . . . physically see" and "physically engage" people in order to renew relationships. In theory, Carl should have been able to "hear" what was going on in the remote office on the phone, but instead, he needed to get the latest gossip and updates face-to-face. Face-to-face communication was instrumental as a means of "cultivating" relationships, and it facilitated the informal conversation—"what's going on in the office"—in a way that the telephone did not.

Kathy, an independent marketing consultant, used another term of physicality, *touchy-feely*, to express how she regarded face-to-face communication:

Kathy: Well, when you're interacting [face to face], you're much more involved, much more—how am I going to say this? I don't know, it's just more touchy-feely, we're in this together kind of thing.

Kathy used the word *touchy-feely* metaphorically to describe the feeling of closeness she got from face-to-face communication. She was not actually touching anyone, but she invoked the power of touch we described in previous examples where people really did touch in face-to-face communication.

Barry, a public relations executive at TelCo, pointed to the importance of sharing physical space and experience in his networking activities:

Barry: Well, I think a tremendous amount of the networking that's done on a business level is personal, spatial, geographical. It's being in and of the same space and having the same experience of the surroundings. So I've never experienced a situation in which we've been able to use technology as an effective substitute to travel. Even though we've tried many times—we've done interviews by videoconference with reporters in one city, with [our people] in another city.

Barry emphasized shared physical space as critical to face-to-face in his use of the words *spatial* and *geographical*, and having "the same experience of the surroundings." Having a common experience of surroundings is undoubtedly partly related to practicalities such as deictic reference and having easy access to shared artifacts (Clark and Brennan 1990; Olson and Olson 2000; Whittaker et al. 1994). However, our interviews also support a social bonding interpretation. Phrases such as "physical connection," "being in and of the same space," and "we're in this together" signify the social and emotional connection people can establish when engaged in face-to-face communication

Evidence for the fact that informants thought of the communication zone as a space came from their metaphorical use of locational terms to describe mediated communication. Rachel, a producer at MediaMax, told us how she managed phone communication with contractors working out of their homes:

Rachel: [And] what I try to foster in all of our independent contractors is an allegiance to the company—to this company. . . . I realize that they are at home in their home setting. I don't call them up and talk business right away. I'll call them up, for example one of my programmers off site is working on fixing up his house. I'll call him up and say, "Hey! How's your floor going?" or "Your windows!" and kind of get into his world. And he'll talk to me and we'll chat about this and that and then I'll get to work stuff. 'Cause I know, I've worked at home before. I know what it's like when you get this business call and you're in your home setting. It's just kind of sometimes invasive or intrusive, and you need to walk a fine line whereby you have that kind of intermediary language. And I don't think it's a ruse. I think it's just a part of conversation that you're meeting each other somewhere.

Rachel was getting into the contractor's world, managing the communication zone, attempting to shape it to her own ends, which were, quite calculatingly to "foster . . . allegiance to the company." She defended her tactical use of language, claiming it was "not a ruse." Rachel could not share physical space with the contractor, but she tried to do the next best thing, which was to imagine and respond to the contractor's space. Her topic of informal conversation was the contractor's physical space—his floor and windows. Rachel was crafting an effective communication zone by taking account of the physical surroundings of the contractor in order to manage the contractor's transition from home to work. Rachel denoted the communication zone as a space, saying that she and the contractor were "meeting each other *somewhere*." To Rachel, this meeting "somewhere" was intrinsically part of communication. As she said, "*. . . It's just a part of conversation* that you're meeting each other somewhere."

In conclusion, then, sharing a common space has many of the same emotional effects as touching or eating and drinking together. It allows connections to be established or strengthened and also provides an ideal context for informal conversation.

Showing Commitment by Showing Up "In Person"

A more symbolic aspect of face-to-face communication can serve to underscore the importance of a particular social bond. Informants described the value of simply "showing up" and what that communicated about social bonds:

Barry: And you know, relationships are managed and fed over time, much as plants are. [You] demonstrate an enormous amount of unconscious commitment when you actually take the time and the trouble to put yourself in the same place as the person you want to build a relationship with. And if you arrive early at a seminar in advance of the time you're to give a presentation, and if you give a presentation and then remain for an hour or two or the rest of the day and participate in other discussion, that's noted and remarked upon, versus the busy executive who comes in, gives the presentation and leaves, or the person who in some fashion is participating as a disembodied voice over television. The information is still received; but the relationship management aspects are not really . . . are not really handled at all.

Barry echoed our views about relationship management in communication by distinguishing the "information being received" from "the relationship management aspects." He remarked that mediated communication—the "disembodied voice over television"—did not work for relationship management. Instead, the body itself was required to achieve the highest levels of bonding. Showing up differs from sharing experience in a common space: informants drew attention to the fact that one party had made a decision to attend "in person" and communicate face-to-face, often at some cost to themselves. In Barry's case, not only was the executive traveling to his colleagues' location, he was generously offering his time in staying around for further discussion, and "that's noted and remarked upon." In a similar vein, Nora, an independent public relations consultant, explained why she preferred to work with local clients:

Nora: Well, actually I prefer to work with local clients because I think that face-to-face contact is important. It certainly helps me to see them even every week, but a couple of times a month is good. I think what we call "face time" is very important.

Interviewer: Why is that?

Nora: Because they tell you stuff they don't tell you over the telephone. You see other people in the office. They know that, "Oh, we really do have a PR person; it's not just some disembodied voice out somewhere in Palo Alto."

The disembodied voice again. Both Barry and Nora stated that mediated communication in which a voice has no body does not serve the same ends as face-to-face communication. Informants made a kind of habeas corpus argument about commitment and face-to-face communication. Nora noted that her clients needed to know that ". . . we really do have a PR person." The identity of the person could not be established with voice only; Nora's body must be produced.

Like Carl, Nora noted that she received information in informal conversations face-to-face that was not forthcoming over the phone. She also talked about "seeing," as Carl and many others did. Bonding happens most easily when people see each other in person, with the body in full view. With showing up, any body (not anybody) will do; it is the living flesh that is required. Technology cannot simulate showing up because meaning derives from the symbolic value of people offering their actual bodies in space.

These interviews provide more evidence that communication zones decay. Nora remarked that a regular program of "seeing" was crucial. Barry too had a regularly scheduled bonding program in mind. He compared it with caring for plants (which presumably would wither if not tended). The communication zone is a dynamic, often fragile field of connection that persists only with careful attention. Kathy, who worked out of her home, spoke of face-to-face communication as "replenishing her spirit" with clients, emphasizing how it allowed her to reconnect with them:

Interviewer: So why do you actually go down to [the customer] site?

Kathy: Well, you have to have face time with people . . . They need to see that you're alive (laughs). They do! They need to get reconnected with you. What I've found is that if you don't go and have face time with people periodically, they'll start to make assumptions about you, like very funny, like, "Oh, I couldn't have gotten a hold of Kathy, so she must not be working on my stuff." . . . So you need to go kind of be there and say, "Hi, I'm here," you know? You need to share, talk a little bit, and you go on. And it's kind of like replenishing your spirit with them in a way. . . . It's their needs. I mean, I can stay here (at home) all day, all alone. I don't have to go see them . . . to do my job.

Again the detached language of business calculation is coupled with emotional warmth as Kathy "replenished her spirit" with her clients, while noting that the actual work of the job could be done from home. Her clients wanted her to "go see them." They demanded her body ("see that you're alive") as an assurance that she was really working for them. As a business strategy, Kathy made sure she had sufficient face time with clients to "share" and "talk" as ways of maintaining social bonds within her communication zones. In all of these examples, face-to-face communication signaled the highest level of commitment to others through the presentation of the body. It also afforded the best opportunities for vital informal conversation.

Symbolic interactionist theories point to symbolic reasons for choosing a particular medium such as "a desire for teamwork, to build trust, or convey informality ... urgency, ... personal concern ... or [deference]" (Trevino, Lengel, and Daft 1987). The importance of showing up fits within this paradigm; the symbolism of showing commitment is a key aspect of face-to-face communication.

There are undoubtedly many interesting power relations involved in summoning another's body as a condition of free communication in mutually constituted communication zones. Our data only begin to hint at these relations. The telecommuting literature reveals that managers often feel a loss of control over employees working at home where they cannot see them or talk to them face to face (Kraut 1987). Our data also suggest the flip side of the power of the presentation of the body: while those in power may summon the body of others to ground communication, we can also marshal our own bodies to show up, signaling high levels of commitment and binding others to us. The use of the body as a trading currency in face-to-face communication is an indication of the continual work needed to manage communication zones. It illuminates the lengths to which we sometimes go to accomplish communication.

Managing Attention
Many informants brought up the subject of gaze or "eye contact" as crucial to face-to-face interaction. Eye contact sometimes had to do with social bonding, with making a primitive (mammalian?) connection to others by "looking people in the eye," a phrase many used. This fits with our understanding of making connection through body work. But informants also discussed how eye contact served a shorter-term purpose of commanding people's attention. Our interviews suggest that attention is activated within communication zones. The potential zone becomes an active field of communication when attention is engaged.

Wanda, a technology transfer specialist at TelCo, was one of many informants who referred to the importance of eye contact in face-to-face communication. Her language strongly suggests a communication zone:

Wanda: When you're in a conference room and you're at a conference table and all these conversations are going on and people are going back and forth and they look at each other, and they look at the other people in the room, and they're trying to convey a point or trying to persuade someone, uhm, eye contact and body language mean a lot. If your eyes are on a computer, you may as well not even be there. You may as well be a secretary taking notes.

Wanda's "you may as well not even be there" posits a "there" that we interpret as a communication zone bounded by those who were at minimum making eye contact. She contrasted those within the zone and those outside it; a hypothetical secretary could be physically present but outside the zone, as would anyone who was looking at the computer. The secretary is also not a participant in the activity. A zone is bounded by an activity in which some people are legitimate participants and others are not.

Accounts of information richness stress how people read facial expressions and body language as clues to the speaker's meaning and affective state. These accounts take the recipient's perspective in decoding information about the content of messages being sent. By contrast, Wanda described how speakers use eye contact and body language to engage the others in the room. When attention is commanded, the communication zone is activated for information exchange.

Ashley, a producer-manager at MediaMax, observed that face-to-face meetings were useful for managing her staff because people and things were ready-to-hand. She then noted less fluently, but with feeling, the uniqueness of face-to-face communication for engaging attention:

Ashley: Well, there's nothing like everybody being in the same place and working on the same problem. It's just—there's an immediacy that you're never far away from what's going on, whereas when people are off site, it takes a lot more management time because you've got to [keep track of things]. On the phone, or setting up those meetings, it's harder to check in on the minute process of a project. . . . Every time you walk to the back of the office, you are passing someone's computer and you see what they are working on, you see what the mood is on their face. You know, if a question comes up you can ask that person as opposed to writing yourself a note to e-mail them or call them later on. It definitely facilitates interaction, there's no question about. And there's also you know, face to face, which—we're all human beings. That's the best way to interact with people is to look them in the eye and talk to them, and, you can't do that over the telephone as easily. Certainly not e-mail. E-mail!

Ashley juxtaposed the practicalities of face-to-face ("you see what they are working on") with the vague but far-reaching notion that face-to-face is effective because "we're all human beings." Attention is engaged at a deeper level through looking people in the eye while talking to them. Ashley seemed quite sure this same kind of attention was not achieved on the phone or by e-mail. As often happened when people discussed the more profound aspects of face-to-face communication, hesitation and searching for words characterized Ashley's discourse. People seemed to feel deeply about face-to-face but (like researchers) did not always have the vocabulary to describe its unique features precisely.

Negative Aspects of Face-to-Face Communication

We have described advantages of face-to-face communication and located them in our theory of communication zones. Our account thus far, and the bulk of other research (Short et al. 1976; Daft and Lengel 1984; Kraut, Galegher, and Egido 1987; Clark and Brennan 1990; Nohria and Eccles 1992; Hallowell 1999; Olson, Teasley, Covi, and Olson, chapter 5, this volume) paint a very positive picture of the benefits of face-to-face communication. However, data from our interviews and observations also revealed significant negative aspects of face-to-face communication in many situations: interruptions, expense, and low-productivity in the common face-to-face setting of meetings.

For many workers, a little face-to-face may go a long way. Being "radically colocated" (Olson and Olson 2001)—for example, in studio configurations or in "war rooms" lacking private space—may not be optimal for many kinds of work. Our data show that despite the many advantages of face-to-face communication, people still sought to avoid it at certain times. Sometimes they chose to remove themselves from the office or other venues of face-to-face communication, or they chose other communication media to avoid the negative aspects of face to face.

Interruptions

We have all been interrupted just when we were finally about to accomplish something. People may try to gauge availability, but they can be so taken with their own problems that they interrupt anyway, or they misread the cues. Informal, unscheduled face-to-face communication exhibits strong participant asymmetry; the intended recipient of a communication has less control over the exchange than does the initiator, due to norms of politeness (Nardi et al. 2000; O'Conaill and

Frohlich 1995; Whittaker et al. 1997). There is often a social cost to refusing communication.

Kathy explained that for her marketing research, she felt she was more productive in a consulting role because she had greater control of her time:

Kathy: A lot of times in order for me to be effective [I must do concentrated work]. . . . The benefit of a consultant is that they *don't* work inside the company, therefore, they're not interrupted all the time.

In our study, almost everyone described strategies for withdrawing from communication (mediated and face-to-face), including leaving the site of face-to-face communications and turning off pagers, phones, and other devices. We will concentrate here on strategies to avoid face-to-face, but the general point is that most people need time alone, when they can concentrate on difficult work.

Managers worried about the productivity of their staff and the effect of too many meetings and informal conversation, or "chitchat in the hallways" as one put it:

Rachel: There is an advantage to having people work off site in that often they can concentrate more and they're not badgered by company meetings or chitchat in the hallways or whatever.

Many people in our study discussed separating themselves from the interruptions of the office by working at home on a regular basis or when they had specific deadlines:

Interviewer: So what would be the kinds of activities where you don't want to be distracted? Where you feel like you want to work from home?

Alan: Uhm, when I have to get a deliverable done, a presentation, or white paper or something. And it's just, I need a chunk of time to just focus, and that's hard to do from the office, because it's so easy to be distracted.

Nevertheless, our informants rarely chose to cut themselves off completely and found that being accessible by phone and e-mail often sufficed. Jane, in business development at an Internet portal company, described how she could stay accessible enough when working at home one day a week:

Jane: So, internally, people know I'm at home working. And normally they don't have the number. My secretary has it, but unless they've like gone out of the way to ask my secretary for the number, they [don't call].

Interviewer: So they have to go one more step.

Jane: Right. So they will send me e-mail. But you can avoid answering e-mail. You don't have to answer it.

It is easy to overlook the significance of interruptions in assessing face-to-face communication. A focus on the creation and maintenance of communication zones encourages us to pay more attention to interruptions as we consider the processes surrounding and scaffolding information exchange and not just the information exchange itself. Strategic efforts to withdraw oneself from communication arenas are not visible if self-contained interactions are the sole focus of attention.

Meetings

Reactions to interruptions were mild compared with the intense annoyance people in our study expressed about formal meetings. While informants described many productive meetings (especially the ones they themselves called), more often meetings were seen as a time-wasting drain. Meetings, a ubiquitous occurrence in virtually all organizations, often failed both to transmit rich information and to deepen social bonds. Some organized themselves to work remotely, usually from home, to avoid this distasteful form of face-to-face interaction. Jane observed:

Jane: And there's just a lot of meetings. I mean, there's—you can't fit 'em in all every day. But when I can work from home, it's amazing, it's just amazing how much work I get done. . . . It's just, uh, heaven!

Jane went on to describe how meetings were generally recognized to be problematic in her organization and the generally unsuccessful attempts to address this:

Jane: Fred [an executive] is very keen on, I mean, we have these timers on here, these hour glasses.

Interviewer: Oh!

Jane: And you start a meeting and they're an hour, and there should be like no more than six or seven people in a meeting, there should be an agenda set, it should only have to go an hour, and you should get everything completed. And if you don't have those, if you don't have an agenda and you have more people in the room than you need, then cancel the meeting and schedule it when you're ready, because it's not going to be useful.

Nora liked working at home because she could avoid the "tedious" and "goofy" meetings her clients had to attend. Ella, an independent consultant to nonprofit organizations, noted that perhaps meetings are becoming even worse as people work on their laptops and respond to pagers.

Ella: I hate it [being in meetings]. I remember, I mean I've been in meetings where everyone's been looking at their laptop, typing, and no one's, you know, to me it's like, "Why are we here? Let's go home." That's a perfect example where we should be using a computer conference or something. Rather than being in person. If we're all gonna be typing on our computers. . . .

Ella proposed a remote experience in lieu of a degraded face-to-face experience. Of course, laptops and pagers in meetings are themselves symptoms of the low productivity of meetings. The feeling seems to be, "If I have to be there, I might as well get something done."

Jane did not like to bring her laptop or pager to meetings, and she wished others would not. On the other hand, she sympathetically explained why she believed others read e-mail during meetings:

Jane: I mean . . . the reason why people do that is you're really busy, right? So if you have eight hours of meetings and then you go back to your desk and you have 200 e-mails, right? And you don't want to work 14 hours a day, then what do you do, right?

Interviewer: You try to do your e-mail in meetings.

Jane: You try to do your e-mails in meetings . . . And like it's a bad habit, but once you get used to using that meeting time to do e-mail, you're caught up, you actually don't have to work those 14 hours.

Interviewer: Yeah, but on the other side, the meeting cannot be as effective.

Jane: Well, you wouldn't think so. So one of the challenges that we've had here and we're trying to balance a lot, is if you're just there to be there, and it's so ineffective for you that you can sit there and do e-mail, then just leave and go back to your desk and do e-mail. And we have a lot of these "Oh, but you have to be there" meetings, and we're trying to really cut them back to be like only if you want to, only if it's valuable, type meetings so that we can get out of the habit of actually bringing in computers and doing e-mail during those meetings.

Meetings seemed to be so universally loathed because they routinely assembled fairly sizable groups of people (too large for any but covert chitchat) to convey standard information that could be delivered in other media such as e-mail. Meetings brought bodies together, then frustrated body work and informal conversation. At the meeting's end, often little had been learned. Few but the speaker had talked.

Expense

Informants often followed discussions of the benefits of face-to-face contact with discussion of its limits. Here, Nora had been describing how much more impact she could have when describing a new product to a client in person:

Interviewer: Now from all you're saying it would be always preferable to actually meet with them in person. So then why . . .

Nora: Well, no, because sometimes it costs too much. And sometimes the news isn't earth-shattering and it doesn't warrant a face-to-face meeting.

Interviewer: Oh, I see.

Nora: You can talk to them, you can talk to them for 10 minutes or 15 minutes and that's all they need. And they don't want to spend the time to meet with you, because if you're gonna go to Boston and drive in Framingham, to spend 15 minutes . . . that doesn't serve anyone. So the face-to-face meetings are really best reserved for major announcements or big developments in the life of the company.

Many informants told the same tale: face-to-face is an "expensive" medium that has to be used judiciously. People also spoke of the emotional expense of face-to-face: the need to pay attention, engage in diverting chat, be pleasant, wear presentable clothing. Sometimes face-to-face communication was exhausting. Gary described how as a manager he struggled to keep communication alive in his small company. He needed meetings, but their emotional cost was sometimes felt by all:

Gary: The best way to get the information out is to have, is to have everybody in the room. I mean, it's amazing with a 10-person company, communications can totally break down. It's unbelievable. . . . If you don't really make a conscious effort, the human mind would rather not have to communicate because of all the issues involved in it. It's a pain in the ass. [There can be] conflict sometimes.

Interviewer: Why is that?

Gary: Because it usually means work for the individual. . . .

Gary is saying that communication is necessary but effortful, so people will try to avoid it. These examples also illustrate the hidden costs of preparing for face-to-face communication—for example, travel and wearing presentable clothes.

Media Ecologies

Given that we know what is good and what is bad about face-to-face communication, how can we best utilize it in distributed work? We propose the design of *media ecologies*, where a particular mix of media is specified depending on the nature of the work and contextual aspects of the workplace situation. Our findings on the costs and benefits of face-to-face show that searching for a single technology to substitute for face-to-face communication misconstrues the problem. Rather, we need to devise an appropriate mix of face-to-face and other media depending on the work, its temporal sequence, the context, and the distances to be traveled. These congenial patterns of mixed media operate within media ecologies. Media ecologies are an "information ecology"—local habitations of people, practices, technologies, and values (Nardi and O'Day 1999).

A key question for the design of a media ecology for distributed work is, How much face-to-face communication is needed? Our findings and other research suggest that the appropriate infusion of face-to-face communication depends on the context of the work. The automotive engineers in the successful war rooms described by Olson et al. (see Chapter 5, this volume) had no other concurrent projects to do. They were in a phase of the design requiring frequent interchanges, and some of them had left their homes and moved temporarily to where the work was being done. In other words, intense face-to-face communication with a small, tightly knit group of people was a likely route to productivity.

By contrast, our informants were almost always engaged in multiple projects, they worked within broad social networks that crossed many organizational boundaries, and their concurrent projects ranged from trying to get new business to wrapping up existing projects. The blitzkrieg nature of the software project at the automotive plant may be a less common scenario for work in the information economy than the more typical networked, overlapping projects of our informants (Ancona and Caldwell 1988; Nohria and Eccles 1992; Smith 1994; Castells 1996; Oravec 1996; Wildeman 1998; Engeström, Engeström, and Vähäaho 1999). Nevertheless, the war room provides an excellent empirical anchor defining one end of a spectrum of media ecologies, the end in which prolonged, intense face-to-face communication aids productivity.

On the opposite end of the spectrum, fully mediated communication may be adequate under some circumstances (see for example, Moon and Sproull, chapter 16, this volume). Dale, a secretary in public relations at TelCo, was located on the West Coast. She described how she supported a group on the East Coast after a layoff. She had never met anyone in the East Coast group, but there just was no one else to do the work:

Interviewer: So, was it hard to do this without ever having met them?

Dale: No, it was, I dealt with them on the phone a lot.

Interviewer: So that worked okay?

Dale: Oh, yeah. It was no problem. The only occasional problem was the hours— the difference in the hours, you know, as far as we're still working like three hours after they've gone home. . . . And so, if we needed something, it was like "Okay. We can't get 'em at work, you know? We have to page 'em." But in P. R. [public relations], people are on call 24-hours a day.

Interviewer: So they expected that they would be paged?

Dale: Oh, yes. . . . In fact, most of them had like fax machines and computers at home, and they most likely were still working, you know, but at home. A lot of them telecommuted, so calling them at home or work was no problem.

In this situation, even a three-hour time difference was not an impediment because people worked in well-equipped home offices. This situation was probably not optimal, but it does show what can be done with phone, fax, and e-mail when necessary, and apparently without undue stress. The telecommuting literature also documents examples of certain types of work such as consultancy or answering phone help lines that can be executed in an exclusively distributed way (Kraut 1987).

Another informant, Lynn, a contract attorney who appealed life sentence cases for the state of California, used U.S. mail and phone calls to deal with her clients on death row. When she was first undertaking a case, she wrote to the client and offered her phone number:

Lynn: I get a little bit of information about the case and the client's address. I then write to the client. That often starts a letter writing campaign back and forth depending on, you know, how interested in the process the person is. I also accept collect phone calls from them. You can't call somebody who's in prison, but they can call you.

In twenty years of practice, Lynn had met only a tiny handful of her clients face-to-face. The state did not fund trips to prisons for contract attorneys, so she used the phone. She felt that she could establish good rapport with many of her clients through phone conversation:

Interviewer: What about the contact with your clients? Do you ever miss that? That's the first thing I would think of because you work for a client, you want to get an impression who the person is, you want to understand the case from their perspective and all that. . . .

Lynn: No. You know, I think that I do have relationships with certain of them that are very intense. There are others—it really sort of comes from the client. I'm available to them if they want to contact me. I never refuse a phone call, ever, and so I have some people who get to the phone all the time. The woman that I have in Federal Court right now I've been representing since 1994 maybe. She calls me all the time. We've become not exactly friends, but our conversations go far beyond what's going on with her case.

In her policy of never refusing a phone call, Lynn was showing commitment to clients, much as people do with face-to-face communication. In the media ecology of Lynn and the prisoners, with its peculiar constraints, the open phone was an effective substitute for the commitment usually signaled through face-to-face communication. Again, although the situation was not optimal, Lynn was able to find ways to use mediated communication to establish working relationships. This example underscores our point that a media ecology is designed with respect to some particular set of circumstances and that we experience the media themselves differently under different circumstances.

A number of researchers have argued against a strong form of media determinism (Cherny 1999; Lea and Spears 1991; Walther, chapter 10, this volume). They observe that when there are established relationships between participants, the so-called leaner media such as e-mail and the phone can indeed be very expressive and adequately fulfill the demands of many situations. Our own observations bear this out. Jill at CreativePix remarked:

Jill: We know Ed very well, so if he were on his phone at home, I think there would still be a tight link between us and him, as opposed to the reading between the lines that one does on a conference call with somebody else you don't know as well.

A key part of the context of an interaction is the quality of the relationship between participants. Shared personal history and social bonds often make it possible to overcome the limitations of mediated communication.

On the other hand, although Lynn used the phone effectively with her clients, she was adamant about her dislike of arguing a case by phone (which is allowed in some courts in California). Again, this is consistent with other research showing the problematic nature of emotional communication in mediated settings (Morley and

Stephenson 1969; Short et al. 1976; Williams 1977). While Lynn could have fruitful interactions with clients on the phone because of their personal relationship and circumstances, this was not possible in court:

Lynn: . . . San Francisco and Fresno are the two courts that allow argument by telephone.

Interviewer: Oh.

Lynn: Which is a disaster! I've done it once, I will never do it again.

Interviewer: What is that like? Describe it to me.

Lynn: Well, I've been in San Francisco when I was in court and my opponent wasn't, and it's a very strange thing of being in this courtroom with the three judges and a voice coming from a speaker. When I've done it, I did it rather than go to Fresno, once. It was horrible. I could not read where these people were coming from, who was speaking, how they were taking my argument, what I should sort of—you can pick up a lot from watching somebody's face.

Interviewer: Mm-hm. Mm-hm.

Lynn: Plus, this included one judge who was extraordinarily rude who was yelling at my co-counsel and I who were both on the telephone. The AG [Attorney General], I think might have been there, my opponent might have been in the room, but it was a very awkward and unpleasant thing. I would never do it again. As much as I hate going to Fresno, I would be there.

We present these somewhat extreme examples from our data to make the point that the context of work varies tremendously so that there is no single recipe for a balanced media ecology. Three key elements of context for designing media ecologies are (1) the work tasks themselves, (2) the quality of the relationships between participants, and (3) the temporal flow of the work.

Our informants talked about the desirability—necessity, in some cases—of early face-to-face meetings to establish relationships. Research suggests that videoconferencing works more effectively when people already know each other (Short et al. 1976; Johansen 1984). Judicious use of face time can have large impacts on subsequent mediated communications by "priming" those other interactions.

We know from our research that communicative zones degrade over time. Thus, some regular program of face-to-face contact would also appear desirable in many settings. Nohria and Eccles (1992) suggest that in the networked organizations of the global economy, the ratio of face-to-face to mediated communication will have to increase to accommodate the personal relationships that buttress the network.

Hallowell (1999) and Olson and Olson (2000) prescribe regular face-to-face contact.

While there is a strong case for some face-to-face communication in distributed projects, the issue of the cost of face-to-face communication in distributed projects looms large. At stake are the costs to organizations of transporting and housing people remotely and the costs to workers of being away from their local work setting, families, and communities. When the costs of distribution are too high, projects may be abandoned, the work reorganized (Olson and Olson 2000), or workers may seek other jobs. If distributed projects are to function effectively, we see a strong incentive to use the technologies of mediation to keep the costs to organizations and workers within bounds. For example, while the workers in the war rooms reported on by Olson, Teasley, Covi, and Olson (chapter 5, this volume), seemed to have a generally positive experience, it is also possible that workers who had to relocate temporarily incurred hidden personal costs that did not come to light because the research focused on measuring productivity

We believe that in general, as little travel as possible is the optimal solution to the problem of distributed work to minimize the substantial personal and organizational costs. However, quantifying "as little as possible" is not straightforward. It depends on many varied situational factors, as our data indicate. Moreover, the realities of distributed work sometimes place workers astride the horns of a dilemma. Too little face time may lead to miscommunication and stress (Hallowell 1999). In our study, informants told us that they sometimes lost business or worked under duress when they could not meet with people face-to-face. Nora described difficulties in dealing with a San Diego client from her San Francisco base:

Nora: Yeah, there was actually a client that I felt in retrospect would have stayed with me longer if I had insisted on face to face meetings. They were located in San Diego, and frankly the manager was a bit of a cheapskate, so I only had a few face to face meetings with them. But I think that that really hampered our effectiveness. And I really should have noticed, jumped up and down and pounded the desk and said, "We have to see each other! If I can't come down there, you HAVE to come up here." Because I think we needed more face time.

Here the expense of face-to-face communication ran directly counter to the communicative demands of the work. Nora paid by losing a client. She not only lost money but paid an emotional price in blaming herself for the problem. Such costs to workers have been largely invisible in the overheated rhetoric enjoining "virtual teams," "virtual organizations," "anywhere, anytime work" (Bishop 1999; Schwarz, Nardi, and Whittaker, in press). Nora needed to be *with her clients*, at a particular time, in a real place where they could look each other in the eye. As she said, "We have to see each other!"

The competitive marketplace may make scenarios such as those Nora experienced all too common. High-level executives such as Barry at TelCo will demand face-to-face communication and will have the status to access the resources of their organizations to get it. Small businesses such as MediaMax and CreativePix will be compelled to find ways to meet their clients and prospective clients. The workers who will be most compromised in the rush to virtuality will be midlevel employees in medium to large organizations who cannot access organizational resources or reorganize themselves (as Nora later did) to build face time into their work. They will shoulder the burden of failed projects, additional stress at work, the increased work of undertaking mediated communication when face-to-face would have served better, and they will miss the satisfactions of social bonding.

Despite the importance of face time, we are optimistic that some technologies can aid a sense of social connection. One of those technologies is instant messaging. In a study of instant messaging in two workplaces (Nardi, Whittaker, and Bradner 2000) we found that people using the system experienced a strong sense of others that helped them establish effective communication zones. People were extremely positive about knowing who was "around" even if they did not want to communicate directly. These experiences, which we call *"awareness moments,"* were no substitute for face-to-face communication, but they provided a sense of social connection when people could not meet face-to-face. Awareness moments slow the degradation of communication zones when people are not collocated. On the other hand, technologies such as videoconferencing, which attempt to replicate the face-to-face experience, may fail because they provide neither the high-fidelity interactivity of face-to-face nor the social benefits of sharing a common physical space (Doherty-Sneddon et al. 1997; Heath and Luff 1991; O'Conaill et al. 1993; Whittaker 1995). Videoconferencing may create misleading assumptions about shared space that can be highly disruptive of communication (Heath and Luff 1991).

Designing "convivial" media ecologies, to borrow Illich's (1973) term, remains a challenge, not least because technologies and markets change so rapidly. A paradox is at hand as well. The diverse distributed webs of personal relationships and crosscutting organizational coalitions that underlie the new economy depend for their existence on sophisticated communication and transportation technologies. But even as our day-to-day activity is enacted in increasingly complex global organizations and social networks, we cannot do without our most basic form of human interaction: face-to-face communication.

References

Allen, T. (1977). *Managing the flow of technology*. Cambridge, MA: MIT Press.

Ancona, D., and Caldwell, D. (1988). Beyond task and maintenance. *Group and Organizational Studies, 13,* 468–494.

Bishop, L. (1999). Visible and invisible work: The emerging post-industrial employment relation. *Journal of Computer Supported Cooperative Work, 8,* 115–126.

Castells, M. (1996). *The rise of the network society*. Malden, MA: Blackwell Publishers.

Cherny, L. (1999). *Conversation and community*. Stanford, CA: CSLI Press.

Clark, H., and Brennan, S. (1990). Grounding in communication. In L. Resnick, J. Levine, and S. Teasley (eds.), *Perspectives on socially shared cognition* (127–149). Washington, DC: APA Press.

Daft, R., and Lengel, R. (1984). Information richness: A new approach to managerial behavior and organizational design. *Research in Organizational Behavior, 6,* 191–233.

DeSanctis, G., and Gallupe, R. (1987). A foundation for the study of group decision support systems. *Management Science, 33,* 589–609.

Doherty-Sneddon, G., Anderson, A., O'Malley, C., Langton, S., Garrod, S., and Bruce, V. (1997). Face-to-face and video mediated communication: A comparison of dialogue structure and task performance. *Journal of Experimental Psychology: Applied, 3,* 105–125.

Engeström, Y., Engeström, R., and Vähäaho, T. (1999). When the center doesn't hold: The importance of knotworking. In S. Chaiklin, M. Hedegaard, and U. Jensen (eds.), *Activity theory and social practice: Cultural-historical approaches*. Aarhus, Denmark: Aarhus University Press.

Hallowell, E. (1999, January–February). The human moment at work. *Harvard Business Review,* 58–66.

Handy, C. (1995). Trust and the virtual organization. *Harvard Business Review, 73,* 40–50.

Heath, C., and Luff, P. (1991). Disembodied conduct: Communication through video in a multi-media environment. In *Proceedings of CHI'91 Conference on Computer Human Interaction* (99–103). New York: ACM Press.

Hollan, J., and Stornetta, S. (1992). Beyond being there. In *Proceedings of CHI'92 Conference on Human Computer Interaction* (119–125). New York: ACM Press.

Illich, I. (1973). *Tools for conviviality*. New York: Harper and Row.

Isaacs, E., Walendowski, A., and Ranganathan, D. (2001). Hubbub: A wireless instant messenger that uses earcons for awareness and for sound instant messages. In *Proceedings of CHI 2001*. New York: ACM Press.

Jarvenpaa, S., and Leidner, D. (1999). Communication and trust in global virtual teams. *Organization Science, 10,* 791–815.

Johansen, R. (1984). *Teleconferencing and beyond.* New York: McGraw-Hill.

Kiesler, S., Siegel, J., and McGuire, T. W. (1984). Social psychological aspects of computer-mediated communication. *American Psychologist, 39,* 1123–1134.

Kraut, R. E. (1987). Predicting the use of technology: The case of telework. In R. E. Kraut (ed.), *Technology and the transformation of white collar work* (113–134). Hillsdale, NJ: Erlbaum.

Kraut, R. E., Egido, C., and Galegher, J. (1990). Patterns of contact and communication in scientific research collaboration. In J. Galegher and R. Kraut (eds.), *Intellectual teamwork: The social and technological bases of cooperative work* (149–172). Hillsdale, NJ: Erlbaum.

Kraut, R., Fish, R., Root, R., and Chalfonte, B. (1990). Informal communication in organizations. In S. Oskamp and S. Spacapan (eds.), *People's reactions to technology in factories, offices and aerospace* (145–199). Thousand Oaks, CA: Sage.

Kraut, R., Galegher, J., and Egido, C. (1987). Relationships and tasks in scientific research collaboration. *Human Computer Interaction, 3,* 31–58.

Kraut, R. E., and Streeter, L. A. (1995). Coordination in software development. *Communications of the ACM, 38,* 69–81.

Lea, M., and Spears, R. (1991). Computer-mediated communication, de-individuation and group decision-making. *International Journal of Man-Machine Studies, 24,* 283–301.

Morley, I., and Stephenson, G. (1969). Interpersonal and interparty exchange: A laboratory simulation of an industrial negotiation at the plant level. *British Journal of Psychology, 60,* 543–545.

Nardi, B., and Engeström, Y. (1999) (guest eds.). Special issue on invisible work. *Journal of Computer Supported Cooperative Work, 8,* 1–167.

Nardi, B., and O'Day, V. (1999). *Information ecologies: Using technology with heart.* Cambridge, MA: MIT Press.

Nardi, B., Whittaker, S., and Bradner, E. (2000). Interaction and outeraction: Instant messaging in action. *Proceedings of CSCW 2000 Conference on Computer Supported Cooperative Work* (79–88). New York: ACM Press.

Nardi, B., Whittaker, S., and Schwarz, H. (2000, May). It's not what you know, it's who you know: Work in the information economy. *First Monday.* Available at: www. firstmonday.org.

Nohria, N., and Eccles, R. (1992). *Networks and organizations.* Boston: Harvard Business School Press.

O'Conaill, B., and Frohlich, D. (1995). Timespace in the workplace: Dealing with interruptions. *Proceedings of CHI'95 Human Factors in Computing Systems* (262–263). New York: ACM Press.

O'Conaill, B., Whittaker, S., and Wilbur, S. (1993). Conversations over videoconferences: An evaluation of the spoken aspects of video mediated interaction. *Human-Computer Interaction, 8,* 389–428.

Olson, G. M., and Olson, J. S. (2000). Distance matters. *Human-Computer Interaction, 15,* 139–179.

Olson, J. S., Teasley, S., Covi, L., and Olson, G. (2002). The (currently) unique advantages of collocated work. In P. Hinds and S. Kiesler, *Distributed work* (113–135). Cambridge, MA: MIT Press.

Oravec, J. (1996). *Virtual individuals, virtual groups.* Cambridge: Cambridge University Press.

Pratt, J. (1999). *Cost/benefits of teleworking to manage work/life responsibilities.* Arlington, VA: International Telework Association and Council.

Rutter, M. (1987). *Communicating by telephone.* Oxford: Pergamon Press.

Schwarz, H., Nardi, B., and Whittaker, S. (1999). The hidden work in virtual work. In *Proceedings of Critical Management Studies Conference.* Available at www.mngt.waikato.ac.nz/ejrot/cmsconference/default.htm

Short, J., Williams, E., and Christie, B. (1976). *The social psychology of telecommunications.* New York: Wiley.

Smith, V. (1994). Institutionalizing flexibility in a service firm: Multiple contingencies and hidden hierarchies. *Work and Occupations, 21.*

Sproull, L., and Kiesler, S. (1992). *Connections: New ways of working in the networked organization.* Cambridge, MA: MIT Press.

Trevino, L., Lengel, R., and Daft, R. (1987). Media symbolism, media richness, and media choice in organizations: A symbolic interactionist perspective. *Communication Research, 14,* 553–574.

Walther, J. (1994). Anticipated ongoing interaction versus channel effects on relational communication in computer mediated interaction. *Human Communication Research, 20,* 473–501.

Whittaker, S. (1995). Rethinking video as a technology for interpersonal communication. *International Journal of Human Computer Studies, 42,* 501–529.

Whittaker, S., Frohlich, D., and Daly-Jones, O. (1994). Informal workplace communication: What is it like and how might we support it? In *Proceedings of CHI'94 Conference on Human Factors in Computing Systems* (130–137). New York: ACM Press.

Whittaker, S., Swanson, J., Kucan, J., and Sidner, C. (1997). TeleNotes: Managing lightweight interactions in the desktop. *ACM Transactions on Computer-Human Interaction, 4,* 137–168.

Whittaker, S., Nardi, B., Isaacs, E., Creech, M., Hainsworth, J., and Ong, S. (2000). "ContactMap: Constructing and exploring personal social networks". Unpublished manuscript.

Wildeman, L. (1998). Alliances and networks: The next generation. *International Journal of Technology Management, 15,* 96–108.

Williams, E. (1977). Experimental comparison of face-to-face and mediated communication: A review. *Psychological Bulletin, 84,* 963–976.

© 2000 DILBERT reprinted by permission of United Feature Syndicates, Inc.

5

The (Currently) Unique Advantages of Collocated Work

Judith S. Olson, Stephanie Teasley, Lisa Covi, and Gary Olson

Today's technologies promise that remote work can be as good as face-to-face. We disagree. We show that radically collocated teams are twice as productive as teams that are merely nearby. Teams in these situations have interactive, continuous communication, making coordination and learning easier. From this observation, we infer two things: what tools might make their work even more productive, and how remote work could benefit from attempting to mimic some of these features.

In spite of all the new ways to connect remote teams—e-mail, chat, videoconferencing, shared whiteboards, and the others—it is still the case that there is nothing quite so humanly effective as being collocated. We make this as a research claim and back it up with evidence presented in this chapter. The research we report here focuses on the collocated work, in fact *radically* collocated work, and describes its effect on productivity, how people work in this environment, and what aspects of this environment seem to contribute to that success.

We describe this work with a caveat. We do not believe that collocated work is the gold standard and that remote work will succeed only if it mimics it (Hollan and Stornetta 1992). There are many aspects of collocated work that are poor (e.g., many meetings where nothing happens), yet there are some aspects that are excellent and worth attempting to achieve. We take the view that for some of kinds of work, being collocated with colleagues is beneficial.

In this chapter, we describe the nature of collocated work—both its advantages and disadvantages. There are three reasons to examine collocated work. First, we may uncover difficult aspects of today's collocated work and suggest tools (either technology or process) to help overcome the difficulties. Second, once we know what the desirable features of collocated work are, we may be able to develop technologies that support those aspects remotely. Third, if we find that the really good aspects of collocated work cannot be duplicated in remote work, perhaps we can define better what kinds of work can be done remotely and what must be done face-to-face. This chapter is intended to inform this goal by setting out many of the details about what happens when people are collocated.

What Do We Mean by Collocation?

Allen (1977) and Kraut, Egido, and Galegher (1990) have summarized extensive data that indicate that communication frequency among individuals drops considerably with distance and that after about thirty meters, it reaches asymptote. This means that if two people reside more than 30 meters apart, they may as well be across the continent. After 30 meters, they are mentally distant because they are in a different work state: out of sight, out of mind. Communication beyond thirty meters is difficult.

While most people think of collocation referring to nearby cubicles or offices, the purest, most extreme form of collocation is being within a few feet of each other—in the same cubicle or office, adjacent offices, or a shared study. Indeed, in this chapter we examine two variants of the most extreme kind of collocation: the *project room*, where all the artifacts of a particular type of work reside, though the team members come and go, and the *team room*, which we call *radical collocation*, where all team members and their artifacts are in a room for the duration of the project.

Project rooms include laboratories with specialized, shared equipment over which people coordinate their work; conference rooms taken over by a particular project or engagement, common in the world of consulting; and perhaps training rooms that have specialized equipment and materials. Team rooms, in contrast, are rooms in which people who are engaged in the same project reside as their primary work site. We find them to be more common for projects where there is a high need for coordination: architects, research teams, designers of a family of appliances, and software engineers. These two types of rooms are similar in that both hold the material of the work for the duration of the project. They differ in whether the team members reside exclusively in them.

Is Radical Collocation Good?

To address the value of collocated work, we report on a number of studies, including an interview study of team and project rooms and one in-depth study of one team room (Covi, Olson, and Rocco 1998, Olson, Covi, Rocco, Miller, and Allie 1998). We start with our most extensive study: a longitudinal study of six teams that used team rooms for software development. The teams consisted of six to eight members: software engineers, a manager, and the customer. Team members were diverse in both gender and country of origin and were mixed in whether they had worked together before. All team members resided in the team room; they did not have other offices to go to or other work responsibilities outside the project. The team rooms were the size of a large conference room with arrays of desks with workstations, a center worktable and chairs, and whiteboards and flip charts arrayed around the room. Bays of hoteling cubicles—offices not assigned to anyone and available as needed for privacy—were nearby for solo work or private phone calls, and conference rooms were available for more formal meetings with outside people. Each team was to produce a software product that was scoped to be completed in six to eight weeks with a team of this size. The products ranged from client-server applications to new Web sites, and they originated from a number of areas in the company, including marketing, manufacturing, and sales.

We administered a survey at the start and end of the project. We observed two of the teams in depth, visiting about eight to ten hours a week for the duration of the projects. At the project's completion, we conducted interviews with the members of two teams we studied in depth. In addition, the company took standard measures of productivity of the six teams, including cycle time and function points per staff month. The company also had the team members, the project sponsor, and the user fill out satisfaction questionnaires at the end of the project. (The details of this study are reported in Teasley, Covi, Krishnan, and Olson 2000.)

In measuring how the work changed in team rooms, we report two measures of productivity that are widely used in measuring software development. The first is the number of function points produced per staff month. Function points are commonly accepted units of complexity in software development (Jones 1996, Albrecht and Gaffney 1983). The second measure is cycle time—the number of months from the start of the project to the end, normalized for the size of the project: the number of months per 1,000 function points.

Teams who experienced radical collocation—pioneer teams—were much more productive than standard teams at both this company and in the industry as a whole. Table 5.1 shows these metrics. These teams produced twice as much as other teams did in their multitasked work, in standard office cubicles, in projects with more variable scoping. The collocated teams got the job done in about one-third the amount

Table 5.1
Comparative statistics on productivity in team rooms

Productivity	Pioneer teams	Company baseline	Industry standard
Function points per staff month (higher is better)	29.49	14.35	20.00
Cycle time (lower is better)	7.64	19.47	24.00

Table 5.2
Productivity of pioneer teams versus follow-on teams

Productivity	Pioneer teams	Follow-on teams	Significance	*df*
Function points per staff month (higher is better)	29.49	51.32	$p < .01$	15
Cycle time (lower is better)	7.64	6.58	N.S.	12

Note: The degrees of freedom were adjusted for unequal variance.

of time compared to the company baseline—and even faster than the industry standard. Both of these differences are significant using a z-score against company baseline ($p < .001$).

We worried that we might be seeing a Hawthorne effect (Mayo 1933), in that the newness of this situation and the fact that we were closely monitoring the teams may have made them more productive. To test this notion, we assessed the productivity of the eleven teams that followed the six pioneering teams. Table 5.2 shows the comparative statistics.

Follow-on teams were even more productive than the pioneer teams; function points per staff month doubled again while cycle time stayed about the same. We believe this second increase has to do in part with the fact that some of the team members now had experience (some pilot team members served on follow-on teams), and there was some organizational learning about how to run and manage such groups.

For both of these sets of teams, we have team, sponsor, and end user satisfaction measures. Satisfaction was measured using a standard scale for the company, which ranges from 1 to 5, where 5 is "very satisfied." (See table 5.3.) We have no baseline to compare these scores to, but overall the scores are high and not significantly different between the pioneer teams and the follow-on teams.

Table 5.3
Satisfaction of pioneer teams versus follow-on teams

Satisfaction	Pioneer teams	Follow-on teams	Significance	*df*
Team	4.15	4.30	N.S.	13
Sponsor	4.56	4.29	N.S.	8
End user	3.68	3.97	N.S.	4

Table 5.4
Changes in preferences at entry and exit

Preference	Entry	Exit	Significance	*df*
For team rooms	3.53	4.00	$p < .01$	5
For cubicles	3.86	3.42	$p < .04$	5

From the surveys we did of all members of the six teams, we found that the team members liked radical collocation. They had little experience with this style of work prior to this project, rating it 2.17 on a 5-point scale where 5 is "very frequent use." Working in the facility increased their preferences for working in the team rooms and decreased their preference for working in cubicles. (See table 5.4.)

In summary, the work was more productive, the satisfaction of the work and the product was high, and the team's preferences for working in this intense collocated environment increased with experience.

What Happened in the Team Rooms?

What did radical collocation give these teams? To address this question, we draw on data from two sources: the team room study detailed above and a very similar study of one team in another company in comparable circumstances (Covi et al. 1998). This other study examined a team that consisted of six people doing software engineering while experiencing advanced training in a new computer language. They resided in a large conference room outfitted the same way as the rooms in the team room study. Like the six teams reported above, they worked for six weeks, had no other responsibilities during this time, and were mixtures of genders and background. Some knew each other from previous work, and they developed an internal application for salespeople.

Figure 5.1
A team working using an object-oriented development method, creating, editing, and referring to the material on the flip charts throughout the six weeks.

Figure 5.1 shows a typical situation for collocated teams. The team members in this group lived among their artifacts. The group depicted produced a large number of flip charts in the early part of their work (the artifacts represented use cases, object hierarchies, to-do lists, and so forth). As the group worked, they referred to the posted lists and diagrams often, occasionally moving the artifacts so that comparisons could be made and marking on them to reflect mutually agreed-on changes.

Team Room Process
The team rooms supported interactive, continuous communication. The close quarters of the team rooms supported impromptu communication and allowed people to overhear each other. Subgroups could form and re-form. Over time, this physical reality produced a number of advantages. First, team members found it easy to develop common ground (Clark 1996), engaging in standard procedures or methods without having to talk explicitly about them. Furthermore, the team members knew each other. They had transactional memory (Moreland, Argote, and Krishnan 1996;

Moreland 1999) and expectations about each other's talents, working style, and moods. They could read each other moment by moment to know, for example, whether someone was having trouble or was deep in thought while coding (and therefore should not be disturbed). They could use various aspects of the context to assess what was going on at this moment—the position, sound, and gestures of the teammate; the recent history; and the shared local context (some from non-task-related conversation as they enter or take breaks, for example).

While being collocated, each member had local control over what he or she was attending to at each moment, so that different people were paying attention to different people or artifacts to suit their current goals. This situation contrasts sharply with videoconferencing, when everyone sees the same thing because there is only one camera. And typically the team members responded immediately to each other. When someone looked at another with a question, the natural reaction was to respond immediately, even if only to say that he or she would look something up or work on something and get back to the person making the inquiry. This situation is in marked contrast to working remotely through e-mail or voice mail, where responses are most commonly delayed, and the sender has no information about when to expect a response.

In the broad interview study reported in Covi et al. (1998), there were numerous stories about the value of being aware of each other's work. One room we visited housed an emergency response team that helped salespeople worldwide broker special large pricing and packaging deals for important customers. Team members had desks about fifteen feet apart. They were close enough to overhear other team members' conversations if they chose and note for future reference what customer was involved, what salesperson called, and what kinds of deals were eventually made. The desks were far enough apart, however, to make this attention a matter of choice. Also, when one person was inundated with calls, others in the same room could seamlessly take over with nearly the same knowledge of the situation as the key person.

The awareness afforded in collocation also allowed people to engage in informal training sessions. In the study of the single team (Covi et al. 1998), trainers could see over students' shoulders, allowing them to monitor progress over time and intervene only when necessary. Similarly, people learned implicitly by imitating others in the room. They learned quickly from the more experienced people "how things are done," how to make a request by phone, and how to gauge the progress of others.

People learned routines from each other without instruction that made the work proceed smoothly (Cohen and Bacdayan 1994).

We also noted that typically projects involve a number of subactivities—some that seemed best done in the whole or subteams and some that required individual work. For example, conversations with the customer, problem solving of major architectural issues, and status meetings involved a lot of both dissemination of information and clarification and negotiation. The left side of figure 5.2 shows an activity involving the whole group, where they are understanding the overall function of the software they are building and the architecture that will support it. The right side of the figure shows the same group gathered to be tutored on an issue that is needed in the next step of their design, called just-in-time learning. At other points during the project, people worked individually. Figure 5.3 shows people in the same room working individually on their pieces of code. In these situations, team members are quiet, concentrating on their own work. But even in the quiet individual work, however, learning is happening. The man in the middle is looking to his neighbor on the right to find out how to do something.

One of the advantages of being collocated, then, was the ability to move between these various subactivities of work—some requiring individual work and some group interaction. When people had questions, often the person who could answer it (e.g., the customer, the tutor, a fellow worker who had more experience or expertise on a topic) was at hand.

Figure 5.2
On the left, a team working huddled around a table with cards on it, attempting to understand the architecture of the whole system they are designing. On the right, the same group huddled around a computer for a just-in-time tutorial.

Figure 5.3
The same team using the room to work individually.

On the other hand, the fact that the team members were in interactive, continuous communication had several disadvantages. First, people reported that the room was strikingly chaotic, with visitors and team members coming and going. Overhearing was distracting for those who were trying to concentrate. Informal nearby meetings can interrupt the "flow state" of those team members doing programming. Team members requiring quiet often left the room to go to nearby hoteling areas, but they left reluctantly, knowing they might miss something important. Some team members came in early or left late, hoping to have some uninterrupted time but in the room with posted shared artifacts available when they needed them. We also noted, however, that collocation works well when the team is in a large enough room, with about fifteen feet between people, and when the group develops norms of behavior about being sensitive to the state of the person someone wished to interrupt.

An additional limitation of team room work is that there is no privacy in the room. Team members reported feeling uncomfortable making private telephone calls in the team room. They also reported discomfort having the customer constantly in the room; programmers worried about revealing half-baked ideas or inelegant

Table 5.5
Changes in reported attitudes about activity in the team rooms

Attitude item	Entry	Exit	Significance
I am susceptible to distraction.	3.37	2.68	$p < .001$
People should work near each other.	3.86	4.27	$p < .009$

solutions. Also, since the manager resided in the room, many team members felt their work could be too closely monitored. Furthermore, the fact that everyone lived in such close quarters affected motivation. The psychological literature has documented this phenomenon well (Allport 1920, Forsyth 1998). We could document social impact, both positive and negative. Five of the six teams were high-energy teams; motivation indeed rose by contagion. In one team, the contagion was negative; motivation dropped very quickly because all behavior was visible to everyone. Nevertheless, even in the low-motivation team, productivity was still remarkably higher than the company norm.

Questionnaire results showed how attitudes changed over time. The questions asked the degree to which the respondent agreed with a statement such as, "I am personally susceptible to distraction," with 5 being high agreement. As shown in table 5.5, team members coming in to the team rooms thought they would be distracted by such close quarters. At project completion, however, people were significantly less distracted by the presence of others in the room. They also increased their reported value of being near each other in getting their work done.

What is striking about all of this is how effortlessly human perceptual and cognitive capabilities come into play in order to support the easy flow of interactions in such situations (Hutchins 1995a, 1995b). Participants working face-to-face seldom feel disoriented or without context. These features of the process are hard to duplicate in today's distance technology, but are key to successful conduct of tightly coupled remote work (Olson and Olson 2000).

Team Artifacts
The artifacts generated by the teams we studied were easy to create (flip chart and pen) and were placed on the walls for everyone to see and use. Their spatial arrangement was important, since artifacts were often put up in the order in which they were produced. People knew where to look for something because they knew when it was produced, and they could tell something about another person's attention by

seeing where that person was looking. These artifacts also served various meetings. People would huddle around an artifact to clarify their understanding and make changes with everyone's knowledge. Whittaker and Swartz (1995) noted the same kind of advantage when developers used a large-scale project plan on the wall with notations and cards affixed to it to monitor and meet about the project.

A second key feature of the artifacts in the team rooms was that they were constantly visible. When the team members wanted to access information generated, in some cases weeks previous, they merely glanced at the portion of the wall where the diagram or list was posted. They lived in the interface. The group members so valued this visibility that they covered even the pictures used to decorate the room and asked for a ladder to post new artifacts high on the wall. Figure 5.4 shows the group using the wall surface for the diagrams. When these people were asked about the design of new rooms, they wanted more tackable surface instead of windows.

At another site, human resource people used a project room to plan various moves in the organizational staffing. Two long walls of the room, covered with whiteboard

Figure 5.4
People working in a team room with the organizational chart made of magnets and connectors in electrical tape—a nondigital editable large display.

material from floor to ceiling, displayed the entire organizational chart of the organization, from the top down to four layers of management. (See figure 5.4.) The people on the chart were represented with small magnets (1 by 4 inches) with their pictures, names, and some other notations. The connectors in the chart were indicated with narrow electrical tape. The whole chart was thus physically editable, though not electronic. Career paths of managers were planned in this room. The magnet of the manager under discussion was removed from the chart and held on the table, while the planners gazed at the entire display to decide the implications of various moves of that person (for example, whom this person would replace and which positions were currently vacant). They reported that holding the magnet of the person in hand while the discussion ensued was important; there was something compelling about the materiality of the magnet representing the magnitude of the decision on peoples' lives.

In another of our field studies (Olson and Olson 2000), we noted that at an automobile manufacturer, a competitor's model was permanently displayed on the hall wall, "exploded" so that each piece was examinable and related parts were near each other. Engineers gathered around the wall display to consider issues and possible alternative designs in informal meetings, aided by the parts and their locations on the wall.

We also have seen an extreme form of the spatial location being important for artifacts. On occasion, people explain things to others by drawing in the air (the "air board" referred to in Olson and Olson 1991). Later in the conversation, people referred to "that idea" by pointing to the spot in the air where the first person had "drawn" the idea.

When everyone focuses their attention on the same object and points to the various places on it, they can easily come to a shared understanding. In our early work on design meetings (Olson, Olson, Storrøsten, and Carter 1992), we noted an example where the meeting participants lacked this ability. All people in the meeting were given individual copies of a system diagram at the start of the meeting. As they discussed and agreed to things, they took notes on their own copy of the diagram, adding things and crossing things out. We noted at the end of the meeting that different people had made different marks, implying different understandings of what they had agreed to. This group could have benefited from referring to the same object, perhaps on a whiteboard, because without it, they ended up not "singing from the same sheet of music".

The Interaction of Artifacts and Process

Room sizes are limited and human perception is limited, and thus one cannot have all the information needed in a project visible. But when artifacts are limited, it affects the process. For example, we witnessed a brainstorming meeting in which the emerging ideas were recorded on the whiteboard. The brainstorming stopped as soon as the board was full. Furthermore, because the board was not editable without a great deal of effort, some synergies and similarities among the ideas were lost. Flexibility and editability were important for this task, but there may be other situations in which inflexibility is important and annotations (not cleaned-up versions) are important to the task. For example, the editing marks may signal to someone not present at the moment of change that something has changed. The point is that different situations call for different features of the artifact, and getting these features right is important.

At yet another site we observed, a project room contained three full walls of tack boards. On the walls were plastic sleeves $8\frac{1}{2}$ by 11 inches with Velcro on the back, holding paper artifacts from various project presentations (like printouts of Power-Point slides) of successful engagements of the past. New clients could come to the room with project planners to discuss these past projects, pulling down the various relevant "pages" to discuss, but seen in the context of the entire project and of other projects. The whole context was afforded by the entire room; they could walk around the room and focus in on various points (Covi et al. 1998).

Other artifacts in the team room helped in the coordination of the group's individual work. The software development team constructed a to-do list consisting of the objects and modules to be built, with individuals' names assigned to each. Tick marks indicated which items were completed, and new items were added as they were discovered to be necessary. As people worked individually in parallel, they could keep track of their upcoming workload and monitor the progress of others. This provided both a coordination aid and a subtle motivator. If others had ticked off their modules and one had not, that person knew that he or she might be responsible for delay. That knowledge was a motivator to work harder and perhaps encourage others to help out.

We were surprised at how many of the rooms had artifacts intended to motivate the occupants. In one project room at an appliance manufacturer, the walls were covered with posters of their planning principles, similar in spirit to Deming principles. Another touted the company slogan about being fast on their feet, adapted to being fast in producing software. The rapid response team for closing large sales deals had the same motivational poster in each of the walls, viewable from anywhere in the room.

In the settings where we were able to observe teams, we saw that the work in team rooms varied. Sometimes all team members focused on a single issue, sometimes they worked in small subgroups, and sometimes they divided the work into modules they could work on individually in parallel. In all the cases, however, the team member had control over the view and editing of the artifact. Several people held pens when working with a use case (a scenario of the anticipated use of a to-be-built software) on a flip chart; work proceeded in parallel in both the subgroup and individual work. Neither solely individual views nor always WYSIWIS (what you see is what I see) is the solution. One has to move flexibly from co-reference to separate views and back. People naturally gravitate to these styles the best they can with the artifacts that are available. There is likely some newer technology that can help even more.

In summary, radical collocation affords a great deal of ease in coordinating the work among people. People have common ground and information about the current and recent context. They can control what they see as well as what they do, and their teammates command rapid responses by virtue of being so close. People share artifacts that are spatially meaningful and constantly visible and can coordinate easily about references to the artifacts. The artifacts are often large, displaying a huge amount of information accessible at a single glance. Some of the artifacts are editable and flexible, adding to their support of emerging, changing work. Individuals can move around the artifact space as their needs change, seeing the large-scale overview or zooming in on aspects they want to focus on, either individually or in small groups. The artifacts also help coordinate the work of individuals through editable to-do lists with tick marks indicating progress. Today's technologies (flip charts, individual workstations) do not yet support well all the activities we seen in radical collocation.

Designing Effective Resources for Collocated Work

Effective teams embody a lot of tacit knowledge that is difficult to articulate and requires extensive observation to tease out, and artifacts play a critical role in shaping the social and cognitive interactions among teams (Hutchins 1995a, 1995b; Suchman 1996; Olson, Olson, Storrøsten, and Carter 1992). The design challenges are to understand the process and artifacts of skilled work and the ways in which new tools might help.

Optimal Design of the Work Space

Hunt and Poltrock (1999) redesigned a workspace at Boeing with the goal of enhancing the environment for collaborative work. Their redesign was guided by a work flow analysis coupled with innovative thinking about how to reconfigure the space. They looked at who needed to work with whom, who needed access to whom, and how the overall flow of work activities proceeded. Their redesign created more collaborative space and eliminated dedicated private spaces such as enclosed offices. In the first seven and a half months following the redesign, they found marked improvements in productivity, as well as increases in job satisfaction. In recent years, there has been increased attention to the issues of how to design space to facilitate collaboration. Two recent Cooperative Building conferences contain a number of references to designs and studies of these issues (Streitz, Konomi, and Burkhardt 1998; Streitz, Siegel, Hartkopf, and Konomi 1999).

Shared Electronic Objects

Artifacts of various kinds, such as whiteboards, flip charts, printouts, and paper, are critical elements of work. Driven by our observation that the physical limits of the artifacts constrained the work of the groups, we built software, called ShrEdit, that allowed shared access to the same editable document. To test ShrEdit's efficacy, we had groups of three work on a design problem that was modeled on those we had studied in the field (Olson, Olson, Storrøsten, and Carter 1992, 1993). Half of the thirty-eight groups worked in the traditional way. They discussed their design and captured it on a large whiteboard along with paper and pencil. The other half used ShrEdit with networked computers that were embedded in the tables of the same meeting room the other group used. The results showed that the groups using ShrEdit produced better-quality designs in the same amount of time as the groups using traditional media. ShrEdit fit the work of these groups quite well, although the ShrEdit groups reported less satisfaction with their work processes than the traditional groups. Undoubtedly, the relative newness of working with ShrEdit played some role in this.

Elsewhere (Olson and Olson 1996) we have argued that simple artifacts with a few well-chosen features can be powerful tools in the hands of groups. There is a tradition of group support systems that have developed much more structured and complex suites of tools for the support of group work. These tools have had some limited success in certain kinds of formal situations (Nunamaker, Dennis, Valacich, Vogel, and George 1991), but on the whole they have not had a big impact on teamwork. Group processes are subtle and delicate, and providing flexibility through simplicity seems to be a better design strategy. But we still lack the kind of deep understanding of group processes and the role of artifacts in their mediation to develop more detailed design guidelines.

Large High-Resolution, Editable Objects

ShrEdit provided a number of desirable features but lacked constant visibility and spatial arrangements that seemed helpful in team rooms. Others have explored variants of the digital wall. Colab (Stefik et al. 1983) had both individual workstations and a shared large display. Tivoli on LiveBoards allowed writing directly on the surface of a large wall-mounted display with a light pen, and operated with handwriting and gestures that do sensible things on the marks by recognizing their structure, not their content (Elrod et al. 1992; Pederson, McCall, Moran, and Halasz 1993; Moran, van Melle, and Chiu 1998a, 1998b; Moran, Chiu, and van Melle, 1997; Moran et al. 1996, 1997; Moran, Chiu, van Melle, and Kurtenbach 1995; Moran, McCall, van Melle, Pederson, and Halasz 1995). The ZombieBoard and Collaborage allow easy transfer to and from paper and remote access, using cameras and digitized images (Saund 1999, Moran et al. 1999). Flatland is an electronic marker board designed for use in an individual's office (Mynatt, Igarashi, Edwards, and LaMarca 1999). Dynawall in I-Land (Streitz et al. 1999) has extended the size of the digital surface to a wall and allowed more than one pen to be operative at a time. I-Land also extends the information access to personal laptops and a group table.

Some of these ideas have made it into the commercial world. Xerox made a commercial product out of the LiveBoard through a spin-off company, LiveWorks. Other large pen-based interactive displays exist, including MicroGraphix SoftBoard and Smart Technology's SmartBoard (Martin 1995). Others are exploring novel hardware solutions (Winograd and Guimbretiére 1999). With the advent of Microsoft's NetMeeting, some of the boards are being used with audioconferencing to support remote work as well as collocated meetings, with some success (Mark, Grudin, and Poltrock 1999).

Moran and associates (1996) conducted a two-year longitudinal study of the use of Tivoli for regular intellectual property management meetings at Xerox. The Live-Board was combined with audiotaping of conversations, a linked laptop for note taking, and a thoughtful arrangement of the physical space. Special tailored features were developed in Tivoli to support the specific tasks that were carried out through these meetings. More than sixty meetings were observed. While much work went into developing the specialized tools and to keeping the technology working, the work process was facilitated by the innovative way in which the display and the capture of process linked the meetings with the interspersed solitary work of the intellectual property coordinator. His task of mining the meeting material ("salvaging") to create documents for management seemed to be particularly facilitated by these tools.

We had an opportunity to study the Xerox LiveBoard running Tivoli in our laboratory. We ran groups of three on a task that required a fair amount of sketching and problem solving. We compared Tivoli to two other tools, the whiteboard and a workstation-based drawing tool called Aspects, which was similar in a number of respects to ShrEdit. In our comparisons of both process and outcome, Aspects finished a distant third. In this study, we wanted to focus on the comparison of Tivoli and the conventional whiteboard. Figure 5.5 shows examples of teams working at these technologies.

Groups did a series of tasks to familiarize themselves with whatever tool they were using. In our analysis, we focus on the third, longest, and last task they did

Figure 5.5
Groups working at the whiteboard, Tivoli, and Aspects, respectively, from left to right.

in the series: the design of the interface to an automatic post office. We videotaped these sessions for analyzing group process and captured their final design. Five groups used Tivoli, and seven used the whiteboard.

The performance conditions of whiteboard and Tivoli use were quite close. The whiteboard was easier to use (as evidenced by the increased amount of time the Tivoli groups spent on technology management), but both tools produced the same number of features in the design, and participants reported equal levels of satisfaction. It is clear from an analysis of details of performance, however, that the limited display size and resolution of the Tivoli system were drawbacks to its effective use. A contemporary whiteboard has very high resolution, and we found our subjects writing and drawing very small things on it. Combined with the large spatial layout of many whiteboards, it is possible to put a lot of information on a visually accessible layout. With Tivoli, there were no space limitations in principle, but this was achieved through large numbers of relatively low-resolution layered pages. Thus, the electronic whiteboard allowed people to talk while referring to the same object (by being large) and it was editable, but visibility was not constant. Furthermore, teams using the true whiteboard were able to write in parallel at various points in their work. That was impossible with Tivoli.

Large, editable displays are a winning idea for collocated work. As the resolution of such displays approaches the whiteboard and as it becomes economically feasible for such displays to cover entire walls in the same way that whiteboards do, these will become powerful tools for group work. Furthermore, being electronic, editable displays offer the immediate advantage of being able to interface with other devices (file systems, mobile devices of various kinds) and of being able to share displays between remote meeting rooms. Where collocated work has the distinct advantage of process, there is room to improve the artifacts used by collocated groups.

Virtual Collocation: Tomorrow's Promise

As Olson and Olson (2000) reported, today's distance technologies fall short in supporting the tightly coupled work of remote groups. In the future, some technologies might be able to support the features of communication and artifact sharing that we have highlighted here as being important in radical collocation. Figure 5.6 shows a conceptualization of what a virtual team room might look like. Artifacts are large, editable, and shared, as well as under individual parallel control, shown

Figure 5.6
Conceptualization of a virtual team room with a video wall and digital walls.

on a wall-size display with various views on individuals' laptops. Remote participants have life-size views of each other, with good stereo audio adjusted to conform
to natural physical space. Although there may not be the flexibility of moving
around wherever you wish to congregate with remote partners, this configuration
goes a long way to produce riche, large, multiple channels of information. If people
work in such a room over longer periods of time, aspects of common ground would
strengthen as well, making the whole interaction smoother yet.

Before we build such a room, however, we must realize that there still are some
limits. We have argued elsewhere (Olson and Olson 2000) that even with the best
of tools, there are some major complications to work at a distance. All of them arise
from the fact that the more remote the partner, the more likely cultural boundaries
will be crossed, with all its concomitant effects on trust, common ground, and
different local contexts. However, with training on cultural variations in work
practice and with extra effort to ensure that people are working with a common
understanding, a number of the features of awareness and shared work flow that
are easy in radical collocation are possible over long distances.

We close this chapter with one final point. Several people have asked us whether
the people who experienced radically collocated work would be better able to
conduct distance work. We do not know. There is certainly widespread belief
that a period of face-to-face interaction to facilitate team building is important for
distributed groups. In fact, Rocco (1998) found that a few minutes of face-to-face

interaction prior to playing a competitive social dilemma game under distributed conditions led to cooperation, whereas purely distributed interactions (via e-mail) led to competitive behavior. We are currently studying whether such facilitation can come through video interactions. Clearly, the interaction of collocated and noncollocated work needs further analysis and investigation.

Note

This work was supported in part by grant ISI 9977923 from the National Science Foundation, and corporate support from Steelcase, Inc., Ford Motor Company, and Sun Microsystems. We are grateful for comments from the participants in the workshop on Distributed Work, in Carmel, California, August, 2000.

References

Albrecht, A., and Gaffney, J. (1983). Software function, source lines of code, and development effort prediction: A software science validation. *IEEE Transactions on Software Engineering (SE-9:6)*, 639–647.

Allen, T. J. (1977). *Managing the flow of technology.* Cambridge, MA: MIT Press.

Allport, F. H. (1920). The influence of the group upon association and thought. *Journal of Experimental Psychology*, 3, 159–182.

Clark, H. H. (1996). *Using language.* Cambridge: Cambridge University Press.

Cohen, M. D., and Bacdayan, P. (1994). Organizational routines are stored as procedural memory: Evidence from a laboratory study. *Organizational Science*, 5, 554–568.

Covi, L. M., Olson, J. S., and Rocco, E. (1998). A room of your own: What do we learn about support of teamwork from assessing teams in dedicated project rooms? In N. Streitz, S. Konomi, and H. J. Burkhardt (eds.), *Cooperative buildings* (53–65). Amsterdam: Springer-Verlag.

Elrod, S., et al. (1992). LiveBoard: A large interactive display supporting group meetings, presentations, and remote collaboration. In *Proceedings of the CHI'92 Conference on Human Factors in Computer Systems* (599–607). New York: ACM Press.

Forsyth, D. R. (1998). *Group dynamics.* Pacific Grove, CA: Brooks/Cole.

Hollan, J., and Stornetta, S. (1992). Beyond being there. In *Proceedings of CHI 92* (119–125). New York: ACM Press.

Hunt, R., and Poltrock, S. E. (1999). Boeing operations fleet support: A case study in integrated worksplace design. In N. Streitz, J. Siegel, V. Hartkopf, and S. Konomi (eds.), *Cooperative buildings: Integrating information, organizations, and architecture: Proceedings of the Second International Workshop (CoBuild'99) LNCS 1670* (2–11). Heidelberg: Springer.

Hutchins, E. (1995a). *Cognition in the wild.* Cambridge, MA: MIT Press.

Hutchins, E. (1995b). How a cockpit remembers its speeds. *Cognitive Science, 19,* 265–288.

Jones, C. (1996). *Applied software measurement: Assuring productivity and quality.* New York: McGraw-Hill.

Kraut, R. E., Egido, C., and Galegher, J. (1990). Patterns of contact and communication in scientific research collaborations. In J. Galegher, R. E. Kraut, and C. Egido (eds.), *Intellectual teamwork: Social and technological foundations of cooperative work* (149–171). Hillsdale, NJ: Erlbaum.

Martin, D. (1995). SMART 2000 conferencing system: What we learned from developing the system. In S. Greenberg, S. Hayne, and R. Rada (eds.), *Groupware for real-time drawing: A designer's guide* (179–197). New York: McGraw-Hill.

Mark, G., Grudin, J., and Poltrock, S. E. (1999). Meeting at the desktop: An empirical study of virtually collocated teams. In S. Bodker, M. King, and K. Schmidt (eds.), *Proceedings of the Sixth European Conference on Computer Supported Cooperative Work ECSCW '99* (159–178). Dordrecht: Kluwer.

Mayo, E. (1933). *The human problem of an industrial civilization.* New York: Macmillan.

Moran, T. P., Chiu, P., Harrison, S., Kurtenbach, G., Minneman, S., and van Melle, W. (1996). Evolutionary engagement in an ongoing collaborative work process: A case study. In *Proceedings of the CSCW'96 Conference on Computer Supported Cooperative Work* (150–159). New York: ACM Press.

Moran, T. P., Chiu, P., and van Melle, W. (1997). Pen-based interaction techniques for organizing material on an electronic whiteboard. In *Proceedings of the UIST'97 Conference on User Interface Software and Technology* (45–54). New York: ACM Press.

Moran, T. P., Chiu, P., van Melle, W., and Kurtenbach, G. (1995). Implicit structures for pen-based systems within a freeform interaction paradigm. In I. R. Katz, R. Mack, L. Marks, M. B. Rosson, and J. Nielsen (eds.), *Proceedings of the CHI'95 Conference on Human Factors in Computer Systems* (487–494). New York: ACM Press.

Moran, T. P., McCall, K., van Melle, W., Pedersen, E. R., and Halasz, F. G. (1995). Some design principles for sharing in Tivoli, a whiteboard meeting-support tool. In S. Greenberg, S. Hayne, and R. Rada (eds.), *Real-time group drawing and writing tools* (24–36). New York: McGraw-Hill.

Moran, T. P., Palen, L., Harrison, S., Chiu, P., Kimber, D., Minneman, S., van Melle, W., and Zellweger, P. (1997). "I'll get that off the audio": A case study of salvaging multimedia meeting records. In *Proceedings of the CHI'97 Conference on Human Factors in Computer Systems* (202–209). New York: ACM Press.

Moran, T. P., Saund, E., van Melle, W., Gujar, A. U., Fishkin, K. P., and Harrison, B. L. (1999). Design and technology for Collaborage: Collaborative collages of information on physical walls. In *Proceedings of the UIST'99 Conference on User Interface Software and Technology.* New York: ACM Press.

Moran, T. P., van Melle, W., and Chiu, P. (1998a). Tailorable domain objects as meeting tools for an electronic whiteboard. In *Proceedings of the CSCW'98 Conference on Computer Supported Cooperative Work* (295–304). New York: ACM Press.

Moran, T. P., van Melle, W., and Chiu, P. (1998b). Spatial interpretation of domain objects integrated into a freeform electronic whiteboard. In *Proceedings of the UIST'98 Conference on User Interface Software and Technology* (175–184). New York: ACM Press.

Moran, T. P., van Melle, W., and Chiu, P. (1999). *Domain objects as meeting tools in Tivoli: An electronic whiteboard.* Videotape. Palo Alto, CA: Xerox PARC.

Moreland, R. L. (1999). Transactive memory: Learning who knows what in work groups and organizations. In L. Thompson, J. Levine, and D. Messick (eds.), *Shared cognition in organizations: The management of knowledge* (3–31), Hillside, NJ: Erlbaum.

Moreland, R. L., Argote, L., and Krishnan, R. (1996). Socially shared cognition at work: Transactive memory group performance. In J. L. Nye and A. M. Brower (eds.), *What's social about social cognition? Research on socially shared cognition in small groups* (57–84). Thousand Oaks, CA: Sage.

Mynatt, E. D., Igarashi, T. Edwards, W. K., and LaMarca, A. (1999). Flatland: New dimensions in office whiteboards. In *Proceedings of the Conference on Human Factors in Computer Systems CHI'99* (346–353). New York: ACM Press.

Nunamaker, J. F., Dennis, A. R., Valacich, J. S., Vogel, D. R., and George, J. F. (1991). Electronic meeting systems to support group work. *Communications of the ACM, 34,* 40–61.

Olson, J. S., Covi, L., Rocco, E., Miller, W. J., and Allie, P. (1998). A room of your own: What would it take to help remote groups work as well as collocated groups? In *Short Paper: The Conference on Human Factors in Computing Systems CHI'98* (279–280). New York: ACM Press.

Olson, G. M., and Olson, J. S. (1991). User-centered design of collaboration technology. *Journal of Organizational Computing, 1,* 61–83.

Olson, G. M., and Olson, J. S. (1996). The effectiveness of simple shared electronic workspaces. In R. Rada (ed.), *Groupware and authoring* (105–126). New York: Academic Press.

Olson, G. M., and Olson, J. S. (2000). Distance matters. *Human-Computer Interaction, 15,* 139–179.

Olson, G. M., Olson, J. S., Carter, M., and Storrøsten, M. (1992). Small group design meetings: An analysis of collaboration. *Human Computer Interaction, 7,* 347–374.

Olson, J. S., Olson, G. M., Storrøsten, M., and Carter, M. (1992). How a group-editor changes the character of a design meeting as well as its outcome. In *Proceedings of the Conference on Computer Supported Cooperative Work* (91–98). New York: ACM.

Olson, J. S., Olson, G. M., Storrøsten, M., and Carter, M. (1993). Group work close up: A comparison of the group design process with and without a simple group editor. *ACM: Transactions on Information Systems, 11,* 321–348.

Olson, G. M., Olson, J. S., Storrøsten, M., Carter, M., Herbsleb, J., and Rueter, H. (1995). The structure of activity during design meetings. In J. Carroll and T. Moran (eds.), *Design rationale* (217–239). Hillsdale, NJ: Erlbaum.

Pedersen, E. R., McCall, K., Moran, T. P., and Halasz, F. G. (1993). Tivoli: An electronic whiteboard for informal workgroup meetings. In *Proceedings of the InterCHI'93 Conference on Human Factors in Computer Systems.* New York: ACM.

Rocco, E. (1998). Trust breaks down in electronic contexts but can be repaired by some initial face-to-face contact. *Proceedings of the Conference on Human Factors in Computing Systems—CHI'98* (496–502). New York: ACM Press.

Stefik, M., Foster, G., Bobrow, D. G., Kahn, K., Lanning, S., and Suchman, L. (1987). Beyond the chalkboard: Computer support for collaboration and problem solving in meetings. *Transactions of the ACM, 30,* 32–47.

Streitz, N., Geisler, J., Holmer, T., Konomi, S., Muller-Tomfelde, C., Feischl, W., Rexroth, P., Seitz, P., and Steinmetz, R. (1999). I-Land: An interactive landscape for creativity and innovation. In *Proceedings of the Conference on Computer Human Interaction, CHI'99* (120–127). New York: ACM Press.

Streitz, N., Konomi, S., and Burkhardt, H. J. (eds.). (1998). *Cooperative buildings.* Amsterdam: Springer-Verlag.

Streitz, N., Siegel, J., Hartkopf, V., and Konomi, S. (eds.). (1999). *Cooperative buildings—Integrating information, organizations, and architecture. Proceedings of the Second International Workshop (CoBuild'99) LNCS 1670.* Heidelberg: Springer.

Suchman, L. (1996) Constituting shared workspaces. In Y. Engestrom and D. Middleton (eds.), *Cognition and communication at work* (35–60). Cambridge: Cambridge University Press.

Teasley, S., Covi, L., Krishnan, M. S., and Olson, J. S. (2000). What does radical collocation give a team? In *Proceedings of CSCW 2000* (339–346). New York: ACM Press.

Whittaker, S., and Schwarz, H. (1995). Back to the future: Pen and paper technology supports complex group coordination. In *Proceedings of the Conference on Human Factors in Computing Systems, CHI'95* (495–502). New York: ACM Press.

Winograd, T., and Guimbretiére, F. (1999). Visual instruments for an interactive mural. In *Proceedings of the Conference on Human Factors in Computing Systems CHI'99, Extended Abstracts* (234–235). New York: ACM Press.

Winograd, T. (1988). A language/action perspective on the design of cooperative work. *Human Computer Interaction, 3,* 3–30.

6

Understanding Effects of Proximity on Collaboration: Implications for Technologies to Support Remote Collaborative Work

Robert E. Kraut, Susan R. Fussell, Susan E. Brennan, and Jane Siegel

This chapter analyzes why computers and telecommunications have not created computer-mediated work environments for collaboration that are as successful as physically shared environments. Our goals are, first, to identify the mechanisms by which proximity makes collaboration easier, concentrating on the way it facilitates interpersonal interaction and awareness; and second, to evaluate how current computer-mediated communication technologies provide or fail to provide the key benefits of proximity. We use a decompositional framework that examines how visibility, copresence, mobility, cotemporality and other affordances of media affect the important collaborative tasks of initiating conversation, establishing common ground, and maintaining awareness of potentially relevant changes in the collaborative environment.

Increasingly, collaborating with other people is as likely to take place over distance or time as it is face-to-face. An abundance of new communication technologies has been developed to mediate remote collaboration: e-mail, bulletin boards, instant messaging, document sharing, videoconferencing, awareness services, and others. Yet collaboration at a distance remains substantially harder to accomplish than collaboration when members of a work group are collocated. For example, in collaboration at a distance, communication is typically less frequent, characterized by longer lags between messages, and more effortful.

In this chapter we consider why these computer-mediated work environments are not as successful as physically shared ones. Our goals are to identify the mechanisms by which proximity makes collaboration easier, concentrating on the way it helps interpersonal communication and awareness, and to evaluate how current computer-mediated communication technologies provide or fail to provide the key benefits of proximity. We extend a decompositional framework, first proposed by Clark and Brennan (1990), to analyze these technologies and their impact on collaboration in remote work groups. We illustrate our discussion with evidence and examples from the domain of scientific research, but believe that the principles here apply to almost all interpersonal collaborations involving communication and coordination of tasks.

An Example of the Effects of Proximity

Even in the age of telecommunication and the Internet, physical proximity increases the likelihood of collaboration. This phenomenon was demonstrated for scientific collaboration in the 1960s by Hagstrom (1965), and it is still true among scientists who have access to the Internet and are heavy users of telecommunications and computer-mediated communications. Consider, for example, a reanalysis of data originally reported in Kraut, Egido, and Galegher (1990), predicting the probability of successful collaboration among scientists and engineers in a large telecommunications company.[1] This company had been using Internet-based e-mail since its founding, and at the time of data collection, every member of the research division had an e-mail account and a personal workstation or computer, and most used e-mail heavily.

Kraut, Egido, and Galegher examined which of the 164 scientists and engineers in the sample actually collaborated as a function of the pairs' organizational proximity (an ordinal measure of how close they were in the organizational chart—same supervisory group, same department, same laboratory, or different laboratory), research similarity (an index of the semantic similarity of a pair's solo publications), and physical proximity (an ordinal measure of how close the office of potential collaborators were—same corridor, same floor, same building, different buildings). (See Kraut et al. 1990 for more details.)

Results showed that even in this environment, pairs of researchers were unlikely to complete a technical report together unless their offices were physically near each other, even if they had previously published on similar topics or worked in the same department in the company. As figure 6.1 shows, virtually all joint publications occurred among researchers with similar research interests. But researchers with the most similar interests were more than four times as likely to publish together if their offices were on the same corridor as they were if their offices were on different floors of the same building, and researchers whose offices were in different buildings almost never collaborated regardless of their research interests.

The association of organizational proximity with collaboration was similar. Most successful collaboration occurred among people who were in the same department. However, among researchers in the same department and those in different

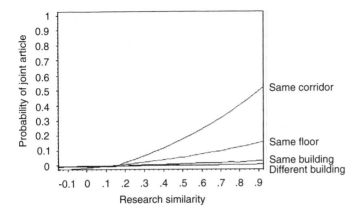

Figure 6.1
Association of research similarity and probability of collaboration at different levels of physical proximity.

departments, researchers physically close to each other were more likely to collaborate than those farther apart. The positive statistical interactions between physical proximity and both research similarity and organizational proximity suggest that physical proximity stimulates collaboration among people who might otherwise not work together. For example, if two people were in the same department, they were two-thirds more likely to collaborate if their offices were on the same corridor than if the offices were only on the same floor. If they were not in the same department, then being on the same corridor boosted their likelihood of collaborating over eight times.

Generic Collaborative Actions

The preceding analyses demonstrate that something about physical proximity encourages or enables collaboration among researchers with the right fit—common research interests or organizational membership—and may even compensate for poor fit. However, this demonstration tells us little about the mechanisms through which proximity works its magic. Collaborative projects are complex endeavors, often taking a year or more to move from an initial idea to a first paper submission (Garvey, Lin, and Nelson 1970) and involve overcoming many social and work-oriented hurdles (Kraut, Galegher, and Egido 1990). In particular, to be successful, potential collaborators must identify and form connections to others whom they believe are both competent and relevant with respect to a work project. They must move from the discussion of an often vague research topic to a detailed research plan. Finally, they must execute the plan. These processes are not linear and consist of many active subtasks as well as active and passive monitoring of information. During these processes, there are important ways in which proximity might facilitate collaboration.

In the remainder of this chapter, we look more closely at how relevant features of proximity affect interpersonal interaction and awareness in collaborative work. We focus on a small number of generic collaborative actions or subtasks that previous research and everyday observation lead us to believe are essential to all collaboration: initiating communication, conducting a conversation, and maintaining awareness of the state of the environment, task, and team.

We discuss how the features and affordances of physical proximity help or hinder accomplishing these tasks. We are mindful, however, that there are other important generic subtasks, and these may depend on the domain within which collaboration takes place. For example, the need to exchange physical objects is likely to differ among mathematicians and surgeons. Similarly, our discussion ignores the processes by which potential collaborators build liking and trust, even though this achievement may be a necessary precondition for many sorts of collaborations (see Nardi and Whittaker, chapter 4, this volume, for a discussion of such issues). Our approach builds on earlier more holistic research (Chapanis, Ochsman, Parrish, and Weeks 1972; Daft and Lengel 1984; Short, Williams, and Christy 1976; Sproull and Kiesler 1991), which examined how types of media influence the success of collaboration. It also aims to extend other recent decompositional analyses of media effects, including Daly-Jones, Monk, and Watts's (1998) analysis of the different functions of audio and visual information and Clark and Brennan's (1990) analysis of the affordances of communication media for grounding in conversation.

Initiating Communication

When people are collocated, it takes relatively little effort for them to start interacting. For this reason, physical collocation has consequences for the frequency of encounters, the likelihood that chance encounters lead to conversations, people's comembership in a community, and the common ground that they develop due to repeated encounters.

Frequency of Communication

Proximity increases frequency of communication. All else being equal, people communicate most with those who are physically close by. Researchers since Zipf (1949) have observed that physical proximity leads to communication. This occurs among potential friends (Festinger, Schacter, and Back 1950), potential work partners (Allen 1977), and people who are already working together (Kraut, Egido, and Galegher 1990).

Frequent communication with collaborators is useful both during the initiation phases of a collaboration, when people are sizing up potential partners and refining vague ideas, and during the execution phase, when they are actively carrying out a plan, performing joint actions, and coordinating individual ones. Each communication episode provides the potential for people to learn something new about their partners, make decisions, monitor the state of the work, take corrective action, and perform other joint activities. If the communication episode does not take place, then the information exchange and joint action will not occur.

Likelihood of Chance Encounters

In part, physical proximity increases the frequency of communication by putting people who have the prerequisites for conversation in each other's presence (Monge, Rothman, Elsenberg, Miller, and Kirste 1985). As a result, they have chance encounters with others inhabiting or visiting the same location, which provide opportunities for conversation. For example, Kraut, Fish, Root, and Chalfonte (1990) showed that in the university and research labs they examined, the majority of conversations were opportunistic, planned by neither party before they happened. Architectural features like common rooms and public events like seminars increase the likelihood that inhabiting a common location leads to opportunities for interaction (Allen 1977).

Proximity facilitates even planned meetings. Being in the same environment as another allows one to pick up information opportunistically about another's availability. One can learn, for example, whether someone keeps morning or afternoon hours, whether the light is on in an office, or whether a conference room is free. Because meetings at a distance incur higher time and transportation costs than local ones, rational actors are likely to ration in-person communication sessions with distant collaborators.

Transitions from Encounters to Communication

In addition to increasing the likelihood of chance encounters, physical proximity leads to more communication by increasing the likelihood that a chance encounter results in conversation. Physical space helps people engage in conversation because when two people encounter each other, they are reminded of each other's existence, can assess each other's availability for communication, have a channel to signal intent for communication, and have the resources to carry it out. Kendon and Ferber (1973) have described the choreography and precise timing that occurs as people make the transition from sighting others to engaging them in conversation. Both physical mobility and the visual channel are important. People frequently wait until the other is not engaged in other activity, catch the other's eye to signal intent to communicate, and then move to an appropriate interpersonal distance before actually speaking. Other media do not support this well-honed routine.

Community Comembership and Repeated Encounters

Merely being in the presence of another does not automatically lead to communication. People frequently ride on mass transit, go to public amusements, and sit in a doctor's waiting room without conversing with the strangers they meet there. The organization of encounters in universities, research labs, and another venues for collaboration helps to increase the likelihood that encounters lead to conversation and that conversation is conducive to collaboration.

Many universities and companies organize office space so that people who have the most need to communicate are collocated. The consequence is that people who are likely to encounter each other in these spaces are likely to have a common history and common purpose.

People inhabit space in a physical work environment such as an office building or laboratory for a relatively long period. As a result, a person one encounters at the coffee station or printer table on one day is likely to be encountered again in the future. Festinger and associates (1950) demonstrated how repeated encounters help relationships form among unacquainted individuals. Although chance conversations tend to be short (Kraut, Fish, Root, and Chalfonte 1990; Whittaker, Frohlich, and Daly-Jones 1994) they typically take place within a broader context of more enduring work or social relationships, with a history and a future. In addition, the inhabitants of these spaces are often mutually exposed to events such as fire drills, seminar speakers, and memos from administrators. The common ground established in prior interactions and from immersion in a shared environment may serve as the stimulus for informal conversations. The knowledge that one will likely encounter colleagues in the future may introduce an obligation to speak to them.

Disadvantages of Physical Proximity for Initiating Communication
Up to this point, we have stressed the mechanisms through which physical proximity facilitates communication and collaboration. But dependence on physical proximity imposes substantial costs as well and may undercut successful collaboration. At a mechanistic level, the most important problem is that when conversation is initiated in person, the people must be simultaneously present. The precise timing in greetings described by Kendon and Ferber (1973) is necessary only because participants must attend to the same thing at the same time. E-mail, telephone answering machines, and computer bulletin boards remove the requirement for synchrony and as a result may facilitate the initiating of communication among people whose schedules do not easily align. Of course, these media can be used by people working together whether their offices are distant or close by.

A second problem with physical proximity for initiating communication is that the opportunistic and spontaneous communication that it supports is not always welcomed. Physical proximity leads to interruptions and loss of privacy, when more disciplined communication might be less disruptive and more productive (Perlow 1999).

Finally, physical proximity by definition privileges communication with people who are nearby. But in many cases, these are the wrong people to communicate with to get productive work done. In particular, these may be people who have too much overlap in orientation and knowledge to support productive collaboration (Burt 1992). Ancona and Caldwell (1992), for example, demonstrated that problems can arise when people concentrate communication within a supervisory group and fail to exchange enough information with others outside the group.

Initiating Communication in Other Media
If people try to use the same strategies to initiate conversation in a remote medium as they do face-to-face, the probability that an encounter will lead to communication is reduced. For example, Fish, Kraut, and Chalftone (1990) evaluated video-conferencing systems that kept an open visual and auditory connection between separated physical environments. Although spontaneous conversations did occur across these video links, they occurred less frequently than communication among

people who met spontaneously within a single location. In part, the low resolution of the video images and the asymmetries between what individuals on opposing sides of the video link could see and hear prevented conversational attempts from being consummated. A less exotic technology, the common telephone, is not as successful as physical proximity in supporting spontaneous communication because it severs an assessment of availability from the signaling channel. People place phone calls with no guarantee that the called party is available or amenable to interruption. As a result, the majority of office-to-office telephone calls are not completed on the first try.

Also, asymmetries in the information available to people who are not perceptually copresent may prevent mutual awareness and lead to difficulties with initiating communication. In the world of cellular phones, briefcases ring in inappropriate settings because the caller does not know the called party's state when placing the call. Caller ID is another interesting case: The called party can assess the identity of the caller and choose whether to take the call, but the caller does not know (for sure) whether he or she is being assessed. The result is that the caller is left to guess whether the called party is absent or unwilling to take the call. An analogous situation occurs when it is ambiguous to the sender of an e-mail message as to whether the message is yet unread or is being ignored. Although this asymmetry in knowledge is a disadvantage to the sender, it is quite an advantage to the recipient when privacy is a priority.

Chatrooms and MUDs (Curtis and Nichols 1993) are virtual places where people come together and exchange messages with each other. These are synchronous text services in which text typed at one terminal is displayed on another person's terminal, in close to real time. Almost all have mechanisms to show who is in attendance. For example, in the generic chat interface in figure 6.2, the list of recipients on the right side shows who is available; this list is updated as members enter or leave, although there is ambiguity when people walk away from their machines without logging out or fail to announce themselves when they return. Seeing that others are available stimulates communication with them.

The new generation of instant messaging services also fosters spontaneous and opportunistic communication. In these services, such as America Online's Instant Messenger and ICQ (a mnemonic for I Seek You; see figure 6.3), people agree to make information about themselves and their activities available to a set of others. When people subscribe to the service and run the instant messaging application, their personal computer sends a notification to a server announcing their

Today's Topic		Participants
Sue:	Hi folks :)	@chanserv machine @address
Sam:	Hey sue	@John-away
Peter:	((((((sue))))))	@Sue
Sally:	How are you?	Sam
Sue:	Fine, u?	Peter
		Sally
		Linda

Figure 6.2
Sample communication in internet relay chat (IRC).

availability. Others who subsequently run the instant messaging application are notified when people on their "buddy lists" go on-line.

Chatrooms also lead to chance encounters and the development of social and work relationships among the previously unacquainted because they lead to repeated interactions, which fosters common ground. Many chatrooms are organized around special topics, such as health, investments, politics, or games. In the most successful of these virtual environments, a subset of participants who are especially interested in these topics attend repeatedly. Together, such characteristics enable these virtual places to support spontaneous and opportunistic communication among the participants at the moment, much as physical proximity does. Like collocation, extended copresence in chatrooms and MUDs leads to the formation of personal relationships (Parks and Roberts 1998).

Conducting Conversation

Almost all collaborative work involves communication. People talk, write, gesture, and participate in multimodal interactive exchanges that serve both instrumental and social ends. For example, at the beginning of a scientific collaboration, people may have extended discussions to develop a common view of the research problem and approach. Later, they might argue the pros and cons of particular research decisions, evaluate and revise experimental protocols, instruct research assistants, apprise each other about the status of the work, or outline manuscripts.

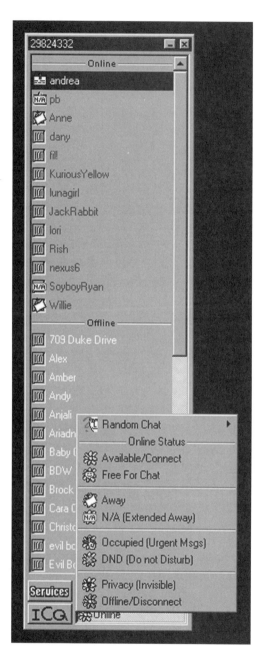

Figure 6.3
User interface for instant messaging.

Table 6.1
Affordances of communication media

Affordance	Definition
Audibility	Participants hear other people and sounds in the environment.
Visibility	Participants see other people and objects in the environment.
Tangibility	Participants can touch other people and objects in the environment.
Copresence	Participants are mutually aware that they share a physical environment.
Mobility	People can move around in a shared environment.
Cotemporality	Participants are present at the same time.
Simultaneity	Participants can send and receive messages at the same time.
Sequentiality	Participants take turns, and one turn's relevance to another is signaled by adjacency.
Reviewability	Messages do not fade over time but can be reviewed.
Revisability	Messages can be revised before being sent.

Source: Adapted from Clark and Brennan (1991).

All language use rests on a foundation of information of which participants are mutually aware, termed *mutual knowledge* or *common ground* (Clark and Wilkes-Gibbs 1986, Clark and Marshall 1981). People can assume common ground prior to an interaction if they know they are members of the same group or have experienced the same events. They also develop common ground by more active means. The term *grounding* refers to the interactive process by which communicators exchange evidence about what they do or do not understand over the course of a conversation as they accrue common ground (Clark and Wilkes-Gibbs 1986). As Clark and Brennan (1990) proposed, different media offer different resources or affordances that shape communication (see table 6.1). As a consequence, different media incur different grounding costs, including those of starting up a conversation, formulating and producing an utterance, receiving and understanding it, delaying in order to plan it more carefully, changing speakers, dealing with the inability to time the placement of a turn precisely, displaying or referring to something, and repairing misunderstandings.

While physical proximity does not preclude collaborators from conversing electronically, we focus here on the affordances of face-to-face conversation that make communication particularly efficient. Face-to-face conversation facilitates the process of grounding utterances in the following ways.

The Use of Common Ground

Whether communication is face-to-face or remote, speakers can rely on what common ground they have with addressees and side participants when they formulate utterances. To the extent that collocated collaborators may be more likely to be members of the same organization, they may have more common ground than remote collaborators. To the extent that speakers and listeners share a common work environment and culture, they can draw on this shared knowledge in planning and interpreting utterances. Experts, for example, can rely on specialized vocabulary in their domain of expertise that can lead to more efficient conversation (Isaacs and Clark 1987). Or collaborators might rely on their joint membership in a specific work culture (e.g., one in which the day ends at 6 P.M.) to clarify an utterance such as, "I'll have this to you by the end of the day."

When a speaker and listener are mutually aware that they are present in the same physical setting (copresence), the speaker generally has a good idea of what the listener can see or hear at any moment and uses these inferences in formulating an utterance. For example, speakers assume that elliptical references to salient objects and events in the environment will be understood (Clark, Schreuder, and Buttrick 1992). Hearing an unexpected noise, a speaker might ask, "What was that?" assuming that the listener had heard the same sound. In addition, the mobility of copresent speakers and listeners gives them greater flexibility in adapting each other's perspectives—for example, by moving closer to see what a partner is looking at.

When people are physically copresent, they can also use a full range of linguistic, paralinguistic, and nonverbal behaviors to communicate. They can use deictic gestures (pointing) to refer quickly and easily to people, locations, and objects. Although these nonverbal behaviors can be replaced with verbal substitutes, the substitutes take more time and effort (Brennan 1990). For example, when coauthors are jointly revising a manuscript, it is easier for one of them to say, "change this," while pointing to a specific sentence, rather than "Change the second to the last sentence in paragraph three on page 24." Of course, pointing can also be done effectively with a mouse and cursor during electronic communication. But sometimes the cursor may not be very salient, it may be delayed, or the person doing the pointing cannot easily monitor whether the remote partner is attending. Such visual evidence about joint attention is most important when speakers are discussing objects and activities that have a spatial character or that are changing. In addition, paralinguistic evidence such as facial expression, intonation, and timing are potentially helpful in detecting speakers' confidence in or attitudes toward what they are saying (Brennan and Williams 1995).

The Precise Timing of Cues

Because face-to-face communication is produced in real time and interpreted on-line and because it affords visual, auditory, and gestural cues, speakers have feedback on how a message is being understood as it is being delivered. Speakers often deliver utterances in installments, and listeners often precisely synchronize visual and verbal backchannels (e.g., head nods or "uh-huh") with these installments, providing evidence of understanding and interest. The features of face-to-face conversation that make it real-time (cotemporality, simultaneity, and sequentiality) are probably more important than its visual nature, since some information in visual and verbal backchannels may be redundant (Short, Williams, and Christie 1976). However, seeing others' actions can enable people to infer comprehension and clarify misunderstandings more efficiently. If a speaker says, "Adjust the red dial," but the addressee instead tries to turn a red screw, the speaker can see that the message was misunderstood and that the problem lies in the identification of the dial (Fussell, Kraut, and Siegel 2000).

The Coordination of Turn-Taking

When speakers are located in the same physical space, their contributions to conversation tend to be timed so that there is little overlap between speaking turns, and when such overlap does occur, it is usually resolved quickly, so that one person is speaking (Sacks, Schegloff, and Jefferson 1974). Although one turn can lead to another by explicit verbal means (e.g., when one person asks another for an opinion), gesture and eye gaze can facilitate the process, and these features are especially important in multiparty conversation. Speakers frequently direct their eye gaze to indicate whom they are addressing and whom they expect to respond (Duncan and Fiske 1977). Since spoken utterances are usually grounded in the order they are produced, adjacent utterances tend to be relevant to one another, and people strongly expect such relevance. This is not the case in chatroom conversations, where multiple threads typically emerge.

The Repair of Misunderstandings

The real-time nature of face-to-face conversation improves the prospects for repairing misunderstandings and other problems. Because speakers have moment-by-moment evidence of what addressees understand and accept, they can repair problems immediately, often in mid-utterance. The more quickly a problem is repaired, the less costly it is likely to be (Clark and Brennan 1990).

Disadvantages of Physical Proximity for Conducting Conversation

Just as the real-time character of face-to-face interaction makes grounding so efficient, it also places cognitive demands on both speaker and listener due to the fact that conversation must be done spontaneously. Speakers have to plan and execute their utterances simultaneously at multiple levels. They need to formulate a relatively long-term conversational strategy (e.g., stage an argument), design the substance and syntax of sentences, find particular words to fill slots in the sentences, and articulate the result; they may begin speaking while they are still planning (Levelt 1989). They need to do all this rather rapidly or risk losing their listeners' attention. Simultaneously, they must monitor what they are saying to ensure that it is consistent with their intentions. They must also monitor feedback from the listener and reformulate their speech accordingly. Not surprisingly, with all these cognitive demands, spoken conversation is littered with sentence fragments, pauses, sounds such as *um* or *uh*, imprecise word choices, and other departures from idealized language. However, because listeners can give feedback in real time about their comprehension and because speakers can quickly reclarify, these errors are often not consequential.

Listeners are also faced with cognitive burdens. Because spoken utterances are ephemeral, unlike messages on an answering machine or in a written document, the listener cannot pause or reread the message when some portion is difficult. Again, however, the ability to ask for clarification partially compensates for the ephemeral nature of speech. When there are many listeners, however, it is far more costly for a single one whose attention has wandered to stop the speaker for clarification.

Other Technologies for Conducting Conversation

People can conduct efficient, productive, and satisfying conversations other than face-to-face, but how they accomplish this varies across media. According to Clark and Wilkes-Gibbs's (1986) principle of least collaborative effort, people try to ground their conversations with as little combined effort as possible. In response to the costs imposed by different media, people adapt different strategies in grounding. In this section we consider the implications of conversing over media that do not support real-time communication (lacking cotemporality, simultaneity, or sequentiality), compared with those that enable physical and linguistic copresence.

As we have seen, spoken language can be filled with disfluencies and still be comprehensible because the costs of turn taking, feedback, and repair are relatively low. Listeners can indicate precisely where in an utterance they are confused, and speakers can repair just this section (Kraut, Lewis, and Swezey 1982). Communication media that introduce even small delays make grounding substantially more difficult to accomplish (Krauss and Bricker 1966). Research suggests that such disrupted conversations are less successful in the sense that participants communicate information less well, feel the conversations are less natural, and terminate them sooner (O'Conaill, Whittaker, and Wilbur 1993).

The telephone supports interactive grounding well, even though it lacks visual evidence and is used remotely. Indeed, early studies of media differences in communication found that full-duplex phone communication was indistinguishable from face-to-face communication for many referential communication tasks (Williams 1977). Speakers partially compensate for the lack of visual channels by producing more verbal backchannels than they would in face-to-face conversations.

Asynchronous text-based communication, such as e-mail, is neither cotemporal, simultaneous, nor necessarily sequential. Because writers of e-mail messages do not have feedback from an audience during the composition process, they need to be more explicit in forming a message. And the often long delays between sending a message and receiving a reply (not to mention the other messages that may arrive in between) often mean that linguistic context is not well preserved. Many of us have received an incomprehensible yes or no answer to a question asked days before by e-mail. For messages to be interpretable, writers may need to reintroduce quotations from previous messages into the body of the message itself. Indeed, many e-mail systems offer commands for this. Even so, it is more effortful to ground utterances in e-mail than in spoken conversation. Linguistic copresence accrues over hours or days by e-mail, as opposed to within minutes in person, by telephone, or in synchronous computer-mediated chats.

We believe that a difficulty in grounding is one reason that collaborators with a choice of communication media try to use face-to-face conversation for tasks that require consensus or negotiation, while using e-mail for coordination (Finholt, Sproull, and Kiesler 1990) and that teams forced to rely on e-mail tend to work more independently, especially in the early stages of a project when they are setting direction (Galegher and Kraut 1994). On the other hand, the fact that e-messages can be stored, consulted when they are replied to, and reviewed later makes linguistic copresence easier to achieve and maintain over longer time periods, compared to the imperfect memory or notes resulting from ephemeral face-to-face meetings. Having such a record can be a real advantage for long-term collaborations.

Because synchronous text services are by definition cotemporal, people ground utterances in chatrooms very differently than in e-mail. On the one hand, the relatively quick exchanges in chatrooms and instant messaging systems make feedback and repair much easier. The potential for rapid interaction has led to a style of communication more like spoken conversation, with short installments and frequent responses.

With respect to video teleconferencing, early research suggested that being able to see a conversational partner's face is surprisingly unimportant in communication. Subjects in problem-solving experiments rated video that simply provided a link to a communication partner as less valuable than video used to share data (Anderson, Smallwood, MacDonald, Mullin, and Fleming 1999). Having a shared visual environment (visual copresence) especially improves communication when it contains the objects being talked about (Karsenty 1999; Fussell et al. 2000; Whittaker and Geelhoed 1993). For some collaborative tasks, such as giving instruction about the operation of a software package, being able to share screens on a computer might provide sufficient shared visual space to improve communication (Karsenty 1999). For tasks where the objects are not computationally generated, higher-bandwidth video may be more important. However, because of quality problems, video may not be sufficient to achieve a shared visual space (Anderson et al. 1997, Fussell et al., 2000). For example, limitations in mobility and fields of view mean that not everything visible to one party in a conversation might be visible to others. Similarly, limitations on resolution and field of view often mean that one party in a conversation cannot easily assess the focus of attention of the other party.

Maintaining Task and Team Awareness

To achieve the coordination required for collaborative action, people maintain an ongoing awareness of events in their work environment and beyond. Many types of awareness may play a role in successful collaborations, varying by domain (e.g., environment, team, and task) and temporal granularity (with timescales ranging from months to fractions of a second; Cooke, Salas, Cannon-Bowers, and Stout

2000). People keep up with information about the demand for their work in the real world, how particular tasks are progressing, what fellow workers are doing, who is communicating with whom, what equipment is out of order, and many other details of the collaboration that concern them directly or tangentially. Here we distinguish between awareness of the task (e.g., what steps need to be taken next; Seifert and Hutchins 1992) and awareness of the collaborative team, (e.g., who knows what among the members; Liang, Moreland, and Argote 1995). Developing and maintaining this awareness is much more difficult in distributed teams than collocated ones (Cramton 2001).

Task awareness, which includes collaborators' beliefs about the overall project, including its history, current status, and future directions, is crucial for successful coordination. When collaborators divide work, they need to monitor their partners' activities for personnel management and to understand the impact of their partners' progress on their own work. This monitoring can help people determine when and which collaborative actions are required (e.g., whether it is time to nag someone to complete his or her section of the project). The granularity with which collaborators need to maintain task awareness differs depending on the nature of the task and the type of collaborative actions they wish to perform. For activities such as collaborative writing, which are characterized by periods of individual work followed by integration of efforts, it may suffice to know that a coauthor will be working on the article at some point during the week. However, under deadline pressure, the same task may require awareness that is more frequently updated. For other tasks, such as a medical team working together in an operating room, a much more finely grained awareness of the current state of the task is needed.

Team awareness, on the other hand, refers to collaborators' beliefs about both stable and changing attributes of their partners. Detailed and accurate models of each other's knowledge, skills, and motivation help collaborators assign tasks appropriately and solicit and offer appropriate help (Liang et al. 1995). Collaborators share beliefs about project roles and responsibilities, interdependencies among team members, the current status of each person's assigned tasks, their availability for interaction, and the like (Cannon-Bowers, Salas, and Converse 1993; Levine and Moreland 1991).

When teams members are collocated rather than distributed, they can provide and receive up-to-date information about the status of current tasks and each other's capabilities relatively easily. Proximity increases the frequency of communication, and each episode of communication provides a setting in which teammates can explicitly exchange information about task status, personal competence, and availability. Equally important, when teammates are collocated, they can passively monitor activities going on around them and pick up relevant information without explicit communication. In face-to-face settings, people display what they are doing simply by doing it, with no special communicative intent. When people share a physical and social work environment, for example, they can attend meetings where others are expressing views, pass by an ongoing activity en route to the printer, overhear a conversation, or view a diagram on a hallway whiteboard.

This passive monitoring of other's activities aids collaboration. For example, Liang and associates (1995) demonstrated that members of a team pick up information about each other while training side by side, which allows them to allocate tasks more effectively. Seifert and Hutchins (1992) demonstrated that team members can assess the competence of new recruits and correct their errors by overhearing conversations.

Not only do collocated teams pick up information implicitly, but they also share a context that helps them accurately interpret this information. Cramton's study of distributed project teams (2001) showed that the lack of shared context leads to misattributions for behavior, resulting in poorer coordination and distrust. For example, one member may send another mail asking for an update, but does not get a response because the recipient is on vacation. In a distributed team, the lack of shared context often led to ambiguity about interpreting silence, which in turn resulted in failures of coordination and distrust. In the teams Cramton (2001) studied, failure to respond to mail was attributed negatively to the person (that person is unreliable) rather than to the situation (the mail did not get through or the team was on vacation). By contrast, in a collocated setting, vacation schedules and availability would likely be known.

The Disadvantages of Physical Proximity for Maintaining Awareness

Because proximity supports frequent communication and passive information gathering, people in collocated teams are more aware of the shared environment, the team, and the tasks than are members of distributed teams. This information is necessary for internal communication but not sufficient. Success in research and development teams also depends on keeping up with changes in the broader social and technical environment (Allen 1977, Ancona and Caldwell 1992). When competing for the Nobel Prize, for example, Watson and Crick needed to know what was happening in Linus Pauling's lab as well what was happening in their own (Watson 1968). We hypothesize that the ease of local communication and information acquisition may bias the information tracked by a work group, causing them to overattend to local information at the expense of more remote, contextual information.

Maintaining Awareness Through Other Technologies

A long-standing goal for research in both information retrieval and computer-supported cooperative work (CSCW) has been to develop tools that aid passive awareness. The major design challenge is that the information needed to maintain awareness of team, task, and environment may overwhelm team members and prevent them from actually doing work. It is difficult, for example, to craft a document if one is continually checking on a teammate's progress. What is needed are automatic ways of detecting relevant changes to the collaborative state and then presenting these changes to interested parties without overwhelming them.

Automated techniques for selectively distributing information have existed for at least a quarter of a century (Salton and McGill 1979) and are designed to match changing information with a subscriber's interests. Using these techniques helps scientists keep aware of new publications in their research areas. Many e-mail systems apply analogous techniques to filter private and group correspondence, with the goal of highlighting the important messages.

Another stream of research builds tools to provide collaborators with knowledge of other team members. Many of the CSCW tools for passive awareness have used images and video to provide a view into the work environments of remote team members (Dourish and Bly 1992, Fish et al. 1992) to show availability and progress. Others use social network techniques to show someone's communication partners (Ackerman and Starr 1996).

Other approaches have concentrated on awareness of people's use of shared documents. For example the edit–read–wear systems (Hill and Hollan 1992) display which aspects of documents were more frequently read and changed. Similarly, the TeamSCOPE system (Yang, Steinfield, and Pfaff 2000) attempted to provide members of a distributed collaborative team up-to-date information about which project documents had changed, who had read them, and which team members had been active. One problem with these systems is that inferences about teammates activities are often fragmentary, ambiguous, or wrong. For example, just because software notices that someone has downloaded a document, there is no guarantee that he or she has read it. Moreover, even when users get detailed and accurate information about other teammates' work activities, this information may not improve their coordination. For example, Espinosa and others (2000) gave teams accurate information about documents their partners had read. As a response, individuals assumed, erroneously, that they did not need to read material their partners had read; this decision prevented them from deliberating over jointly read documents.

Details in design can strongly influence whether information for awareness will overload its users. Awareness systems differ on whether they broadcast information to users or require them to poll a database. Consider two techniques to allow a team member to monitor discussions among collaborators. These discussions could be delivered to recipients through distribution lists or listservs, a broadcast technology. Alternatively, they could be deposited in a Web site or electronic bulletin board, which users must poll to see if new material has arrived. The value and costs of these mechanisms are likely to depend on the granularity and frequency of updates. The broadcast technique is genuinely passive. In a listserv, for example, people see the awareness information whenever they check their personal e-mail. Broadcasting awareness information, however, can be highly intrusive. Butler (1999) showed that each message sent to a listserv drives some subscribers away, even as it attracts others, with more members lost than gained per message sent. To alleviate this problem, highly active listservs allow members to subscribe to a digest, which concatenates messages and delivers them once per day. Polling techniques are much less intrusive but require people to check whether new material has arrived. Because awareness techniques based on polling are not passive awareness mechanisms, they are likely to be ineffective at keeping people up to date unless polling is done frequently.

In addition to information delivery mechanisms, the success of passive awareness systems strongly depends on the details of the user interface. Interfaces to instant messaging systems, which support passive awareness of friends' and colleagues' availability, illustrate one way to announce new information without demanding excess attention. In figure 6.3, a user has entered more than twenty individuals in his "buddy list," of whom he wants to keep aware. When a buddy goes on-line, his screen name moves to the upper part of the window, alerting the user that he is on-line and hence potentially available for communication. When one of the buddies attempts a conversation, the icon representing the buddy flashes. Other icons allow users to indicate that they are on-line but not accepting calls, and other variations on their availability.

Conclusions

This chapter has explored how copresence, visibility, mobility, cotemporality, and other affordances of media affect the important collaborative tasks of initiating conversation, establishing common ground, and maintaining awareness of potentially relevant changes in the collaborative environment. Although not perfect, collocation and face-to-face communication bundle together affordances for these generic collaborative tasks, making collaboration easier to accomplish among people who are collocated than among those who are apart. People, however, can and do collaborate over distance, using whatever technologies they have available. In the nineteenth century, Darwin corresponded with naturists around the globe on the role of emotional expression in humans and animals (Darwin 1965). In such cases, people adapt, within limits, to the means of communication they have available. One can ask questions by letter and get explanations in response, but because of delays and the extra effort required to write text, using this method of communication changes the nature of the communication and the collaboration. For example, communication will be less social, more focused on the topic at hand, more planned, less ambiguous, and more likely to contain misunderstandings than communication conducted in person.

We discussed results in terms of media affordances, but it is difficult to differentiate physical attributes of the media from long-standing adaptations of social systems and individual behavior to media with specific features. For example, it is because media influence the probability of chance encounters that organizations collocate people who need to talk to each other. Because typing is more effortful and slower than speaking, people who interactively communicate in chats, MUDs, and instant messaging systems write in abbreviations that get their meaning across with less typing (see figure 6.2). Communities of users have developed conventions of abbreviations, where, for example, LOL means "laughing out loud," IMHO means "in my humble opinion," and BBFN means "bye bye for now."

E-mail and instant messaging are both text-based computer-mediated communication, but they differ from each other in the likely delay between a message's being sent and being received. We have treated the greater interactivity of the instant messaging systems as a matter of media. However, to some extent, these differences are a matter of convention. Although it is possible to use conventional e-mail so that a dyad rapidly exchanges messages as soon as they arrive, in practice most e-mail is exchanged with substantial delays between when a message is sent, when it is read, and when it is replied to.

This chapter has not been an exhaustive treatment of either collaboration or media differences. Rather, the goal has been to illustrate an approach that examines how the affordances of media influence important tasks within a larger social process such as collaboration. We have treated only several media affordances. We have skimmed only three generic collaborative subtasks, and there are numerous domain-specific tasks we have not discussed at all. Although our conclusions are limited, they illustrate the value of the decompositional approach.

Note

We thank Sara Kiesler, Pam Hinds, Judy Olson, Gary Olson, Takeshi Okada, and other members of the Distributed Work Workshop for their very helpful comments. This material is based on work supported by the National Science Foundation under grants 9980013 and 0082602.
1. We thank David Krackhardt for help in conducting this analysis.

References

Ackerman, M. S., and Starr, B. (1996). Social activity indicators for groupware. *IEEE Computer, 29*(6), 37–44.

Allen, T. (1977). *Managing the flow of technology*. Cambridge, MA: MIT Press.

Ancona, D. G., and Caldwell, D. F. (1992). Bridging the boundary: External activity and performance in organizational teams. *Administrative Science Quarterly, 37*, 634–665.

Anderson, A., O'Malley, C., Doherty-Sneddon, G., Langton, S., Newlands, A., Mullin, J., Fleming, A., and Velden, J. (1997). The impact of VMC on collaborative problem solving: An analysis of task performance, communication process, and user satisfaction. In K. Finn, A. Sellen, and S. Wilbur. (eds.), *Video-mediated communication* (133–156). Mahwah, NJ: Erlbaum.

Anderson, A., Smallwood, L., MacDonald, R. Mullin, J., and Fleming, A. (1999). Video data and video links in mediated communication: What do users value? *International Journal of Human-Computer Studies, 51*, 1–23.

Brennan, S. E. (1990). *Seeking and providing evidence for mutual understanding*. Unpublished doctoral dissertation, Stanford University.

Brennan, S. E., and Williams, M. (1995). The feeling of another's knowing: Prosody and filled pauses as cues to listeners about the metacognitive states of speakers. *Journal of Memory and Language, 34*, 383–398.

Burt, R. S. (1992). *Structural holes: The social structure of competition.* Cambridge, MA: Harvard University Press.

Butler, B. S. (1999). *The dynamics of cyberspace: Examining and modeling online social structure.* Unpublished doctoral dissertation. Carnegle Mellon University.

Cannon-Bowers, J. A., Salas, E., and Converse, S. A. (1993). Shared mental models in expert decision-making teams. In N. J. Castellan, Jr. (ed.), *Current issues in individual and group decision making* (221–246). Hillsdale, NJ: Erlbaum.

Chapanis, A., Ochsman, R. B., Parrish, R. N., and Weeks, G. D. (1972). Studies in interactive communication: I. The effects of four communication modes on the behavior of teams during cooperative problem solving. *Human Factors, 14*, 487–509.

Clark, H. H., and Brennan, S. E. (1990). Grounding in communication. In L. B. Resnick, R. M. Levine, and S. D. Teasley (eds.), *Perspectives on socially shared cognition* (127–149). Washington, DC: American Psychological Association.

Clark, H. H., and Marshall, C. R. (1981). Definite reference and mutual knowledge. In A. K. Joshi, B. L. Webber, and I. A. Sag (eds.), *Elements of discourse understanding* (10–63). Cambridge: Cambridge University Press.

Clark, H. H., Schreuder, R., and Buttrick, S. (1992). Common ground and the understanding of demonstrative reference. In H. H. Clark (ed.), *Arenas of language use* (78–99). Chicago: University of Chicago Press.

Clark, H. H., and Wilkes-Gibbs, D. (1986). Referring as a collaborative process. *Cognition, 22*, 1–39.

Cooke, N. J., Salas, E., Cannon-Bowers, J. A., and Stout, R. J. (2000). Measuring team knowledge. *Human Factors, 42*(1), 151–173.

Cramton, C. D. (2001). The mutual knowledge problem and its consequences in geographically dispersed teams. *Organizational Science, 12*, 346–371.

Curtis, P., and Nichols, D. (1993). MUDs grow up: Virtual reality in the real world. In *Proceedings of the Third International Conference on Cyberspace.* Palo Alto, CA: XEROX Palo Alto Research Center. Available at: ftp.lambda.moo.mud.org/pub/MOO/papers/MUDs-GrowUp.txt.

Daft, R. L., and Lengel, R. H. (1984). Information richness: A new approach to managerial behavior and organization design. In B. Staw and L. L. Cummings (eds.), *Research in organizational behavior* (Vol. 6, 191–233). Greenwich, CT: JAI Press.

Daly-Jones, O., Monk, A., and Watts, L. (1998). Some advantages of video conferencing over high-quality audio conferencing: Fluency and awareness of attentional focus. *International Journal of Human-Computer Studies, 49*, 21–58.

Darwin, Charles. (1965). *The expression of the emotions in man and animals.* New York: Appleton. (Originally published 1872.)

Dourish, P. , and Bly, S. (1992). Portholes: Supporting awareness in a distributed work group. In *Proceedings of CHI'92* (541–547). New York: ACM, Press.

Duncan, S., and Fiske, D. W. (1977). *Face-to-face interaction: Research, methods and theory.* Hilldale, NJ: Erlbaum.

Endsley, M. (1995). Toward a theory of situation awareness in dynamic systems. *Human Factors, 37*(1), 32–64.

Espinosa, A., Cadiz, J., Rico-Gutierrez, L., Lautenbacher, G., Kraut, R., and Scherlis, L. (2000, March). Coming to the wrong decision quickly: Why awareness tools must be matched with appropriate tasks. In *Proceedings, Human Factors in Computing Systems, CHI'2000* (392–399). New York: ACM Press.

Festinger, L., Schachter, S., and Back, K. (1950). *Social pressures in informal groups: A study of human factors in housing.* Palo Alto, CA: Stanford University Press.

Finholt, T., Sproull, L., and Kiesler, S. (1990). Communication and performance in ad hoc task groups. In J. Galegher, R. Kraut, and C. Egido (eds.), *Intellectual teamwork: Social and technological bases of cooperative work* (291–325). Hillsdale, NJ: Erlbaum.

Fish, R. S., Kraut, R. E., and Chalftone, B. L. (1990). The VideoWindow system in informal communications. In *Proceedings, ACM Conference on Computer Supported Cooperative Work* (1–12). New York: ACM Press.

Fussell, S. R., Kraut, R. E., and Siegel, J. (2000). Coordination of communication: Effects of shared visual context on collaborative work. In *Proceedings of the ACM 2000 Conference on Computer Supported Cooperative Work* (21–30). New York: ACM Press.

Galegher, J., and Kraut, R. E. (1994). Computer-mediated communication for intellectual teamwork: An experiment in group writing. *Information Systems Research, 5*(2), 110–138.

Garvey, W., Lin, N., and Nelson, C. (1970). Communication in the physical and social sciences. *Science, 170,* 1166–1173.

Hackman, J. R. (2000, October 4). *When teams, when not?* Keynote presentation, Organizational Development Conference, Naples, FL.

Hagstrom, W. O. (1965). *The scientific community.* Carbondale, IL: Southern Illinois University Press.

Hill, W. C., and Hollan, J. D. (1992). Edit wear and read wear. In P. O. Bauersfeld, J. Bennett, and G. Lynch (eds.), In *Proceedings CHI'92* (3–9). New York: ACM Press.

Isaacs, E., and Clark, H. H. (1987). References in conversation between experts and novices. *Journal of Experimental Psychology: General, 116,* 26–37.

Karsenty, L. (1999). Cooperative work and shared visual context: An empirical study of comprehension problems and in side-by-side and remote help dialogues. *Human-Computer Interaction, 14,* 283–315.

Kendon, A., and Ferber, A. (1973). A description of some human greetings. In R. Michael and J. Crook (eds.), *Comparative ecology and behavior of primates* (591–668). London : Academic Press.

Krauss, R. M., and Bricker, P. D. (1966). Effects of transmission delay and access delay on the efficiency of verbal communication. Journal of the Acoustical Society, 41, 286–292.

Kraut, R. E., Egido, C., and Galegher, J. (1990). Patterns of contact and communication in scientific research collaboration. In J. Galegher, R. Kraut, and C. Egido (eds.), *Intellectual teamwork: Social and technological bases of cooperative work* (149–171). Hillsdale, NJ: Erlbaum.

Kraut, R. E., Fish, R. S., Root, R. W., and Chalfonte, B. L. (1990). Informal communication in organizations: Form, function, and technology. In S. Oskamp and S. Spacapan (eds.), *Human reactions to technology: The Claremont Symposium on applied social psychology* (145–199). Thousand Oaks, CA: Sage.

Kraut, R. E., Galegher, J., and Egido, C. (1988). Relationships and tasks in scientific research collaborations. *Human-Computer Interaction*, 3, 31–58.

Kraut, R. E., Lewis, S. H., and Swezey, L. W. (1982). Listener responsiveness and the coordination of conversation. *Journal of Personality and Social Psychology*, 43, 718–731.

Levelt, W. J. M. (1989). *Speaking: From intention to articulation*. Cambridge, MA: MIT Press.

Levine, J. M., and Moreland, R. L. (1990). Progress in small group research. *Annual Review of Psychology*, 41, 585–634.

Liang, D., Moreland, R., and Argote, L. (1995). Group versus individual training and group performance: The mediating role of transactive memory. *Personality and Social Psychology Bulletin*, 21, 384–393.

Monge, P. R., Rothman, L. W., Eisenberg, E. M., Miller, K. L., and Kirste, K. K. (1985). The dynamics of organizational proximity. *Management Science*, 31, 1129–1141.

Nardi, B., and Whittaker, S. (2002). The place of face-to-face communication in distributed work. In P. Hinds and S. Kiesler (eds.), *Distributed Work*. (83–110). Cambridge, MA: MIT Press.

O'Conaill, B., Whittaker, S., and Wilbur, S. (1993). Conversations over videoconferences: An evaluation of the spoken aspects of video mediated communication. *Human Computer Interaction*, 8, 389–428.

Parks, M. R., and Roberts, L. D. (1998). Making MOOsic: The development of personal relationships online and a comparison to their offline counterparts. *Journal of Social and Personal Relationships*, 15, 517–537.

Perlow, L. A. (1999). The time famine: Toward a sociology of work time. *Administrative Science Quarterly*, 44(1), 57–81.

Sacks, H., Schegloff, E., and Jefferson, G. (1974). A simplest systematics for the organization of turn-taking in conversation. *Language*, 50, 696–735.

Salton, G., and McGill, M. J. I. (1979). *Introduction to modern information retrieval*. New York: McGraw-Hill.

Seifert, C., and Hutchins, E. L. (1992). Error as opportunity: Learning in a cooperative task. *Human-Computer Interaction*, 7(4), 409–436.

Short, J., Williams, E., and Christie, B. (1976). *The social psychology of telecommunications*. New York: Wiley.

Sproull, L., and Kiesler, S. (1991). *Connections: New ways of working in the networked organization*. Cambridge, MA: MIT Press.

Watson, J. D. (1968). *The double helix: A personal account of the discovery of the structure of DNA*. New York: Scribner.

Whittaker, S., Frohlich, D., and Daly-Jones, O. (1994). Informal workplace communication: What is it like and how might we support it? In *Proceedings of the ACM Conference on Human Factors in Computing Systems CHI'94* (131–137). New York: ACM Press.

Whittaker, S., and Geelhoed, E. (1993). Shared workspaces: How do they work and when are they useful? *International Journal of Man-Machine Studies, 39,* 813–842.

Williams, E. (1977). Experimental comparisons of face-to-face and mediated communication: A review. *Psychological Bulletin, 84,* 963–976.

Yang, C., Steinfield, C., and Pfaff, B. (2000, December 2). *Supporting awareness among virtual teams in a web-based collaborative system: The TeamSCOPE system.* Paper presented at the ACM International Workshop on Awareness and the World Wide Web, Philadelphia.

Zipf, G. K. (1949). *Human behavior and the principle of least effort.* Reading, MA: Addison-Wesley.

CATHY © 2000 Cathy Guisewite. Reprinted with permission of Universal Press Syndicate. All rights reserved.

III

Group Process in Distributed Work

The chapters in this part address how geographic distribution affects group processes in distributed work. In chapter 7, Armstrong and Cole present a case study of distributed software development teams, showing how geographic distance triggered problems of cultural and organizational distance, which exacerbated barriers to effective communication. In chapter 8, Catherine Cramton pursues the theme of communication difficulties further, showing how they affect the way people think about one another and make attributions of causality and blame that can interfere with the work and group interaction. Elizabeth Mannix, Terri Griffith, and Margaret Neale in chapter 9 apply a large body of research on conflict to the questions of how and why conflict may arise in distributed groups and how groups can manage this conflict. Joseph Walther in chapter 10 discusses the use of communication technology in ongoing distributed work groups. In a critical review of the research on the effects of communication technology, he shows how working and interacting over time changes the way group members use technology and how they adapt to one another and to the needs of the group.

Whereas the first four chapters in this part look at interpersonal relationships and interactions of distributed team members, the last two compare formal versus emergent processes in distributed groups. In a qualitative study of several distributed units of the German government, Gloria Mark in chapter 11 examines how conventions emerge and govern the work processes and interactions between members (and subgroups) of distributed teams. Mark Mortensen and Pamela Hinds in chapter 12 explore the extent to which team boundaries—who is and who is not a member of the team—are clear in distributed versus collocated product development teams. They report that none of the twenty-four teams they studied was in complete agreement on team membership.

The chapter authors generally agree that group processes in distributed groups are fundamentally similar to those of collocated groups. However, as is clear from the empirical studies, conflict and communication difficulties can overtake distributed work groups if they do not adapt their communications and attitudes to the special demands that distance imposes.

7

Managing Distances and Differences in Geographically Distributed Work Groups

David J. Armstrong and Paul Cole

This chapter presents a detailed examination of software product development teams whose members were located in separate offices, some in different countries. The members of these distributed work groups experienced misunderstandings in communications and conflict. Communications were often fragmented, with gaps and misunderstandings among distant group members. Group members had problems forming groups and maintaining ties. Distributed groups showed developmental changes over time, typically with the support of managers who actively intervened to integrate the group. Some teams became better integrated, but they still faced problems due to distance. Differences in national and office site cultures were observed even in integrated groups, and constituted a dimension of distance beyond kilometers and time zones. Also, larger organizational problems sometimes recreated or reinforced differences within the distributed group. To counter these forces, managers must use integrating practices that promote greater understanding and liking between cultural groups (such as enforcing equality, creating superordinate goals, promoting frequent personal and face-to-face contact, and supporting mutual knowledge); these are the same activities that lead to cohesion in collocated work groups.

In the rush to go global, corporations are asking their employees to be effective across distances never before mastered, depending on new innovations in communication technology to tie everyone together. These leaner companies are simultaneously emphasizing flexible team structures as the organizational molecule most responsive to rapid developments in products and markets. Teams of professionals, armed with laptop computers, fax-modems, e-mail, voice mail, videoconferencing, interactive databases, and frequent flyer memberships, are being sent out to conduct business in this global arena.

Working with a Fortune 100 U.S. computer company, which we refer to by the pseudonym Compute Company, we served as consultants to product development teams with members located in separate offices, sometimes on different continents. This chapter summarizes the lessons we learned from consulting with two such distributed groups and from interviewing managers and staff consultants involved in seven other distributed groups. All of these groups were part of the software engineering organization, involved with product development, and consisted of software engineers, marketing specialists, and technical writers.

A Case Study of Distributed Work Groups

We used interviews and document reviews to study nine distributed work groups in Compute Company's software engineering organization. The groups included software product development groups, a product management group, and a group responsible for producing software manuals. We interviewed thirty-eight managers, individual contributors, and staff consultants associated with these groups. In addition, we conducted extensive organizational consultations with two of the groups and visited their work sites.

These distributed work groups ranged in size from 25 employees to 450 (in this largest group, we studied the management team). The groups ranged in dispersion from two to nine sites, located from 15 kilometers apart to worldwide distribution. All groups had offices in or near the software engineering head office (HO) on the U.S. East Coast. Other group sites in the United States were located in Massachusetts, New Hampshire, New Jersey, California, and Washington State. Groups had international offices in the United Kingdom, France, Germany, Italy, Israel, Hong Kong, Taiwan, and Japan.

Members of these distributed groups were linked by e-mail, voice mail, fax, telephone conferences, and computer conferences that allowed sites to work in shared text files. Some sites had videoconference links with their HO counterparts. Computer networks allowed the engineers to ship their software products to other sites for testing, trial assembly, or joint inspections.

Problems across Distances and Differences

The members of these distributed work groups experienced two problem areas that they considered uniquely difficult when working across distance and differences: misunderstandings in communications and strangely escalating conflicts.

Communications were often fragmented, with gaps and misunderstandings among distant group members. There was confusion in telephone conferences, with people on different pages of documents. Group members failed to return telephone calls or respond to inquiries from distant members. Key group members at remote sites were left off e-mail distribution lists. Distant members were not informed of key decisions or information. Misunderstandings developed on the basis of different assumptions about the tasks and assignments. Messages were interpreted differently in different places, sometimes fueling ongoing conflicts among office sites.

Conflicts among sites went unidentified and unaddressed longer than conflicts among members of collocated groups and flared up more suddenly, surprising distant managers. Leaders were surprised by unexpected reactions to their decisions from distant sites. Some of these conflicts seemed to resist reason and play a role in self-perpetuating feuds among different sites. Members of the same group treated each other as if they were members of different groups, with colleagues at one office site described as *us* and group members at distant sites labeled *them*. As a consequence of the conflicts and communication problems, projects often took longer than planned to start up, with frequent delays in work progress.

In addition, managers reported difficulty analyzing performance problems and coaching from a distance. Distances interfered with communications that depended on subtle, often nonverbal behaviors, which were needed to be effective in group work roles such as project leader. In particular, managers had difficulty transferring group culture subtleties (e.g., "how we do things around here") across distance.

Proximity Effects on Work Relations

Chatting in the Hall

Communication with colleagues who worked nearby, on the same floor of the same building, was more frequent and occurred in more situations in both scheduled and coincidental encounters than with distant colleagues. Communication with people at the same site occurred through many media, permitting a broader range of messages and immediate responses. One informal study by an engineer revealed, in fact, that more e-mail messages were sent to collocated group members than to group members on another continent, despite the fact that nearby members were easily accessible face-to-face.

Beyond a very short distance, people began to miss out on spontaneous exchanges and decision making that occurred outside formal meetings. Many people commented on how often key exchanges occurred after meetings and in chance encounters in the hallway, over work cubicle walls, and in the cafeteria. The postmortem analysis of one canceled international project zeroed in on the lack of casual connections: "There was no day-to-day coffee machine conversation, which was needed to make it succeed." Remote group members felt cut off from the key conversations, over lunch or in the hall, that often followed videoconferences.

Feedback

Distance blocked the corrective feedback loops provided by chance encounters. Misunderstandings built up between sites that lacked the casual opportunities that close proximity offered to identify and discuss disagreements. One manager contrasted how employees who worked in his home office related to his decisions, compared with employees 15 kilometers away. Engineers would drop by his office or catch him in the hall or at lunch. "I heard you were planning to change project X," they would say. "Let me tell you why that would be stupid." The manager would listen to their points and clarify some details they were lacking, and all would part better informed.

In contrast, employees at the remote site would greet his weekly visits with formally prepared group objections, which took much longer to discuss and were rarely resolved as completely as the more informal hallway encounters. He concluded, "You don't get coincidental chances to detect and correct perceptions at a distance. Informal channels of face-to-face encounters allow things to be corrected more easily."

Learning by Watching

Distance blocked casual visual observation, which was invaluable to monitoring and mentoring performance. In collocated groups, managers found it useful simply to watch the person work or eavesdrop on casual conversations. Some of the more subtle work roles, such as project leader, were best learned through direct observation and modeling. These roles tended to be unique to particular organizational cultures. The inability of remote employees to watch successful project managers enact their roles, along with the inability to observe the learning employee in action, served as a barrier to effective coaching of such subtle interpersonal skills across distance.

Out-of-Sight, Out-of-Mind

Distant employees tended to be left out of discussions and forgotten—out of sight, out of mind. Remote sites "fell off people's radar screens" and were ignored even during telephone and videoconferences. "The default behavior is to ignore the speaker phone. This is magnified if the smaller group is on the phone [distant]." In a case where the larger part of a group was in the home office and the smaller part was in Europe (and also not native English speakers), the larger face-to-face sub-group would start talking and just roll over the silently listening Europeans. The manager of this group explained that it took discipline and coaching to integrate the smaller distant group of employees into the meetings, but that it was "less of an exercise" in videoconferences than in telephone conferences.

Short Is Long
People described how the effects of close proximity died off quickly with relatively little distance, making short distances equal to long ones in their effects on group interaction. Managers felt there was as much conflict between sites 15 kilometers apart as between sites 800 kilometers apart. One manager, referring to the HO buildings that were joined by a common cafeteria, explained, "Even if you are on the other side of the cafeteria, you are in another sphere of influence. Outside of that range, the next major jump is across a different time zone." Echoed another manager, "You make the same mistakes if the distance is 4,000 miles or 10. You still tend to turn to the person in front of you for the answer. I respond more to people I see more often."

Time Is Distance
Time differences amplified the effects of physical distance. Distributed group members faced the challenge of "finding each other at the same time, in different times." Global conference calls caught people at different times of day. One consultant made conference calls only late at night or early in the morning (her time) because the group members (in Japan, the United States, and Europe) spanned all hours of the day(s). A global group leader listed endurance as one trait necessary in his role, for both the jet lag and the conference calls.

Time differences sometimes highlighted cultural differences. One group, based in the United States and Italy, celebrated a project milestone in their weekly video-conference by sharing foods on the video screen and fax. The East Coast U.S. team, at 9 A.M., sent images of bagels and coffee. The Italian team, at 3 P.M. their time, sent images of champagne and cookies—different times, different tastes.

Several managers felt that time was more of a barrier than physical distance alone for engineers who were used to solving technical problems in spontaneous meetings. They called distant peers into spontaneous video or telephone conferences when they could, but often global time differences meant their counterparts were not available.

The Home Group

People tended to think of their home group as the people they sat beside at work. Geographic sites promoted an informal, spontaneous group identity. This first group identity was reinforced by close physical proximity and the dense communication it promoted. Office site colleagues shared the metacontext of the locale, including similar occupational beliefs and concerns, cultural perspectives, and political viewpoints. People working in an office tended to have friends at the same nearby competitors, hear the same industry rumors, and share similar beliefs about technological trends.

People working at the same geographic site also tended to feel that they shared related organizational fates. In sites that included people from several groups and departments, layoffs in one group would threaten all site members. In other sites, all members relied on the same project in one way or another for their livelihood. As a result, sometimes distant group members did not feel like members of the home site group and were treated accordingly (e.g., left out of decision making).

Site Cultures with Site Attitudes

Site cultures developed shared viewpoints and beliefs about the site in relation to the rest of the company. A site's perspective gave unique meaning to messages sent from other sites or the HO. These shared filters tended to perpetuate the expectations that they were based on, acting as self-fulfilling prophecies. Site cultures seemed comparable to national cultures as sources of misunderstandings and conflicts.

One site, founded by a "rogue pirate" engineer who was too brilliant for the company to lose, developed the belief that the HO always stole the site's best project ideas by reassigning the products to HO teams. Various groups at this site shared similar beliefs and acted accordingly, sometimes hiding promising new ideas. Visitors from the HO complained that site members had a "chip on their shoulder," holding a resentment that resisted solutions.

Recognizing Conflicts

Conflicts were expressed, recognized, and addressed more quickly if group members worked in close proximity. A manager could walk across the hall, "nip it in the bud," and solve the problem quickly. Over distance, the issues were more likely to get dropped and go unresolved, contributing to a slow buildup in aggravation.

Conflicts among sites were often nurtured within sites by shared attitudes, beliefs, and values. People complained to their neighbors, reinforcing local perceptions of events, but did not complain to distant leaders until feelings reached high levels. One experienced manager of distributed groups stated, "With conflicts at a distance, thresholds for expressing the conflicts are higher the greater the geographic and cultural distance. Charges build up to higher levels in remote players before being discharged to the central manager."

Group Dynamics and Distances: Groups Are Formed, Not Assigned

Distributed work groups could be described by the degree of psychological closeness among members. This psychological closeness (or experienced proximity) consisted of many interrelated variables, including the degree of identification with group membership; the similarity of work goals, norms, role, and procedure expectations (task cohesion); the accuracy of mutual comprehension; the degree of motivation toward shared goals; the amount of interdependency and mutual trust; and the frequency of communication among members.

Lines of Conflict Reveal Group Boundaries   Assigning people from distant sites or different departments to one group did not necessarily form a group. A voluntary group identity had to be forged and integrated across distance. Some formally assigned groups were not experienced by the designated members as being groups. They had not coalesced around a genuine shared commitment to the group and its goals.

Fragmented communications or patterns of conflicts between members sometimes revealed the true functional boundaries of working groups (as opposed to assigned boundaries to which few members felt loyalty). In one case, the members of an international group with four sites fought among themselves as if they were enemies. Interviews revealed that the group was not a single group but rather four groups under one manager. Employees indicated that their alliances were stronger to other employees located in different departments at their sites than to their functional colleagues across the continent. Their use of *we* most often referred to people at their site, regardless of work group assignment.

Distributed Groups Coalesce Slowly   The formation of a distributed group had to overcome the lack of physical proximity in order to coalesce across distance. Similarities of shared goals, norms, and expectations were built over time among group members, evidenced by a more frequent spontaneous use of *we*, *us*, and *our way*. Accurately shared expectations and understandings among members were experienced as a growing group closeness, described by some as a group identity or culture. This group culture integrated members from different office sites and national cultures, spanning distances between members.

The group culture that seemed to matter most to work groups entailed accurate understandings about how to work together. It was easy to assume that distant members understood each other's expectations and meant the same thing with words such as *project review*, *phase completion*, and *test procedure*. Experience usually called such assumptions into question, as subtle yet profound differences generated strong feelings of resentment toward the "other" site.

In the case of one failed engineering project, a postmortem analysis revealed significant differences in expectations between the U.S. and European subgroups. Even careful planning did not prevent misunderstandings about specific processes vital to the project's success. The two sites had different definitions of completed product quality and tested their work with different procedures. These differences caused unexpected conflicts and delays and were taken by either side as signs of bad faith and political maneuvering by the other. These two sites were unable to overcome the mistrust that existed between them and never developed a unified group identity.

Distributed groups that reached an invisible line of formation across distances tended to show developmental changes over time. The leader of one global organization described how the management group of twelve site managers and staff developed over time from two separate organizations into one organization with a formal hierarchy and, finally, into a collaboration of team peers.

Multicultural Differences Observed within Groups

Differences in national and office site cultures could be observed even within integrated groups. Several U.S. managers characterized European engineers' relations with management as more formal and hierarchical than they were used to with U.S. engineers, who were more verbally confrontational with objections and questions.

Compute's recognition and reward programs, designed for U.S. engineers, did not always fit the cultures of subgroups in other countries. The leader of a global group met with his Japanese manager to revise the corporate excellence awards. "We agreed that they were not correct for a team culture, not appropriate for some of our Asian sites. They reflected more of the individual hero ethos of our Western sites."

This manager also delegated tasks differently during group meetings, depending on the site manager's nationality. He adjusted his style in telephone conferences, depending on what he felt was culturally appropriate. In delegating to the manager from the United Kingdom, he would ask the manager's opinion and then try to sell him on the merits of a particular approach, whereas he might later turn to the Japanese manager and tell him precisely what to do, with very specific instructions. He then followed up often with the U.K. manager, while leaving the Japanese manager alone.

Managers were particularly surprised when they encountered differences in work cultures in engineering groups within the United States: "I underestimated and was surprised when I found just as strong differences in the U.S. groups, like the New Jersey group. They have a distinct culture. They want to be left alone and autonomous and fear being gobbled up." Another manager experienced a similar surprise with a group located just 15 kilometers from the HO when it delayed individual pay raises to save money for a team-building consultation: "They have a very different socialist culture compared to our hero capitalist culture where some get more and others get less." He was describing two teams in the same U.S. state, but it sounded as if he was describing groups from different continents.

It was difficult to distinguish the source of differences among members of a distributed group. The subtle interplay of personal style, national culture, and organizational and occupational cultures often made accurate attribution of style differences difficult for group members. Deciphering the precise cause of conflicts or performance problems at a distance was almost impossible.

National, Organizational, and Professional Cultural Factors

National cultural differences interacted not only with individual style differences, but also with differences in company and professional cultures. One U.S. manager described a problem that her U.S. group had with an Italian superior. Engineers in her group complained that the superior overdirected them and did not ask for or listen to their opinions enough. The U.S. manager was unsure how much of the superior's style was an expression of an Italian management style, his own personal style, or a reflection of the fact that he was new to Compute Company and came from a marketing instead of software engineering background. She wondered specifically whether her manager related differently to her than to male professionals. She spent a weekend with him and his family, and observed his enthusiastic encouragement of his daughter's professional development. She concluded that the issue was probably not a gender-based dynamic, but rather his history in a more hierarchical company and profession. Notice the complex levels of factors she analyzed (Italian male marketeer from a European company).

Effects of the Organizational Context

In many cases, the larger organizational context was a determining factor in the effectiveness of the distributed group.

Conflict Detoured into the Distributed Group

Often, a host organization sponsored the distributed work group. Conflicts within the host organization were sometimes detoured into the distributed group and played out there. Because the cause of the fight did not originate among group members, resolution of the conflict within the distributed work group was impossible. In one such case, members of a distributed group responsible for product marketing fought among themselves. Interviews revealed that their conflicts paralleled the conflicts of the larger, more influential engineering sites they each served. The distributed product managers acted as proxies for the larger organization, carrying out its duels on the periphery.

Home Office and the Periphery

Most distributed groups included offices in or near the HO, plus one or more sites that were distant from the HO, located on the metaphorical (and often geographically literal) periphery of the organization. The structure of geographic distribution of people and resources was echoed in the language used by managers, who spoke of remote sites on the company's periphery, and the core, or home office region. This HO-centric language reflected the fact that many distributed groups had a greater mass of people and resources at or near the HO complex. This distribution of resources gave the HO-based people more connections and easier access to upper management in software engineering, as well as people in other departments of the company. Many of the issues within distributed groups reflected dynamic tensions between the HO and sites on the periphery.

Home Office Sponsorship and Assigned Group Mission

A critical factor in the life of a distributed group and its remote sites was the work assignment or mission given to each site. The mission was the site's central assignment, the reason for the site's existence, and the area of work owned and controlled by engineers at the site. From the perspective of the larger company, remote software engineering sites were established for many overlapping reasons, such as to reassure local customers, meet import requirements, and even retain star engineers who insisted on moving to remote locations. From the site's perspective, however, the group wanted responsibility for challenging projects that would gratify their needs for achievement. In practice, the remote sites were often given responsibility for small tasks and treated as subcontractors rather than getting critical strategic projects. In other cases, remote sites had multiple HO sponsors (such as sales and design engineering), with conflicting expectations of the remote site.

Influence of Changes between the Home Office and Periphery

No matter how clearly the founding reason was specified, the reason for a site's existence drifted from the original one over the years. Markets and technologies changed, projects were completed, and the site staff looked for new work. Sometimes the site matured and began to lobby for more ownership of strategic, challenging assignments. In other cases, headquarters changed strategies or reprioritized projects, rendering a remote site's mission extinct. The negotiation of changes in missions and associated changes in site resources, budget, and location involved some of the strongest feelings among group members: "Giving things up and getting new things [assigned] is where the pain and suffering is."

The consequences of strategic changes initiated by the HO were often far more dire for remote sites than for the HO. Smaller sites were more vulnerable in that their limited staffs had been hired for one technical purpose. Retraining this same staff in another technology took one site a year and a half. In other cases, it was not possible. By contrast, groups within the HO were more easily dissolved and reconfigured around new assignments because of the much larger mass of talent available to call on.

The forces of change, of course, worked both ways. The remote sites existed in part to bring awareness of new technology and market trends into the core, pushing the company to change. Just as the periphery could drag, so too did the HO resist needed changes. In one case, a remote site made a proposal that the company change its strategy in some key areas where new technology was developing quickly. The company ignored the suggestion for two years while competitors developed advantages over them in this field.

Such mutual resistance was aggravated by the lack of shared context, making mutual understanding more difficult. The periphery existed partly because it offered insight into developments that were foreign to the core. The sites also often had different cultures of influence—informal rules guiding them to influence others successfully. Remote sites without a lot of contact with people in the HO often did not know how to influence the HO. "Out there is almost a naiveté, as with novices," explained one HO manager. The HO culture could be confusing and obscure, however, to remote managers used to different styles of conducting business. One remote manager thought he had succeeded when his contact in the HO agreed to support his proposed new project. But then, mysteriously, the contact told him he now had to go "work" the proposal with other colleagues in the HO, leaving the manager to wonder what that actually meant.

Acculturation to Home Office Work Culture

Newly established remote sites had to import and set up both the physical connections to Compute's core (broadband data networks, computer systems, and telephone links) and, just as critical, the human infrastructure of work roles and procedures. This more subtle infrastructure of shared expectations was often difficult to export to remote sites without at least some learning errors.

Different Meanings in Different Contexts

Remote sites, with unique site cultures and contexts, tended to interpret messages from within their own sets of assumptions and expectations. These filters were not always accurately accounted for in transmissions from the HO, especially in broadcasts from the HO to multiple remote sites. The remote sites often perceived messages that the HO did not intend to send, usually pertaining to power and control over projects and budgets.

Integrating Practices That Span Distances and Differences

Face-to-Face Contact

Group formation was difficult across distances using electronic media alone. The integrating degree of psychological closeness needed to form the group was aided strongly by face-to-face discussions and agreements on the group's purpose, norms, roles, and procedures for working together and communicating effectively across distances. Frequently, distributed groups were formed when people from various sites were reassigned to a new project and placed in a newly designated group. Face-to-face contacts allowed group members to form initial relationships around a group identity, which could then be supported on the reduced bandwidth of e-mail, telephone, and videoconferences.

Face-to-face meetings first focused on gaining commitment to the group's purpose. Developing an accurately shared awareness of a group's mission and goals is a unifying exercise in any work group. Such shared understandings were even more vital when working across distances. The group as a whole, as well as each remote site, required a well-articulated mission and set of goals. Promoting a common vision of the group's mission and strategy was central to promoting a cohesive group culture across distance.

To promote strong group cohesion among site managers around the globe, the leader of a newly designated organization committed his management staff to meeting face-to-face every six to eight weeks. They rotated the location of each meeting around the globe so that they visited each other's country and office several times. Telephone conferences were held every three weeks between the face-to-face meetings. During their first round of visits to each other's site, the assembled management team also met face-to-face with each site's staff in discussions facilitated by a consultant. The group even developed shared humor and jokes, such as requiring each site manager to sing a song in his or her native tongue to the assembled management team at his or her first meeting. This became an entry ritual for new managers as membership turned over.

Group Leadership

Group leadership was important in guiding group members to articulate and embody group norms, roles, and procedures in working together and communicating. An effective leader convened and facilitated repeated group discussions of these issues, captured and followed through reliably on agreements reached, modeled the norms, and coached group members to maintain norms. Sometimes this leadership was distributed among several people and sites.

Leadership took the form of bringing up issues of distance and leading group discussions about the challenges of communicating across distance. Discussions had to reach into the details of procedures, roles, and expectations in order to avoid later confusions. Effective leaders organized discussions of how to use various technologies, such as computer conferences, to communicate across distance. They modeled the desired use of the technology, coached and directed others, and reviewed its use in later meetings.

Leadership was required in showing diligence in monitoring the group's communication practices to ensure that people were not left out. It was demonstrated in articulating norms for videoconferencing, including how to structure the meetings, where to point the cameras, who controlled them, and how to talk in conferences. The manager in one group helped the engineers learn how to ask each other for input. Just saying, "Would you guys read my stuff?" would produce no action. She coached them to make their requests very specific during conferences, such as, "I need you two to review these lines of code for issue X, by next Monday if possible."

Group Learning

Some groups developed an escalating cycle of learning, where members experimented with and shared their developing insights on techniques for communicating, comprehending, and working together smoothly across distances. Such techniques included, for example, habits of updating or checking in with each other, use of computer conferences for information exchange, effective video- and teleconferencing procedures, and operating procedures for working together.

Engineers located in the HO learned to bring up hallway discussions and check out decisions in weekly videoconferences with distant counterparts. Traveling to the other site of a conference was particularly enlightening. One manager of a remote site regularly invited staff from the HO out to his site on some pretext so that they would end up sitting in on his site's end of a videoconference. Similarly, HO staff were sensitized to their relation to remote sites when they observed their own HO colleagues turning up on the video screen. When traveling members returned home, they might be given feedback that they "talked too fast." In various ways, group members learned how to be effective with the technology and, more important, learned how to maintain awareness of the other sites rather than rolling over them during conferences or forgetting about them outside conferences.

Developing Group Norms about Cultural Differences

Cultural differences were addressed by managers who discussed the topic directly with their distributed groups, providing leadership in modeling how cultural differences could be identified and discussed. With such leadership, the group developed its own knowledge over time about cultural differences and the best way for the group to handle them. This group knowledge became part of the culture of the group.

One of the clearest examples of such leadership was provided by the manager of a globally distributed group responsible for translating products into local languages and markets. His company badge listed his name in Latin, Cantonese, and Japanese characters. He coached his managers to watch for and address possible culturally based misunderstandings during their meetings. He would interrupt staff who were discussing an issue to check if one was not fully understanding the other. He encouraged his managers to do the same. He would also meet with his managers privately, like a diplomat, to bring up more sensitive issues, such as the possibility that one manager's style might be offensive to another.

Leadership and Management Practices

One experienced manager explained that leading a distributed group required "focus and discipline," meaning a highly structured, clear style with careful follow-up on action items (assigned tasks). In a distributed group, the great distances involved required that decisions be made clearly, not reversed often, and reliably followed up over time to ensure implementation and necessary revisions. Examples of useful structure in leadership activities included structured, frequent conference calls or video meetings; agendas, slides, and written material distributed in advance and meeting minutes with action items published quickly afterward; and customized but structured formats, revised over time to fit the group's needs, including such practices as polling all silent members before making key decisions. Reliably updating distant colleagues on hallway conversations and even delaying key decisions until distant peers could comment on them were related aspects of focus and discipline.

Personal Relations Bridge Distance

Frequent face-to-face contacts among members of a distributed group served to renew their trust in mutual comprehension. Visits to different sites, staff rotations, and large face-to-face meetings convened at junctures of key change in the group all helped to maintain a level of mutual comprehension and trust. This trust acted as a buffer, keeping misunderstandings from escalating into conflicts. One manager had better relations with distant sites than with sites near his office. He attributed this to the fact that he tended to visit nearby sites with a very tight schedule of formal meetings, then rush back to his office that same day. With distant sites, he would go for ten days and spend much time in unstructured conversations, where he learned useful details about the site's work and concerns.

Layered Communication Technology with Norms for Use

Distributed groups were supported by having ready access to multiple, simultaneous channels of communication among members. Such a layered network ideally included voice mail and e-mail (both of which bridge time differences), fax, telephone conferencing, computer conferencing, and videoconferencing. Work group software support (groupware) that allowed group scheduling or the sharing of technical designs and convening of technical review meetings across distance was also very useful.

A shared agreement across distance concerning how to use the technology was just as important as the technology itself. Much of the critical group leadership and learning involved facilitating and teaching clear group norms and skills about how to use the communication technology effectively.

Integrated Leaders Sent out to the Periphery

An old joke in the United States is that organizational failure leads to an assignment "to Alaska." Sending a manager to a distributed group's remote site as punishment would, in fact, be destructive to the site and the organization as a whole. Remote sites of distributed groups prospered best when they had leaders or staff who were successful in the HO and brought with them informal contacts, influence, and knowledge that greatly improved the remote site's connection to the HO. Sending out leaders who had already peripheralized themselves while at the HO (through clashes in style, fundamental disagreements, or rebellious relations) made remote sites more remote.

Conclusion

Our findings lead us to three propositions, which may be used as testable hypotheses but can only be informally supported by the experiences described in our findings.

First, distance among members of a distributed work group is multidimensional. Objective measures of distance include not just geographic distance, but also time difference (time zones), organizational distance (different departments, functions, and levels), and cultural difference (both national culture and organizational office site culture). Our findings suggest that national and organizational cultures are experienced as dimensions of distance in distributed work groups, along with kilometer and time zones. The culture that matters most to work groups is that concerning work roles, procedures, and methods. Surprisingly, members can have very different national cultures but establish closer work cultures or be very close nationally and geographically but be very different in work cultures (as between an engineer and a marketing specialist).

Second, the impact of such distances on the performance of a distributed work group is not directly proportional to objective measures of distance. Some work groups are more effective than others, even if their memberships span a greater geographic distance and encompass more time zones and cultures than less effective groups. This proposition is supported by the experiences of managers who have worked in several distributed groups with varying degrees of success. It may be judged more accurately with controlled outcome measures.

Third, the differences in the effects that distance seems to have on work groups are due at least partially to two sets of integrating practices: practices that help members effectively span distances and an organizational context and structure that support the group as its members work across distance. The integrating practices within distributed groups emphasize group and leadership process variables in work groups (Hackman 1983). Personal contacts serve to refresh De Meyer's (1991) "half-life" of trust among members. In a manner akin to Bartlett and Ghoshal's flow of knowledge (1991), informal networks of relations transmit knowledge about subtle work processes, such as how to influence the HO, that are needed to span distances in multinational corporations. The larger organizational contexts that help distributed groups to span distances include structure and design variables such as stable, long-term sponsorship and a clear mission.

Geographically distributed work groups are inherently diverse, at least on some dimensions. Managing a distributed group requires addressing its diversity so that the group forms effectively across distances. McGrath, Berdahl, and Arrow (1995) point to the importance of time as a process variable in groups. They observed that groups grow less diverse over time on some dimensions. This fits closely with our observation of how groups form across distances over time. To form successfully, group members become much less diverse in their definition of work culture, including goals, methods, roles, and procedures for collaborating across distance. This decreasing diversity is along the dimension of group task cohesion (Bernthal and Insko 1993).

We do not consider distributed work groups to have qualitatively different dynamics from collocated groups. Many of the integrating practices are the same for both, such as gaining commitment to shared goals and articulating and monitoring norms. In distributed groups, these common factors were essential for even basic group formation. Other practices are more uniquely crucial to groups operating across distances, such as structured communication practices, informal networks of relations, face-to-face contacts, and a reliance on layered communication technology. Distributed work groups are very sensitive to the structural features of their host organization, but the ability of any work group to integrate differences is affected by the structure and values of the larger organization.

Many of the integrating practices that help form a work group across distances and differences are similar to the positive factors Triandis (1994) has described in multicultural research on in-groups/out-groups and social distance. The conditions that promote greater understanding and liking between cultural groups (such as equality, superordinate goals, frequent contact, and mutual knowledge) also promote cohesion in distributed work groups. We can even say that the leadership and group learning necessary to articulate detailed work norms and procedures contribute to isomorphic attributions (accurate understandings of each other). The networks of personal relationships provide a buffer of trust that slows down nonisomorphic attributions that can fuel in-group/out-group rivalries.

According to this same model, members of cultural groups that have a history of prior conflict, competing goals, and power differences tend to exaggerate the perceived differences, thereby increasing conflict and mutual dislike. This conclusion from Triandis (1994) reads like a case description of a distributed group gone bad. Several of the failed distributed work projects we studied met these criteria closely:

a history of resentment and conflict with the HO or other sites, competition for limited resources, and lack of influence in the HO.

As with current group theory, based largely on face-to-face contact, the cultural models of in-group/out-group dynamics often assume that physical proximity is the source of cultural contact and networks of connecting acquaintances. It will be of interest to study cultural relations between physically distant groups linked by media and technology, such as sister cities in the United States and Russia.

Distributed work groups are created entities, formed over time for the accomplishment of defined goals and for the provision of work and income to its members. The groups that formed and performed most effectively competed with the local work scene to capture a degree of commitment to a common goal from its scattered members. Aided by leadership, group members developed a shared sense of group culture that clarified role and procedure expectations. They became less diverse and more of an in-group. Clearly articulated norms on how to use technology to communicate across distance and on how to handle cultural differences were of key importance in this process, as were frequent face-to-face contacts.

Success served to solidify the group identity and in-group culture, whereas serious setbacks taxed group identity. Distributed work groups that achieved major success in high-visibility projects were remembered fondly by their former members years after the group was dissolved, much like a circle of friends or a winning sports team.

Note

This chapter is abridged from D. J. Armstrong and P. Cole (1995). Managing distances and differences in geographically distributed work groups, in S. E. Jackson and M. N. Ruderman (eds.), *Diversity in work teams: Research paradigms for a changing workplace* (187–215). Washington, DC: American Psychological Association. (The summary was added by the editors.) Reprinted with permission of the American Psychological Association. An earlier paper, *Managing Geographic, Temporal and Cultural Distances in Distributed Work Groups*, was presented at the 102nd Annual Convention of the American Psychological Association in Los Angeles, California, August 1994.

References

Bartlett, C., and Ghoshal, S. (1991). *Managing across borders*. Boston: Harvard Business School Press.

Bernthal, P., and Insko, C. (1993). Cohesiveness without groupthink: The interactive effects of social and task cohesion. *Group and Organization Management, 18*, 66–87.

De Meyer, A. (1991). Tech talk: How managers are stimulating global RandD communication. *Sloan Management Review, 32*, 49–58.

Hackman, J. (1983, November). *A normative model of work team effectiveness* (Tech. Rep. No. 2). New Haven, CT: Yale School of Organization and Management, Research Program on Group Effectiveness.

McGrath, J. E., Berdahl, J. L. and Arrow, H. (1995). Traits, expectations, culture, and clout: The dynamics of diversity in work groups. In S. E. Jackson and M. N. Ruderman (eds.), *Diversity in work teams: Research paradigms for a changing workplace* (17–45). Washington, DC: American Psychological Association.

Triandis, H. (1994). *Culture and social behavior*. New York: McGraw-Hill.

Addendum to Chapter 7

Virtual Proximity, Real Teams

David J. Armstrong and Erika Bill Peter

In the six years since "Managing Distances and Differences" first appeared, research and advice on working across distances has grown dramatically. So too has the technology designed to support working across distances, transformed most obviously by the Web. The idea of virtual team has captured people's imaginations. Reflecting on our consulting experiences, we add to the observations presented in the original chapter.

What Is a Virtual Team?

The term *virtual team* is frequently used to describe teams that span distance and organizational boundaries. Many of our clients and writers in the field use the term *virtual team* to refer to a range of groups, from a real team to an anonymous loose network of people with a shared interest. However, most distributed groups do not attain the ideal of being a real team: a work group with stable and defined membership that has established a shared working process in the pursuit of a common goal that they can only achieve together (Hackman 2000). On the other hand, we have become impressed with the qualities of those few distributed work groups we have observed that have become real teams. Such teams are often most effective when modest in size (between six and eight members) and stable over time so that the members get to know each other and establish a track record. Why should one care about whether a distributed or virtual team is "real" in this perhaps conservative or restrictive sense? We think the distinction is valuable because real teams are more capable of showing a level of commitment to shared goals that overrides even individual members' interests.

We have observed members of globally distributed account teams who sacrificed business in hand for the good of the team, with a short-term (negative) impact on their own commissions. These teams worked against the incentive plan, the financial control systems, and the priorities of their own local line management for the larger good of the account. The team members believed that their actions would increase customer satisfaction and loyalty, thereby paying off for both the company and themselves personally in the long run. They saw their actions as strategically constructive. This uncharacteristic behavior sprang from their team commitment.

Gaining Commitment: The Achilles Heel

In much distributed work, the example above is an exception. In most geographically distributed account teams, for example, salespeople pay primary attention to well-defined short-term goals. They do what adds value to their goal attainment, client satisfaction being a core goal. The team members score their team poorly on such items as, "Team members speak and act in a unified way," "Members are willing to sacrifice personal interests for the good of the team," and "Members fulfill their commitments to this team." This is an Achilles heel that becomes apparent as competing issues, local work demands, and priorities override commitments made to the team effort. Over the course of three to nine months, promised delivery dates on tasks slip significantly, as does voluntary participation in conference calls.

It is not entirely clear whether the eroding priority given to team tasks is a result of distance or an effect of the tactically urgent overriding the strategically important. However, distributed teams seem particularly vulnerable to the primacy of not just the short term but also the proximate urgent demand.

Face-to-face team formation meetings are essential. Such meetings allow hard questions to be asked ("I am very busy. Why should I give this team's calls priority over client calls?") and support the informal social contact that nurtures mutual understanding and trust. In subsequent teleconferences and e-mails, every meeting ought to include a review of the team's goals and the value of the team to its members, reminding members why the team effort deserves their commitment. Care must be taken not to reopen debates over what these goals should be. Such debates can leave a distributed team feeling unfocused and threaten the sense of progress that has been achieved. Leadership is critical in calling the question of commitment at its first manifestation, yet in a facilitative manner that does not put members on the defensive but rather invites reflection and dialogue. Team discussions about what is eroding commitment and competing for time often produce useful realignments in process and practices.

We also see one-on-one conversations between members and with the leader increasing the degree of commitment, allowing concerns and barriers to be vetted privately and strengthening trust in the team leader, especially when the leader visits the local site and talks with the member while they work together.

Importance of Strategic Alignment: Occasions of Wishful Thinking

The strategic alignment or justification for a team working across distances must be compelling and visibly supported by the organization. We have seen organizations that acted with ambivalence and mixed priorities in creating distributed teams. These teams face an uphill battle and often fail. In one company, virtual teams were chartered from the top of the house and aligned with an explicit goal of increasing customer satisfaction. But senior executives hesitated to reformulate their financial control and incentive systems, thereby severely handicapping the capacity of the distributed teams to change customers' experience. Lack of alignment between a global customer focus and the organization's systems of financial control, budget allocation, planning and compensation doomed these teams' hopes for committing to and attaining a shared goal.

Straining the Bones of the Organization

Hackman (2000) argues that real teams are fragile social structures that lose when placed in opposition to the dominant cultural forces. Although that is usually true, we have observed rare distributed teams that seemed to pull on the very bones of the organization, straining the existing systems rather than being overcome by them, at least in the short run. One team in particular, a global account team, moved forward on the strength of personal relationships, a commitment to seizing the opportunity for coordinated global account strategy, and a belief that their customer contacts would appreciate their efforts, despite a lack of organizational alignment from their own senior management. Distributed teams can sometimes overcome organizational inertia, becoming a temporarily viable force of change. For enduring or more widespread change to occur, however, the larger organization must realign its systems, measures, objectives, and talent management to support the distributed team and its strategic objectives.

Reference

Hackman, J. (2000). *When teams, when not?* Keynote presentation, Organizational Development Conference, October 4, 2000, Naples FL: Linkage Inc.

"I've never trusted cows."

8

Attribution in Distributed Work Groups

Catherine Durnell Cramton

The fundamental attribution error is likely to be exacerbated for dispersed collaborators relative to collocated collaborators, with grave consequences for group cohesion and viability. Working across dispersed locations typically reduces the situational information that collaborators have about each other, affects how they process information, and fosters the development of in-groups and out-groups based on location. These processes bias perceptions of causes of behavior toward dispositional explanations rather than situational explanations.

Attribution is the process by which people make inferences about the causes of events. There is a long tradition of research by social and organizational psychologists that investigates why people make the attributions they do. For example, the attributions that the CEO of a company makes concerning a team's failure to produce an innovative product might range from poor leadership skills on the part of the team leader, to a shortage of qualified engineers because of the company's salary structure, to an organizational culture that is not conducive to cross-functional collaboration and innovation, to lack of support for the team's efforts in the rest of the company. The attributions people make play an important role in determining their subsequent actions, feelings and thoughts. Depending on what attribution the CEO makes, she might feel angry at the team leader or apologetic about not having exerted more pressure on other functions to support the team's work. She might order a review of the company's hiring policies and salary scales or focus on developing cross-functional familiarity and respect in the company.

The fundamental psychological process of attribution influences people's thoughts, feelings, expectations, and behaviors in all domains of their lives. However, scholars of organizational behavior have focused on the significance of attribution processes in workplace settings. These processes have been shown to influence how credit and blame are allocated and performance is evaluated (Feldman

1981), motivation (Brockner and Guare 1983, Dorfman and Stephan 1984, Teas and McElroy 1986, Weiner 1985), leader-member relations (Adams, Adams, Rice, and Instone 1985), the performance-satisfaction relationship (Norris and Neibuhr 1984), attitudes and efforts toward safety (DeJoy 1994), and resistance to the introduction of information technologies (Martinko, Henry, and Zmud 1996). In work groups and teams, attributions also affect willingness to collaborate (McDonald 1995), group cohesion (Brawley, Carron, and Widmeyer 1987; Turner, Hogg, Turner, and Smith 1984), performance and satisfaction (Wang 1994), and group viability (Novell and Forsyth 1985).

A new kind of work group has come into practice recently, composed of people in dispersed locations who collaborate with the aid of new communication technologies. This chapter shows how distance and technology affect the antecedents of attribution in work groups, with consequences for cohesion and group viability.

Characteristics of Distributed Work Groups

The defining characteristic of a distributed work group is that it incorporates members who are based at locations remote from each other. Sometimes group membership is distributed evenly across locations, one member at each location. Often, however, there are clusters of people at locations. Because of physical dispersion, group members typically make heavy use of communication technologies such as e-mail, telephone, and groupware. Three other common characteristics of distributed work groups are membership spanning cultural, organizational, or professional boundaries, temporary status, and limited history as a group. These characteristics grow out of the purposes for which distributed work groups are created. A distributed group design may be chosen because it permits the collaboration of people from different countries, organizations, or professions. Or it may be chosen because the task is short term in nature and it is undesirable to relocate members. All these defining and associated characteristics of distributed work groups can affect attribution.

How Attributions Come About

Weiner (1986) describes three underlying dimensions of attribution that have withstood multiple empirical investigations: (1) the extent to which behavior is inferred to be determined by forces inside or outside the actor (distinguishing personal traits from responses to situational pressures), (2) the degree to which internal causes are perceived to fluctuate or remain stable (distinguishing effort from ability, for example), and (3) the degree to which internal causes are considered to be controllable or not by the individual (distinguishing strategy from passion). Of these dimensions of attribution, the one with the strongest empirical support and an undisputed place in the literature is the distinction concerning the locus of activity: whether behavior is determined internally, by the disposition of the actor, or externally, by characteristics of the situation (Bell, Wicklund, Mando, and Larkin 1976; Deaux and Farns 1977; Regan, Straus, and Fazio 1974; Weiner 1986; Weiner, Russell, and Lerman 1978; Zuckerman 1979). In the example of the product development team above, the CEO makes an internal or dispositional attribution when she questions the skills of the team leader. She makes an external or situational attribution when she reviews company hiring and salary policies or focuses on developing a company culture more conducive to cross-functional collaboration and innovation.

Antecedents of Internal and External Attributions

Research shows that the likelihood that an event or behavior will be perceived as being driven by internal as opposed to external causes tends to vary with the role of the person making the attribution—whether he is the actor or an observer. In addition, factors such as culture, motivation, and personality influence the making of internal versus external attributions.

Actors tend to think that situational factors shape events or behaviors, while observers of the same events or behaviors are more likely to attribute causality to the disposition or personality of the actor (Jones and Nisbett 1972, Ross 1977). For example, a speaker who is late for her engagement may understand her lateness to result from the heavy traffic that day and the directions given to her (*situational determinants*). However, observers of her lateness, such as the organizer and audience, are more likely to conclude that she is a disorganized or careless person (*dispositional determinants*). According to Jones and Nisbett (1972), this difference stems from differences in the information before the actor and observer and characteristics of information processing from these two vantage points. Typically, the actor has more information than the observer concerning the situation and the way it affected her behavior. In addition, the physiology of perception leads observers to focus on what they see: the actor rather than her situation (Storms 1973). The overweighting of dispositional relative to situational determinants of behaviors and events is known as the *fundamental attribution error* (Heider 1944, Ross 1977).

The first part of this chapter shows how geographic dispersion and use of technology-mediated communication seem to exacerbate differences between actors and observers in information and information processing, in turn exacerbating the fundamental attribution bias.

Attributions also are affected by motives such as self-enhancement, self-protection, and positive presentation of self to others (Kelley and Michaela 1980). Actors often veer from situational explanations of their own behavior toward dispositional explanations when the behavior reflects well on them but not when the behavior reflects badly on them. While a speaker attributes her late arrival to give a speech to traffic and poor directions, she may attribute the audience's warm reception of her remarks to her own knowledge and skill rather than to aspects of the situation such as the composition and mood of the audience.

In recent years, scholars have considered the role of motive on attribution at the group level of analysis. Pettigrew (1979) coined the term *ultimate attribution error* to describe a tendency toward systematic differences in attributions concerning members of one's own social group when compared with attributions concerning members of other social groups. He proposed that negative behavior by members of one's own group is more likely to be explained in situational terms than negative behavior by members of other groups. He also suggested that positive behavior by in-group members is more likely to be explained in dispositional terms than positive behavior by out-group members. Since then, Pettigrew's work has been used to understand biased attribution in work teams in which subgroup identities are strong and in-groups and out-groups develop. Karakowsky and Siegel (1995) have proposed that the social integration of a work group will be negatively related to egocentric bias in in-group member attributions. In other words, members of more integrated groups will be less likely to blame out-group members for group failings or claim credit on behalf of one's in-group for successes. The second part of this chapter will show how geographically dispersed, technology-mediated groups are vulnerable to the development of in-groups and out-groups based on location and weak social integration, increasing the risk of ultimate attribution error.

The attribution literature also has explored whether individuals show characteristic attributional tendencies across situations. Although the findings are not conclusive, efforts to develop and validate an Attributional Style Questionnaire (ASQ) have indicated some consistency in individual style (Henry and Campbell 1995, Kent and Martinko 1995). The ASQ distinguishes people who have "pessimistic" and "optimistic" styles. The former tend to blame themselves for negative events and expect that the cause will continue into the future, while the latter tend toward the opposite, blaming negative events on circumstances that are not likely to recur (Seligman and Schulman 1986).

Finally, it is important to note that the research described thus far has been carried out by Western researchers on samples of mostly Western subjects. Recently, researchers have been investigating whether the making of internal versus external attributions varies across cultures. They have concluded that the attributions of observers from individualistic Western cultures tend to be biased more toward individual dispositional causes than the attributions of observers from collectivist East Asian cultures such as China, Korea, and Japan (Morris, Nisbett, and Peng 1995; Morris and Peng 1994). However, the underlying cognitive processes and structures that result in these differences are not yet clear. For example, it appears that East Asians are more likely than North Americans to attribute causality to group dispositions as distinguished from both individual dispositions and nonsocial situational causes (Menon, Morris, Chui, and Hong 1999). Therefore, it is important to keep in mind that the following discussion of attribution in dispersed collaborations is grounded in a Western literature and perspective and may not hold in contexts influenced by East Asian values. In addition, cultural differences in attribution tendencies probably will affect distributed work groups whose membership is culturally broad.

How Attribution Will Differ in Distributed and Face-to-Face Teams

The distinctions between perceptions of internal versus external causation and the vantage points of actors and observers are significant for geographically dispersed collaboration. This section explores how geographic dispersion and use of technology-mediated communication are likely to affect the information available to actors and observers, and their information processing and motivation, resulting in attribution biases.

Differences in Information
Jones and Nisbett (1972) describe how the information that collocated actors and observers have to make attributions often differs. They discuss both effect data and cause data.

Effect Data   Jones and Nisbett define effect data as what was done, the environmental outcomes of what was done, and the actor's experience at the time. Assuming that actors and observers are collocated, they point out that they are likely to have equivalent information about what was done and its outcomes, but that actors are likely to have more information about their own experience than observers have concerning the actor's experience. Consider their example of a person who has delivered an insult to another person. An observer of the two of them may know that the actor has delivered an insult and that the recipient is angered. However, with regard to the feelings of the actor (glee or regret, for example), the observer can only make inferences from the actor's face, gestures, and tone and judgments based on the observer's knowledge of what others and he himself have felt in similar situations. This difference in the information held by actor and observer often results in actors' making situational attributions and observers' making dispositional attributions.

Actors and observers in a dispersed team will likely have less common information concerning effects than the collocated actors and observers that Jones and Nisbett describe. Not only may they lack common information about what the actor experiences, but also about what was done and its environmental outcomes. Both the action and its outcomes are likely to occur at a location that only part of the team can observe directly. Furthermore, exchange of information across locations appears to be a leaky process. Cramton (2001) shows how members of dispersed teams end up with different information because of undetected human and technical transmission errors and because people fail to distribute information to all team members without awareness of all the consequences. When Armstrong and Cole (Chapter 7, this volume) studied nine distributed software development teams, they observed that "key group members at remote sites were left off e-mail distribution lists" and "not informed of key decisions or information." One consequence is that what was done and its outcomes may not always be communicated to remote partners. Finally, remote observers using electronically mediated communication often lack the few cues to the actor's experience that collocated observers enjoy: observation of facial expression, tone of voice, and gestures. Therefore, differences in the data concerning effects held by actors and observers in a dispersed team are likely to be even more pronounced than they are when actors and observers are collocated, making it more likely that the attributions of actor and observer will differ.

Abel (1990) provides an example in his description of a Xerox PARC work group that was distributed between laboratories in Palo Alto, California, and Portland,

Oregon. The two subgroups were linked by a sophisticated cross-site video network. Each subgroup had prepared a presentation for a corporate VIP who had arrived at Palo Alto to visit the video-linked labs. The Portland subgroup gave its presentation first by video. Then all but one member of the Portland contingent left to go to an off-site meeting without announcing their departure to their remote collaborators. Abel (1990, 500) describes the subsequent events and attributions:

At the same time (that the Portland subgroup left), the Palo Alto manager began his presentation with a videotape that wasn't transmitted to Portland. The remaining Portlander saw a blank screen and could hear almost nothing. Thinking that the Portland folks were being intentionally excluded and not wanting to interrupt, the remaining Portlander went to his office, leaving an empty couch in video view. When the videotape was completed in Palo Alto, the Portland image returned to the Palo Alto monitor, showing an empty couch. To Palo Alto, it appeared that Portland had given their presentation and then left, showing no interest in the Palo Alto presentations. In other words, it appeared to Palo Alto that Portland was being extremely rude. It affected the rest of the meeting because the empty Portland couch was constantly in view. From Portland's perspective, it appeared that Palo Also had intentionally excluded them by turning off Portland's "eyes and ears." So it appeared to Portland that Palo Alto had been rude.

There were at least three parties involved in this incident, each of which was located in a different place and consequently had different information about what was done: the Palo Alto group, the Portland group that went to the off-site meeting, and the Portland representative who remained behind to participate in the video conference. Only the group in Palo Alto saw Portland's empty couch on the monitor. They interpreted this to mean that all the Portlanders had left after the Portland presentation, although this inference was not accurate. Only the Portland person who stayed behind knew that the Palo Alto video was not shown in Portland. He also was the only one who knew that he had left the meeting only after the video link with Palo Alto went blank, not at the conclusion of the Portland presentation. Only the Portland representative and the group that went to the off-site meeting knew that they had indeed left a representative behind to continue the video meeting with Palo Alto.

Groups also had different information about the consequences of what occurred. The Portland representative knew he had left the video meeting because he was receiving no video or sound from Palo Alto. The Palo Alto group knew that the rest of the meeting had been affected by uneasiness about the empty couch and presumably by the inability to ask questions of or share comments with the Portland collaborators. The group from Portland that went to the off-site meeting knew how their attendance at that meeting affected Xerox PARC's overall objectives.

Finally, each of the three groups had information about their own experience and reactions that the others did not have. The Palo Alto group was annoyed with the Portland group, but the Portland group did not know this. The Portland representative was annoyed about not being able to see the video, but the Palo Alto group and the Portland group that went off-site did not know this. Finally, the Portlanders who went off-site had no reason to be concerned about the group's relationships, even though these relationships in fact had come under stress. As a consequence of all these differences in information, members of the dispersed group attributed the behavior of other members to rudeness, a dispositional assessment, rather than to aspects of the situation.

Causal Data   According to Jones and Nisbett (1972), the two types of causal data that are important for attributions are proximal environmental stimuli operating on the actor and the intentions of the actor. Under collocated conditions, actor and observer in theory could have equal knowledge of proximal environmental stimuli, say Jones and Nisbett. In practice, however, they conclude that completeness is rarely approximated. For example, the actor may be responding to events more extended in time than those available to observation. It is even more difficult for the observer to gain accurate knowledge of the actor's intentions. The observer "may infer intentions from the actor's expressive behavior or from the logic of the situation. But . . . knowledge of intentions is indirect, usually quite inferior and highly subject to error," they conclude (1972, 84).

Geographic dispersion further erodes the quality of the information available to the remote partner who is making a causal attribution. Unlike a collocated observer, he may have little or no knowledge of the proximal environmental stimuli affecting the actor. He also may have little historical perspective on the behavior of the actor and few cues with which to discern the actor's intent. In addition, if the dispersed team incorporates cultural or professional diversity, the remote observer's inferences from what he perceives to be the logic of the situation also may be flawed. For example, Cramton (2001) observes that partners sometimes do not understand the topography of their remote collaborators' locations. They may assume—without thinking much about it—that the drive to a collaborator's test facility is short because one's own local test facility is only a short drive away. In fact, a remote partner's test facility may lie at the end of a multihour, traffic-clogged drive. It can be a long time before such differences in proximal environmental stimuli are recognized. All the while, one partner seems inexplicably reluctant to go to the test facility (i.e., lazy) while the other seems disrespectful of the time and energy required to make a long and difficult trip.

Olson and Olson (2000, 171) describe a talk given to a group of U.S. executives by a U.S. professor via desktop video during a period in which the professor was working in the Netherlands. When arranging for technical support in the Netherlands, it was discovered that the day chosen for the talk was the fiftieth anniversary of the liberation of Holland after World War II. "As the question and answer period went on after the talk (moving on to 10 P.M. Dutch time), the speaker and the technical support person noted wistfully the fireworks and revelers outside the window. The audience in the United States was oblivious to the situation."

The professor and technical person found the questions of the executives to be "slow-paced" and "irritating." As the session continued, the executives may have experienced the professor as increasingly curt. These reactions were driven by the differences in the proximal environmental stimuli affecting the people in each location—situational factors—even though they may have been interpreted at the time as resulting from the dispositions of the participants. Cramton (2001) observes that people involved in dispersed collaborations often fail to figure out which aspects of their local situation and environment differ from the situation and environment of their remote partners and must be explained to remote partners.

Overall, studies suggest that there is a "gradient of dispositional attribution as an inverse function of the total amount of information known about other persons" (Kelley and Michaela 1980, 477). On average, members of geographically dispersed teams are likely to have much less information about remote partners and their situations than members of collocated teams. In addition, members of collocated subgroups of dispersed teams are likely to have more information about each other and the local situation than remote subgroups of the team. As will be discussed further, this can give rise to tensions between subgroups.

Differences in Information Processing

Geographic dispersion and use of communication technology influence attribution by affecting not only the availability of information but also information processing. The three information processing antecedents of attribution that seem to be most affected are the salience of different pieces of information, the cognitive load, and perceptions of temporal contiguity.

Salience   Even in collocated situations, actors and observers often differ in their processing of information. According to Jones and Nisbett (1972), "Different aspects of the available information are salient for actors and observers and this differential salience affects the course and outcome of the attribution process" (85). These differences stem in part from the physiology of perception. Sources of movement or change tend to be salient to observers. Usually, the actor, rather than the situation, is the locus of movement or change and, consequently, the locus of attribution. On the other hand, actors are not physically equipped to view themselves as they act. Their attention tends to be focused on the details of the situation in which they are operating. Interestingly, when Storms (1973) used videotape to give actors the perspective on themselves that observers would have and vice versa, the attributions of each group shifted significantly. Attributions of actors who viewed themselves on videotape shifted toward the dispositional from the situational, and the attributions of observers who were given the vantage point of actors shifted toward the situational from the dispositional.

Remote partners are likely to be further removed than collocated partners from the activities of actors in context. Actors must describe their situation to remote partners if the situation is to have any salience for them. Otherwise, what is likely to be salient are the few behaviors of the actor that can be observed directly by remote partners. Thus, attribution is likely to be biased by these observable behaviors and fail to take unobservable behaviors and aspects of the situation into account.

A study conducted by Storck and Sproull (1995) is suggestive of this point. They studied the impact of videoconferencing on the formation of impressions of remote others and found that "the impressions people form of remote others are different from and less positive than the impressions they form of face-to-face others, starting from an equal baseline" (197). With regard to salience, they showed that people communicating by interactive video use different kinds of information in forming their impressions of their partners than do people communicating face-to-face. Specifically, those evaluating others using video relied "less on task competence information and more on communication competence information" (211). The authors suggest that this occurs because the communication behaviors of remote partners are more salient to observers than behaviors related to competent task performance, which often occur outside the camera's eye.

Cognitive Load   Jones and Nisbett (1972) also describe how the demands placed on the observer affect information processing activities and attributions. In the case of a mutual contingency interaction, each actor observes and is affected by the other. The observer must respond to the actor, becoming an actor himself, rather than enjoying leisurely passive observation. When caught up in action and under pressure to respond, observers fall back on "convenient simplifying assumptions," say Jones and Nisbett. One such assumption "is that action implies a disposition to continue acting in the same manner and to act in such a manner in other situations as well" (87). In other words, when under pressure, people tend to fall back on uncomplicated dispositional attributions rather than taking into account the nuances of a complex situation. This includes failing to take into account how their own actions have contributed to what has occurred. In other words, they fail to see themselves as actors in a complex interaction.

These pressures are likely to be even greater for dispersed than collocated teams. Cramton (2001) has suggested that dispersed teams typically operate under a heavy cognitive load, which disrupts controlled processing of information. Maher (1995) defines cognitive load as occurring "when a person's cognitive resources are tapped or engaged" (194). In addition to the cognitive demands of the task in which the team is engaged, geographically dispersed teams are likely to function in a complex situational structure. This complexity grows with each additional location from which members work. Information about multiple locations must be gathered, organized, integrated, and updated. Multiple possible explanations for unexpected behaviors must be weighed and investigated. Technical problems must be solved. Exchanges between subgroups must be reported to the whole. Lags in communication among locations may be unpredictable. There is considerable evidence that cognitive load exacerbates the tendency to make dispositional rather than situational attributions (Gilbert and Hixon 1991; Gilbert and Osborne 1989; Gilbert, Pelham, and Krull 1988) and biases impression formation (Ford and Kruglanski 1995, Hinds 1999).

Differences in Temporal Contiguity   Distance and the use of technology also can disrupt the timing of communication. The electronically mediated communication tools that members of dispersed teams typically use to collaborate are subject to time lags and even the occasional disordering of messages (Cramton 2001). This is significant because research shows that events are more likely to be perceived as cause and effect if they appear close together in time (Killeen 1978, Siegler and

Liebert 1974, Shultz and Ravinsky 1977). Thus, time lags and disordering of messages may affect team members' perception of causal links between events and the attributions that they make.

For example, Cramton (2001) describes a team composed of two members in Australia and four in the United States, two of them on the East Coast and two in the Southwest. The team held five synchronous text-based "chats" during which tensions between the members in the United States and Australia were evident. Near the end of the team's fifth chat, an American team member observed that the Australian members always seemed to be "twenty-five minutes behind the discussion" and suggested that this could be an artifact of the speed of transmission between the continents. Investigation suggests that parts of the team were indeed communicating at different rates—one rate between the two sites in the United States and another rate between the U.S. and Australia. The team members at the two U.S. locations could carry on a relatively rapid exchange until being "interrupted" by team members in Australia, who were referring to prior topics. If the members in Australia responded to messages the instant they received them, their responses still would appear in the chat traffic well after the conversation between the U.S. partners had moved on because of time lags coming and going. Moreover, from the perspective of the Australian partners, a stream of unrelated comments by the U.S. partners always would follow their messages. It would appear that their comments were ignored. These problems of temporal contiguity were invisible to the American and Australian team members during most of their work together and instead were attributed to lack of manners and conscientiousness on the part of remote partners. In other words, dispositional rather than situational attributions were made.

The points discussed thus far concerning the availability of information and information processing suggest the following propositions:

Proposition 1a: Members of geographically dispersed teams are more likely to make dispositional attributions concerning the activities of remote partners than members of collocated teams will make concerning the activities of local partners.

Proposition 1b: Exchange of situational information across locations will moderate this effect for dispersed teams.

Proposition 2a: Members of collocated subgroups of geographically dispersed teams are more likely to make situational attributions concerning the activities of local partners than remote partners will make concerning those same partners and activities.

Proposition 2b: Exchange of situational information across locations will moderate this effect.

Subgroup Identities and Ultimate Attribution Error

Dispersed teams may be subject not only to exacerbation of the fundamental attribution error, but also the ultimate attribution error, the term Pettigrew (1979) used to describe a tendency toward systematic differences in attributions concerning members of one's own social group when compared with attributions concerning members of other social groups. In other words, attributions are biased in favor of one's in-group and against a perceived out-group. There seems to be a tendency for dispersed teams to develop subgroup identities based on location. This section suggests that under certain conditions, these subgroups can function as in-groups and out-groups, fueling attribution biases.

Hewstone (1990) examined nineteen studies that tested Pettigrew's propositions and found evidence across studies of an in-group bias: more dispositional attribution for positive acts and less dispositional attribution for negative acts by in-group than out-group members. However, the evidence differed from Pettigrew's propositions concerning attribution of out-group behavior. Attributions concerning out-group behaviors tended to be dispositional, whether positive or negative in nature. In other words, the frequency of dispositional attribution of out-group behavior did not differ on the basis of whether the behavior was positive or negative. One explanation for this that is relevant for dispersed collaboration is that people lack information about out-group members' situations and have difficulty placing out-group members in situational context. Hewstone (1990) also examined studies of ultimate attribution error concerning group outcomes, as distinguished from group behaviors. For outcomes, Pettigrew's propositions hold in their entirety: Out-group failure is more likely than in-group failure to be explained in dispositional terms (e.g., lack of ability), and out-group success is more likely than in-group success to be explained away (e.g., attributed to aspects of the situation). Hewstone proposes that intergroup competition accounts for the less charitable assessments of out-groups' outcomes relative to behaviors.

In geographically dispersed teams, factors affecting the incidence of ultimate attribution error may include the development of strong subgroup identities by location, weak social integration of the dispersed team as a whole, a paucity of situational information concerning remote subgroups, information processing biased toward dispositional attribution concerning remote subgroups, and the challenging nature of collaboration under dispersed conditions, encouraging the creation of scapegoats. If the social integration of the team as a whole is weak, attribution may be affected by egocentric bias. In other words, there may be a tendency to make attributions in ways that enhance the self-esteem and self-protection of one's own subgroup.

For example, Armstrong and Cole (chapter 7, this volume) describe how subgroup identities developed around location in the software development teams they studied:

People tended to think of their home group as the people they sat beside at work. Geographic sites promoted an informal, spontaneous group identity. This first group identity was reinforced by close physical proximity and the dense communication it promoted. Office site colleagues shared the metacontext of the locale, including similar occupational beliefs and concerns, cultural perspectives, and political viewpoints. People working in an office tended to have friends at the same nearby competitors, hear the same industry rumors, and share similar beliefs about technological trends. (p. 172)

On the other hand, Armstrong and Cole observed what they called self-perpetuating feuds among different sites: "Members of the same group treated each other as if they were members of different groups, with colleagues at one office site described as *us* and group members at distant sites label *them* (p. 169).

Herbsleb and Grinter (1999) observed subgroup tensions between software developers involved in a large project that was distributed across two locations, Germany and Britain. Team integration was weak, and there was reluctance to share information across sites for fear that one site might be closed down and work consolidated at the other site. In this competitive atmosphere, Herbsleb and Grinter note the incidence of "uncharitable" attributions across dispersed subgroups: "When someone would say, 'We can't make that change,' it was often interpreted as, 'We don't want to make that change,' whether it would benefit the overall project or not. . . . Each side tended to assume the other was just being difficult, rather than trying to understand the concerns behind their position. . . . The situation improved considerably over time, and visits across sites seem to have been pivotal" (93).

Finally, Cramton (2001) observed a tendency in the dispersed teams she studied for collaborators under stress to generalize dispositional attributions, particularly negative ones, to locational subgroups. Remote subgroups were described as "lackadaisical," "aggressive," and having an "inferiority complex." She also observed that once in-group/out-group dynamics had arisen, there was a tendency for members of the subgroups to withhold information from each other. Withholding information may escalate problems by further eroding the basis for situational as opposed to dispositional attribution.

In light of the preceding discussions of the antecedents of fundamental attribution error and ultimate attribution error, the following propositions are suggested:

Proposition 3: In both collocated and dispersed work groups, there will be a negative relationship between the level of social integration of the group and egocentric bias in attributions.

Proposition 4: In teams containing dispersed and collocated members, subgroup identities will tend to reflect differences in location.

Proposition 5: In teams containing dispersed and collocated members, parties will attribute a remote group member's negative behavior to dispositional causes more than they will a collocated member's negative behavior. This effect will be moderated by the level of social integration of the group as a whole.

Proposition 6: In teams containing dispersed and collocated members, parties will be equally likely to attribute the positive behaviors of collocated and remote members to dispositional causes.

Implications for Research and Practice

The use of distributed work arrangements is predicted to be the number one trend in the workplace over the next ten years (Kemske 1998). Such arrangements offer many advantages to individuals and organizations. However, much remains to be learned about the interpersonal and group dynamics of dispersed collaboration. This chapter identifies issues of considerable importance. It explains why the fundamental attribution error may be exacerbated for dispersed collaborators, such that they overweight dispositional factors in explaining the behavior of their remote partners. It also suggests that dispersed collaborators may be vulnerable to the ultimate attribution error: bias in favor of a collocated in-group and against remote out-groups.

Common structural characteristics of geographically dispersed work groups can affect the antecedents of attribution. Geographic dispersion restricts partners' information about each other's local situations. In addition, use of computer-mediated communication makes it difficult for people to discern the intent and internal experience of remote partners. These factors contribute to the tendency for observers to attribute behavior to the disposition of the actor rather than considering whether the observed behavior is a response to the situation at hand. In addition, mediated communication is subject to time lags and disordering of messages, which can affect attributions of causality. Because the systemic and technical nature of these problems often is invisible to dispersed team members, attribution may fault individuals or subgroups.

Preliminary data collected by Cramton and Wilson (2001) show this rationale concerning the impact of geographic dispersion and mediated communication on attribution behavior to be promising. Their sample consisted of twelve dispersed and six collocated teams of graduate students based at three different universities and assigned a complex group project. The researchers established a baseline by querying students about their prior experience with group projects and their attributions concerning partners' behavior when it differed from expectations. There were no significant differences on these items between students assigned to the dispersed and collocated conditions. After the dispersed and collocated teams finished their three-week project, students were queried about their attributions concerning their most recent partners' behavior. The respondents who had worked in dispersed teams were significantly more likely to report dispositional attributions concerning remote partners' behavior than the respondents who had worked in collocated teams (see table 8.1).

This chapter also has presented a rationale for why geographic dispersion can contribute to the ultimate attribution error, a bias in attributions in favor of one's in-group and against a perceived out-group. The likelihood of this problem increases when the social integration of the dispersed team as a whole is weak and the team develops subgroup identities based on location. Shared location provides a natural basis for the development of strong subgroup identities because such clusters of people typically enjoy more interaction and more common information with each other than they do with remote partners. In addition, membership in dispersed teams often spans cultural, professional, and organizational boundaries. If these sources of subgroup identity coincide with divisions by location, the result could be a greater likelihood of the formation of in-groups and out-groups. However, if these sources of shared identity cut across location, they may provide a source of social integration for the dispersed team and weaken tendencies toward egocentric attribution on the basis of location.

Table 8.1
Comparison of attributions made by dispersed and collocated team members

Postproject attributions	Condition	Number	Mean	Standard deviation
On this project, when team members did not meet my expectations, it could generally be attributed to: 1 = Something within the team member 2 = Circumstances outside the member's control	Dispersed team	25	1.6	.5
	Collocated team	6	2.0	.0

Independent samples test

	t-test for equality of means				95% confidence interval of the mean	
Equal variances not assumed	*t*	*df*	Significance (two-tailed)	Mean difference	Lower	Upper
	−4.0	24	.001	−.4	−.6	−.2

Source: Cramton and Wilson (2001).

Finally, the temporary nature and short common history of many geographically dispersed teams also can affect attribution. Members cannot draw on much experience with each other in making attributions. In addition, if members perceive a group to have a limited future, they may fail to give and seek adequate social and contextual information to ground their attributions.

The problems of attribution described here can have serious consequences for the maintenance of working relationships in dispersed teams. When things go wrong, people may blame individuals rather than examine the characteristics of the situation. This directs attention away from team-level learning and lasting solutions and harms team cohesion and cooperation. Herbsleb and Grinter (1999) and Cramton (2001) have observed that when people make negative attributions about remote partners, they also tend to withhold information from them.

How such problems affect team performance probably depends on the degree to which each team members' knowledge and cooperation are necessary for success. Some teams are able to isolate individuals or subgroups and still accomplish their task. However, members of such teams will go on to their next assignment ignorant of the structural factors and processes that shaped their attributions and they will be vulnerable to repeating mistakes.

Future research should explore the propositions offered here, comparing the strength and consequences of these phenomena in dispersed and collocated situations. Impacts on both team relationships and performance should be measured. Potential moderators of the relationships such as exchange of situational information and team social integration also should be investigated.

In the meantime, members of dispersed teams and people communicating by computer mediation might want to think carefully before making assumptions about the situation and constraints of remote others. Instead, they should seek out such information. One also should take care to explain one's own situation to remote partners and try to see it through their eyes. It is important for individuals to monitor the tendency to leap to dispositional attributions about remote partners. This may be quick and easy, but could also be inaccurate and destructive to collaboration. Situational causes should be considered routinely, even if information to support them is not immediately available. Giving remote partners the benefit of the doubt when questions or problems arise is a simple but powerful practice.

Leaders of newly formed teams whose members will be working from dispersed locations typically are advised to bring the team members together for a face-to-face meeting at least once at the outset in order to build relationships and trust (see Mannix, Griffith, and Neale, chapter 9, this volume). Building the social integration of a dispersed team in this way is a good idea. Still better, however, is for people who will collaborate remotely to visit each other's locations at least once. This gives them an opportunity to see how a partner's situation differs from their own and absorb details that a partner may neglect to mention, as well as allowing partners to get to know each other better. If this is not possible, an alternative might be sending influential team members or people in leadership positions to visit the locations remote from their own. Should problems across locations arise, these more informed members may be able to guide colleagues toward constructive interpretations of the behavior of partners in the remote locations.

In designing and launching dispersed teams, leaders should give careful attention to the communication system and norms. They should educate team members about the pitfalls of failing to share situational information and making assumptions about remote partners and locations. Team leaders should monitor the effectiveness of communication processes across locations as a regular part of their job.

When confusion or problems do occur, teams should analyze collectively their operating practices and look for opportunities to improve them. Although blame could be laid on an individual, it is important to recognize how complex the situation and processes of dispersed teams tend to be. The perspectives of individuals and subgroups often differ far more than the group as a whole realizes. If people involved in dispersed collaboration learn from these differences, they are likely to strengthen their overall effort.

Note

I thank Pamela J. Hinds, Sara Kiesler, Margaret A. Neale, Joseph B. Walther, and colleagues at the 2000 Carmel Conference on Distributed Work for their thoughtful contributions to the development of this chapter.

References

Abel, M. (1990). Experiences in an exploratory distributed organization. In R. Kraut and C. Egido (eds.), *Intellectual teamwork: Social and technological foundations of cooperative work* (111–146). Hillsdale, NJ: Erlbaum.

Adams, J., Adams, J., Rice, R., and Instone, D. (1985). Effects of perceived group effectiveness and group role on attributions of group performance. *Journal of Applied Social Psychology, 15,* 387–398.

Armstrong, D., and Cole, P. (2002). Managing distances and differences in geographically distributed work groups. In P. Hinds and S. Kiesler. *Distributed work* (167–186). Cambridge, MA: MIT Press.

Bell, L., Wicklund, R., Mando, G., and Larkin, C. (1976). When the unexpected behavior is attributed to the environment. *Journal of Research in Personality, 10,* 316–327.

Brawley, L., Carron, A., and Widmeyer, W. (1987). Assessing the cohesion of teams: Validity of the group environment questionnaire. *Journal of Sport Psychology, 9,* 275–294.

Brockner, J., and Guare, J. (1983). Improving the performance of low self-esteem individuals: An attributional approach. *Academy of Management Journal, 26,* 642–256.

Cramton, C. (2001). The mutual knowledge problem and its consequences for dispersed collaboration. *Organization Science, 12,* 346–371.

Cramton, C., and Wilson, J. (2001). *Psychological contract violations and attribution behavior in dispersed teams.* Unpublished manuscript.

DeJoy, D. (1994). Managing safety in the workplace: An attribution theory analysis and model. *Journal of Safety Research, 25,* 3–17.

Deaux, K., and Farris, E. (1977). Attributing the causes of one's own performance: The effects of sex, norms, and outcome. *Journal of Research in Personality, 11,* 59–72.

Dorfman, P., and Stephan, W. (1984). The effects of group performance on cognitions, satisfaction, and behavior: A process model. *Journal of Management, 10,* 173–192.

Feldman, J. (1981). Beyond attribution theory: Cognitive processes in performance appraisal. *Journal of Applied Psychology, 66,* 127–148.

Ford, T., and Kruglanski, A. (1995). Effects of epistemic motivations on the use of accessible constructs in social judgment. *Personality and Social Psychology Bulletin, 21,* 950–962.

Gilbert, D., and Hixon, J. (1991). The trouble with thinking: Activation and application of stereotypic beliefs. *Journal of Personality and Social Psychology, 60,* 509–517.

Gilbert, D., and Osborne, R. (1989). Thinking backward: Some curable and incurable consequences of cognitive busyness. *Journal of Personality and Social Psychology, 57,* 940–949.

Gilbert, D., Pelham, B., and Krull, D. (1988). On cognitive busyness: When person perceivers meet persons perceived. *Journal of Personality and Social Psychology, 54,* 733–740.

Heider, F. (1944). Social perception and phenomenal causality. *Psychological Review, 51,* 358–374.

Henry, J., and Campbell, C. (1995). A comparison of the validity, predictiveness, and consistency of a trait versus situational measure of attributions. In M. Martinko (ed.), *Attribution theory: An organizational perspective* (289–313). Delray Beach, FL: St. Lucie Press.

Herbsleb, J., and Grinter, R. (1999). Splitting the organization and integrating the code: Conway's law revisited. In *Proceedings of the International Conference on Software Engineering ICSE '99* (85–95). New York: ACM Press.

Hewstone, M. (1990). The "ultimate attribution error"? A review of the literature on intergroup causal attribution. *European Journal of Social Psychology, 20,* 311–355.

Hinds, P. (1999). The cognitive and interpersonal costs of video. *Media Psychology, 1,* 283–311.

Jones, E., and Nisbett, R. (1972). The actor and the observer: Divergent perceptions of the causes of behavior. In E. Jones, D. Kanouse, H. Kelley, R. Nisbett, S. Valins, and B. Weiner (eds.), *Attribution: Perceiving the causes of behavior* (79–94). Morristown, NJ: General Learning Press.

Karakowsky, L., and Siegel, J. (1995). The effect of demographic diversity on causal attributions of work group success and failure: A framework for research. In M. Martinko (ed.), *Attribution theory: An organizational perspective* (289–313). Delray Beach, FL: St. Lucie Press.

Kelley, H., and Michaela, J. (1980). Attribution theory and research. *Annual Review of Psychology, 31,* 457–501.

Kemske, F. (1998, January). HR 2008. *Workforce,* 47–60.

Kent, R., and Martinko, M. (1995). The development and evaluation of a scale to measure organizational attribution style. In M. Martinko (ed.), *Attribution theory: An organizational perspective* (289–313). Delray Beach, FL: St. Lucie Press.

Kiesler, S., and Sproull, L. (1992), Group decision making and communication technology. *Organizational Behavior and Human Decision Processes, 52,* 96–123.

Killeen, P. (1978). Superstition: A matter of bias, not detectability. *Science, 199*, 88–90.

Maher, K. (1995). The role of cognitive load in supervisor attributions of subordinate behavior. In M. Martinko (ed.), *Attribution theory: An organizational perspective* (193–209). Delray Beach, FL: St. Lucie Press.

Mannix, E. A., Griffith, T., and Neale, M. A. (2002). The phenomenology of conflict in distributed work teams. In P. Hinds and S. Kiesler (eds.), *Distributed work* (213–233). Cambridge, MA: MIT Press.

Martinko, M., Henry, J., and Zmud, R. (1996). An attributional explanation of individual resistance to the introduction of information technologies in the workplace. *Behavior and Information Technology, 15*, 313–330.

McDonald, D. (1995). Fixing blame in n-person attributions: A social identity model for attributional processes in newly formed cross-functional groups. In M. Martinko (ed.), *Attribution theory: An organizational perspective* (273–288). Delray Beach, FL: St. Lucie Press.

Menon, T., Morris, M., Chiu, C., and Hong, Y. (1999). Culture and the construal of agency: Attribution to individual versus group dispositions. *Journal of Personality and Social Psychology, 76*, 701–717.

Morris, M., Nisbett, R., and Peng, K. (1995). Causal attribution across domains and cultures. In G. Lewis, D. Premack, and D. Sperber (eds.), *Causal cognition: A multidisciplinary debate* (577–612). Oxford: Clarendon Press.

Morris, M., and Peng, K. (1994). Culture and cause: American and Chinese attributions for social and physical events. *Journal of Personality and Social Psychology, 97*, 949–971.

Norris, W., and Niebuhr, R. (1984). Attributional influences on the job performance–job satisfaction relationship. *Academy of Management Journal, 27*, 424–431.

Novell, N., and Forsyth, D. (1985). The impact of inhibiting or facilitation causal factors on group members' reactions after success and failure. *Social Psychology Quarterly, 47*, 293–297.

Olson, G., and Olson, J. (2000). Distance matters. *Human-Computer Interaction, 15*, 139–178.

Pettigrew, T. (1979). The ultimate attribution error: Extending Allport's cognitive analysis of prejudice. *Personality and Social Psychology Bulletin, 5*, 461–476.

Regan, D., Straus, E., and Fazio, R. (1974). Liking and the attribution process. *Journal of Experimental Social Psychology, 10*, 385–397.

Ross, L. (1977). The intuitive psychologist and his shortcomings: Distortions in the attribution process. *Advances in Experimental Social Psychology, 10*, 174–220.

Seligman, M., and Schulman, P. (1986) Explanatory style as a predictor of productivity and quitting among life insurance agents. *Journal of Personality and Social Psychology, 50*, 832–838.

Shultz, T., and Ravinsky, F. (1977). Similarity as a principle of causal inference. *Child Development, 48*, 1552–1558.

Siegler, R., and Liebert, R. (1974). Effects of contiguity, regularity, and age on children's causal inferences. *Developmental Psychology, 10*, 574–579.

Sproull, L., and Kiesler, S. (1986). Reducing social context cues: Electronic mail in organizational communication. *Management Science, 32*, 1492–1512.

Storck, J., and Sproull, L. (1995). Through a glass darkly: What do people learn in video-conferences? *Human Communication Research, 22*, 197–219.

Storms, M. (1973). Videotape and the attribution process: Reversing actors' and observers' points of view. *Journal of Personality and Social Psychology, 27*, 165–175.

Teas, R., and McElroy, J. (1986). Causal attributions and expectancy estimates: A framework for understanding the dynamics of salesforce motivation. *Journal of Marketing, 50*, 75–86.

Turner, J., Hogg, M. Turner, P., and Smith P. (1984). Failure and defeat as determinants of group cohesiveness. *British Journal of Social Psychology, 23*, 97–111.

Wang, Z. (1994). Group attributional training as an effective approach to human resource development under team work systems. *Ergonomics, 37*, 1137–1144.

Weiner, B. (1985). An attributional theory of achievement motivation and emotion. *Psychological Review, 92*, 548–573.

Weiner, B. (1986). *An attributional theory of motivation and emotion.* New York: Springer-Verlag.

Weiner, B., Russell, D., and Lerman, D. (1978). Affective consequences of causal ascriptions. In J. Harvey, W. Ickes, and R. Kidd (eds.), *New directions in attribution research* (Vol. 2, 59–90). Hillsdale, NJ: Erlbaum.

Zuckerman, M. (1979). Attribution of success and failure revisited, or: The motivational bias is alive and well in attribution theory. *Journal of Personality, 47*, 245–287.

9

The Phenomenology of Conflict in Distributed Work Teams

Elizabeth A. Mannix, Terri Griffith, and Margaret A. Neale

New organizational forms are arising that allow flexibility and speed. One feature of these new organizations is the distributed work group. Teams whose members are distributed in time or space have tremendous potential, yet they also face great challenges. In this chapter, we focus on conflict as one of the keys to effective group process and performance in distributed teams. We define the special hurdles these teams face in managing conflict, specifically focusing on creating a common social identity and managing compositional diversity. We then examine the antecedents to productive conflict management, including the enactment of swift trust, the development of a shared reality and strong team culture, and the belief in team efficacy derived from a highly developed transactive memory system and a strong sense of psychological safety. We end with a consideration of the role of leadership in distributed team dynamics.

Conflict, and its resolution, are fundamental to group functioning. Conflict is an awareness by the parties of differences, discrepancies, incompatible wishes, or irreconcilable desires (Boulding 1963). There has been a debate in organizational research regarding whether agreement or disagreement within groups is advantageous (Eisenhardt and Zbaracki 1992). One key to unlocking this complex relationship lies in the differentiation of conflict as either relationship or task related (Crosier and Rose 1977, Guetzkow and Gyr 1954, Jehn 1995, Pinkley 1990, Wall and Nolan 1986). Relationship conflict is an awareness of interpersonal incompatibilities. Relationship conflict often includes personality clashes, animosity, and annoyance between individuals. Studies show that relationship conflict is detrimental to individual and group performance, member satisfaction, and the likelihood that the group will work together in the future (Jehn 1995, Shah and Jehn 1993, Jehn and Mannix 2001). When group members have interpersonal problems or feel friction with one another, they may be distracted from the task, work less cooperatively, and produce suboptimal products (Argyris 1962; Kelley 1979; Staw, Sandelands, and Dutton 1981; Roseman, Wiest, and Swartz 1994).

Task, or cognitive, conflict is an awareness of differences in viewpoints and opinions pertaining to the group's task. Examples are disagreement among group members' ideas about the task being performed, disagreement regarding an organization's current hiring strategies, and conflict about the information to include in an annual report. In contrast with relationship conflict, moderate levels of task conflict have been shown to be beneficial to many kinds of group performance. Teams performing complex cognitive tasks benefit from differences of opinion about the work being done (Bourgeois 1985, Eisenhardt and Schoonhoven 1990, Jehn 1995, Shah and Jehn 1993, Jehn and Mannix 2001). Teams improve decision quality as they drop old patterns of interaction and adopt new perspectives; the synthesis that emerges from the conflict is generally superior to their individual perspectives (Schweiger and Sandberg 1989, Schwenk 1990).

Unfortunately, recent research in this domain (for a review, see Simons and Peterson 2000) indicates that perceptions of task and relationship conflict are often highly correlated. One reason for this correlation may be misattribution—for example, mistaking a task-focused comment as a personal attack (Jehn 1997, Amason 1996; see Cramton, chapter 8, this volume). Misattribution can occur because people experience conflict as negative and infer malevolent intentions on the part of those with whom they disagree. Misattribution may be more likely in newly formed or highly diverse teams, where a lack of deep knowledge of others may cause members to confuse task conflict with relationship conflict (Gruenfeld, Mannix, Williams, and Neale 1996). Similarly, in highly political or competitive environments, comments that are meant to generate task conflict may be misperceived as relationship conflict (Amason 1996). Thus, by facilitating task conflict, a team runs considerable risk in also increasing the level of relationship conflict.

The existence of trust seems to break this cycle in teams (Simons and Peterson 2000). Trust necessarily requires a different set of behaviors from those that lead to the negative effects of relationship conflict (Zand 1972). Simons and Peterson (2000) note that teams with low levels of intragroup trust evidenced a significantly stronger positive association between task and relationship conflict than did groups with high levels of intragroup trust (see also Mayer, Davis, and Schoorman 1995). Trust helps people avoid interpreting conflict as relationship based even when task conflict is high. Further, the sense of trust helps resolve conflict when it does occur.

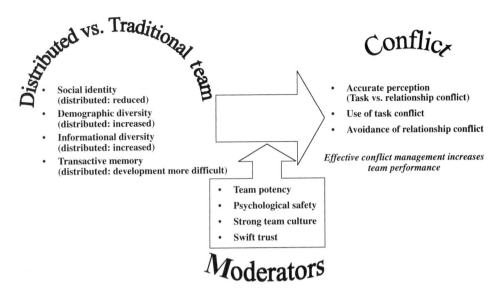

Figure 9.1
Conceptual model of distributed teams and conflict.

Conflict in Distributed Teams

Several factors may make it difficult for distributed teams to engage in productive types of conflict as compared with traditional teams. These factors pose challenges to the team's ability to achieve high levels of performance We focus on two of the particular challenges distributed teams must overcome that are directly antecedent to conflict: lack of a common social identity and increased compositional diversity. Both arise because distributed teams are likely to be drawn from diverse locations and populations and may be composed of individuals who never or rarely meet face-to-face (Griffith and Neale in press). Figure 9.1 provides a conceptual summary of these issues.

Common Social Identity
Distributed teams are often groups of strangers rather than people who have worked together in the past or friends. For example, a distributed team may be composed of employees from several locations, chosen to capitalize on disparate skills not available at a common site. They may feel little common social identity. A common social identity benefits group process and performance by increasing team members'

knowledge of one another's skills, perspectives, and interpersonal styles (Harrison, Price, and Bell 1998; Wittenbaum and Stasser 1996). It also focuses teams on a common set of goals and values (Jehn and Mannix 2001; Jehn, Northcraft, and Neale 1999). We suggest:

Proposition 1:   A common social identity will be more difficult to achieve in distributed work teams, potentially decreasing beneficial task conflict and reducing performance when compared to traditional work teams.

Preexisting ties also can reduce conformity and the suppression of alternative perspectives and judgments (Asch 1952, Nemeth 1986, Schachter and Singer 1962). Gruenfeld and associates (1996) found that teams composed of individuals with preexisting relationship ties were more comfortable with disagreement and better able to pool unique information to arrive at the correct solution to a complex problem than were groups of strangers. Similarly, Shah and Jehn (1993) report that task groups composed of friends exhibited greater task and emotional conflict while working on a complex decision task than did groups of strangers. Because the task required critical inquiry and analysis of assumptions, the willingness of familiar groups to engage in this type of conflict gave them a performance advantage. Thus, we propose that:

Proposition 2a: Limited previous interactions among distributed team members will have the potential to increase detrimental conflict and make it more difficult to resolve.

Proposition 2b: Due to their lack of relationship, team members are likely to have more difficulty distinguishing task conflict from relational conflict, thus decreasing team performance.

Diversity

Because distributed teams tend to be drawn from different populations, they are likely to comprise individuals who are diverse on multiple dimensions. Social category diversity refers to mainly visible demographic characteristics such as age, sex, and race (Tsui, Egan, and O'Reilly 1992). Although such differences often are not relevant to completing the task, they do shape people's perceptions and behaviors through mechanisms of categorization and prejudice (Pelled 1996). People report being more committed, satisfied, and likely to remain in groups and organizations that are more demographically homogeneous (O'Reilly, Caldwell, and Barnett 1989; Tsui et al. 1992; Verkuyten, de Jong, and Masson 1993). Demographic dissimilarity among team members also is associated with poor communication, lower integration, increased conflict, and negative affective relations in the group (Bantel and Jackson 1989, Jackson et al. 1991, Jehn et al. 1999, Tsui and O'Reilly 1989, Zenger and Lawrence 1989).

Recent empirical work demonstrates that demographic diversity is linked to increased relationship conflict in traditional teams (Jehn et al. 1999). Of course, ascriptive characteristics may initially be invisible to distributed team members, reducing the impact of stereotyping on team process and performance. For example, in a study of co-located groups, computer-mediated groups focused on the content of member contributions, whereas face-to-face discussion groups showed gender bias in their evaluations (Bhappu, Griffith, and Northcraft 1997). However, if ascriptive characteristics become known in distributed groups, they may exacerbate social distance because positive contact is limited (see Armstrong and Cole, chapter 7, this volume).

Proposition 3: Demographic diversity has the potential to create higher levels of relationship conflict in distributed work teams when compared to traditional work teams.

Another dimension of diversity, informational diversity, includes attributes such as work experience, education, and functional background that influence how an individual perceives and approaches problems. Many theorists argue that knowledge or skill diversity can enhance group performance by enhancing the group's creative problem-solving ability (Nemeth 1986), primarily through task conflict (Damon 1991; Jehn 1995; Levine, Resnick, and Higgins 1993). For example, educational diversity in top management teams has been found to be positively related to a firm's return on investment and growth in sales (Smith et al. 1994). Jehn and associates (1999) found that informational diversity increased task-related conflict in teams, improving overall performance. Hambrick, Cho, and Chen (1996) found that top management teams that were diverse in terms of education, functional background, and company tenure exhibited a greater propensity for strategic action than did homogeneous teams. However, these teams made slower decisions than homogeneous groups. Ancona and Caldwell (1992) found that as functional diversity increased, team members communicated more often with outsiders, and this external communication helped them develop more innovative products, but their diversity also had some negative performance effects. For example, diverse teams were more likely to overspend their budgets and miss important deadlines.

Resolving task conflict in distributed teams may require more coordination overhead than is experienced in face-to-face teams. For example, investment clubs (where members pool their money and then make joint investment decisions) that used greater numbers of communication technologies had higher portfolio values if they also had greater attention to procedural roles; the opposite effect was found for more traditional clubs (Griffith and Meader 2000). Similarly, group support systems (software providing electronic meeting support) usually require a facilitator to manage the technology (Limayem, Lee-Partridge, Dickson, and DeSanctis 1993). Even with facilitation, decision making using such tools often takes longer than in comparable face-to-face groups (McGrath and Hollingshead 1994). Thus:

Proposition 4:   Distributed teams with more informational diversity will have more potential for creative and high-quality decisions, but may take longer than more homogeneous teams to resolve conflicts, reach agreement, and implement those decisions.

Effective Conflict Management in Distributed Teams

Distributed teams face greater risks than traditional teams in developing commitment to the team. With diversity and lack of a common, compelling social identity, conflict has the potential to be considerably more disruptive to the distributed team than to more traditional teams. Given that distributed teams face these challenges, what interventions are necessary for distributed teams to achieve high performance? We discuss the importance to distributed teams of trust, a strong team culture, team efficacy, and a team leader or coach.

The Development of Trust

Distributed teams may be perceived as more temporary than their more traditional counterparts (see Meyerson, Weick, and Kramer 1996). If so, these teams do not have the luxury of time and face-to-face interactions typically necessary for the development of trust.

Myerson and associates (1996) claim that trust does exist in these temporary systems, but it is formed in response to a different set of antecedents than traditional trust. *Swift trust* is likely to occur when people are drawn from a known labor pool or network, interact through role-based norms, and have moderate levels of interdependence and when time pressure pushes them to use category-based information processing (especially categories that are made salient—and positive—by the institution). From this analysis, we would expect that swift trust will develop in distributed teams whose members have clear roles and well-defined specialties, value their professional reputations as well as the reputations of their group of origin, and are assigned tasks that require only moderate levels of interdependence among members.

Swift trust may be enacted through an autoreinforcing mechanism. That is, as members of distributed teams act as if trust existed (Jarvenpaa and Leidner 1999), their behavior provides the social proof to other members of the team that trust does exist (Cialdini 1993). Each individual's trusting behavior contributes to the shared reality that trust exists within the distributed team. As a result:

Proposition 5: Distributed teams that have enacted swift trust will be more willing to interpret conflict as task based rather than relationship oriented. As such, conflict will be beneficial, improving both team process and performance.

Shared Reality and Team Culture

The notion of a shared reality is an old one in social psychology; shared reality lends reliability, validity, generality, and predictability to individual experience (Sherif 1936, Asch 1952, Festinger 1950, Heider 1958). Hardin and Higgins (1996) claim that an individual's experience of reality is created and maintained through sharing this reality with others, social interaction is predicated on and regulated by shared reality, and shared reality achieved through social interaction influences self-regulation. Hardin and Higgins (1996) argue that efforts to establish a shared reality will dominate social interaction, guiding its course and consequences.

Recently, Levine and Higgins (in press) have extended the concept of shared reality to the group context, arguing that a shared reality is critical to the formation, maintenance, and functioning of groups. When a newly formed group faces an interactive task, they are as likely to be as concerned with social acceptance as they are with task performance (Schachter 1951, Deutsch 1949). This concern can affect the tendency to suppress or misattribute conflict. For example, team members may experience evaluation apprehension (Zajonc 1965), leading to the cognitive suppression of alternative perspectives and judgments (Carver and Scheier 1981, Sanna and Shotland 1990). In addition, team members might attempt to behave like other group members, regardless of the nature of their private beliefs (Davis 1973, Tanford and Penrod 1984), to avoid missteps that might lead to ostracism. Indeed, even if team members are able to overcome these hurdles and express disagreement, they may find that their fellow team members have difficulty interpreting their comments, a problem likely to be exacerbated in distributed work groups.

Over time, however, teams develop a shared reality, resulting in informal rules, or norms (Levine and Higgins, in press). The shared understanding and acceptance of norms at the team level result in a team culture (Mannix, Thatcher, and Jehn 2000). While culture must be a system of shared beliefs, teams vary on the content of their beliefs and the degree to which they have a strong culture (Jackson 1966, Katz and Kahn 1978). A strong team culture facilitates and reinforces the development and maintenance of a positive team social identity. Such an identity can help enhance swift trust and move the group toward a level of deeper understanding regarding team member skills, values, goals, and motivations. As a result of these factors, the enactment of conflict becomes less threatening, and the attribution of its meaning becomes clearer. Thus:

Proposition 6:   A strong team culture, fostering open conflict norms, will enhance the ability of distributed teams to interpret conflict as task based, improving team process and performance.

Team Efficacy

For teams to be successful, they must believe that they can accomplish their assigned tasks. This notion of efficacy at the group level has been labeled potency (Shea and Guzzo 1987): the collective belief of a group that it can be effective in performing its task. Potency is determined not only by the availability of resources within a group (e.g., member skill, experience, equipment) or within its environment (e.g., training opportunities, information, access to key people) but also by the willingness of team members to exert effort and share information necessary to solve the problem or accomplish the task at hand. Potency allows team members to take advantage of their knowledge of and be willing to share the various caches of information that exist within the group's boundaries. Team potency contributes to a distributed team's ability to enact and manage task-related conflict and avoid relationship conflict. Two factors—the development of transactive memory and the presence of psychological safety—are likely to have a major impact on the team's perception of its potency.

Transactive Memory   Wegner (1987, 1995) describes transactive memory as a shared system that groups use to encode, store, and retrieve their available information, enabling team members to know where knowledge exists within the team. Moreland and associates (1998) found that groups whose members were trained together performed more effectively than groups whose members were trained apart. They argued that a co-training effect develops as team members learn about other members' domains of expertise through experience and member disclosure. Over time, the team relies on these pools of expertise, and different members become responsible for encoding, storing, and retrieving expert knowledge across domains. Recently, Moreland and Myaskolvsky (2000) reported that the development of transactive memory does not require that group members be trained together on relevant tasks. Conveying the nature of group members' skills to individuals trained separately resulted in the equivalent level of performance as groups trained together, and both performed significantly better than those whose members were trained individually with no subsequent performance feedback. This recent finding suggests that technological systems that provide such a skills map through their documentation capabilities (Gordon and Moore 1999) may enhance the development of transactive memory in distributed teams (Hollingshead, Fulk, and Monge, chapter 14, this volume). Computer-based systems may allow distributed teams to resolve process conflicts more smoothly as it becomes apparent which team members are responsible for which tasks. In addition, a readily available knowledge base should enhance the ability of teams to have constructive task-related conflict—and also to resolve such conflict through the use of data and expertise. However, documentation alone is insufficient. Transactive memory requires more than the storing and retrieving of knowledge; interaction may be necessary to update old information and create new information (Griffith, Sawyer, and Neale in press). As such:

Proposition 7: Distributed teams are likely to have more difficulty in developing transactive memory than groups whose members work together.

The difficulty distributed teams have in establishing transactive memory may stem, first, from problems of coordination. Wittenbaum, Vaughan, and Stasser (1998) suggest that explicit coordination is more difficult in larger groups because larger groups have more problems communicating. In distributed groups, a lack of media richness and member inattention is likely to be greater than in traditional groups, so one would expect that the knowledge about who knows what would be more opaque to the group members.

Second, because distributed groups are likely to be diverse, member expertise and access to unique knowledge pools may have greater variance. This diversity would exert greater need and value for the development of a transactive memory (Moreland, Argote, and Krishnan 1998; Watson, Kumar, and Michaelsen 1993). In diverse teams where members have considerable face-to-face interaction, various physical markers such as style of dress, gender, and age provide cues to this diversity. These cues can facilitate the processing of information about different team members and aid the development of transactive memory. However, when team members are distributed, the amount and value of these visual cues are dramatically reduced.

Thus, distributed teams may have considerable diversity but the cues (visual, interpersonal) associated with this diversity may be unavailable. The experience of these teams, because of the distributed nature of their interaction, may be more akin to that of homogeneous teams that must use more explicit mechanisms than visual cues to identify the specific skills and expertise that their members possess. Especially in these types of teams, embedding knowledge in both team members and the technology (using documentation and technologically mediated communication systems) is likely to be more effective in transferring knowledge and the development of transactive memory across individuals, time, and distance (Galbraith 1990, Rothwell 1978). Individuals can capture the tacit nuances of the knowledge, while technology can capture the explicit knowledge reliably and consistently (Argote, Gruenfeld, and Naquin 1999, Griffith et al. in press).

Proposition 8:   Transactive memory is a precursor to team potency, increasing the ability of team members to see how each might contribute to accomplish their task. Distributed teams that achieve team potency will more easily engage in task conflict, increasing their level of performance.

Psychological Safety   Edmondson (1999) suggests that for team learning to occur, members must have a willingness to discuss mistakes, experiment with new actions, ask for feedback, and speak up about problems and concerns—in other words, to engage in constructive task conflict. This state of psychological safety is necessary for teams to learn.

Psychological safety (Edmondson 1999) is a team climate characterized by interpersonal trust and mutual respect. If team members feel a sense of psychological safety, risk-taking behaviors are more likely to occur. Edmondson, Bohmer, and Pisano (2000) report that psychological safety led to greater innovativeness and greater openness and comfort in speaking up about difficult issues. In distributed teams, the development of swift trust may lead to the perception of psychological safety. Edmondson (1999) provides support for the hypothesis that access to resources and information is an antecedent of psychological safety—the argument being that such context support will reduce the insecurity and defensiveness of team members. Having greater communication with teammates, through either face-to-face interaction or electronically, could provide access to resources and information.

The relationship between distributed work and psychological safety is a complex one, depending largely on the social construction processes within the group. We propose an interaction between level of technological support and time necessary to develop a group's sense of psychological safety (and, through psychological safety, on the willingness of team members to share information). It may be that no level of technological support can completely offset the challenge to openness and innovation posed to the development of psychological safety by physical distance; however, technologies that facilitate information exchange, making explicit the transactive memory of distributed groups, may fulfill part of the requirements for team-level psychological safety. Further, technologies that also provide groups with greater access to their members because of increased opportunities for communication are likely to facilitate the development of norms of openness and perceptions of psychological safety.

Proposition 9a: Distributed teams that develop psychological safety are more likely to experience team potency than are those teams (distributed or traditional) that do not develop psychological safety.

Proposition 9b: In general, teams (either distributed or traditional) that develop psychological safety and a sense of the team's potency are likely to increase the distribution and discussion of relevant information, thus facilitating task conflict and avoiding relationship conflict.

The Role of Leadership

To manage conflict effectively, some distributed teams may be able to rely on a strong organizational culture that provides individuals with norms and beneficial patterns of behavior that readily transfer to the team. Other distributed teams may be composed of relatively similar others, making the creation of a strong team culture more readily attainable. Still other distributed teams may have the advantage of working together in the past, thus being able to take advantage of previously established relationships or common social identities. When groups do not have these advantages, another solution is available: effective leadership and coaching.

To understand the role of a team leader we refer to the classic work by McGrath (1984), who argued that team leaders must engage in two primary behaviors: monitoring and taking action. Hackman and Walton (1986) combined McGrath's model of leadership with their model of work group effectiveness to create a functional view of leadership in teams. Hackman and Walton (1986) argued that effective work groups require three conditions: a clear and engaging direction, an enabling performance situation (comprising a facilitative group structure, a supportive organizational context, and available expert coaching), and adequate material resources. Thus, the critical leadership functions can be arranged in a matrix, with the two types of leadership functions for each of the three team effectiveness conditions.

A clear and engaging direction can be defined as a shared sense of why the group exists and what it is trying to accomplish (Wageman 1997). In numerous studies of traditional teams, a clear and engaging direction has been shown to distinguish effective teams from ineffective ones (Hackman 1990). Clear, simple, and specific direction in ends but not in means allows team members to use their own skills, abilities, and creativity to discover how best to accomplish the task. This level of freedom can make a task more engaging. In distributed teams, members may belong to several different project groups (and perhaps their local projects are more salient), making multiple commitments a problem. Thus, for distributed teams even more than for more traditional teams, leadership behavior at the moment of team formation is crucial. It sets the tone for subsequent expectations, directs focus to the project, and creates shared commitment toward the task. It may also be a window of opportunity (Tyre and Orlikowski 1994) to implement technological tools to keep the team's direction in the forefront.

Having set the direction, leaders of distributed teams should vigilantly monitor group process and performance (see Weisband, chapter 13, this volume). While the ability to monitor group process may be supported in distributed teams (for example, by documentation of the work process; Griffith et al. in press), applying the knowledge gained from this monitoring by keeping the group on track and engaged is likely to be more difficult when dealing with distributed, as compared to traditional, teams. There is some empirical evidence that teams may be most receptive to interventions to refocus at the midpoint of their interactions (Jehn and Mannix 2001, Gersick 1989), and the monitoring capabilities of distributed teams may be advantageous in doing so.

The organizational context of the team is also a crucial focus for leadership behaviors. The organizational context has three primary components: group structure, performance context, and coaching. Beginning with group structure, the leader has the opportunity to set boundaries around the task itself, determine the group composition, and influence the core norms that regulate team behavior. The leader's greatest leverage on these factors is likely to be at the inception of the team (Wageman 1997, Bettenhausen and Murnighan 1985). Later, the team itself may be best placed to create and manage task conflict effectively based on the boundaries set by the leader.

According to Hackman and Oldham (1980), a motivating task is one that team members view as meaningful, for which they share responsibility and accountability. Thus, a strong team leader should draw performance and contextual links between a particular project and the objectives of the organization. Such a scenario provides a foundation on which to manage conflicts more effectively. In addition, to strengthen responsibility and accountability, individuals should be explicitly chosen for the team and assigned specific roles based on their expertise. Again, building a foundation, specifically here one that relates to the ability of the group to generate transactive memory based on individuals' expertise, group composition should link the team's diversity to task needs. These role assignments, combined with clear objectives, should facilitate the development of swift trust as well as the reinforcement of open communication and beneficial conflict norms.

The second aspect of the organizational context is the performance environment, or infrastructure, including the reward system, the educational system, and the information system. First, leaders should ensure that organizational rewards are strongly linked to team rather than individual performance. This may be more difficult when the team is distributed because team-based recognition by the organization is less likely to occur. However, if rewards are linked to individual performance rather than team performance, it is likely to increase the focus on political status-seeking behavior within the group and reduce the opportunity to develop swift trust and a shared team culture. As a result, the perception of relationship-based conflict may increase, creating a team in which conflict is destructive.

The technological infrastructure is also a resource to be supported by the leader. In distributed teams, this might include supplying teams with particular databases, educating team members in the use of group support systems, or developing distributed communication skills. As a value is placed on learning in the team, a sense of psychological safety can be created where risks can be taken and opinions challenged without fear of social ostracism or rejection. Coaching can be directed at effort, knowledge and skill, or team performance strategies. For example, the leader can increase team members' effort by minimizing coordination costs, increase the synergy of a team by integrating individual knowledge, and sharpen performance strategies by enhancing creativity. Providing teams with the tools to develop a transactive memory system is one way to accomplish all three of these goals. With such a system in place, knowledge can be easily accessed, diversity taken advantage of, and innovation enhanced. Again, the coach facilitates the conditions necessary to move the team toward a greater sense of team efficacy.

The final ingredient to effective team performance is the provision of adequate material resources—time, space, budgets, and tools. Clearly, an effective team leader takes responsibility for monitoring team needs and providing needed resources. The resources that distributed teams need may be very different from those demanded by traditional teams. In distributed teams, these resources may be specific databases, operating systems, computer resources, or group support systems. They may even include money for travel to meet face-to-face. In many ways, these resources are the crucial linchpin holding group process and performance together. Without the needed databases, distributed teams may not be able to develop systems for creating a transactive memory. Without shared access to Web-based information, individual team members may not be able to fulfill their assigned roles, reducing the reinforcement of swift trust and eliminating the opportunity to build a strong team culture. Without adequate time or travel budget, distributed team members may never interact sufficiently to learn from one another and thereby build a sense of psychological safety. All of these factors are the building blocks of effective conflict management and strong team performance.

Thus, the leader of a distributed team must, more than his or her traditional counterpart, monitor and carefully attend to the needs of distributed teams for structure. While some moments will be more critical for intervention than others, distributed groups are likely to benefit considerably more by face-to-face interaction early in their development rather than later. Further, leaders of distributed teams must also be vigilant at other times to ensure the successful development of appropriate norms and task-based progress.

Proposition 10: Because of the additional challenges of creating successful distributed teams, team leaders who set a clear and engaging direction, establish clear boundaries around the task, effectively compose the group, define an appropriate reward structure, and help set the core norms around conflict, communication, and trust will be more effective than team leaders of distributed teams with a more laissez-faire approach.

Proposition 11: Leaders of distributed groups will have greater impact on the performance of their groups to the extent that they monitor and intervene at specific times (early, middle) than will leaders of more traditional teams.

Conclusion

Although decades of research suggest that the challenges that traditional teams face are considerable, they are likely to pale in comparison to those faced by teams functioning in a distributed environment. Consistent with previous research on traditional teams, we expect that a major factor in the success or failure of distributed teams' performance will hinge on the way they manage conflict.

A distributed environment may also provide some interesting advantages to teams. Teams may benefit from the increased diversity of information that exists when they are not constrained by the demands of physical proximity. Components of transactive memory may be more easily developed because of the necessity of documentation. This same documentation may also facilitate the coach or leader's ability to monitor team progress and performance. Indeed, new technologies may provide the opportunity for teams to have new kinds of interactions, new norms, and more dynamic relationships with others.

With the flexibility of technologically enabled environments, the feasible boundaries of organizational design have been expanded. The implication is that applying the principles we have enumerated will require explicit consideration of specific technology capabilities, the implementation process and adaptation to the technology, as well as the development of leadership skills capable of functioning with more (and less) information about the situation. We have applied our knowledge of conflict management to this relatively new arena. This lens serves to identify key areas for attention and to help understand and improve on the early efforts at managing distributed teams.

References

Amason, A. (1996). Distinguishing effects of functional and dysfunctional conflict on strategic decision making: Resolving a paradox for top management teams. *Academy of Management Journal, 39*, 123–148.

Ancona, D., and Caldwell, D. (1992). Demography and design: Predictors of new product team performance. *Organization Science, 3*, 321–341.

Argote, L., Gruenfeld, D. H., and Naquin, C. (1999). Group learning in organizations. In M. Turner (ed.), *Groups at work: Advances in theory and research*. Hillsdale, NJ: Erlbaum.

Argyris, C. (1962). *Interpersonal competence and organizational effectiveness*. Homewood, IL: Dorsey Press.

Armstrong, D. J., and Cole, P. (2002). Managing distances and differences in geographically distributed work groups. In P. Hinds and S. Kiesler, *Distributed work* (167–186). Cambridge, MA: MIT Press.

Asch, S. E. (1952). *Social psychology*. Englewood Cliffs, NJ: Prentice Hall.

Bantel, K., and Jackson, S. (1989). Top management and innovations in banking: Does the composition of the top team make a difference? *Strategic Management Journal, 10*, 107–124.

Bettenhausen, K., and Murnighan, J. K. (1985). The emergence of norms in competitive decision-making groups. *Administrative Science Quarterly, 30*, 350–372.

Bhappu, A. D., Griffith, T. L., and Northcraft, G. B. (1997). Media effects and communication bias in diverse groups. *Organizational Behavior and Human Decision Processes, 70*, 199–205.

Boulding, K. (1963). *Conflict and defense*. New York: Harper and Row.

Bourgeois, L. J. (1985). Strategic goals, environmental uncertainty, and economic performance in volatile environments. *Academy of Management Journal, 28*, 548–573.

Carver, C., and Scheier, M. (1981). The self-attention-induced feedback loop and social facilitation. *Journal of Experimental Social Psychology, 17*, 545–568.

Cialdini, R. (1993). *Influence: Science and practice*. New York: HarperCollins.

Cramton, C. D. (2002). Attribution in distributed work groups. In P. Hinds and S. Kiesler, *Distributed work* (191–212). Cambridge, MA: MIT Press.

Crosier, R., and Rose, G. (1977). Cognitive conflict and goal conflict effects on task performance. *Organizational Behavior and Human Decision Processes, 19*, 378–391.

Damon, W. (1991). Problems of direction in socially shared cognition. In L. B. Resnick, J. M. Levine, and S. D. Teasley (eds.), *Perspectives on socially shared cognition* (384–397). Washington, DC: American Psychological Association.

Davenport, T. H., and Pearlson, K. (1998, Summer). Two cheers for the distributed office. *Sloan Management Review*, 51–65.

Davis, J. H. (1973). Group decision and social interaction: A theory of social decision schemes. *Psychological Review, 80*, 97–125.

Deutsch, M. (1949). An experimental study of the effects of cooperation and competition upon group process. *Human Relations, 2*, 129–152.

Edmondson, A. (1999). Psychological safety and learning behavior in work teams. *Administrative Science Quarterly*, *44*, 350–383.

Edmondson, A., Bohmer, R., and Pisano, G. (2000). Collaborating to learn: Effects of organizational and team characteristics on successful adoption of new medical technology in hospital-based surgical teams. In M. A. Neale, E. A. Mannix, and T. L. Griffith (eds.), *Research on managing groups and teams: Technology* (Vol. 3, 29–51). Stamford, CT: JAI Press.

Eisenhardt, K., and Schoonhoven, C. (1990). Organizational growth: Linking founding team, strategy, environment, and growth among U.S. semiconductor ventures. *Administrative Science Quarterly*, *35*, 504–529.

Eisenhardt, K., and Zbaracki, M. (1992). Strategic decision making. *Strategic Management Journal*, *13*, 17–37.

Festinger, L. (1954). A theory of social comparison processes. *Human Relations*, *7*, 117–140.

Galbraith, C. S. (1990). Transferring core manufacturing technologies in high technology firms. *California Management Review*, *32*(4), 56–70.

Gersick, C. (1988). Time and transition in work teams: Toward a new model of group development. *Academy of Management Journal*, *31*, 9–41.

Gordon, M. D., and Moore, S. A. (1999). Depicting the use and purpose of documents to improve information retrieval. *Information Systems Research*, *10*(1), 23–37.

Griffith, T. L., and Meader, D. (2000). *Prelude to virtual groups: Leadership roles and technology variety within investment clubs*. Working paper.

Griffith, T. L., and Neale, M. A. (in press). Information processing in traditional, hybrid, and distributed teams: From nascent knowledge to transactive memory. In R. Sutton and B. Staw (eds.), *Research in organizational behavior* (Vol. 23.) Stamford, CT: JAI Press.

Griffith, T. L., Sawyer, J. E., and Neale, M. A. (in press). Information technology as a jealous mistress: Competition for knowledge between individuals and organizations. In A. Segars, J. Sampler, and B. Zmud (eds.), *Redefining the organizational roles of information technology in the information age*. Minneapolis: University of Minnesota Press.

Gruenfeld, D. H., Mannix, E. A., Williams, K. Y., and Neale, M. A. (1996). Group composition and decision making: How member familiarity and information distribution affect process and performance. *Organizational Behavior and Human Decision Processes*, *67*, 1–15.

Guetzkow, H., and Gyr, J. (1954). An analysis of conflict in decision making groups. *Human Relations*, *7*, 367–381.

Hackman, J. R. (ed.). (1990). *Groups that work (and those that don't): Creating conditions for effective teamwork*. San Francisco: Jossey-Bass.

Hackman, R., and Oldham, G. (1980). *Work redesign*. Reading, MA: Addison-Wesley.

Hackman, R., and Walton, R. (1986). Leading groups in organizations. In P. Goodman (ed.), *Designing effective workgroups* (pp. 72–119). San Francisco: Jossey-Bass.

Hambrick, D., Cho, T., and Chen, M.-J. (1996). The influence of top management team heterogeneity on firms' competitive moves. *Administrative Science Quarterly*, *41*, 659–684.

Hardin, C., and Higgins, E. T. (1996). Shared reality: How social verification makes the subjective objective. In R. M. Sorrentino and E. T. Higgins (eds.), *Handbook of motivation and cognition* (Vol. 3, pp. 28–84). New York: Guilford Press.

Harrison, D. A., Price, K. H., and Bell, M. P. (1998). Beyond relational demography: Time and the effects of surface- and deep-level diversity on work group cohesion. *Academy of Management Journal, 41,* 96–107.

Heider, F. (1958). *The psychology of interpersonal relationships.* New York: Wiley.

Hollingshead, A. B., Fulk, J., and Monge, P. (2002). Fostering intranet knowledge sharing: An integration of transactive memory and public goods approaches. In P. Hinds and S. Kiesler, *Distributed work* (335–356). Cambridge, MA: MIT Press.

Jackson, J. (1966). A conceptual measurement model for norms and roles. *Pacific Sociological Review, 9,* 35–47.

Jackson, S., Brett, J., Sessa, V., Cooper, D., Julin, J., and Peyronnin, K. (1991). Some differences make a difference: Individual dissimilarity and group heterogeneity as correlates of recruitment, promotions, and turnover. *Journal of Applied Psychology, 76,* 675–689.

Jarvenpaa, S. L., and Leidner, D. E. (1999). Communication and trust in global virtual teams. *Organization Science, 10,* 791–815.

Jehn, K. A. (1995). A multimethod examination of the benefits and detriments of intragroup conflict. *Administrative Science Quarterly, 40,* 256–282.

Jehn, K. (1997). A qualitative analysis of conflict types and dimensions in organizational groups. *Administrative Science Quarterly, 42,* 530–557.

Jehn, K., and Mannix, E. (2001). The dynamic nature of conflict: A longitudinal study of intragroup conflict and group performance. *Academy of Management Journal, 44,* 238–251.

Jehn, K. A., Northcraft, G. B., and Neale, M. A. (1999). Why differences make a difference: A field study of diversity, conflict, and performance in workgroups. *Administrative Science Quarterly, 44,* 741–763.

Katz, D., and Kahn, R. (1978). *The social psychology of organizations* (2nd ed.). New York: Wiley.

Kelley, H. H. (1979). *Personal relationships.* Hillsdale, NJ: Erlbaum.

Levine, J., and Higgins, E. T. (in press). Shared reality and social influence in groups. In F. Butera and G. Mugny (eds.), *Social influence in social reality.* Bern, Switzerland: Hogrefe and Huber Publishers.

Levine, J. M., Resnick, L. B., and Higgins, E. T. (1993). Social foundations of cognition. *Annual Review of Psychology, 44,* 585–612.

Lewicki, R., and Litterer, J. A. (1997). *Negotiation* (3rd ed.). Homewood, IL: Irwin.

Limayem, M., Lee-Partridge, J. E., Dickson, G. W., and DeSanctis, G. (1993). Enhancing GDSS effectiveness: Automated versus human facilitation. In *Proceedings of the 26th Hawaii International Conferences on System Sciences* (95–101). Los Alamitos, CA: IEEE Computer Society Press.

Mannix, E., Thatcher, S., and Jehn, K. A. (2000). Does culture always flow downstream? Linking group consensus and organizational culture. In C. Cooper, C. Early, J. Chatman, and W. Starbuck (eds.), *Handbook of organizational culture.* New York: Wiley and Sons.

Mayer, R. C., Davis, J. H., and Schoorman, F. D. (1995). An integrative model of organizational trust. *Academy of Management Review, 20*(3), 709–734.

McGrath, J. E. (1984). *Groups: Interaction and performance.* Englewood Cliffs, NJ: Prentice Hall.

McGrath, J. E., and Hollingshead, A. B. (1994). *Groups interacting with technology: Ideas, evidence, issues, and an agenda.* Thousand Oaks, CA: Sage.

Meyerson, D., Weick, K. E., and Kramer, R. M. (1996). Swift trust and temporary groups. In R. M. Kramer and T. R. Tyler (eds.), *Trust in organizations: Frontiers of theory and research* (166–195). Thousand Oaks, CA: Sage.

Moreland, R. L., Argote, L., and Krishnan, R. (1998). Training people to work in groups. In R. S. Tindale, L. Heath, J. Edwards, E. J. Posvoc, F. B. Bryant, Y. Suarez-Balcazar, E. Henderson-King, and J. Myers (eds.), *Applications of theory and research on groups to social issues* (Vol. 4, 37–60). New York: Plenum.

Moreland, R., and Myaskovsky, L. (2000). Exploring the performance benefits of group training: Transactive memory or improved communication? *Organizational Behavior and Human Decision Processes, 82,* 117–133.

Nemeth, C. J. (1986). Differential contributions of majority and minority influence. *Psychological Review, 93,* 23–32.

O'Reilly, C., Caldwell, D., and Barnett, W. (1989). Work group demography, social integration and turnover. *Administrative Science Quarterly, 34,* 21–37.

Pelled, L. H. (1996). Demographic diversity, conflict, and work group outcomes: An intervening process theory. *Organization Science, 7,* 615–631.

Pinkley, R. (1990). Dimensions of the conflict frame: Disputant interpretations of conflict. *Journal of Applied Psychology, 75,* 117–128.

Roseman, I., Wiest, C., and Swartz, T. (1994). Phenomenology, behaviors and goals differentiate emotions. *Journal of Personality and Social Psychology, 67,* 206–221.

Rothwell, R. (1978). Some programs of technology transfer into industry: Examples from the textile machinery sector. *IEEE Transactions on Engineering Management, 25,* 15–20.

Sanna, L. J., and Shotland, R. L. (1990). Valence of anticipated evaluation and social facilitation. *Journal of Experimental Social Psychology, 26,* 82–92.

Schachter, S. (1951). Deviation, rejection and communication. *Journal of Abnormal and Social Psychology, 46,* 190–207.

Schachter, S., and Singer, J. (1962). Cognitive, social and physiological determinants of emotional state. *Psychological Review, 69,* 379–399.

Schweiger, D., and Sandberg, W. (1989). The utilization of individual capabilities in group approaches to strategic decision making. *Strategic Management Journal, 10,* 31–43.

Schwenk, C. (1990). Conflict in organizational decision making: An exploratory study of its effects in for-profit and not-for-profit organizations. *Management Science, 36,* 436–448.

Shah, P., and Jehn, K. (1993). Do friends perform better than acquaintances? The interaction of friendship, conflict and task. *Group Decision and Negotiation, 2,* 149–166.

Shea, G., and Guzzo, R. (1987). *A theory of workgroup effectiveness.* Working paper, Wharton School.

Sherif, M. (1936). *The psychology of social norms.* New York: Harper.

Simons, T., and Peterson, R. (2000). Task conflict and relationship conflict in top management teams: The pivotal role of intragroup trust. *Journal of Applied Psychology, 85,* 102–111.

Smith, K. G., Smith, K. A., Olian, J. D., Sims, H. P., O'Bannon, D. P., and Scully, J. A. (1994). Top management team demography and process: The role of social integration and communication. *Administrative Science Quarterly, 39,* 412–438.

Staw, B. M., Sandelands, L., and Dutton, J. (1981). Threat-rigidity effects in organizational performance. *Administrative Science Quarterly, 28,* 582–600.

Tanford, S., and Penrod, S. (1984). Social influence model: A formal integration of research on majority and minority influence. *Psychological Bulletin, 95,* 189–225.

Trist, E., and Murray, H. (eds.). (1993). *The socio-technical perspective.* Philadelphia: University of Pennsylvania Press.

Tsui, A. S., Egan, T. D., and O'Reilly, C. A. (1992). Being different: Relational demography and organizational attachment. *Administrative Science Quarterly, 37,* 549–579.

Tsui, A. S., and O'Reilly, C. A., III. (1989). Beyond simple demographic effects: The importance of relational demography in superior-subordinate dyads. *Academy of Management Journal, 32,* 402–423.

Tuckman, B. W. (1965). Developmental sequences in small groups. *Psychological Bulletin, 63,* 384–399.

Tyre, M. J., and Orlikowski, W. J. (1994). Windows of opportunity: Temporal patterns of technological adaptation in organizations. *Organization Science, 5,* 98–118.

Verkuyten, M., de Jong, W., and Masson, C. N. (1993). Job satisfaction among ethnic minorities in the Netherlands. *Applied Psychology: An International Review, 42,* 171–189.

Wageman, R. (1997, Summer). Critical success factors for creating superb self-managing teams. *Organizational Dynamics, 26,* 49–60.

Wall, V., and Nolan, L. (1986). Perceptions of inequity, satisfaction, and conflict in task oriented groups. *Human Relations, 39,* 1033–1052.

Watson, W. E., Kumar, K., and Michaelsen, L. K. (1993). Cultural diversity's impact on interaction process and performance: Comparing homogeneous and diverse task groups. *Academy of Management Journal, 36,* 590–602.

Wegner, D. M. (1987). Transactive memory: A contemporary analysis of the group mind. In B. Mullen and G. R. Goethals (eds.), *Theories of group behavior* (185–208). New York: Springer-Verlag.

Wegner, D. M. (1995). A computer network model of human transactive memory. *Social Cognition, 13,* 319–339.

Weisband, S. (2002). Maintaining awareness in distributed team collaboration: Implications for leadership and performance. In P. Hinds and S. Kiesler, *Distributed work* (311–334). Cambridge, MA: MIT Press.

Wittenbaum, G. M., and Stasser, G. (1996). Management of information in small groups. In J. L. Nye and A. M. Brower (eds.), *What's social about social cognition? Social cognition research in small groups* (3–28). Thousand Oaks, CA: Sage.

Wittenbaum, G. M., Vaughan, S. I., and Stasser, G. (1998). Coordination in task-performing groups. In R. S. Tindale, L. Heath, J. Edwards, E. J. Posvoc, F. B. Bryant, Y. Suarez-Balcazar, E. Henderson-King, and J. Myers (eds.), *Applications of theory and research on groups to social issues* (Vol. 4, 177–204). New York: Plenum.

Zajonc, R. B. (1965). Social facilitation. *Science, 149,* 269–274.

Zand, D. E. (1972). Trust and managerial problem solving. *Administrative Science Quarterly, 17,* 229–239.

Zenger, T. R., and Lawrence, B. S. (1989). Organizational demography: The differential effects of age and tenure distributions on technical communication. *Academy of Management Journal, 32,* 353–376.

10

Time Effects in Computer-Mediated Groups: Past, Present, and Future[1]

Joseph B. Walther

Technology affects distributed groups in an interplay with characteristics of time. A review of empirical research on temporal factors in on-line interaction focuses on (1) teams' development over time and their adaptation to media, (2) the way information rates promote impersonal or interpersonal reactions, the timing of electronic communication, and the use of real-time message systems to manage interaction, and (3) members' anticipated group longevity, which shapes members' interactions and the character of their associations.

Contemporary distributed work teams rely to an increasing extent on e-mail and computer conferencing to accomplish their work (Weisenfeld, Raghuram, and Garud 1999). Because of their vital role in such groups, the impact of electronic communication media on the ways people work and relate to one another is critically important. Yet these media do not have simple effects. Distributed teams typically work on extended tasks over some period of time, and temporal variations affect the way such relationships work in a variety of potent ways. This chapter focuses on the interactions of temporal factors and media in distributed interaction.

Williams, Rice, and Rogers (1988) recommended that "researchers studying new media use theories, designs, and methods that take change over time into account in order to improve the meaningfulness of their results and to capture the social dynamics of the new media" (68; see also Hesse, Werner, and Altman 1988; McGrath 1991, 1992, 1993), but few have specified theoretically what the effects of time might be when groups use communication technology (Menneke, Hoffer, and Wynne 1992), and little evidence about temporal dynamics in electronic groups exists (Chidambaram 1996; Chidambaram, Bostrom, and Wynne 1991; Maznevski and Chudoba 2000; Rice 1982). Nevertheless, some studies have empirically examined temporal issues and electronic communication, and a review of these works may provide researchers and practitioners some guidance as they continue to ponder time's influence in electronic communication.

This chapter reviews research on several dimensions of temporal forces. The *past dimension* includes the adaptation of electronic partners to media and each other as they develop a shared history. The *present dimension* includes the impact of the rate of communication and how technology retards information flow, a phenomenon that comes into play most clearly as groups face time limits and deadlines. It includes the timing with which messages are sent and to which they are replied, which stimulate interpersonal reactions among distributed partners. It also includes the ways that new messaging technologies are being used to maintain connectedness among distributed workers. The *future dimension* includes the expectation of whether an electronic group is enduring and not a short-term affiliation, and the effects of that expectation on the ways members envision and treat one another. These dynamics help shape whether electronic groups find their working together onerous, productive, or enjoyable. Advantages and disadvantages to electronic groups due to variations of temporal factors are summarized in table 10.1.

Effects of a Past: Group Tenure and Development

The first studies of e-mail and computer conferencing focused on the constraints on social context cues but generally ignored the remarkable ways people can adjust over time to constraints on their communication. Outcomes associated with the lack of nonverbal cues included findings that mediated groups reach decisions less quickly than unmediated groups, that on-line groups exhibit equal status and participation, and that communication on-line is relatively impersonal and hostile (see for review Garton and Wellman 1995, Walther 1996).

While such findings attribute the group behaviors to the restrictions of the media, temporal factors within these studies may hide an interaction effect, which, when examined, offers a different view of the nature of on-line interaction. By and large, these studies examined group interaction within restricted times and time periods (typically twenty minutes). Groups need time to adjust to communication technology and to coalesce as a group, and depending on the task, they often do quite well if they are given time. Differences between face-to-face and electronic groups are reduced over time as members interact. In studies in which time periods were unrestricted, different outcomes often accrued. For instance, regarding participation equality, Weisband's (1994; Weisband, Schneider, and Connolly 1995) studies in

Table 10.1
Temporal effects in computer-mediated groups

	Past	Present		Future
	Effects of history/ adapatation	Effects of time pressure	Effects of time cues	Effects of real-time messaging	Effects of anticipation of future interaction
Advantages	• Positive interpersonal impressions accrue more rapidly • Message content shifts to social • Improves some decision making	• More task-oriented content • Greater participation equality • Greater attenuation of status differences	• Chronemic cues signal affection, status, urgency	• Affords management of other interactions • Provides persistent connection to partner	• Improves interpersonal relations • Overcomes media effects or photos
Disadvantages	• Status differences increase • Participation inequality increases	• Suppression of affective content • Rational discourse gives way to hurried consensus	• Different time zones may ambiguate chronemics	• Often unattended	• Does not apply to ad hoc or temporary work groups

which participants had no time restrictions showed that despite anonymous on-line interaction, preexisting status differences among group members were associated with disproportionate contributions to group discussions, like those seen in face-to-face interaction. Additionally, field investigations using cross-sectional or longitudinal designs showed more friendly interpersonal relations among communicators than in brief studies (Rice and Love 1987; see for review Walther, Anderson, and Park 1994). In response to these results, researchers began to consider more formally whether timing may have important developmental effects on groups using technology in different ways than nonmediated groups experience.

Technology, Time, and Tasks

McGrath and colleagues addressed various aspects of time, technology, tasks, and groups in a series of essays and empirical studies. Their time, interaction, and performance (TIP) theory focuses on the temporal dynamics of groups and the intellectual and coordination requirements of different tasks, although it does not specify any media effects (McGrath 1991). Their task-media fit hypothesis extends information richness theory (Daft and Lengel 1986), which presents a set of contingencies with which to make effective media choices based on the ambiguity or equivocality of the message one is sending. For very simple messages, a lean medium such as e-mail is not only sufficiently effective but most efficient because extraneous information is eliminated (see Daft and Lengel 1986). For more complex information tasks, richer (i.e., multichannel, interactive) communications are recommended.

McGrath and colleagues (Hollingshead, McGrath, and O'Connor 1993) studied computer conferencing, tasks, and time in the JEMCO studies (the name of the fictitious company in which their student-participants pretended to work). Small groups worked on a succession of thirteen different tasks (four different task types) for two hours each over a period of thirteen weeks. Half the groups used synchronous computer conferencing, and half operated face-to-face (with one exposure to the opposite mode along the way). These were not distributed teams; all partners worked in the same physical space (raising questions about generalizability to bonafide distributed groups), but they did work exclusively on-line. Results were that unmediated groups produced superior results on the initial three tasks, but after that point, mediated and unmediated groups' decision recommendations were of equally high quality. The researchers concluded that over time, users accumulate experience and adapt to computer conferencing. While a "practice-makes-perfect" finding may not be very compelling, the notion that computer-based groups need to acclimate to the medium is valuable as a potential explanation of why mediated communication differed from face-to-face communication in previous nonlongitudinal research. There may have been a decrement in performance when using technology for certain types of tasks, but those results were not as clear.

In JEMCO 2, Lebie, Rhoades, and McGrath (1995/1996) examined the amount and kinds of statements made in synchronous computer-based and face-to-face groups. They found that computer-based groups made fewer statements across tasks over time and that the nature of their comments differed from face-to-face groups in early stages, but not in successive ones. At first, electronic groups devoted a significantly greater proportion of their comments to the use and mechanics of the technology; face-to-face groups, unsurprisingly, did not. This illustrates the accommodations that electronic groups must make that can offset the amount of time they have to address more substantive tasks or interpersonal issues—at least when the amount of time they have is fixed and limited, as was the case in this and much other research. Early prognoses about the promise of computer-mediated communication suggested that it would help prevent groups from being distracted by interpersonal and nontask issues. The JEMCO 2 findings suggest that such groups are distracted instead by the medium itself and that this problem remedies itself as users grow accustomed to it.

When difficulties adjusting to system requirements occur in distributed teams, serious tensions and interlocation hostilities often arise, but they can be remediated. Jonas, Boos, and Walther (2000) experimented with international electronic teams comprising students taking similar courses at universities in the northeastern United States and in Germany. To see if the effects of inexperience could be managed without disrupting distributed teams, two rounds of projects were designed. For the first round of group projects, writing collaborative reports, students were placed in teams comprising only local partners whom they saw almost daily. They were admonished to use only a "virtual seminar" (Web-based bulletin board) for all of their collaborative interaction. It was expected that by using the Web-based system exclusively yet with partners whom they knew, they would come to recognize the adjustments that are needed in order to accommodate asynchronous interaction, response lags, the time required to type rather than talk, and other facets of communication that electronic communication entails, before confronting distributed teams. Whatever frustrations the members encountered would not be attributed to out-group foreign partners, but rather to their own difficulties adapting to electronic meetings. Indeed, anecdotal reports by participants indicated that they had difficulty adapting to the timing and pacing that the system required and would approach things differently were they to try again.

Participants then joined international electronic groups for the second round of projects. Their reports were notably more positive after the distributed round. Many participants reported enjoying the work—some reporting they had never had so much fun in a group project—and all seemed to adjust to the system and the time constraints effectively. These results suggest that insufficient time and inexperience in electronic groups affect more than mere performance; experience and competence with computer-based systems may also be at the core of relational dynamics that also accrue over time in electronic groups. Poor performance and frustration in initial endeavors can be interpreted through a "fundamental attribution error" (Ross 1977; see also Cramton, chapter 8, and Mark, chapter 11, both this volume). That is, rather than blame events on situational causes or on themselves, electronic team members blame distant partners' personalities for their communication and performance problems in their early collaborative work, interpretations from which it is difficult to recover. However, by interacting with known, local partners on-line, they refocus the attributions of difficulty to the self and the system rather than an anonymous out-group and avert the kinds of problems often seen in distributed teams, so that positive distributed relations may accrue more quickly.

Tasks and Time

Despite McGrath and colleagues' deliberate focus on tasks, technology, and time, research has not clearly answered questions about the optimal match of different kinds of tasks to different media. In one sense, this is unsurprising: the information richness theory on which McGrath's research was based is not well supported in studies with unlimited interaction times. Numerous surveys show that managers evaluate different communication media in accordance with prescriptive matches between media richness and task equivocality (Rice 1993), but these prescriptions consistently fail to predict actual media use (Fulk, Schmitz, and Steinfield 1992), communication effectiveness (Markus 1994), or task quality and communication satisfaction (Dennis and Kinney 1998). There appears to be an attitude-behavior disjuncture when it comes to selecting communication media. Moreover, since Hollingshead and associates (1993) did not include a complete rotation of tasks through time, causes and effects are not clear. Some task types were presented both early and late in the research design, some were not, and some were presented more frequently than others. The design was not fully crossed or counterbalanced in a manner necessary to identify the true effects of the independent variables of time and task type. Performance improvements may be due to time × medium effects, or task × time × medium effects, or a task sequence × medium effect. These are not trivial differences. Some combinations would override a main effect for time, others override a task main effect, and some do both. So while the temporally oriented findings in McGrath and colleagues' research seem robust, the task effects are not as clear.

More research is needed with respect to the kinds of tasks that electronic groups undertake and the timing decisions they make. In a study of face-to-face groups, Gersick (1988, 1989) observed three phases of group work: a general co-orientation phase, followed by an energizing midpoint at which serious commitments were made, and finally an active production phase. Gersick's observations suggest that group activity follows an innate and uniform progression across time, but electronic groups may or may not be able to manage this progression in the same way. For instance, in a study of groups working face-to-face and using a group decision support system (GDSS), Poole and Holmes (1995) studied the decision paths undertaken by these groups: the ordering of different activity sequences, the repetition of activity types, and the simplicity versus complexity of these sequences. They showed that the communication conditions had a significant effect on the decision paths that groups adopted. GDSS groups' paths differed more from a standard, unitary sequence than did face-to-face groups with agendas. The impacts of these variations within long-term working groups and on interpersonal or decisional outcomes are not entirely clear, but they deserve further exploration.

Research on at least one electronic group suggests that a distributed team using mediated communication orients to events rather than to calendars or clocks. Orlikowski and Yates (1998) found that activity in the distributed group was as likely to respond to events—the occasional passing of document drafts—as it was to predetermined or ad hoc deadlines. How virtual groups orient to critical incidents rather than linear time lines seems to hold promise for additional study.

In sum, it appears that electronic groups require some period of time to adjust to the mediated environment. Forgoing this adaptation is likely to result not only in poor performance but in hostilities directed toward others. Steps toward the remediation of these problems can be taken through adaptation time outside of critical teamwork. Whether some tasks are better suited for some media is not yet clear. Finally, with respect to how distributed groups time themselves and their work is not yet known, but what seems to be emerging is a sense that expectations for electronic groups to follow the same timing and sequences that face-to-face groups show are misplaced.

Present: Rates, Chronemics, and Connectivity

In e-mail and conferencing, people are writing, which takes longer than speaking. Partners must give and adjust to task and social feedback in words and perhaps explain themselves and their context more fully than normally. These requirements imply that many tasks will take longer too, and groups might be frustrated by a lack of time—ironic, since computer-based communication technologies are supposed to be fast. These effects of time and technology on groups are moderated by organizational or environmental forces, especially how much time the groups are given to finish their work and the kinds of tasks they are doing. Time limits have a dramatic impact on the interpersonal nature of on-line work. Additionally, the dispersion of technology into homes and offices, its portability, and its increasing ubiquitousness mean that colleagues can send messages to each other around the clock and across time zones. The scheduling of messages between colleagues conveys interpersonal signals, which constitute another form of temporal effects. Finally, real-time messaging, or even its persistent potential, creates connectedness between electronic partners. These aspects of the pace of life in on-line partnerships describe how communicators using technology shape the present.

Time Limits, Deadlines, and Information Rates

Some distributed work may be ongoing and deliberative, while other projects must be turned around quickly. Some tasks, such as a group's development of a document or program, allow for a great deal of independent work and some coordination; other tasks, such as decision making, require coordinated sharing and evaluation of ideas. In either case, the amount of time collaborators have to work with each other may have an impact that differs somewhat from the impact of time in traditional, nonmediated groups. Research examining decision making and collaborative writing suggests that the amount of time collaborators have interacts with the nature of the medium they use, due to differences in the communication rates afforded by technology. Lebie and associates (1995/1996) allowed fifteen minutes for face-to-face groups and twenty minutes for mediated groups, which "might need additional time, at least at first, to overcome the relative slowness of communicating by typing versus talking" (134). Yet even a three-to-four differential may not be enough. Computer communication takes longer than speech, and time restrictions seem to have extraordinary impacts on it.

A few experimental studies of computer-mediated and face-to-face groups provided participants in both conditions as much time as they needed to complete their tasks. Among these, Dubrovsky, Kiesler, and Sethna (1991) and Weisband (1992) found that mediated groups took four to five times as long as face-to-face groups to complete the same tasks, yet the average number of messages exchanged did not differ between these groups. Thus, it appears that mediated and face-to-face groups operate at different rates.

Reid and colleagues examined the impact of computer-based versus face-to-face communication rates, establishing that equal time intervals create different effects due to time scarcity communicating by computer. In an experiment comparing computer-mediated and face-to-face responses to alternative time frames, Reid, Ball, Morley, and Evans (1997) found that in the mediated groups, rational discourse gave way to pressure to reach hurried consensus when time was restricted. Reid, Malinek, Stott, and Evans (1996) found that messages conveying affective content were suppressed in computer-mediated groups when time was scarce. In experiments without time limits, the equalized participation seen in short-term computer-based studies seemed to dissipate (Straus and McGrath 1994, Weisband 1994, Weisband et al. 1995). In a time-related field study, Steinfield (1986) found that computer-based communication became more task oriented as users neared project deadlines; otherwise, it was more socially oriented. These efforts reinforce the notion that the time an electronic group has to work exerts a significant effect on group processes and that the difficulty in computer-based systems of conveying task and social messages simultaneously is accentuated when time is, or becomes, short.

Rate differences may affect groups' instrumental effectiveness and participation as well as their socioemotional processes. Many studies on the progression of small groups through decision-making stages typically describe the first exchanges in work group development as heavily task oriented, followed by conflict and then solidarity (see for review Fisher 1974, Menneke et al. 1992). If computer-mediated groups work more slowly than face-to-face groups, then previous findings that mediated groups reach decisions less often or are more task oriented (in time-limited experiments) may be the result of cutting off their interaction before they can get through their different task and socioemotional phases, including conflict and getting to know one another.

Social Information Processing: Rate and Relating Online

The social information processing (SIP) perspective (Walther 1992a) focuses explicitly on media communication rates in the development of interpersonal relations on-line. Although there is less social information per message in computer-mediated communication because of the absence of nonverbal cues, users adapt to linguistic codes for task and social information available in written messages. However, this social and task information travels through one code system—a system in which even verbal messages are processed more slowly than they are in speech. It follows that the expression and deciphering of these cues are retarded in computer-mediated communication relative to face-to-face communication. Social information effects therefore are expected to be slower in time and to develop in proportion to the accumulation of message exchanges.

Several studies emanating from this perspective show a significant effect of time on the development of the interpersonal dynamics of mediated groups, and some extend the theory as well. Walther and associates' (1994) meta-analysis examined whether time-limited experiments differed from time-unlimited studies in relational communications of mediated groups. Ratios of socially oriented to task-oriented communications were computed and standardized across previously published reports and compared on the basis of time limits, which proved a statistically significant effect. Studies in which time periods were not restricted showed more positive socioemotional communication on average than did those studies where electronic groups were cut off.

In a direct examination of SIP, Walther (1993) examined impression development among decision-making groups meeting using computer conferencing, and their face-to-face counterparts, over six weeks. SIP predicted that face-to-face communicators would develop impressions quickly, whereas computer-based communicators' interpersonal impressions would be initially less developed than those in face-to-face, would develop more gradually, and would finally equal those in face-to-face groups. Results generally confirmed these hypotheses, with mediated impressions developing in a positive linear trend over time. Computer-mediated and face-to-face scores never matched, but at the end they were no longer statistically different either.

Walther and Burgoon (1992) tested relational development in face-to-face and computer-mediated groups over time. Sixteen face-to-face and computer-mediated groups addressed three policy deliberation tasks in three unlimited meetings each (one and a half months of asynchronous computer conferencing). Results of repeated measurement of relational communication revealed very few initial differences between conditions, and the relational communication (affection, similarity, trust, and informality) in both conditions increased over time to similarly affiliative levels. These results added partial support to the SIP perspective, but the lack of differences between computer- and face-to-face teams after only the first meetings was unexpected.

Chidambaram and associates (1991) examined interpersonal effects in GDSS and face-to-face groups over four meetings. Groups worked on a series of tasks and used a variety of GDSS support tools. Over time, the computer-supported groups became more cohesive and handled conflict better. This research was not designed to test SIP theory, but the results are nevertheless consistent. Another study, drawing explicitly on SIP, showed that groups did develop in their social relations, over repeated episodes, in ways predicted by SIP (Chidambaran 1996).

Impressions were also subject to participation rates in other studies. Weisband and associates (1995) studied groups in which real-world status differences were either correctly or incorrectly conveyed to participants through experimental manipulation. The amount of contribution each participant made to the group's discussions corresponded with that person's actual status. When the experimentally assigned status label was accurate, these participants were rated as more influential and positive by their partners. When the higher-contributing members were thought by others to have lower status, however, they were evaluated negatively. These findings depart from SIP in the sense that a context × participation effect, rather than the content of communication effect, prevailed. However, they do show that interpersonal judgments accrue rather simply in computer-mediated communication based on cues that traverse the medium.

Chronemics

The choice of when to communicate is quite different in e-mail or computer conferencing than in face-to-face, and there are social consequences of these temporal choices. In studying how timing affects interpersonal judgments, Walther and Tidwell (1995) drew on the literature of chronemics—the nonverbal cue system regarding "how we perceive, structure, and react to time and . . . the messages we interpret from such usage" (Burgoon and Saine 1978, 99). The researchers varied pairs of organizational e-mail message transcripts so that by their time stamps, they appeared to be sent during business hours or after hours. Message pairs also varied in terms of whether the response was sent immediately or after a day's delay. Such information is commonly perceived by e-mail users and helps them track the flow of electronic information (Rice 1990). One set of messages depicted a socially oriented exchange (gossip and plans to visit), and the other pair was task oriented (a request for information).

Walther and Tidwell drew from the the chronemics literature and from Lea and Spears's (1992) social identification/deindividuation (SIDE) theory. They predicted different reactions to these messages depending on the time day or night the first message appeared to have been and how long a delay occurred before their reply took place. Results partially supported predictions. If a task-oriented message was sent at night, it was perceived to be more dominant, and to signal less relational equality, than if the same message was sent during the day. The amount of affection ascribed to a message resulted from a complex interaction including the time a message was sent, its content, and the promptness to which it was replied. Messages were rated most affectionate when one replied quickly to a task message sent in the day, but least affectionate when giving a prompt response to a nighttime task message (respondents appeared slavish perhaps). A slow reply to either day or night task messages signaled moderate affection. As for social messages, more affection was perceived in a slower reply to a daytime message than a fast reply, but a fast reply at night showed more affection than a slow one. Perhaps we prefer people to take their time to get back to us socially during a busy day, but after hours, we are flattered if they drop what they are doing to reply as fast as they can. Ironically, in the chronemics literature, a slow reply is also associated with more rather than less intimate relations (think of a first date versus a long-married couple, and which must keep a fast conversational pace). And as we will see, sporadic message exchanges seem perfectly acceptable during business hours when it comes to other new media. "One of the advantages of e-mail and many forms of computer conferencing is the ability to communicate asynchronously, at one's discretion and convenience," Walther and Tidwell (1995) concluded. "Accompanying this choice, however, are relational implications affected by normative standards regarding the time of day in which certain topics are discussed, and regarding the latencies communicators employ in responding to others" (371).

This research demonstrates that communicators using asynchronous text-based communication do not have all nonverbal cues filtered out: chronemic time cues are potent. It also shows that communicators' choices about how to manage the present—when to transmit and when to reply—affect social responses. One implication of this research is that in distributed work with distributed partners, differences in time zones make time management in communication—anticipating lead time, conveying urgency, and spending time maintaining social ties—at once necessary and difficult. Johanson and O'Hara-Devereaux (1994) suggest that e-mail should be used across time zones primarily to establish a time for telephone calls and videoconferences, but it is far more likely that distributed workers will rely on e-mail to do substantive work. The way that collaborators manage or fail to manage time differences on such projects will have significant impact on their work and relationships.

Instant Messaging, Polychronics, and Persistence

The relatively new technology of instant messaging (IM) brings a new temporal element into computer-mediated communication. In IM, the user creates a dyadic chat window with another (as opposed to virtual group chat environments, which have also been used in organizational settings; Churchill and Bly 1999). Recent research by Nardi, Whittaker, and Bradner (2000) describes how distributed employees used IM to exchange quick questions, facts, and other kinds of content. Users perceived IM to be less intrusive than a phone call but more likely to garner a fast reply than e-mail. Employees also initiated communications about the timing of future communications—asking if someone would be free for a phone call or a visit or signaling unavailability via automatic "away" messages. These messages essentially negotiated the chronemics of interaction.

Another chronemic dimension of IM is its frequent polychronic use. Polychronic use of time is the conduct of several tasks or communications simultaneously (as opposed to monochronic, that is, one thing at a time; Hall 1983; for a review see Ballard and Seibold 2000). We violate convention to talk on the phone with one person while having a face-to-face with another, but some users dash off IM during phone calls, allowing two unseen communications to take place at once—one using fingers and one using voice. The most extraordinary aspect of IM, according to Nardi and associates (2000), is its use to create a persistent connection to a partner. It is common for people to establish dyadic IM connections that stay open on their computer displays for hours, even if they send messages sporadically. By keeping this connection open, Nardi and associates suggest, people create a virtual common space in which conversations can be advanced at any time. Are intermittent (rather than quick) responses associated with greater familiarity and closer working relations, as is the case with e-mail? More research on this emerging technology will be interesting to see.

The adaptation of users to text-based media holds imminent danger and imminent reward, depending on how media are employed with respect to duration and scheduling. On-line groups, communicating more slowly through words, require greater periods in which to develop interpersonal relations and successful tasks, while constraints on their time lead to adverse consequences. Within this temporal frame, the timing of messages affects relations and impressions, a factor to which colleagues distributed not only across space but in different time zones (or time preferences) should be observant. For those who can afford real-time interaction, new messaging systems add new ways of coordinating communication and new levels of presence among electronic partners.

Future: Anticipated Group Longevity and Interpersonal Perceptions

Motivation to affiliate may play a role in how well groups adjust to technological constraints and opportunities in communication. One source of this motivation is the anticipation of future interaction (Walther 1992b). When members of groups know they will be communicating with, and interdependent on, their partners over time, they experience what Bouas and Arrow (1995/1996, 157) call "the shadow of the future." Anticipated future interaction increases a number of interpersonal behaviors and feelings, including the amount of personal information exchanged, self-disclosure, feelings of similarity, positive and friendly self-presentations, and cooperation in negotiations (for a review, see Kellermann and Reynolds 1990). Several studies have shown that "the shadow of the future" has similar effects in computer-mediated interaction, sometimes to a surprising degree.

In a study on anticipated future interaction in electronic groups, Walther (1994) formed groups of three who met face-to-face through an asynchronous computer conferencing system or synchronous conferencing. Half of the groups were led to expect that they would work on three tasks with the same partners over eight weeks; the other half were told they would work with different partners each time. The manipulation of long-term versus short-term partnerships had a larger impact on the anticipated future interaction reported by computer-mediated than among face-to-face partners. Further, once the variation attributable to perceived anticipation of future interaction was controlled, there was no difference between relational communication in computer-mediated and face-to-face groups. These findings recall those of Hiltz, Turoff, and Johnson (1989), who found no differences in flaming, or negative affective interaction, in anonymous and nonanonymous electronic exchanges of corporate employees. These researchers concluded that in professional settings or communities "when the participants ... have ongoing expectations of common group identity and shared activities to accomplish, the mode of communication does not necessarily produce high levels of disinhibited behavior" (225).

In some studies, researchers have observed that electronic exchanges were more social than face-to-face exchanges. In a study of GDSS versus face-to-face interaction of groups with a history and expected future interaction, McLeod and Liker (1992) found the electronic groups were significantly more socially oriented than nonelectronic groups. In a field experiment, Walther (1997) examined the extent to which anticipated future interaction, coupled with history and a salient group identity, would affect interpersonal judgments. Student groups were formed combining members from universities in two different countries to work on two projects over several weeks. Groups expected either to work together across the two projects—and did so—or to work together on only one project. These manipulations were crossed with instructions inducing a group identity for some groups, while other groups were asked to look for intermember differences. It was expected that a strong group identity would exaggerate the effects of long-term or short-term expectations, making them either more interpersonally positive or more impersonal and task oriented, respectively, and that individually oriented groups would be immune to these temporal frames. A significant interaction effect obtained as predicted. Long-term, high-group-identity teams experienced greater affection, enjoyed interacting with each other more, worked harder, and even rated their electronic partners as more physically attractive (even though they never saw the partners) than their short-term, high-group-identity counterparts. In contrast, teams that were looking for individual differences had average rather than extreme interpersonal ratings.

This study offers the first deliberate investigation of what Walther (1996) calls the "hyperpersonal communication" effect. When electronic partners experience commonality, anticipate longer-term associations, and are able to conduct them, they idealize their partners, present themselves to one another through text in selectively positive and intimate ways, and reciprocate these exaggerated impressions. Communication becomes more intimate and positive than even accrues in parallel face-to-face settings.

A follow-up study explored whether the effects of anticipated future interaction in electronic communication might be strictly cognitive and perceptual or lead to differential communication behaviors (Tidwell and Walther 2000). Anticipation might affect partner perceptions, whether or not they really act differently in short-term or long-term groups. Alternatively, the "shadow of the future" might prompt real communication differences. Tidwell and Walther had dyads communicate either face-to-face or using e-mail, with explicit instructions that there would be a future meeting or no future meeting. E-mail partners who anticipated a longer relationship exchanged more frequent and more intimate self-disclosures and asked more personal questions of their partners than face-to-face partners did. Moreover, there was a significant difference in their judgments about such behavior depending on the medium used. The more face-to-face partners stayed away from personal questions and disclosures, the more effective they were perceived to be. In e-mail, however, the more frequent the personal questions, the more conversationally effective partners rated each other.

Hyperpersonal communication effects can blossom as time goes on. Walther, Slovacek, and Tidwell (2001) assessed the effects of a long-term versus short-term computer-mediated association, crossed with the effects of seeing photos of one's group partners. In this study, international student teams worked on class projects. Half had been working on projects together all term, and the other half had never worked together and would not do so after a single group decision task. Half of the long-term groups and half of the short-term groups were shown photos of each other in World Wide Web pages prior to their discussion. Significant interaction effects showed that for zero-history groups, a photo improved affection and social attractiveness, helping to reduce uncertainty more quickly than text-based conferencing alone would allow. However, for long-term computer-mediated groups whose partners had gotten to know each other under conditions facilitating hyperpersonal relationships, the photos were a disappointment, reducing affection and social attraction among the long-term groups who saw each other on-line. The researchers concluded that when time is short, a picture can help give a head start to normal interaction, but when electronic groups are given the time and opportunity, they are better off getting to know each other slowly, selectively, and, ultimately, more positively.

In sum, the results of these studies provide further indications that technology does not have direct effects on communication. Rather, media act as a moderator, accentuating the effects of anticipation of future interaction. This process portends greatly for the nature of groups' interaction, affecting the microbehaviors of intimacy and acquaintanceship formation and higher-level judgments of affection, attraction, and work production. Long-term groups, or groups that believe they will exist long term, seem to be more effective and manage to adapt to time and one another remarkably well, just as short-term groups without richer media seem to have remarkably poor experiences.

Conclusion and "Future" Directions

There is little theory and comparatively few deliberate studies of the effects of temporal dimensions on computer-mediated communication. Yet temporal effects are crucial. Some studies show that temporal effects can outweigh media effects on decision quality when groups have a chance to develop common experiences. The management of the present through rate and time limited interactions has significant effects on the regulation of task versus social messages in electronic communication. Tests of the SIP perspective on relationship development provide some answers and raise new questions about the effects of time and media on groups' interpersonal communication. Communicators' judicious consideration of chronemic behaviors may enhance their interpersonal impressions, and the anticipation of a common future also leads to more personal types of interactions using mediated systems.

The practical implications of the literature as a whole suggest an ironic picture of the effectiveness of electronic meetings. Despite their transmission speed, computer-based systems seem to operate most effectively for long-term associations. Short-term or ad hoc groups, especially those with a narrow time frame and limited opportunity to exchange messages, may find the media difficult for managing relations and reaching optimal conclusions. Although many aspects of business projects may be handled through brief contacts and ad hoc committees (Galagher and Kraut 1990) and computer tools such as distribution lists are clearly very useful for casting a wide net for quick information (Constant, Sproull, and Kiesler 1996), the potential of electronic support for complex projects and decision making and for satisfying relational outcomes appears to require longer-term, deliberative projects than faster ones. This observation is based on the following principles, which we can draw from the empirical literature on time and media. When time is plentiful, people adapt to their systems and each other, reach decisions and finish tasks, build impressions, and manage positive interpersonal relations. As they do, they may also enact and discover status differences and participate unequally. When time is constrained, people are more harsh, assertive and less friendly, and they are less likely to come to agreements. At the same time, there is greater participation equality and greater attenuation of status differences. The timing of messages—sending and responding to e-mail—constitutes symbolic cues that interact with message content in the shaping of status and affection attributions. When real-time messaging is available, it can be used to time substantive interaction, as well as to provide a virtual space for ongoing contact among partners.

When electronic partners anticipate future interaction, people change their interpersonal communication strategies, manage positive interpersonal relations to an extent that media effects disappear, and in some cases, surpass that of unmediated groups. The research on electronic groups has come a long way since early studies looking for the true nature of computer-based interaction. Clearly, the effects depend to a large extent on temporal factors.

A concern should be noted about the level of theorizing and the kinds of predictions that a developmental approach implies. In most work dealing with time and media, the passage of time has been said to prompt various effects—for example, "group member behaviors and activities change as the group develops over time" (Menneke et al. 1992, 544). In this and other developmental work, groups are said to evolve over time. This places the entire theoretical explanation at the foot of time's mere passage and does not explain variations and the mechanisms for adaptation. For example, the propositions of the TIP model do not specify temporal predictions. In the SIP research, outcome-level measures do not provide direct evidence that the developmental processes specified by the model have in fact occurred. Lebie and associates' work (1995/1996) is a valuable exception to the rule, demonstrating that electronic groups' conversational topics shift from mechanics toward tasks and relations as they gain experience with the medium. The anticipated-future-interaction and chronemics research, which specifies alternatively better or less favorable reactions to temporal variables, and the recent work on disclosure and personal questions in mediated interaction also provide interesting contrasts to strictly developmental views. Future research must attend to and assess other mechanisms that may accompany the interactions of media, time, and groups and the behavioral correlates of these interactions.

Finally, research will need to assess the extent to which our theories and findings may be subject to another kind of temporal phenomenon: their historical embeddedness. No one needs a reminder that communication technology has changed a great deal and should continue to do so and that it is pervading professional and public sectors at incredible rates. The time that collaborators have and the rates at which they communicate become marvelously complicated as the number of messages in the in box grows from a few a day to several an hour, from a variety of sources in a myriad of relationships. On-line chat, once arcane and recreational, is now so pervasive on wired college campuses that hardly a moment goes by that one is not paged by someone wanting to discuss something—from details about a group project due that day, to how tedious the lecture has become at the front of the same location where the message emanates. As Nardi and associates (2000) show, some distributed workers are multitasking in ways we are just starting to apprehend, dividing their attention among messages that are coming more quickly, which take just as long to compose and to which to reply.

Although our current theories may be sufficiently abstract and flexible to maintain some relevance in the light of changes in technology and organizational developments, it is hard to predict how workers will achieve equilibrium in their management of distributed projects and relationships. New technology may allow us to detect interactions of time, technology, and groups that have not been apparent. New technologies may allow new insights on our technological management of time and time's management of our responses to one another through technology.

Note

I thank Sara Kiesler, Pamela Hinds, Steve Whittaker, John Walsh, and Ronald Rice for their helpful comments during the development of this chapter.

References

Ballard, D. I., and Seibold, D. R. (2000). Time orientation and temporal variation across work groups: Implications for group and organizational communication. *Western Journal of Communication, 64*, 218–242.

Bouas, K. S., and Arrow, H. (1995/1996). The development of group identity in computer and face-to-face groups with membership change. *Computer Supported Cooperative Work, 4*, 153–178.

Burgoon, J. K., and Saine, T. (1978). *The unspoken dialogue: An introduction to nonverbal communication*. Boston, MA: Houghton Mifflin.

Chidambaram, L. (1996). Relational development in computer-supported groups. *MIS Quarterly, 20*, 143–163.

Chidambaram, L., Bostrom, R. P., and Wynne, B. E. (1991). The impact of GDSS on group development. *Journal of Management Information Systems, 7*, 3–25.

Churchill, E. F., and Bly, S. (1999, February). Virtual environments at work: Ongoing use of MUDs in the workplace. In *Proceedings of the International Joint Conference on Work Activities Coordination and Collaboration* (99–108). New York, NY: ACM Press.

Constant, D., Sproull, L., and Kiesler, S. (1996). The kindness of strangers: The usefulness of electronic weak ties for technical advice. *Organization Science, 7,* 119–136.

Cramton, C. D. (2002). Attribution in distributed work groups. In P. Hinds and S. Kiesler (eds.), *Distributed work* (191–212). Cambridge, MA: MIT Press.

Daft, R. L., and Lengel, R. H. (1986). Organizational information requirements, media richness, and structural determinants. *Management Science, 32,* 554–571.

Dennis, A. R., and Kinney, S. T. (1998). Testing media richness theory in the new media: The effects of cues, feedback, and task equivocality. *Information Systems Research, 9,* 256–274.

Dubrovsky, V. J., Kiesler, S., and Sethna, B. N. (1991). The equalization phenomenon: Status effects in computer-mediated and face-to-face decision-making groups. *Human-Computer Interaction, 6,* 119–146.

Fisher, B. A. (1974). *Small group decision making: Communication and the group process.* New York: McGraw-Hill.

Fulk, J., Schmitz, J., and Steinfield, C. W. (1990). A social influence model of technology use. In J. Fulk and C. Steinfield (eds.), *Organizations and communication technology* (117–140). Thousand Oaks, CA: Sage.

Galagher, J., and Kraut, R. (1990). Technology for intellectual teamwork: Perspectives on research and design. In J. Galegher, R. Kraut, and C. Egido (eds.), *Intellectual teamwork: Social and technological foundations of cooperative work* (1–20). Hillsdale, NJ: Erlbaum.

Garton, L., and Wellman, B. (1995). Social impacts of electronic mail in organizations: A review of the research literature. In B. R. Burleson (ed.), *Communication yearbook 18* (434–453). Thousand Oaks, CA: Sage.

Gersick, C. J. G. (1988). Time and transition in work teams: Toward a new model of group development. *Academy of Management Journal, 31,* 9–41.

Gersick, C. J. G. (1989). Marking time: Predictable transitions in task groups. *Academy of Management Journal, 32,* 274–309.

Hall, E. T. (1983). *The dance of life: The other dimension of time.* Garden City, NY: Anchor/Doubleday.

Hesse, B. W., Werner, C. M., and Altman, I. (1988). Temporal aspects of computer-mediated communication. *Computers in Human Behavior, 4,* 147–165.

Hiltz, S. R., Turoff, M., and Johnson, K. (1989). Experiments in group decision making, 3: Disinhibition, deindividuation, and group process in pen name and real name computer conferences. *Decision Support Systems, 5,* 217–232.

Hollingshead, A. B., McGrath, J. E., and O'Connor, K. M. (1993). Group task performance and communication technology: A longitudinal study of computer-mediated versus face-to-face work groups. *Small Group Research, 24,* 307–333.

Johansen, R., and O'Hara-Devereaux, M. (1994). *Globalwork: Bridging distance, culture, and time.* San Francisco: Jossey-Bass.

Jonas, K. J., Boos, M., and Walther, J. B. (2000, July). *The influence of media-competence on behavior, language use and participation in a virtual seminar.* Paper presented at the Seventh International Conference on Language and Social Psychology, Cardiff, Wales.

Kellermann, K., and Reynolds, R. (1990). When ignorance is bliss: The role of motivation to reduce uncertainty in uncertainty reduction theory. *Human Communication Research*, 17, 5–75.

Lea, M., and Spears, R. (1992). Paralanguage and social perception in computer-mediated communication. *Journal of Organizational Computing*, 2, 321–341.

Lebie, L., Rhoades, J. A., and McGrath, J. E. (1995/1996). Interaction processes in computer-mediated and face-to-face groups. *Computer Supported Cooperative Work*, 4, 127–152.

Mark, G. (2002). Conventions for coordinating electronic distributed work: A longitudinal study of groupware use (259–281). In P. Hinds and S. Kiesler (eds.), *Distributed work*. Cambridge, MA: MIT Press.

Markus, M. L. (1994). Electronic mail as the medium of managerial choice. *Organization Science*, 5, 502–527.

Maznevski, K. L., and Chudoba, K. M. (2000). Bridging space over time: Global virtual team dynamics and effectiveness. *Organization Science*, 11, 473–492.

McGrath, J. E. (1990). Time matters in groups. In J. Galegher, R. E. Kraut, and C. Egido (eds.), *Intellectual teamwork: Social and technical foundations of cooperative work* (23–61). Hillsdale, NJ: Erlbaum.

McGrath, J. E. (1991). Time, interaction, and performance (TIP): A theory of groups. *Small Group Research*, 22, 147–174.

McGrath, J. E. (1992). Groups interacting with technology: The complex and dynamic fit of group, task, technology, and time. In J. Turner and R. Kraut (eds.), *CSCW '92: Sharing Perspectives (Proceedings of the Conference on Computer-Supported Cooperative work)* (4). New York: ACM Press.

McGrath, J. E. (1993). Introduction: The JEMCO workshop—description of a longitudinal study. *Small Group Research*, 24, 285–306.

McLeod, P. L., and Liker, J. K. (1992). Electronic meeting systems: Evidence from a low structure environment. *Information Systems Research*, 3, 195–223.

Menneke, B. E., Hoffer, J. A., and Wynne, B. E. (1992). The implications of group development and group history for group support system theory and practice. *Small Group Research*, 23, 524–572.

Nardi, B., Whittaker, S., and Bradner, E. (2000). Interaction and outeraction: Instant messaging in action. In *Proceedings of Conference on Computer Supported Cooperative Work* (79–88). New York: ACM Press.

Orlikowski, W. J., and Yates, J. (1998, August). *It's about time: Temporal structuring in organizations.* Paper presented at the annual meeting of the Academy of Management, San Diego, CA.

Poole, M. S., and Holmes, M. E. (1995). Decision development in computer-assisted group decision making. *Human Communication Research*, 22, 90–127.

Reid, F. J. M., Ball, L. J., Morley, A. M., and Evans, J. S. B. T. (1997). Styles of group discussion in computer-mediated decision making. *British Journal of Social Psychology, 36,* 241–262.

Reid, F. J. M., Malinek, V., Stott, C., and Evans, J. S. B. T. (1996). The messaging threshold in computer-mediated communication. *Ergonomics, 39,* 1017–1037.

Rice, R. E. (1982). Communication networking in computer-conferencing systems: A longitudinal study of group roles and system structure. In M. Burgoon (ed.), *Communication yearbook 6* (925–944). Thousand Oaks, CA: Sage.

Rice, R. E. (1990). Computer-mediated communication system network data: Theoretical concerns and empirical examples. *International Journal of Man-Machine Studies, 32,* 627–647.

Rice, R. E. (1993). Media appropriateness: Using social presence theory to compare traditional and new organizational media. *Human Communication Research, 19,* 451–484.

Rice, R. E., and Love, G. (1987). Electronic emotion: Socioemotional content in a computer-mediated network. *Communication Research, 14,* 85–108.

Ross, L. (1977). The intuitive psychologist and his shortcoming: Distortions in the attribution process. In L. Berkowitz (ed.), *Advances in experimental social psychology* (Vol. 10). New York: Academic Press.

Steinfield, C. W. (1986). Computer-mediated communication in an organizational setting: Explaining task-related and socioemotional uses. In M. L. McLaughlin (ed.), *Communication yearbook 9* (777–804). Thousand Oaks, CA: Sage.

Straus, S. G., and McGrath, J. E. (1994). Does the medium matter? The interaction of task type and technology on group performance and member reactions. *Journal of Apllied Psychology, 79,* 87–97.

Tidwell, L. C., and Walther, J. B. (2000, July). *Getting to know one another a bit at a time: Computer-mediated communication effects on disclosure, impressions, and interpersonal evaluations.* Paper presented at the Seventh International Conference on Language and Social Psychology, Cardiff, Wales.

Walther, J. B. (1992a). Interpersonal effects in computer-mediated interaction: A relational perspective. *Communication Research, 19,* 52–90.

Walther, J. B. (1992b). A longitudinal experiment on relational tone in computer-mediated and face to face interaction. In J. F. Nunamaker and R. H. Sprague (eds.), *Proceedings of the Hawaii International Conference on System Sciences 1992* (Vol. 4, 220–231). Los Alamitos, CA: IEEE Computer Society Press.

Walther, J. B. (1993). Impression development in computer-mediated interaction. *Western Journal of Communication, 57,* 381–398.

Walther, J. B. (1994). Anticipated ongoing interaction versus channel effects on relational communication in computer-mediated interaction. *Human Communication Research, 20,* 473–501.

Walther, J. B. (1995). Relational aspects of computer-mediated communication: Experimental observations. *Organization Science, 6,* 186–203.

Walther, J. B. (1996). Computer-mediated communication: Impersonal, interpersonal, and hyperpersonal interaction. *Communication Research, 23*, 3–43.

Walther, J. B. (1997). Group and interpersonal effects in international computer-mediated collaboration. *Human Communication Research, 23*, 342–369.

Walther, J. B., Anderson, J. F., and Park, D. (1994). Interpersonal effects in computer-mediated interaction: A meta-analysis of social and anti-social communication. *Communication Research, 21*, 460–487.

Walther, J. B., and Burgoon, J. K. (1992). Relational communication in computer-mediated interaction. *Human Communication Research, 19*, 50–88.

Walther, J. B., Slovacek, C., and Tidwell, L. C. (2001). Is a picture worth a thousand words? Photographic images in long term and short term virtual teams. *Communication Research, 28*, 105–134.

Walther, J. B., and Tidwell, L. C. (1995). Nonverbal cues in computer-mediated communication, and the effect of chronemics on relational communication. *Journal of Organizational Computing, 5*, 355–378.

Weisband, S. (1992). Group discussion and first advocacy effects in computer-mediated and face-to-face decision making groups. *Organizational Behavior and Human Decision Processes, 53*, 352–380.

Weisband, S. (1994). Overcoming social awareness in computer-supported groups: Does anonymity really help? *Computer Supported Cooperative Work, 2*, 285–297.

Weisband, S. P., Schneider, S. K., and Connolly, T. (1995). Electronic communication and social information: Status salience and status differences. *Academy of Management Journal, 38*, 1124–1151.

Weisenfeld, B. M., Raghuram, S., and Garud, R. (1998). Communication patterns as determinants of organizational identification in a virtual organization. *Journal of Computer-Mediated Communication, 3* (4). Available at: www.ascusc.org/jcmc/vol3/issue4/wiesenfeld.html.

Williams, F., Rice, R. E., and Rogers, E. M. (1988). *Research methods and the new media.* New York: Free Press.

11

Conventions for Coordinating Electronic Distributed Work: A Longitudinal Study of Groupware Use

Gloria Mark

Conventions are essential for governing cooperation. In electronic work, conventions help regulate the use of shared objects. A critical factor for the emergence and functioning of conventions is the information available that communicates the group context. In distributed work, groups have difficulty forming and maintaining conventions. A longitudinal study of groupware use showed that it took considerable time for a distributed group to recognize coordination situations where conventions were needed. Conventions were difficult to define, incongruent conventions were formed, and when an implicit convention was adopted, it violated organizational procedures. Explicit agreements on convention use were frequently violated. These difficulties can be attributed to multiple factors inherent in distributed groups, which affect the ability to learn about others' activities, engage in ongoing articulation, and reinforce appropriate behaviors.

"There must be ground rules established for working together and dealing with the groupware. The culture is lacking to be able to handle this problem with the new technical possibilities. The stronger the technical flexibility, the more rules must exist for how we can handle this." These words were spoken by the leader of a distributed group about eighteen months after the introduction of a groupware system. The leader expressed his realization that merely learning about technical operations of a groupware system is not sufficient for work practice. Users must develop social agreements for how they will interact and conduct their work electronically. These agreements apply to all aspects of electronic work—for example, determining who has access rights for documents, how shared information should be named and structured, when to send a query, and perhaps even how to end an electronic conference.

In this chapter, I discuss the difficulties in forming and establishing conventions for distributed groups that conduct their work electronically. A physically collocated team that has a long history of working together may have already established conventions for many of its cooperative activities, but a team that is formed to cooperate together using a groupware system must establish new conventions. Such agreed-on rules of interaction increase the chances that cooperative work can result in process gain rather than process loss if, for example, one member should restructure or rename files, resulting in extra effort by other cooperating partners to find the documents. One user's action on a shared document, such as changing text or even access rights, affects all users working on the shared document. Especially in asynchronous distributed work, conventions are important in that they enable people to keep track of, and predict processes, for example, of stages of document completion. Also important, conventions are a means for new members to adapt to electronic work.

Conventions are important in group interaction in that they reduce trial and error and confusion by regulating mutually interdependent activities so that they do not interfere with each other. The conventions thus provide a modus vivendi for making interactions proceed smoothly (Feldman 1984, Conte and Castelfranchi 1995, Biddle and Thomas 1966). Conventions can regulate almost all types of group interactions—among them, communication (Lenke, Lutz, and Sprenger 1995), interpersonal distance (Hall 1966), the use of artifacts, and the control of negative social processes such as cheating.

I use the term *convention* rather than *social norm* in this chapter because I am interested in describing routine ways that group members do things rather than moral principles. *Conventions* are defined in the *Merriam-Webster Dictionary* (1998) as "general agreement about basic principles or procedures" and "a rule of conduct or behavior." This meaning is similar to what Cialdini, Reno, and Kallgren (1990) call a *descriptive* norm—a guide to behavior that informs people what most others do in a situation.

A Normative Model of Convention Use

Whereas in physically collocated work, a number of social forces operate to ensure development and conformity to a convention, these forces are weak or absent in distributed groups. This limited social information combined with incomplete activity information from cooperating partners makes it difficult for distributed group members to form and maintain conventions. In order to examine these difficulties, I present a definition of normative convention behavior in physically collocated work, according to Lewis (1969):

A regularity in the behavior of members of a population when they are agents in a recurrent situation is a convention if and only if it is true that, and it is common knowledge in the population that, in any instance of the recurrent situation among members of the population,

• everyone conforms to the regularity;
• everyone expects everyone else to conform to the regularity;
• everyone prefers to conform to the regularity on condition that the others do, since the recurrent situation is a coordination problem and uniform conformity to the regularity is a coordination equilibrium in the recurrent situation. (42)

Although in its strictest form Lewis's definition requires that everyone conform to the convention, in this chapter, I refer to his relaxed alternative where "almost everyone" in the group conforms to, expects to, and prefers conformity to the regularity. Following this normative model, as a consequence of conforming to the convention, group members develop expectations that others in the group will continue to conform. This leads to commitments that sustain the convention. Every new instance of conforming to the convention increases the expectations that when the situation arises, people will use the convention. And the expectation that others will conform in the future is reason to continue to conform: If I conform, then others will. This conformity leads to a number of higher-order expectations that are instrumental in sustaining the use of conventions.

The convention represents mutual knowledge in the group. The existence of a convention indicates that all in the group have common knowledge that this convention leads to solving a coordination problem. Moreover, according to this normative view, to belong to the group indicates that each member possesses the common knowledge associated with the group convention. The distinguishing characteristic, then, of conventions is that they are emergent properties of the group rather than of individual members (Turner and Oakes 1989).

Limited Information and Communication Affects Convention Use

Conventions do not develop as efficiently in distributed groups as they do in groups that are physically collocated. A critical factor for the emergence and functioning of conventions is the information available that communicates social, behavioral, and environmental aspects of the group. In physically collocated work, people can detect the finest nuances of behavior and expression in other people. They see how others are handling or changing artifacts, and from the context they can infer previous changes made to artifacts (Robinson 1993). By watching others, they generally can get a clear understanding of the other's subjective expressions and can use this to correct and fine-tune their responses (Schutz 1970).

Common information and artifacts available to interacting actors can include people; physical objects such as documents, keys, or books; communicative signals such as signs of approval, feedback, gestures, status indicators, and facial expressions; and the state of the environment, such as closed doors, placement of telephones, or noise level. The placement, occurrence, and changes of artifacts embedded within a context affect the knowledge and affective states of group members (Hackman 1976). This common information affects each member's knowledge and beliefs about the group and the work activity. It can also affect the group's attitude, such as what outcomes are desirable. When artifact use, behavior, and expression are easily communicable in a group, the group can discover where coordination situations exist. Common information and artifacts are the basis for forming conventions: the group can then develop methods for regulating their actions.

However, in distributed settings, this information is not readily available. Distributed team members do not share a common physical environment, and so actors do not have common orientations and reference points. Environmental information for physically separated actors is local and distinct from one another. Any (environmental, behavioral, and artifact) information common to the group is mostly constrained to an electronic environment. The reduced communication, as well as varying contexts of actors and stimuli, affect the ability for cooperating actors to understand interaction in the same context. Thus, it is difficult for actors to know how their collaborating partners are handling electronic artifacts (e.g., storing documents) or naming files.

An Empirical Study of Conventions in Distributed Electronic Work

To illustrate my argument about the difficulties of forming conventions in distributed groups, I present observations of a group conducting electronic work over a period of five years. Recently in Germany, historical and political circumstances led to the development of a prototype groupware system to support distance cooperation. Bonn served as the capital of West Germany from 1949 until German reunification in 1990, and in 1991, the parliament chose Berlin as the new capital. Until the government fully relocates, there will be a large division of labor spread between the old and new capitals. The PoliTeam groupware system was specifically designed to build a telecooperation bridge between Bonn and the new capital of Berlin, supporting distributed work with shared workspaces and electronic circulation folders (Prinz and Kolvenbach 1996).

Research Setting and Methods

The shared workspace in PoliTeam is used in a cooperative arrangement by two different groups in a federal ministry: typists in a central writing office and members of a ministry unit. The ministry unit consists of nine members whose job is to support the minister whom they work for through activities such as speechwriting, information dissemination, and answering citizens' queries. The writing office consists of a coordinator and three typists who type electronic versions of documents for the ministry unit members. The two groups can be distinguished by differences in jobs, tasks, education levels, career path orientations, salaries, computer experience, and even more. The two groups are spatially distributed: most users are located on different floors of the same building in Bonn, and two users are in Berlin.

After PoliTeam was introduced, the exchange of documents was done through the shared workspace. The shared workspace has two purposes. First, it provides shared document access for the writing office and the ministry unit, thus enabling intergroup cooperation. Second, it provides shared access to people within the ministry unit, enabling intragroup cooperation (e.g., when unit members coauthor documents). And finally, it provides access to common information sources about the ministry, which all users update.

The results are from a case study involving a collection of material: workshops, site visits, design-team-user discussions, and user interviews. Initial semistructured interviews were conducted before the system was introduced in order to learn about the potential users' work practices. Transcripts were also used from workshops in which the design team met with users—shortly after the first system version was finished and about every six months thereafter.

Twice after system introduction, a series of semistructured interviews with the users was conducted. In the first set of interviews, which lasted one to three hours each, users were asked about training and support, individual and collective work with the system, cooperation and use of information, the search facility, awareness of others, the shared workspace, and conventions: how the users had established some conventions, disturbing actions from others, conventions needed, violations, views on conventions, and their effect on work styles. A second set of interviews was conducted shortly before the project ended in order to develop an overview of costs and benefits of system use. Information was also used from a log of reported problems and results from the user hot line and weekly site visits of design team members.

Problems in Establishing Conventions in Distributed Work
Problems were observed in the group with respect to conventions. First, it took considerable time for the users to discover what Lewis (1969), in his definition of a convention, describes as a coordination problem. Second, once the coordination problems were recognized, it was difficult for the users to define what form the conventions should take. This was especially hard for emerging work processes, which the new shared workspaces enabled. Third, different groups applied conventions based on their prior work, and these conventions conflicted when both groups worked together. Fourth, all the users did adopt the same convention implicitly, but this convention violated a ministry procedure. I now describe each of these problems.

The Slow Discovery of Coordination Problems in Distributed Work The distributed group recognized the need for many conventions only after the users passed through different phases in their use of the groupware system. From logbooks, where problems were carefully recorded from biweekly site visits, two types of events were coded:

Group use events: Problems and experiences that concerned system handling and understanding of shared objects

Individual use events: Problems and experiences that concerned system handling of all aspects except shared objects (e.g., setting up individual document templates, organizing personal directories)

Usage was divided into six-month intervals, and events in these intervals were coded. As a result of this categorization, rough phases of group development with the system were identified, and are shown in figure 11.1. In the first eighteen months, group functionality was set up, and growing pains with system usage were evident. Groupware functionality was slowly refined, and individual use events show that users were beginning to customize features of the system (e.g., setting up personal document template collections).

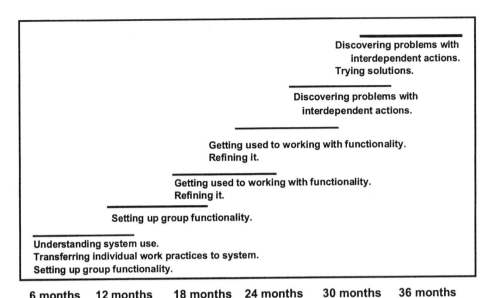

Figure 11.1
Approximate stages of groupware learning.

After two years of system use, a definite change was evident in the events. Many users were reporting problems that they were having as a result of other users' actions: users were concerned that files were taken out of the shared folder and were lying on others' personal desktops, and there was confusion reported in how addresses in the shared address book were organized. First trials of electronic circulation folders were initiated by the newly connected managers of the units that led to the report of stalled folders (as with paper folders).

In the last six months of the project, more problems were reported that concerned other users' actions (e.g., only owners can delete documents). The Berlin users wanted to identify only changes from specific users in Bonn. The Berlin and Bonn unit leaders defined requirements for editing, and other users defined requirements for reporting changes made on shared objects within a shared work space.

What is interesting is that after about two years, now that group functionality had been set up and work patterns seemingly firmly established, the group members began to report problems that concerned coordinating their work patterns. The group members recognized the consequences of their interdependencies. Some evidence shows that the same types of problems with interdependencies occurred very early on in the system use, yet were not considered by users to be due to the actions of other members. For example, in the first three months of system use, a typist reported a system problem because an icon that usually turned blue was now turning black. The typist did not make a connection that the color change reflected a status change due to another user's action. These experiences illustrate how in distributed work, it can require a long time for team members to identify what Lewis terms coordination situtations.

Why Did It Take So Long to Discover Coordination Problems?   Two years seems to be an exceptional amount of time for people to become aware of the need to regulate interdependencies in a shared workspace. In addition to limited information about other users' actions, other factors may have also contributed to this long delay.

One factor was the need to regulate interactions because of the design of the groupware system, which was intended to serve as a medium for cooperation, as opposed to a prescribed cooperation mechanism (Prinz, Mark, and Pankoke-Babatz 1998; Bentley and Dourish 1995). The flexible cooperation media included both electronic circulation folders, where plans for work sequences could be configurable, and shared work spaces, where material could be flexibly stored and accessed for a number of different purposes. This flexibility allowed for different working styles but imposed a burden on the group to regulate its interdependent activities.

A shared workspace is characterized by properties that Hewitt (1985) describes to be generally true for open systems. The shared workspace is continually changing and evolving, and there may be no direct access to internal information from other users, so that it is difficult to infer reasons behind the actions. In many cases, the shared workspace involves decentralized decision making, which introduces problems for regulating actions. Shared workspaces sometimes cross organizational boundaries, and so users may have different perspectives about work. Finally, shared workspaces do not meet the assumption of a closed world, which imposes the additional burden for users of needing to take external information into account.

The design approach may have served inadvertently to reinforce particular patterns of system usage, which delayed the discovery of coordination situations. The design approach was an evolutionary cycle (Mambrey, Mark, and Pankoke-Babatz 1997), where system requirements were gathered in the course of the users' actual work. In hindsight, the stages of use and system development follow in a logical order: supporting first individual and then group needs. The design approach reinforced the users' current patterns of system usage rather than promoting the users to evolve in their usage. What happened was a cycle. The system developers implemented requirements to support the users' current pattern of usage. When the users were primarily using the shared workspace as a personal workspace, then the system was enhanced to support individual work better. In this way, the users may have been less aware of the potential of the system to support group work. Consequently, the users may then have used the system less as a group system. Whether coordination situations can be recognized earlier with a different design approach is a fertile area of research.

Cooperation among the users was not continuous. This discontinuity made it difficult for people to learn their interdependencies, to learn where coordination problems lay, and to provide timely feedback. Ackerman, Hindus, Mainwaring, and Starr (1997) describe a group that used a media space for continuous informal interaction, and the group quickly developed conventions to make public who was present, as well as to govern other communication. By contrast, the PoliTeam users worked mostly on their personal desktops and then used the shared workspace to exchange and store information. Often, feedback was given long after the action or not at all. Communicative behaviors may in fact have a certain period of time relevance for partners (Frey 1975). It seems plausible that notification of others' behaviors must be presented at points when it is relevant for the receiver in order to optimize learning. Thus, the discontinuity of cooperation and feedback made it difficult for the users to learn interdependencies and consequently to form conventions.

The Difficulty in Defining Conventions for Distributed Electronic Work   Once coordination problems were recognized, the users identified a number of requirements for conventions in their distributed work—for example:

- Conventions for a common information structure and for archiving information
- Conventions regarding shared tasks (e.g., managing shared document work)
- Conventions for determining public and private workspaces
- Conventions for access rights for different document types
- Conventions for an electronic circulation folder (e.g., notification)

People had difficulty defining exactly how such conventions would manage the coordination problems. Most users reported that they did not have a clear idea of the activities of other users. The Bonn-Berlin users had met each other only infrequently, so they were unfamiliar with each others' work practices. The users reported a lack of awareness of shared object use:

We must think over, depending on the information that we have, which shared work areas would be sufficient. But I'm not in the situation where I can see that, i.e., where I get information other than that for my own workspace.

For my own archive, what I set up myself, then I can look at my own example. But for a real archive [shared] that would be set up for others, then we must really think it over: what the system offers and what is necessary. But I can't evaluate that at this point.

Conventions were especially difficult to identify for new work processes that emerged in the course of using the groupware. For example, a shared folder opportunistically set up between ministry departments in Bonn and Berlin enabled documents to be accessed almost immediately, whereas before PoliTeam, they were exchanged by regular mail. This new ability to transact information fast and to make it accessible posed a new kind of question to the users. They needed to determine conventions for the shared workspace between Bonn and Berlin: on organization, types of information, and access. As one unit member reported:

When we use more information together with Berlin, then we must really think what shared work areas would be useful. For example, should we have things where we pack five things inside or something else? It also depends on what it is, what kind of information. I think that in certain folders, it must be this way. It is necessary. Otherwise we have chaos—or someone has chaos for themselves.

Limited Communication Affects the Ability to Define Conventions   Whereas physically collocated group members can easily learn a great deal of information about others' work simply through peripheral observation and conversation (see Olson, Teasley, Covi, and Olson, chapter 5, this volume; Kraut, Fussell, Brennan, and Siegel, chapter 6, this volume), the PoliTeam group communicated about their work mainly through e-mail, an occasional telephone call, or simple automatic document notification. It is the common information available to the group, about artifact use, behavior, communicative signals, and environment, that serves as the basis for forming conventions. In the case of the PoliTeam users, the group had to construct this information through their intermittent communication.

Workshops, where the users met face-to-face in structured meetings every six months, were a means to supplement the users' communication about group work. Here the users discussed shared object use. The insightful unit leader pointed out in one workshop discussion that the user group needed to develop new cultural thinking involving group agreements in their electronic work. As one user reports:

We must simply try. I can't imagine that there is a scientific method to use. We are forced to formulate them [conventions]. What we can do is help with that. And for us, the conventions are also a help. If I had time, I would spend two days working on it. But it's a question of time for us. If we would meet for a day workshop, then that would be good. It's the preparation that's hard. We need a meeting to formulate them.

Articulation is needed in order for a group to achieve a standard representation or convention for handling boundary objects (Gerson and Star 1986). But carrying out articulation in a distributed group, as in the case of PoliTeam, is extremely difficult when communication and information about the handling of common objects are limited, and especially when feedback must explicitly be given.

The Problem of Different Groups Forming Incongruent Conventions   Whereas members of the same work team may develop similar interpretations for some objects, often cooperation has to be implemented among members of heterogeneous groups, whose perspectives can be quite diverse. Especially when cooperating partners cross organizational boundaries, the same object or piece of information is subject to different specialized activities, opinions, perspectives, and interests, which can lead to different handling. The two heterogeneous groups in the ministry did in fact develop different conventions for organizing and using the same information in the shared workspace.

The writing office developed a solution to organize documents in the shared workspace using a two-level hierarchy: first, according to the units and then by the members of a unit. This convention for how the shared workspaces were organized was logical for the work process of the writing office: their sorting convention used the name of the document owner and date of creation. A second convention concerned the naming of documents. The typists named documents according to date and unit member.

In contrast, the unit members developed a convention to organize their documents in the shared workspace according to their work processes. They collected documents produced by the writing office in folders that each represented a distinct task. This procedure resulted in a rather deep multilevel structure. Users' sorting and naming criteria for documents in the workspace were based on the content of a document—for example, a speech on a senior citizen initiative.

Conventions Are Logical for Each Group   The organization for each group (the typists and unit members) was logical for their work processes. The problem for the group as a whole arose because the shared workspace lacked a common information structure for its documents. Most of the users employed a location-based finding strategy for documents (Wulf 1997), and some unit members reported that they could not find documents in the vast array of information in the shared workspace because the system supported only the writing office view. One unit member described his perspective:

For me, the subject is the most important. Plus additional information. It answers the question, What is inside? It's easier to find. The date has to do with the order of the closet. The subject is what tells me the content. It's important for me that the subject tells me what's in the document and that the reference code is precisely written. The subject is important when we look for an old document. I need subject [field], content, and reference code.

With different file structures in use between the typists and unit members, how are documents exchanged between the groups? The method was ad hoc. As one typist reported:

J has many subdirectories. Each has a special name. When a document comes from J, it is very clear to us where the document should be placed back—she writes it on the paper document. However, we can't pay attention to and can't keep track of which subdirectories everyone has. When I get exact instructions where to lay a document or when I know where it goes, then it is not necessary to think about where the document goes.

For this unit member, who has a one-level file structure, he need not specify where the shared documents should be placed. However, he confirms how the other the other unit members' individualized file structures create overhead for the typists:

[A unit member:] They put the documents back in my folder. F [typist] knows this already. It says my name. I have only one level. It's always clear for me where it lies. The newest version always lies on top. The others have something else. N has many levels.

Thus, each user had to specify in which directory the finished document should be replaced. This unit member was an exception for having one level in his file structure. The solution worked fine for some individuals who were careful about specifying locations, but broke down when this information was not provided to the typists. It was extra overhead for the typists to determine which subdirectory the finished document had to be placed into. In contrast, the method used for exchanging documents *intragroup,* within the unit, was more uniform in task-specific folders.

The contrast in the use of the shared workspace by the heterogeneous groups is evident in other respects. First, the typists and unit members had different needs for notification:

[A typist:] After returning from vacation, it's not relevant for us in the typing office to know what has happened in the shared folders.

In contrast, it was important for unit members to catch up on work missed during absences since their tasks were interdependent (e.g., collaborative writing and responding to citizens' requests). Thus, they needed to know if information had changed. Renaming and erasing documents were also done differently:

Renaming, erasing—that comes less into question for us [typists]. Who should erase a document, that should come from the unit. I don't do that at all with PoliTeam. The other directories we clean them up a bit when there are too many. But since in PoliTeam, each person has their own directory, I don't go into another person's directory and clean up. If we create a document that's similar or a new document under another name, then we can erase it.

For some operations, implicit conventions evolved naturally. This typist indicated that it was logical that the unit members were responsible for doing certain operations such as deleting documents: this decision was based on content.

Conventions Formed in Previous Work Different precedents for conventions existed for the typists and unit members and led to the development of conflicting naming and storing conventions. Before PoliTeam, the unit members used a task-based storage scheme for paper documents with the registrar department; the typists used a name and date storage scheme with documents that they stored electronically in a house system.

Conventions from previous work, which were appropriate and logical for different group work practices, were not congruent when the groups worked together. For typists of the department, accessing a document by the creator (or owner) made much more sense to them than accessing a document by the subject. Their primary task was to type documents for unit members; their system was an efficient means for them to access a document. To the unit members who were speechwriters, accessing a document by its subject was efficient for them. The dates of the documents had less meaning for them, since they might work on multiple projects within the same time frame.

Users can face difficulties in forming conventions when they hold different mental models of their work processes, the system. Orlikowski and Gash (1994) refer to this difference as different technological frames. With different technological frames, perceptions of each others' behaviors may not be accurate, as Schutz expresses (1970, 229): "Each expects that the other's interpretive scheme will be congruent with his own." In PoliTeam, the typists and unit members had different models of cooperation, the organization, and their work (see also Mark and Mambrey 1997). To the unit members, typing is a mechanical process and they felt that their interaction with the typists was not cooperation. On the other hand, the typists felt that they were members of a cooperative group. This difference in notions of cooperation could have contributed to the unit members' lack of commitment in following the naming conventions.

The Problem of Adopting an Implicit Convention That Violates Organizational Procedures   Conventions in physically collocated work can often be formed swiftly and implicitly. People may consciously or unconsciously model the behavior of other group members (Bandura 1971). For instance, people canoeing fall automatically into a smooth rhythm. Implicit conventions also may be formed from precedents of analogous situations. If group members share the same experience of a previous convention, then this can be applied as precedent in a new situation. For example, in a new work team, members may apply a precedent of democratic decision making, which all experienced in their former work teams. The problem is that different precedents create ambiguity in the group and would not result in a uniform convention. Feedback also plays an important role in the development of both implicit and explicit conventions by shaping behavior. Positive feedback strengthens responses—for example, through praise or encouragement—whereas negative feedback stops or reverses a behavior. Groups not in close proximity and whose communication is not spontaneous must have far less opportunity for providing immediate feedback for shaping behavior and controlling deviance. Similarly, it is far more difficult to model the behavior of others and to apply uniform precedents.

In the case of PoliTeam, an implicit convention developed quickly: all the users maintained private workspaces and used them for preparing drafts and storing documents. No one explicitly discussed borders of public and private workspaces. Private workspaces were respected; the users reported that no one searched or looked at anyone's private workspace, and conversely expected no one to search theirs.

Ironically, this convention violated a strict ministry policy, which stated that all work in the ministry must be public. Work is organized accorded to the Common Rules of Procedure of the Federal Ministries (the GGO). The GGO specifies how work has to be organized: only official documents exist. This is because the only work allowed is official work, done on behalf of, and by roles that substitute for, the minister in person. Despite this idea of official and public work within the organization, the employees had their own private work, such as early drafts of a speech. In the requirements analysis, the users requested a personal workspace in the system to store their private documents, which was against the formal GGO. Thus, although a formal set of rules existed in the ministry to prescribe and define how work should proceed, the users neglected to follow these prescriptions.

The users described how their earlier nonelectronic work influenced their current convention:

Private areas should be protected. It's good that I can't search L's desk. This corresponds to our earlier experience with our real desks.

There are certainly private areas here, such as my private workspace. If someone looks for a circulation folder here [pointing to the in-box and out-box on her desk], they can search in the out-box but not the in-box. Similarly, what lays on my private desk, that is private.

The distinction between public and private areas was made very natural and implicit.

That is one of the basic conventions that protects the workers. Also when someone develops something on their private workspace, then it's relevant when it's put in a folder and it's accessible to me. Before then, it's not relevant to me. It's their thing. I don't look at it and say, What have you written for the first three sentences? It is a fundamental convention and it has a protection character. On the one side, you want to know the information that someone has, but on the other side, you have to keep in mind that it's a private sphere.

It was obvious to us. The system is an exact technical reproduction of our work. That's the charm of the system. You observed how work functions in the ministry, and then you tried to reproduce it electronically. So it's no wonder that conventions used in our normal work are carried over.

Common Precedents from Prior Work Whereas the typists and unit members applied different precedents of naming and storing conventions, it was also the case that when the precedent of a convention was the same for all group members and when the analogy was clear, the convention was applied to electronic work by the whole group. This was evidenced by the convention of maintaining private and public workspaces. Applying analogy to technology use is a valuable learning tool, since people try to understand new processes in terms of a conceptual framework that they already know (Carroll and Thomas 1982). Before PoliTeam, the users had a clear distinction on their physical desks between public and private workspaces, with private spaces being in-boxes or locked drawers.

Commonly in face-to-face interaction, conventions are formed implicitly (Habermas 1987). Conventions to regulate nonverbal communication are naturally developed since individuals are attuned to others' facial expressions and change their behaviors accordingly (Bakeman and Gottman 1986). Conventions to regulate artifact use within a group are gradually developed by observing how others use artifacts. Ethnographic investigations have shown that actors adjust their behaviors depending on others' actions to stimuli, for example, using telephones in a dealer room (Heath, Jirotka, Luff, and Hindmarsh 1993), using paper airstrips in air traffic control (Hughes, Randall, and Shapiro 1992), or interacting in control rooms (Heath and Luff 1992). A simple and elegant example of how common information influences behavior and leads to conventions can be found in a protocol of children at play, described by Bakeman and Gottman (1986). Two children, coloring next to each other, begin as individuals playing in parallel with crayons. Soon, while observing the colors that the other is using, the play evolves into joint use of the stimuli and a convention: "You want all my blue?" "Yes. To make cookies. Just to make cookies, but *we* can't mess the cookies all up."

In cases where no clear precedent for a convention exists for electronic work, it becomes difficult for users to develop conventions implicitly. The example of the workspace that established a new connection between Bonn and Berlin illustrates that without precedents, conventions are difficult to plan at the outset of a new work process. Orlikowski (1996) cites an example of how specialists, because of their experience, were able to recognize the need for some conventions to fit an emerging work process. However, because the connection with Berlin was new and the work practice between Bonn and Berlin had yet to be refined, the precedents gained from past experiences with shared workspaces could not be easily applied.

Problems Maintaining Conventions in Distributed Work

Conventions can be formed through explicit agreements when a situation is recognized as a coordination problem and a solution is then actively sought. For example, if several people want to use a handbook and only one copy exists, a convention is formed to regulate turn taking. Explicit conventions (see Waldenfels 1994) can take the form of agreements, rules, or even laws (Castelfranchi 1999) and may be introduced by the group itself, an agent in the group, or the organization (Finnemore and Sikkink 1998).

Explicit agreements on conventions were made by the PoliTeam users, and in most cases, these agreements were violated. The first case of explicitly forming group conventions occurred to address the conflicting naming conventions. The conflict was discussed in a workshop that was initiated by user advocates, members of the design team. Several solutions were discussed, and a proposal was made for maintaining the typists' naming and storing conventions. However, most unit members did not follow the conventions. The unit members describe the situation:

With the naming conventions, there was difficulty with the typists.

Naming conventions, reference code, and subject area, I always violate. I give file names that seem to fit.

The naming conventions, what are these? We first write 57 [a pseudonym], then the reference code, which completes it.

This procedure, of course, is not the agreed-on naming convention. Technical means were implemented to prompt users to follow a convention of entering a file code on newly created documents. The code is important since it provides a common reference for electronic documents. Yet all but one user failed to type it in.

We [the writing office] give no file code. We type in 0000. Maybe they [the unit members] give the correct file code afterward.

If I know the file code, I give it. Otherwise I use a fantasy number.

Other convention violations also occurred. An explicit agreement on a convention was made in the second workshop: a document must not be removed from a shared folder. However, in practice, many unit members dragged the document out of the folder shared with the writing office into their task-specific folder, violating the convention:

It gets on my nerves when people don't work on their things in the writing office shared folder. In the case of substituting, when you want to get these things, then it's really difficult.

Another explicit agreement on a convention was made that required all members to update a shared address list. Prior to PoliTeam, the users kept personal address lists and then continued to maintain them. As two users explain:

It doesn't function yet, though, since we don't have conventions for it. Each one does something else. It functions only when all the users use this distribution tool. An address list functions only when all write it into a central place. It doesn't work when each one keeps a list in parallel.

Not everything can be carried over into the computer work. Before, the address lists were organized so that you had it lying in the drawer in your desk. Now, it's being moved from the drawer in your desk into the public workspace as a share. Naturally, technology brings changes here. But it's a big advantage that we can bring it from the private space into the public space.

Reasons for Lack of Commitment to Conventions

Violations among agreements need not be detrimental to a task, as when people need to respond to changes in the environment (Beck and Bellotti 1993) or when violations are "productive laziness" (Rogers 1993). But for PoliTeam users, not following the agreements for conventions brought additional work and annoyance to others. With a few exceptions, the PoliTeam users failed to build up experiences where everyone conformed to a convention. As Lewis (1969) points out, without such a set of experiences, the group does not develop expectations that others will conform in the future; the expectations help lead to commitment. Limited information about other users' system activity prevents users from seeing who had followed the conventions. In particular, knowing *who* accepts the convention is also critical, such as whether it is the unit leader and head typist or a part-time employee. Thus, a basic pattern was set early in the group of nonconformity to conventions. There are several reasons that the users failed to follow conventions.

Reaching an Acceptance Threshold   For a group to commit to a convention, according to Finnemore and Sikkink, (1998), the convention must cross an acceptance threshold, where a critical mass is reached. One way to achieve an acceptance threshold is through persuasion by some agent, such as a manager. In the case of the PoliTeam group, the unit leader could have fulfilled this role, as he was a strong advocate for group conventions. Yet he did not want to issue a mandate: he made sure to communicate that he wanted the group itself to promote convention usage in subtle ways. Nor did the design team force the users to accept a convention; they wanted the users to self-organize.

A second way to cross an acceptance threshold is if the convention becomes part of the institutional procedures. The organizational platform, which supports the ministry's formal procedures, did not determine conventions for the group. The users did not conform to the procedures when they first defined their user requirements. Also, many conventions needed for the electronic work are new and cannot be based on the prior ministry specifications for paper-based work. And because of its nature as a pilot study, the organization did not intervene with rules of operation, as they might have with other ministry workers.

Finnemore and Sikkink propose that when such an acceptance threshold (i.e., a critical mass) is reached, the convention becomes internalized. At this point, conformity to the convention occurs, and the convention is incorporated as a habit.

However, internalized conventions in electronic work may not be desirable. Habits can be difficult to change, and flexibility is needed to adjust conventions to the dynamic nature of work.

Payoffs for Following Conventions From a game theory perspective (Axelrod 1984), conventions would be adopted by the group if their use results in a higher payoff than by not using them. However, payoffs among group members may be uneven, especially in interorganizational cooperation (see Hollingshead, Fulk, and Monge, chapter 14, this volume). For the PoliTeam users, maintaining the conventions would result in uneven payoffs in the group. For the typists, the benefits far outweighed the costs if the whole group followed the naming convention, since they did not have to exert effort to change their file names. For the unit members, it required effort to follow the naming convention, since renaming files would not be logical for their work practices. Even the one unit member who reported using "file names that seem to fit" did not follow the naming convention of those in his own group.

An imbalance in the overhead and benefits existed for the group members in following the convention of updating the shared address list, as found with shared calendar use (Grudin 1988). The users may not have understood the payoffs that they would have gained by sharing an address list. The users continued to maintain personal address lists, resulting in redundant work and incomplete lists.

Social Influence Social pressure can reinforce commitment to a convention. Waltz (1979) describes that emulation, praising conforming behavior, and punishment for deviating from the group influence convention use. The power of peer pressure cannot be underestimated, and in experimental settings, its effect on inducing conformity to norms and conventions has been strongly demonstrated (Asch 1956). Yet such studies have been carried out with actors who are face-to-face; inducing social pressure in a distributed group is difficult to achieve. Social pressure is further weakened in electronic work since everyone's activities are hardly visible to others. This lack of visibility (and related anonymity) shields against social influence and increases the chances for convention violations and free riding to occur. This lack of social pressure was evident in the case of the PoliTeam users during their electronic work. They rarely received praise or punishment for their actions.

Conclusions

If we consider Lewis's description of conventions as a normative model by which we can evaluate convention behavior, then the behavior of the group in the case study rarely followed such a model in their electronic work. It took considerable time for the group to recognize coordination situations where conventions were needed, conventions were difficult to define, and incongruent conventions were formed. When an implicit convention was adopted, it violated organizational procedures. Explicit agreements on convention use were frequently violated, and the group rarely developed what Lewis terms a coordination equilibrium. I argue that the difficulty in forming and following conventions was due to the distributed nature of the group, where it was difficult to learn about others' activities, engage in ongoing articulation, and reinforce and shape individual behaviors to conform to agreements.

But are conventions really necessary, or can standard group representations simply be formed through technical means, remaining invisible so as not to bother users in their work? There are two strong arguments for conventions. The first is that it is an extremely difficult problem to capture the wide range of conventions that a distributed group needs. Conventions are dynamic and must adapt as work evolves, people learn, and emerging work processes form, as the empirical results here show. Even if it were possible to capture conventions formally, it would require a great deal of overhead to continually adapt them in a technology. And who would adapt them: the users or a technical support group? The second argument for conventions rests on social grounds. As a face-to-face group develops by merging individual work styles into a congruent group structure, so should distributed groups, at least to some extent, if they are going to cooperate effectively. Conventions can reinforce and strengthen distributed group members' notion of cooperation. The unit leader defined conventions as follows:

I would use the term *obligation* in order to make working together easier. *Cooperation* is also an important keyword because conventions only make sense in terms of cooperation. Conventions only make sense in terms of others.

Cooperation makes sense in terms of conventions. Their existence serves to strengthen social bonds and reinforce the idea for the users that the use of a groupware system is a cooperative group effort. Knowing the conventions helps group members interpret behaviors and states of affairs in the group. For example, papers that are placed in a pile on a colleague's desktop indicate that they are public and can be looked at; those moved to a closed desk drawer become private. Conventions provide a framework to interpret and predict the group behavior. This is especially valuable in distributed work where information is limited, and actions may need interpretation.

Following norms and conventions has been considered to be rational behavior (Axelrod 1984). Convention violations in the PoliTeam case, however, while superficially seeming irrational, may have been fully rational behavior at the individual level, motivated by self-interest in support of individual work processes. The lesson we may have learned is that a distributed group needs to achieve a level of social development so that people think in terms of what is rational for the group. It appears as if the PoliTeam members did not sufficiently socially accommodate to the group, which would have led to commitment to the group (Moreland and Levine 1989). The experience of the PoliTeam users might be typical for groups cooperating in electronic work, as the unit leader expressed:

It's a problem of the working method of people. There's always a certain tolerance: a certain openness of doing things and a certain stringency. These are the two poles. That means on the one side we must allow individuality, and on the other side, we must arrange conventions. That's the normal daily working style. Each one arranges their desk in their own way, and that's their freedom. The problem is that we are in an evolutionary process here—we need conventions for our normal contact with each other, our process. We don't have this yet with information technology. We need to find a balance between individual operations and conventions. It is a balance. And it's very central. There are things that must be reproducible. It must be clear that people possibly may do things not according to their individual ideas, because it is an improvement for everyone. The success of PoliTeam depends on this.

Note

I thank Catherine Cramton, Paul Dourish, Jonathan Grudin, Thomas Herrmann, Pamela Hinds, Sara Kiesler, Kjeld Schmidt, Christian Schunn, and Carla Simone for their valuable comments. I also thank the PoliTeam design team members, and especially the users.

References

Ackerman, M. S., Hindus, D., Mainwaring, S. D., and Starr, B. (1997). Hanging on the 'wire: A field study of an audio-only media space. *ACM Transactions on Computer-Human Interaction, 4,* 39–66.

Asch, S. E. (1956). Studies of independence and conformity: A minority of one against a unanimous majority. *Psychological Monographs 70,* Whole No. 416.

Axelrod, R. (1984). *The evolution of cooperation.* New York: Basic Books.

Bakeman, R., and Gottman, J. M. (1986). *Observing interaction: An introduction to sequential analysis.* Cambridge: Cambridge University Press.

Bandura, A. (1971). *Social learning theory,* New York: General Learning Press.

Beck, E. E., and Bellotti, V. (1993). Informed opportunism as strategy: Supporting coordination in distributed collaborative writing. In *Proceedings of ECSCW '93* (233–248). Dordrecht: Kluwer Academic Publishers.

Bentley, R., and Dourish, P. (1995). Medium versus mechanism: Supporting collaboration through customization. *Proceedings of ECSCW '95* (133–148). Dordrecht: Kluwer Academic Publishers.

Biddle, B. J., and Thomas, E. J. (eds.). (1966). *Role theory: Concepts and research.* New York: Wiley.

Carroll, J. M., and Thomas, J. C. (1982). Metaphors and the cognitive representation of computing systems. *IEEE Transactions on Systems, Man, and Cybernetics, 12,* 107–115.

Castelfranchi, C. (1999). Prescribed mental-attitudes in goal-adoption and norm-adoption. *AI and Law, 7(1),* 37–50.

Cialdini, R. B., Reno, R. R., and Kallgren, C. A. (1990). A focus theory of normative conduct: Recycling the concept of norms to reduce littering in public places. *Journal of Personality and Social Psychology, 58,* 1015–1026.

Conte, R., and Castelfranchi, C. (1995). *Cognitive and social action.* London: UCL Press.

Feldman, D. C. (1984). The development and enforcement of group norms. *Academy of Management Review, 9,* 47–53.

Finnemore, M., and Sikkink, K. (1998). International norm dynamics and political change. *International Organization, 53,* 887–917.

Frey, S. (1975). Tonic aspects of behavior in interaction. In A. Kendon, R. M. Harris, and M. R. Key (eds.), *Organization of behavior in face-to-face interaction* (127–150). The Hague: Mouton Publishers.

Gerson, E. M., and Star, S. L. (1986). Analyzing due process in the workplace. *ACM Transactions on Office Information Systems, 4,* 257–270.

Grudin, J. (1988). Why CSCW applications fail: Problems in the design and evaluation of organizational interfaces. In *Proceedings CSCW '88* (85–93). New York: ACM Press.

Habermas, J. (1987). *The theory of communicative action.* Boston: Beacon Press.

Hackman, J. R. (1976). Group influences on individuals. In M. D. Dunnette (ed.), *Handbook of industrial and organizational psychology* (1455–1525). Chicago: Rand-McNally.

Hall E. T. (1966). *The hidden dimension.* New York: Anchor Books.

Heath, C., Jirotka, M., Luff, P., and Hindmarsh, J. (1993). Unpacking collaboration: The interactional organization of trading in a city dealing room. In *Proceedings of ECSCW '93* (155–170). Dordrecht: Kluwer Academic Publishers.

Heath, C. C., and Luff, P. (1992). Collaboration and control: Crisis management and multimedia technology in London underground line control rooms. *CSCW Journal, 1,* 69–94.

Hewitt, C. (1985, April). The challenge of open systems. *BYTE, 10,* 223–242.

Hollingshead, A. B., Fulk, J., and Monge, P. (2002). Fostering intranet knowledge sharing: An integration of transactive memory and public goods approaches. In P. Hinds and S. Kiesler (eds.), *Distributed work* (335–356). Cambridge, MA: MIT Press.

Hughes, J. A., Randall, D., and Shapiro, D. (1992). Faltering from ethnography to design. In *Proceedings CSCW92* (115–122). New York: ACM Press.

Kraut, R. E., Fussell, S. R., Brennan, S. E., and Siegel, J. (2002). Understanding effects of proximity on collaboration: Implications for technologies to support remote collaborative work. In P. Hinds and S. Kiesler (eds.), *Distributed work* (137–162). Cambridge, MA: MIT Press.

Lenke, N., Lutz, H.D., and Sprenger, M. (1995). *Grundlagen sprachlicher kommunikation.* Munich: Wilhelm Fink.

Lewis, D. K. (1969). *Convention: A philosophical study.* Cambridge, MA: Harvard University Press.

Mambrey, P., Mark, G., and Pankoke-Babatz, U. (1997). User advocacy in participatory design: Designers experiences with a new communication channel. *Computer Supported Cooperative Work (CSCW): An International Journal, 7,* 291–313.

Mark, G., and Mambrey, P. (1997). Models and metaphors in groupware: Towards a group-centered design. In S. Howard, J. Hammond, and G. Lindgaard (eds.), *Human-Computer Interaction INTERACT'97* (477–484). London: Chapman and Hall.

Moreland, R. L., and Levine, J. M. (1989). Newcomers and oldtimers in small groups. In P. Paulus (ed.), *Psychology of group influence* (143–186). Hillsdale, NJ: Erlbaum.

Olson, J. S., Teasley, S., Covi, L., and Olson, G. (2002). The (currently) unique advantages of collocated work. In P. Hinds and S. Kiesler (eds.), *Distributed work* (113–135). Cambridge, MA: MIT Press.

Orlikowski, W. J. (1996). Improvising organizational transformation over time: A situated change perspective, *Information Systems Research, 7,* 63–92.

Orlikowski, W. J., and Gash, D. C. (1994). Technological frames: Making sense of information technology in organizations. *ACM Transactions on Information Systems, 12,* 174–207.

Prinz, W., and Kolvenbach, S. (1996). Support for ministerial workflows. In *Proceedings of the Conference on Computer Supported Cooperative Work CSCW'96* (199–208). New York: ACM Press.

Prinz, W., Mark, G., and Pankoke-Babatz, U. (1998). Designing groupware for congruency in use. In *Proceedings of the Conference on Computer Supported Cooperative Work CSCW'98* (373–382). New York: ACM Press.

Robinson, M. (1993). Design for unanticipated use. In *Proceedings of ECSCW '93* (187–202). Dordrecht: Kluwer Academic Publishers.

Rogers, Y. (1993). Coordinating computer-mediated work. *Computer Supported Cooperative Work (CSCW), An International Journal, 1,* 295–315.

Schutz, A. (1970). *On phenomenology and social relations.* Chicago: University of Chicago Press.

Turner, J. C., and Oakes, P. J. (1989). Self-categorization theory and social influence. In P. B. Paulus (ed.), *Psychology of group influence* (233–275). Hillsdale, NJ: Erlbaum.

Waldenfels, B. (1994). *Der stachel des fremden.* Frankfurt: Suhrkamp.

Waltz, K. N. (1979). *Theory of international politics.* Reading, MA: Addison-Wesley.

Wulf, V. (1997). Storing and retrieving documents in a shared workspace: Experiences from the political administration. In S. Howard, J. Hammond, and G. Lindgaard (eds.), *Human Computer Interaction: INTERACT 97* (469–476). London: Chapman and Hall.

12

Fuzzy Teams: Boundary Disagreement in Distributed and Collocated Teams

Mark Mortensen and Pamela Hinds

In this chapter, we challenge the prevailing assumption that team members agree on the membership and therefore the boundaries of their teams. In a comparative study of twelve collocated and twelve geographically distributed product development teams, we found that no team was in complete agreement as to its own membership. Preliminary evidence suggests that both tenure and cultural heterogeneity of team members, are associated with increased boundary agreement. Our data also suggest that collocated teams are more likely to add members, whereas geographically distributed teams tend to drop team members, especially those who are distant. However, geographically distributed as compared with collocated teams experience greater boundary agreement, perhaps due to less reciprocal interdependence on distributed teams and increased novelty of distant team members. Boundary agreement also was associated with more awareness of and access to expertise within the team and with overall team performance.

Having just presented their team's redesign of the new user interface, Larry and Alice stood in front of a room full of anxious stares. Finally, Karen, the project head, spoke up: "As you know, we are supposed to go live with this system in two weeks, and as we've just seen, your new redesign won't fully integrate with our product line. I realize we've all been working long hours, but how on earth did this slip by?"

Larry was quick to respond: "I know this is bad, but there's nothing else we could have done. We sent around an e-mail to everyone else on the team. We ran it by Phil, Joan, Chris, and Karl, and none of them foresaw this problem."

"Not to be picky, but you did not run it by everyone in the team. You never mentioned it to me," noted Alex, an engineer on the project, "and I could have helped."

Larry and Alice looked slightly startled. Finally Alice spoke up, "We certainly would have run it by you . . . but we didn't realize you were on the team."

Most scholarly and popular literature on teams assumes that teams have clear boundaries: who is and who is not a member of the team is readily apparent and agreed on. In this chapter, we challenge the notion of unambiguous team boundaries and examine the extent to which individuals agree on the membership of their teams. We present data suggesting that teams, even effective ones, often have ambiguous or fuzzy boundaries. Focusing our investigation on a comparison of collocated and distributed teams, we examine the effects of geographic distribution on boundary agreement. We also consider the effects of fuzzy boundaries on team process and performance.

Traditional View of Teams

Most definitions of teams assume that all members are aware of the team's membership, implying member agreement on team boundaries. Cohen and Bailey's (1997) definition of teams identifies group members as those "who see themselves and who are seen by others as an intact social entity" (241). This notion is also implicit in the definition of team specified by Alderfer (1977), later refined by Hackman (1987), and used in recent reviews of the literature (Sundstrom, De Meuse, and Futrell 1990). They define teams as "small groups of interdependent individuals who share responsibility for outcomes for their organizations" (Sundstrom et al. 1990, 120). This shared responsibility by team members implies an agreement as to the individuals contributing. More recently, Arrow, McGrath, and Berdahl (2000) used as a criteria for "groupiness" whether the people involved "recognize one another as members and distinguish members from non-members" (34).

Studies of geographically distributed teams typically have used definitions similar to those of collocated teams, that is, as "groups of geographically or organizationally dispersed coworkers that are assembled using a combination of telecommunications and information technologies to accomplish an organizational task" (Townsend, DeMarie, and Hendrickson 1998, 18). Like the definition that Alderfer and Hackman used, this definition makes an implicit assumption of mutual awareness of who is, and is not, a member.

This assumption of agreed-on boundaries plays a pivotal role in the theories of team dynamics that form the basis of our understanding of teams. Research on ingroups and out-groups (Abrams and Brown 1989; Tajfel and Turner 1986; Tsui, Egan, and O'Reilly 1992) and group composition (see Moreland and Levine 1992 for a review), for example, rest on the assumption that team members recognize one another as such. Similarly, work on boundary spanning relies on the idea that there is an agreed-on boundary that is crossed when team members interact with outsiders (Ancona and Caldwell 1992).

The assumption of clear boundaries is at least partially based on the methodologies that have been employed to study groups and teams. Much of the early work on teams used laboratory experiments in which membership was experimentally determined. Having been brought together in an artificially created experimental setting, subjects were encouraged to perceive other subjects assigned to work with them as their teammates. This approach was common in classic social-psychological work on group norms and influence (Asch 1953, Milgram 1963, Sherif 1936) and has continued in more recent group research (Kerr 1989, Moreland and Levine 1982). Similarly, in nonexperimental studies, researchers have worked with organizations to identify and delimit the boundaries of the teams being studied. For example, to "ensure that individuals had a common referent," the questionnaire in Ancona and Caldwell's (1992) study of product development teams included a list of team members. Although such methods ensure that questionnaire responses can be accurately aggregated to a team level, they do not allow for the possibility that the boundaries identified by the organization or researchers might not align with the boundaries perceived by team members. As a result, we know relatively little about the extent to which groups agree on their boundaries or the effects that disagreement might have on team functioning and effectiveness.

Our Study

To investigate the effects of geographic distribution on team process, we surveyed twenty-four product development teams. In this survey, each respondent could "correct" the official manager-provided list of team members. This tailoring was done primarily in an effort to reduce respondents' cognitive load by reducing irrelevant items and the survey's length. The result, however, was an unexpected discovery. Of the twenty-four teams surveyed, not a single team was in complete agreement on its team boundary: who was and who was not a member of the team. In fact, the average level of agreement within the sample was only 75 percent, such that that any given team member was likely to disagree with the rest of his or her team on one-quarter of potential team members. Error variance is to be expected in any survey, but this finding is startling when one considers that the lack of agreement occurred despite strong priming in the form of an official list of team members.

Causes of Boundary Agreement

Existing theory of teams and groups suggests a number of ways one might understand boundary agreement. Here, we outline a theoretical model of the causes of boundary agreement, the role of geographic distribution in boundary disagreement, and the effects of boundary agreement on teams.

The first step in understanding the causes of boundary agreement is to understand the mechanisms underlying people's perceptions of membership and team boundaries. By understanding how people identify others as teammates, we can better predict what factors will lead to boundary agreement in a team.

Sensemaking

By definition, team-level boundary agreement relies on individual team members' attribution of membership to others. We speculate that these attributions are assigned as individuals attempt to make sense of their work environment. Research on the process of sense making (Weick 1979, 1995) outlines a process wherein active agents attempt to "structure the unknown" (Waterman 1990, 41). In this view, "reality is an ongoing accomplishment that emerges from efforts to create order and make retrospective sense of what occurs" (Weick 1993, 635). Thus, although a formal organizational structure may exist, employees are likely to use an individual sense-making process to make sense of their own experiences and formulate a model of team membership and group boundaries.

Taking this a step further, we believe that individuals' models of team membership are based largely on the extent to which a person has strong memories of another person acting as a team member. Strong memories may result, in part, from interaction between the two people. When interaction has been extensive, an availability bias (see Tversky and Kahneman 1974) may lead to increased salience of the other's status as a team member. Extensive research on person perception suggests that the extent to which the target dominates the actor's visual field, the relevance of the target person to the actor's goals, and perceived novelty of the target person will increase the salience of a the target person (see Fiske and Taylor 1991) by improving the actor's ability to recall the target person. To the extent that experiences with the target are more available in memory, actors will make more attributions about the target's influence, importance, and so forth (see Pryor and Kriss 1977, Rholes and Pryor 1982). Thus, we expect those targets more salient as colleagues to be more readily perceived as team members when actors are attempting to make sense of team boundaries. The similarity of interaction patterns among team members should affect boundary agreement, as uneven communication will provide team members with different experiences on which to build their models of team membership. To the extent that team members have common perceptions and experiences of one another, we would expect group-level agreement on boundaries to be high. Conversely, to the extent that perceptions and experiences differ, agreement on boundaries is likely to be low.

Proposition 1: Similarity in quantity of interaction between team members, use of visual communication, interdependence among team members, and team members' perceived novelty will increase boundary agreement.

Geographic Distribution
For the purposes of this chapter, we consider distributed teams to be teams in which at least one member is located in a geographically distant location (another city or country). In contrast, we consider collocated teams to be teams in which all members of the team are located within one office building or complex. We further assume that distributed teams will have less face-to-face interaction on average than collocated teams and that they will rely more heavily on mediated communication technologies (e.g., e-mail, telephone, fax, videoconferencing) than will their collocated counterparts. Using the sense-making and salience arguments, there are two plausible alternative predictions of the effect of increased geographic distribution on boundary agreement: one that suggests reduced boundary agreement in distributed teams and the other that suggests increased boundary agreement in distributed teams. A diagram of the relationships is provided in figure 12.1.

Decreased Boundary Agreement   Distributed teams as compared with collocated teams could experience lower levels of agreement about team boundaries because they have less evenly distributed information among members, are less dominant in one another's visual fields, and have less interdependent working relationships. There are several reasons to expect information to be less evenly distributed within geographically distributed teams. People often are more difficult to reach when they are not nearby, as it is more difficult to monitor peoples' patterns of activity and

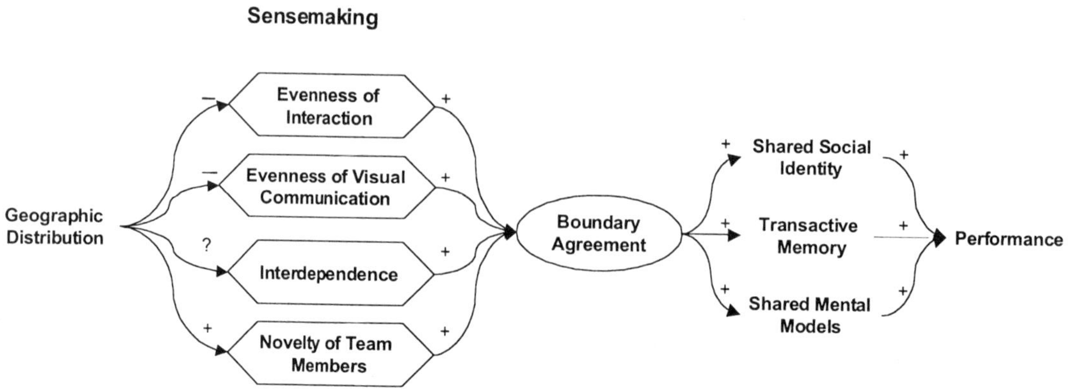

Sensemaking

Figure 12.1
Model of the effect of distribution on boundary agreement and team performance.

thus be aware of when they are available. Furthermore, even when people are accessible, interaction itself can be more difficult when partners are physically distant and technology is required as a mediator. In evidence of this, Cramton (2001) identifies unevenly distributed information as one of the key problems faced by many distributed teams and describes numerous situations in which conflicts arose because team members were not provided full information and were later expected to be aware of what was taking place. Similarly, other studies have demonstrated that information is often not shared equally among remote team members and that remote sites are excluded from important decisions (Armstrong and Cole, chapter 7, this volume; Grinter, Herbsleb, and Perry 1999).

Uneven distribution of information may affect boundary agreement in two ways. First, unevenly distributed information is likely to include information about the task as well as information about team membership. Second, repeated interactions can make others more salient in one's memory. To the extent that interaction is uneven, we posit a difference in team member salience that will result in less agreement on team boundaries.

Another factor likely to lower member salience in distributed teams is reduced visual access to teammates. People who are distant from one another are more likely to rely on mediating technologies, which tend to be text based and not to provide visual access to partners (see Olson and Teasley 1996). Collocated teams are more likely to participate in face-to-face meetings, engage in informal get-togethers by the water cooler, and share an office setting, all factors that increase visual access.

Without such access, those who are seen infrequently and whose interaction is predominantly textual or limited to voice are less likely to be salient as team members. Armstrong and Cole (chapter 7, this volume) describe this as an "out of sight, out of mind" problem in which remote sites are ignored even during joint telephone and videoconferences. It follows that on distributed teams, those who are collocated are more likely to see one another as team members, thus creating subgroups with stronger internal agreement and less overall agreement as to team boundaries. An exception to this line of reasoning may be teams that rely heavily on video technologies for interactions. We anticipate that extensive use of video technologies will mitigate the effect of reduced face-to-face communication.

Member salience also is likely to be reduced due to a lack of interdependence within distributed teams. In comparison with collocated teams, we posit that distributed teams will manage the challenges of distance by decreasing interdependence among team members. This is consistent with Olson and Olson's (2000) finding that technology may not support tight coupling among team members and that work is frequently reorganized to reduce tight coupling between distant locations. They provide an example where software design work was reorganized such that tasks associated with each module of the software were conducted by separate collocated teams. In fact, the only successful distributed teams in their study were those in which the work was modularized in ways that allowed loose coupling of activities across sites (see also Moon and Sproull, chapter 16, this volume). Given that strong goal interdependence among people increases their salience to one another (Ruscher and Fiske 1990), it follows that both lower levels of interdependence and uneven distribution of interdependence on a team are likely to reduce boundary agreement.

Taken together, these factors suggest that a collocated team is more likely to agree on who is and who is not a member than will a geographically distributed one. This proposition is consistent with evidence that face-to-face interaction is more appropriate than mediated interaction for building a shared interpretive context (Zack 1993), with evidence that social contracts diminish when team members are distant from one another (Olson and Teasley 1996) and with Caldwell and Koch's (2000) finding that reduced collocation makes team boundaries more permeable and more difficult to define.

Proposition 2a: Geographically distributed teams will experience lower boundary agreement than collocated teams due to more unevenly distributed information, reduced and uneven visual access, and reduced and uneven interdependence.

Increased Boundary Agreement   In opposition to proposition 2a, we consider the alternative hypothesis that distributed as compared with collocated teams will experience higher levels of agreement about team membership. It is possible that members of distributed teams, as compared with those who are collocated, are more dependent on one another to accomplish their goals, that they will perceive one another as more unique, and that they will find their team interactions more memorable because of the effort required to interact.

One factor related to geographic distribution that is likely to increase salience of membership in distributed teams is that these teams often are composed to take advantage of distributed resources, such as specialized expertise and access to goods, services, or customers unique to a geographic location (see DeSanctis and Monge 1999, Grinter et al. 1999). As a result, the roles or skills held by the members of distributed teams may be more diverse or unique than those of collocated team members. As the explicit and unique reasons for members' inclusion in the team become clear, these people may be more heavily relied on by their teammates. Consequently, they are more likely to be perceived as team members by other members of the team, increasing the overall level of boundary agreement within the team.

In addition to skill diversity, distributed teams may be demographically more diverse than collocated teams. This should be especially true of internationally distributed teams whose membership reflects several different national cultures. This diversity also may increase the novelty and therefore the salience of the individuals with whom the members of geographically distributed teams interact.

Distributed teams might more easily recall their interactions with distant team members due to the cost and effort these interactions require. Distributed teams must rely on technology or travel, or both, to interact; even with fast planes and advanced technologies, though, work is difficult to coordinate across distance and time zones (Olson and Olson 2000). Thus, team members are likely to be acutely aware of the members with whom they put in so much effort to interact. This increased awareness, along with interdependence and novelty, could lead to higher levels of boundary agreement in distributed as compared with collocated teams.

Proposition 2b: Geographically distributed teams will experience greater boundary agreement than their collocated counterparts due to greater interdependence, novelty of team members, and effort required to interact.

Effects of Boundary Disagreement

The extent to which a team agrees on its boundaries is likely to yield a wide range of team-level effects. We posit that fuzzy teams will be less likely to develop shared mental models about their tasks and their team and less likely to develop an effective transactive memory system and a shared team identity. We further argue that reduced shared mental models, transactive memory, and identity will reduce overall team performance.

Shared Mental Models and Transactive Memory

In their extensive review of research on team mental models, Klimoski and Mohammed (1994) point out that being on the same team, sharing experiences, and communicating contribute to the development of shared understandings. To the extent that team members do not agree who is on the team, do not share experiences together, and have uneven communication, their development of shared mental models may be impaired. Most work in this area argues that shared mental models are a precondition for well-coordinated team action (Bettenhausen and Murnighan 1985, Walsh and Fahey 1986, Weick and Bougon 1986) and enable organizations to be flexible and robust (Hutchins 1990). Therefore, through unshared team mental models, a lack of boundary agreement could contribute to poor coordination and structural rigidity.

Closely related is the notion of transactive memory, whereby a team is able to maintain a distributed group-level memory. Transactive memory systems comprise two major components: individually held knowledge and an awareness of the location of that knowledge (see Liang, Moreland, and Argote 1995). Transactive memory systems enable teams to identify the team members who have expertise in a given knowledge domain, which has a positive impact on work group performance (Hollingshead 1998a, 1998b; Liang et al. 1995; Moreland, Argote, and Krishnan 1996). Knowing which team members are good at a particular task allows teams to plan their own work better, thereby improving the team's overall coordination and allowing them to solve unexpected problems more quickly and easily (Moreland and Levine 1992, Moreland et al. 1996). However, if team membership is unclear, it may be difficult to develop and maintain a transactive memory. Hence, transactive memory systems are likely to be weak in teams that do not agree on boundaries. Thus, groups with lower boundary agreement will be less able to coordinate, retrieve, and use the knowledge that they possess.

Proposition 3a: Boundary agreement within teams will increase shared mental model formation and the effectiveness of transactive memory systems.

Shared Social Identity

A group's level of boundary agreement is likely to affect its ability to create a shared social identity. Drawing on social comparison theory (Festinger 1954, Sokol 1992) and closely related to self-categorization theory (Turner, Hogg, Oakes, Reicher, and Wetherell 1987), social identity theory argues that individuals engage in a process of categorization relative to those around them (Gecas, Thomas, and Weigert 1973). In an effort to fulfill a need for favorable self-image and maintain self-esteem, these categorizations are assigned comparative valences, with those most similar to the categorizer being valued most highly. This process results in two basic categorizations of people, in-group and out-group, with members of the in-group viewed more positively than members of the out-group.

Teams with fuzzy boundaries are likely to experience a weaker sense of team identity and be prone to experience out-group feelings toward other team members. If the team does not agree on its membership, by definition there will be some individuals viewed as in-group by some and out-group by others. Such out-group feelings toward teammates "have been shown to lead to decreased satisfaction with the team, increased turnover, lowered levels of cohesiveness, reduced within team communication, decreased cooperation, and higher levels of conflict" (Williams and O'Reilly 1998, 84).

Proposition 3b: Boundary agreement within teams will increase the likelihood of shared social identity formation.

Proposition 3c: Boundary agreement within teams will increase overall team performance.

Method

To test some of the propositions discussed above, we examined the data from our study of collocated and geographically distributed product development teams. Although the study was not designed for this purpose, we use the data to explore our ideas about what may lead to and result from boundary agreement. We hope that this will lead to more informed theory about boundary agreement on collocated and distributed teams.

Our study was designed to investigate the effects of geographic distribution on knowledge sharing, group dynamics, and overall team effectiveness. The survey was sent to 221 individuals in twenty-six teams located in five companies. One hundred forty-one usable responses were returned from twenty-four teams in five companies, a 63 percent response rate. For analysis, the sample was subdivided into twelve collocated and twelve geographically distributed teams.

Although all of these teams were responsible for developing a new product for commercial sale, they differed in many respects. Table 12.1 provides a summary of the characteristics of the twenty-four teams in our sample. The official size of our teams ranged from five to seventeen members.[1] In general, the projects were well underway, with the average project being 69 percent complete.

Data Collection

The primary data collection method used was a Web-based survey, designed to allow for automated real-time customization. Upon beginning the survey, respondents were provided with a list of individuals that reflected their official team membership as reported by the team's manager, who was designated by the organization. Respondents were asked to review the list of team members and to "indicate which of the following people you consider to be members of the team and add any additional team members we missed." To remove team members, respondents needed to switch a radio button from the default value of yes to no. To add team members, respondents had to type the individual's name and switch the associated radio button from its default value of no to yes. The resulting list was used to tailor subsequent questions based on each subject's perception of his or her team's membership.

Measuring Boundary Agreement

To better understand boundary agreement, a measure of the extent to which each respondent agreed with his or her teammates on the composition of the team was created. To create the measure, a pairwise comparison of the membership lists of all respondents within a given team was conducted, yielding a percentage of agreement for each pair of individuals.[3] For example, if person i indicated that j, k, and l were members of the team and person j indicted that i, k, and m were members of the team, the pair ij would receive a score of 60 percent because they were in agreement on three (i, j, and k) of five team members. Averaging across all pairs within a team created a group average of these agreement measures. To better

Table 12.1
Characteristics of teams in sample

Type of team	Team size[a]	Percentage complete	Project certainty[b]	Average tenure (months)	Member agreement	Manager agreement	Percentage dropped	Percentage added
Collocated teams								
High tech	8	72%	3.75	45.75	83%	88%	2%	19%
High tech	6	91	4.00	39.75	74	84	0	29
High tech	9	38	3.39	20.50	79	88	2	20
High tech	9	34	4.11	15.00	51	55	53	25
Computer Peripherals	8	77	3.11	18.33	80	86	4	15
Snack foods	8	71	4.17	9.00	93	96	0	4
Snack foods	6	61	3.50	2.50	40	70	17	33
Snack foods	8	51	4.67	15.50	62	73	6	38
Snack foods	10	71	4.11	7.50	64	80	13	17
Snack foods	9	70	3.53	11.20	64	81	18	13
System design	7	61	3.38	9.71	75	88	12	2
System design	6	91	3.17	15.93	90	83	0	8
Average	7.83	65	3.74	17.56	71	81	11	19

Distributed teams

High tech	14	81%	3.29%	10.75%	73%	83%	17%	13%
High tech	11	77	2.67	17.11	73	85	17	15
High tech	5	91	3.50	7.50	76	82	0	40
High tech	8	86	4.20	10.25	67	82	19	10
Computer Peripherals	17	76	2.89	21.42	84	85	13	4
System design	6	38	1.83	3.50	81	86	6	11
System design	6	76	3.67	20.75	83	92	0	13
Semiconductors	8	56	2.95	18.14	84	89	82	9
High tech	6	75	3.17	29.83	89	83	17	0
Snack foods	14	86	3.37	13.13	69	79	26	6
Snack foods	11	84	3.17	10.29	79	86	13	4
System design	9	57	3.42	8.17	79	92	13	30
Average	9.58	73	3.18	14.24	78	85	18	13
Average, all teams	8.71	69	3.46	15.90	75	83	15	16

a Size is official team size as identified by team managers.
b Ratings given on a scale of 1–5 (1 = low, 5 = high).

understand the nature of boundary agreement, three additional measures were created: agreement with manager, percentage of members added, and percentage of members dropped.

The measure of manager boundary agreement was designed to gauge the extent to which the team, on average, agreed with management's official view of the composition of the team. Similar to the measure of member agreement, the measure of manager agreement was created based on a comparison of the membership lists of each member with that of the team manager. An average across all team members yielded a team-level measure of agreement with the manager.

We also calculated percentage of members added and percentage of members dropped from the official manager-sanctioned team roster. To calculate these measures, each team member's roster was compared with the official manager-sanctioned list. The number of added and dropped team members were then divided by the official team size, thus yielding a percentage added and percentage dropped.

Before assessing the relationship between boundary agreement and the variables discussed, we offer two caveats: those of statistical significance and causality. Although we do not have appropriate data or an adequate number of teams to thoroughly test the propositions we have presented, our data do allow us to look at patterns to identify the most promising propositions. We present statistical analyses designed to illustrate such patterns in the data. Second, the propositions discussed earlier imply causality. Critics will quickly and accurately note that our data are correlational and thus do not lend themselves to tests of causality. In most cases, we believe these relationships to be self-reinforcing (e.g., low levels of boundary agreement lead to low levels of shared identity, which further reduces boundary agreement). Thus, our analyses are meant primarily to suggest possible links between variables. Given these two methodological caveats, we offer these analyses with the purpose of theory building rather than hypothesis testing.

Findings

Boundary Agreement

No groups were in complete agreement as to their membership, suggesting that at least some level of boundary disagreement is common in all teams. The teams in our sample ranged in boundary agreement from a low of 40 percent to a high of 93 percent, with an average agreement of 75 percent. Manager boundary agreement was slightly higher, ranging from a low of 55 percent to a high of 96 percent, with an average of 83 percent. Team members were equally as likely to be added (16 percent) or dropped (15 percent), although the percentage of members dropped had a much larger range (0–82 percent) than the percentage of members added (0–40 percent).

We now explore the potential causes and consequences of boundary agreement. We argued that increased interaction, visual access, interdependence, and novelty of the target person would increase membership salience.

To understand the effects of volume and similarity of interaction as well as visual access on boundary agreement, we created measures of overall, mediated, and visual communication. Overall communication consisted of the aggregate average quantity of communication among team members across all media, including face-to-face. Visual and mediated communication formed overlapping subsets of overall communication. The former consisted of face-to-face communication and video-conferencing, whereas the latter of all mediated (non-face-to-face) communication technologies. To measure the extent to which teams communicated unevenly, we calculated the average Euclidean distance between the reported communication patterns given by the members of each team. This produced a measure of the extent to which teams were dissimilar in their patterns of communication. Finally, in an effort to assess the effects of interaction over time, we averaged self-reported tenure (in months) across team members.

Though not significant, the regressions of boundary agreement on average quantities of overall communication ($\beta = -.06$, $p = .76$) and visual communication ($\beta = -.13$, $p = .46$) yielded negative relationships. In contrast, though also non-significant, the regression of average quantity of mediated communication ($\beta = .13$, $p = .55$) was positive. Although none of these findings were statistically significant, they suggest that while the participants in face-to-face communication are often difficult to delimit (e.g., everyone in a room versus only those talking), mediated communication often requires explicit identification of interaction partners.

To test the effects of unevenly distributed information, boundary agreement was regressed on the dissimilarity of overall, visual, and mediated communication patterns, controlling for quantity of communication. Dissimilarity of overall ($\beta = .19$, $p = .38$), visual ($\beta = .17$, $p = .47$), and mediated ($\beta = .24$, $p = .27$) communication patterns, however, were not significantly related to boundary agreement. Although the regressions of boundary agreement on average quantity and evenness of overall and visual communication did not yield significant results, the regression of boundary agreement on tenure resulted in a significant, positive relationship ($\beta = .41$,

$p < .05$). This suggests that over time, repeated interactions may lead to a shared understanding of who makes up the team, thus providing partial support for our first proposition.

We also argued that interdependence among team members would increase boundary agreement. To test this idea, we used three measures. First, we created a dependency measure from the data provided in the survey. Each respondent was asked to indicate on a five-point scale (1 = "not at all," 5 = "heavily") how much she or he relied on every other member of the team, and an average interdependence score was calculated across all dyads. Second, with the idea that boundary agreement may be linked to the similarity of interdependence between team members, we created a measure of interdependence pattern dissimilarity. This measure consisted of team-level Euclidean distances of the interdependency scores outlined above. Third, we tried to understand the nature of each team's interdependence (pooled, reciprocal, or sequential) by asking them how work was coordinated. We asked each person to rate his or her team on the following items using a five-point scale, where 5 indicated that the description fit "very much." The following descriptions represent types of interdependence as outlined by Mintzberg (1979) in his work on organizational structuring:

Pooled. Like a symphony: We work on the same components of the product at the same time. We are aware of others' activities and continually adjust our own work to match the work being done by other team members.

Reciprocal. Like a baseball team: Each of us works on the product for awhile, hands it off to someone else on the team, and then we get it back when our expertise is required again.

Sequential. Like a factory: As each of us completes a piece of the product, we hand it off to another team member to add his or her piece to it. Each of us rarely works on any model or piece of the product more than once.

Contrary to our propositions, the average level of interdependence between dyads on the team was not associated with boundary agreement. Similarly, no significant relationship was found between similarity of interdependence and boundary agreement. However, our examination of the nature of the interdependence—pooled, reciprocal, or sequential—was more fruitful. The results of these analyses found reciprocal interdependence to be negatively associated with boundary agreement ($\beta = -.43$, $p < .05$). One interpretation of these results is that limited handoffs to people with particular expertise may reduce other interactions on the team and result in less awareness of other team members.

The final factor that we proposed would lead to boundary agreement was perceived novelty of team members. To examine novelty, we calculated several measures of heterogeneity, including cultural (an index of ethnicity, country of origin, and dominant language), gender, age, and functional training. Of these measures, heterogeneity of gender ($\beta = -.10$, $p = .64$), age ($\beta = -.13$, $p = .53$), and functional training ($\beta = -.16$, $p = .46$) were not found to be related to team boundary agreement. Cultural heterogeneity, however, was found to be significantly related ($\beta = .46$, $p < .05$) to boundary agreement, thus providing partial support for our proposition that novelty increases salience of team members and thus boundary agreement.

Taken together, these analyses suggest that tenure in team and cultural heterogeneity increase boundary agreement, while reciprocal interdependence serves to reduce it.

Distributed Teams

We offered alternative hypotheses. On the one hand, distributed teams may experience lower levels of boundary agreement due to less evenly distributed interaction, less visual contact between team members, and less interdependence between team members. On the other hand, distributed teams may experience higher levels of boundary agreement because they may have more novel membership, greater interdependence, and more memorable interactions among team members.

Looking first at descriptive statistics, boundary agreement was slightly higher in distributed teams ($M = 78$ percent) than in collocated teams ($M = 71$ percent). Within distributed teams, our sample included domestic teams (team members in the same country) and international teams (team members in multiple countries). More distance was associated with more agreement (collocated = 71 percent, domestically distributed = 77 percent, internationally distributed = 80 percent). In a regression analysis controlling for tenure, collocation was marginally associated with reduced boundary agreement ($\beta = -.35$, $p = .08$). Though not statistically significant, these findings provide some support for proposition 2b: that distributed teams experience higher levels of boundary agreement than collocated teams.

We also examined the type of boundary disagreement in collocated as compared with distributed teams and discovered that members of distributed teams were more likely to drop rather than add team members, whereas the reverse was true for collocated teams. On average, members of collocated teams dropped 11 percent of the official team members, whereas members of distributed teams dropped an average of 18 percent. Conversely, while collocated teams added an average of 19 percent to the official list, distributed teams added only 13 percent. This observation suggests that the source of disagreement may be different on geographically distributed as compared with collocated teams. It suggests an "out of sight, out of mind" problem, wherein distant team members are forgotten. It also suggests a social noise problem in collocated teams, wherein individuals may have difficulty distinguishing interactions with team members from their large number of non-team-related face-to-face interactions.

An examination of interdependence on distributed teams suggests a more complex story than a simple positive or negative relationship between geographic distribution and interdependence. Our data indicate that collocated and distributed teams have nearly the same level of interdependence ($M = 3.3$ versus $M = 3.2$, on a 5-point scale). However, based on the average Euclidean distance between members with respect to interdependence, distributed teams, as compared with collocated teams, were found to have less evenly distributed interdependence ($M = 1.6$ versus .45 respectively). Recall, though, that similarity in interdependence was not associated with boundary agreement. Therefore, we turned our attention to the amount of reciprocal interdependence on collocated as compared with distributed teams. The results suggest that collocated teams have more reciprocal interdependence than distributed teams ($M = 3.30$ versus 2.64). Given that earlier analyses indicated a negative relationship between reciprocal interdependence and boundary agreement, the data suggest the possibility that being collocated may lead to reduced boundary agreement due to more reciprocal work arrangements.

Turning to the issue of novelty, our data show that distributed teams are likely to be more heterogeneous with respect to factors like functional ($M = .73$ versus .62) and cultural background ($M = .44$ versus .19, on a scale of 0–1). This finding suggests that members of distributed teams are likely to appear different from one another. To test the relationship between heterogeneity and boundary agreement, within a sample restricted to only geographically distributed teams, agreement was regressed on measures of heterogeneity (gender, age, culture, and functional training). Although the results for gender ($\beta = -.12$, $p = .73$) and age ($\beta = .16$, $p = .63$) were not significant, suggestive relationships for these twelve teams were found for functional heterogeneity ($\beta = .56$, $p = .06$) and cultural heterogeneity ($\beta = .47$, $p = .12$). Furthermore, despite their lack of significance, the R^2 values for the models with training heterogeneity (adjusted $R^2 = .25$) and cultural heterogeneity (adjusted $R^2 = .15$) were high, indicating that these effects explained a significant proportion of the variance in boundary agreement in distributed teams. This result provides further support for our argument that geographic distribution increases functional diversity and novelty, thus increasing member salience and subsequently boundary agreement.

Finally, paralleling the tests of the effects of communication run on the entire sample, boundary agreement was regressed on both communication quantity and dissimilarity within distributed teams. Although neither quantity of overall ($\beta = .22$, $p = .47$) nor visual ($\beta = .09$, $p = .77$) communication was significantly related to boundary agreement, a significant relationship was found for quantity of mediated communication ($\beta = .58$, $p = .05$). This result for mediated communication suggests that within distributed teams, the explicit identification of interaction partners typically found within mediated communication may highlight team membership. At the same time, controlling for volume, dissimilarity in patterns of overall ($\beta = -.09$, $p = .80$), visual ($\beta = -.19$, $p = .60$), and mediated ($\beta = .10$, $p = .72$) yielded no significant relationships.

Performance and Other Outcome Measures

In propositions 3a, 3b, and 3c, we posited that disagreement would lead to a reduction in shared mental models, impaired transactive memory, a reduction in shared identity, and subsequently lower overall performance. We do not have the data to examine shared mental models, but our analyses of transactive memory, shared identity, and overall performance provide partial support for these propositions. Although the analyses of shared identity (as measured by a sixteen-item scale based on Tyler 1999) were not associated with boundary agreement, the results suggest that the development of a transactive memory may be impaired on teams with lower levels of boundary agreement. In our survey, we asked respondents about how frequently they experienced "not having access to expertise or information when you need it" and "not knowing who should be responsible for a particular activity." We combined these into a measure of transactive memory. The results indicate that problems with transactive memory are strongly related to boundary disagreement ($\beta = .47$, $p = .02$). Although the direction of causality cannot be established, we believe that this indicates that confusion about the boundaries of the team makes it difficult to know where the expertise resides in the team and to take advantage of it.

Finally, in our survey, we asked respondents to report on how they thought the team was performing. We asked respondents how their team performed with respect to efficiency, quality, technical innovation, adherence to schedule and budget, and work excellence, all rated on a five-point scale where 1 = "poor" and 5 = "excellent." The five performance measures were combined to form a single index of overall performance (α = .80). Although regressing this performance measure on boundary agreement yielded only a marginally significant effect (adjusted R^2 = .09, β = .361, p < .08), the pattern suggests that boundary agreement may positively affect (perceived) performance.

Implications for Research and Practice

In this chapter, we examined a characteristic of teams that has to date remained largely unexplored: team boundary agreement. Although agreement on boundaries and membership has traditionally been a central part of the definition of teams, our data suggest that boundary agreement on teams cannot be expected or assumed. Recently, Arrow and associates (2000) argued that agreement on membership is an indicator of the "groupiness" of the group. Although this perspective is consistent with the data presented in this chapter, we found little link between boundary agreement and our measures of group identity. Boundary agreement may still be an indicator of "groupiness," but it represents a different dimension from group identity or cohesiveness.

Our data suggest that boundary agreement may result from different sources in geographically distributed and collocated teams. In distributed teams, different perceptions of team boundaries were often a result of official team members' being dropped from the team, whereas in collocated teams, the opposite was true. We suspect that this is a reflection of distributed teams' suffering from an "out of sight, out of mind" problem in which distant team members are less likely to be recognized as team members. To evaluate this possibility, we calculated the percentage of dropped individuals who were distant from versus collocated with the respondents. As expected, within distributed teams, individuals were almost twice as likely to drop an individual who was located at a different site (65 percent) than one with whom they were collocated (35 percent).

We argued that team interaction, interdependence between team members, and novelty of team members would increase team member salience, contributing to higher levels of boundary agreement. We found some support for each of these relationships. A shared history measured by average tenure within the team was positively related to boundary agreement, suggesting that boundary agreement is likely to improve over time as repeated interactions take place and more context is shared.

Although neither overall nor similarity of interdependence among team members was related to boundary agreement, reciprocal interdependence was negatively associated with boundary agreement. Reciprocal interdependence is an indicator of the extent to which work is passed back and forth between team members as their expertise is required. Reciprocal interdependence may be characterized by handoffs between team members that do not involve and are not visible to the entire team. Thus, shared team membership may be evident to those involved in the handoff but hidden from others on the team.

We also found some support for the relationship between novelty and boundary agreement. To the extent that team membership differed in ethnicity, country of origin, and dominant language, boundary agreement was higher. These results suggest that cultural heterogeneity may play a role in increasing the salience of team membership and thus increasing boundary agreement. However, we found no similar effects for gender, age, or functional background on collocated teams.

We argued and found support for the idea that boundary disagreement on teams may be associated with a lower perceived performance and a weakened transactive memory system. Although the limitations of our data make it difficult to untangle the relationship between these factors, we hypothesize that boundary agreement disrupts the transactive memory system by making it difficult to identify the location of expertise on the team and subsequently access it. We further posit that the weakened transactive memory system may inhibit performance, a hypothesis consistent with the findings of previous work on transactive memory in teams (Liang et al. 1995).

In addition to contributing a new variable to models of team effectiveness, a better understanding of boundary agreement stands to affect existing research on boundary spanning (Ancona and Caldwell 1992). Underlying this research on activities that span team boundaries is the assumption that boundaries exist, are known, and are agreed on. Given the patterns in our data, we suspect that it may be the case that many such boundary-spanning activities are in actuality perceived by team members as being completely internal to the team. Further complicating matters, given disagreement as to team boundaries, there may also be disagreement as to the extent to which activities are in fact internal versus boundary spanning.

In addition to the theoretical, there are methodological implications of this work. Given evidence that teams may not agree on their membership, investigating teams as though this agreement exists may introduce unnecessary variance. We believe it is possible to address the issues surrounding team boundaries through the use of social network methods. By collecting team data as social networks, membership can be determined through an analysis of the patterns of interconnection among all potential team members. Within this context, teams are defined as "subsets of actors among whom there are relatively strong, direct, intense, frequent, or positive ties" (Wasserman and Faust 1994, 249). Setting a boundary level of interconnection provides a means of differentiating between those considered to be members of the team and those falling outside its boundaries. Thus, the use of network measures to determine group membership provides a step toward including boundary agreement in empirical work on teams.

The work reported here has many methodological limitations, including a small sample and a study that was admittedly not designed to investigate this phenomenon. Furthermore, our sample includes only product development teams. Only future research can validate the findings presented here and determine the extent to which our preliminary work generalizes to other types of teams. Preliminary findings from this study suggest further investigation into the nature and effects of boundary agreement. In particular, validation of the findings regarding the relationship of tenure, reciprocal interdependence, and boundary agreement would provide insight into the underlying causes of this phenomenon. Further exploration of the relationship between transactive memory and team performance is important to establish the importance of boundary agreement for team performance and provide a useful link to an important existing literature. Finally, boundary agreement may be increased on distributed teams, perhaps because of the novelty associated with heterogeneous membership. The link between boundary agreement and geographic distribution, however, remains complex and requires additional empirical work to understand fully.

In the meantime, we cautiously propose several ways that managers and other practitioners can address the issue of boundary agreement. For both distributed and collocated teams, reduced turnover may lead to higher levels of boundary agreement. Reducing turnover has other positive effects on teams and therefore poses little risk. Managers may want to ensure a balance between formal procedures and informal interaction among all team members so that team members do not lose touch with one another. As part of this strategy, managers and team members may want to understand team members' perceptions of team boundaries. They can then use this knowledge to reintegrate members who have inadvertently been forgotten or left out.

Notes

This research was partially supported by a National Science Foundation grant (IIS-9872996) to the second author. We thank Andrea Hollingshead, Jane Siegel, and Sara Kiesler for their helpful suggestions on earlier drafts.

1. Official team size reflects the number of members on the team as reported to us by management.

2. To create a measure of agreement between team members, those who did not respond to the survey were removed as respondents in this measure.

References

Abrams, D., and Brown, R. (1989). Self-consciousness and social identity: Self-regulation as a group member. *Social Psychology Quarterly, 52,* 311–318.

Alderfer, C. P. (1977). Organization development. *Annual Review of Psychology, 28,* 197–223.

Ancona, D. G., and Caldwell, D. F. (1992). Bridging the boundary: External activity and performance in organizational teams. *Administrative Science Quarterly, 37,* 634–665.

Armstrong, D. J., and Cole, P. (2002). Managing distances and differences in geographically distributed work groups. In P. Hinds and S. Kiesler, *Distributed work* (167–186). Cambridge, MA: MIT Press.

Arrow, H., McGrath, J. E., and Berdahl, J. L. (2000). *Small groups as complex systems: Formation, coordination, development and adaptation.* Thousand Oaks, CA: Sage.

Asch, S. E. (1953). Effects of group pressure upon the modification and distortion of judgements. In D. Cartwright and A. Zander (eds.), *Group dynamics: Research and theory* (151–162). Evanston, IL: Row, Peterson.

Bettenhausen, K. L., and Murnighan, J. K. (1985). The emergence of norms in competitive decision-making groups. *Administrative Science Quarterly, 30,* 350–372.

Caldwell, D. F., and Koch, J. L. (2000). The impact of mobile computing on work groups. In M. Neale, B. Mannix, and T. Griffith (eds.), *Managing groups and teams.* Stamford, CT: JAI Press.

Cohen, S. G., and Bailey, D. E. (1997). What makes teams work: Group effectiveness research from the shop floor to the executive suite. *Journal of Management, 23,* 239–290.

Cramton, C. D. (2001). The mutual knowledge problem and its consequences in geographically dispersed teams. *Organization Science, 12,* 346–371.

DeSanctis, G., and Monge, P. (1999). Introduction to the special issue: Communication processes for virtual organizations. *Organization Science, 10,* 693–703.

Festinger, L. (1954). A theory of social comparison processes. *Human Relations, 7,* 117–140.

Fiske, S. T., and Taylor, S. E. (1991). *Social cognition* (2nd ed.). New York: McGraw-Hill.

Gecas, V., Thomas, D. L., and Weigert, A. J. (1973). Social identities in Anglo and Latin adolescents. *Social Forces, 51,* 477–484.

Grinter, R. E., Herbselb, J. D., and Perry, D. W. (1999). The geography of coordination: Dealing with distance in RandD work. In *Proceedings of SIGGROUP Conference on Supporting Group Work* (306—315). New York: ACM Press.

Hackman, J. R. (1987). The design of work teams. In J. Lorsch (ed.), *Handbook of organizational behavior* (315–342). Englewood Cliffs, NJ: Prentice Hall.

Hollingshead, A. B. (1998a). Distributed knowledge and transactive processes in decision-making groups. M. A. Neale, E. Mannix, and D. H. Gruenfeld (eds.), *Research on managing groups and teams* (Vol. 1, 105–125). Stamford, CT: JAI Press.

Hollingshead, A. B. (1998b). Retrieval processes in transactive memory systems. *Journal of Personality and Social Psychology, 74*(3), 659–671.

Hutchins, E. (1990). The technology of team navigation. J. Galegher, R. E. Kraut, and C. Egido (eds.), *Intellectual teamwork: Social and technological foundations of cooperative work* (191–220). Hillsdale, NJ: Erlbaum.

Kerr, N. (1989). Norms in social dilemmas. In D. Schroeder (ed.), *Social dilemmas: Social psychological perspectives*. New York: Draper.

Klimoski, R., and Mohammed, S. (1994). Team mental model: Construct or metaphor? *Journal of Management, 20,* 403–437.

Liang, D. W., Moreland, R., and Argote, L. (1995). Group versus individual training and group performance: The mediating factor of transactive memory. *Personality and Social Psychology Bulletin, 21,* 384–393.

Milgram, S. (1963). Behavioral study of obedience. *Journal of Abnormal Social Psychology, 67,* 371–378.

Mintzberg, H. (1979). *The structuring of organizations: A synthesis of the research.* Englewood Cliffs, NJ: Prentice Hall.

Moon, J. Y., and Sproull, L. (2002). Essence of distributed work: The case of the Linux kernel. In P. Hinds and S. Kiesler (eds.), *Distributed work* (381–404). Cambridge, MA: MIT Press.

Moreland, R. L., Argote, L., and Krishnan, R. (1996). Socially shared cognition at work: Transactive memory and group performance. In J. L. Nye and A. M. Brower (eds.), *What's social about social cognition? Research on socially shared cognition in small groups* (57–84). Thousand Oaks, CA: Sage.

Moreland, R., and Levine, J. (1982). Socialization in small groups: Temporal changes in individual-group relations. In L. Berkowitz (ed.), *Advances in experimental social psychology* (Vol. 15, 137–192). New York: Academic Press.

Moreland, R. L., and Levine, J. M. (1992). The composition of small groups. In E. Lawler, B. Markovsky, C. Ridgeway, and H. Walker (eds.), *Advances in group processes* (Vol. 9, 237–280). Greenwich, CT: JAI Press.

Olson, G., and Olson, J. (2000). Distance matters. *Human Computer Interaction, 15,* 139–179.

Olson, J. S., and Teasley, S. D. (1996). Groupware in the wild: Lessons learned from a year of virtual collocation. *Proceedings of the ACM Conference on Human Factors in Computing Systems* (419–427). New York: ACM Press.

Pryor, J. B., and Kriss, M. (1977). The cognitive dynamics of salience in the attribution process. *Journal of Personality and Social Psychology, 35,* 49–55.

Rentsch, J. R., Heffner, T. S., and Duffy, L. T. (1994). What you know is what you get from experience: Team experience related to teamwork schemas. *Group and Organization Management, 19,* 450–474.

Rholes, W. S., and Pryor, J. B. (1982). Cognitive accessibility and causal attributions. *Personality and Social Psychology Bulletin, 8*(4), 719–727.

Ruscher, J. B., and Fiske, S. T. (1990). Interpersonal competition can cause individuating processes. *Journal of Personality and Social Psychology, 58,* 832–843.

Sherif, M. (1936). *The psychology of social norms.* New York: Harper.

Sokol, M. B. (1992). Time boundaries, task commitment, and the illusion of group immortality. *Consulting Psychology Journal: Practice and Research, 44,* 28–32.

Sundstrom, E., De Meuse, K. P. , and Futrell, D. (1990). Work teams: Applications and effectiveness. *American Psychologist [Special Issue: Organizational Psychology], 45,* 120–133.

Tajfel, H., and Turner, J. C. (1986). The social identity theory of intergroup behavior. In W. G. Austin and S. Worchel (eds.), *Psychology of intergroup relations* (2nd ed., 7–24). Chicago: Nelson-Hall Publishers.

Townsend, A. M., DeMarie, S. M., and Hendrickson, A. R. (1998). Virtual teams: Technology and the workplace of the future. *Academy of Management Executive, 12,* 17–29.

Tsui, A. S., Egan, T. D., and O'Reilly, C. A. I. (1992). Being different: Relational demography and organizational attachment. *Administrative Science Quarterly, 37,* 549–579.

Turner, J. C., Hogg, M. A., Oakes, P. J., Reicher, S. D., and Wetherell, M. S. (1987). *Rediscovering the social group: A self-categorization theory.* Oxford: Blackwell.

Tversky, A., and Kahneman, D. (1974, September 27). Judgment under uncertainty: Heuristics and biases. *Science, 185,* 1124–1131.

Tyler, T. R. (1999). Why people cooperate with organizations: An identity based perspective. *Research in Organizational Behavior, 21,* 201–246.

Walsh, J. P. , and Fahey, L. (1986). The role of negotiated belief structures in strategy making. *Journal of Management, 12,* 325–338.

Wasserman, S., and Faust, K. (1994). *Social network analysis: Methods and applications* Cambridge: Cambridge University Press.

Waterman, R. H. Jr. (1990). *Adhocracy: The power to change.* Memphis, TN: Whittle Direct Books.

Weick, K. E. (1979). Cognitive processes in organizations. In B. M. Staw (ed.), *Research in Organizational behavior* (41–73). Greenwich, CT: JAI Press.

Weick, K. E. (1993). The collapse of sensemaking in organizations: The Mann Gulch disaster. *Administrative Science Quarterly, 38,* 628–653.

Weick, K. E. (1995). *Sensemaking in organizations.* Thousand Oaks, CA: Sage.

Weick, K. E., and Bougon, M. G. (1986). Organizations as cognitive maps: Charting ways to success and failure. In H. P. Simms and D. A. Gioia (eds.), *The thinking organization: dynamics of organization social cognition* (102–135). San Francisco: Jossey-Bass.

Weick, K. E., and Roberts, K. H. (1993). Collective mind in organizations: Heedful interrelating on flight decks. *Administrative Science Quarterly, 38,* 357–381.

Williams, K. Y., and O'Reilly, C. A. III. (1998). Demography and diversity in organizations: A review of 40 years of research. In B. M. Staw and L. L. Cummings (eds.), *Research in organizational behavior* (Vol. 20, 77–140). Greenwich, CT: JAI Press.

Zack, M. (1993). Interactivity and communication mode choice in ongoing management groups. *Information Systems Research, 4,* 207–239.

IV

Enabling Distributed Work

In the previous two parts, the authors emphasized the virtues of collocated work and painted a comparatively poor future for distributed work. In this part, the authors look at how today's distributed work is organized and managed, sometimes with spectacular success.

In chapter 13, Suzanne Weisband examines how members and managers of project groups communicate in ways that reinforce and sustain awareness in the distributed group, attempting to overcome a tendency in these groups to lose a sense of awareness of other people, and the work process. Andrea Hollingshead, Janet Fulk, and Peter Monge in chapter 14 apply two social science theories, public goods theory and transactive memory theory, to consider the problem of knowledge sharing in distributed work. They argue that intranets can be designed to sustain workers' motivations and provide an infrastructure for sharing knowledge in distributed groups. In an empirical study of distributed employees at a global computer company, Thomas Finholt, Lee Sproull, and Sara Kiesler examine in chapter 15 how distributed employees used a computerized archive of e-mail exchanges of advice from peers. They show how records of questions and advice from peers were retrieved far more often than records of question and advice from designated experts doing technical support. In chapter 16, Jae Yun Moon and Lee Sproull describe the development of the Linux kernel by an electronic community of practice. They identify factors that made the Linux distributed project a success.

Taken as a group, these chapters suggest that perhaps successful distributed work is not simply a spread-out version of good collocated work. Successful distributed work seems to engage and require a qualitatively different set of incentives, work structures, and ways of communicating.

13

Maintaining Awareness in Distributed Team Collaboration: Implications for Leadership and Performance

Suzanne Weisband

In distributed work, there is considerable uncertainty about others' behaviors. To reduce uncertainty, group members need information about the remote work and what other group members are doing. This chapter reports a study of the process of collaboration in student teams with a deadline. The study shows how the behavior of the leader and members in creating or reinforcing awareness of others and the work was related to successful collaboration outcomes. Teams in which members periodically gathered information about others and revealed information about themselves performed better than teams in which members did not do this. Project leaders made a substantial difference in how teams performed. Implications for managing teams in distributed work settings are discussed

All interdependent work entails uncertainty about others' behaviors. Will other group members complete their part of the work on time? Will they do the work they said they would do? Will they pay attention to quality? Will they be available to work this weekend? Effectively coordinating behavior and activities among interdependent people at a distance is challenging (DeSanctis, Staudenmayer, and Wong 1999). The need to communicate continuously is essential for sharing information and knowledge of group and individual activities related to the task, informing others about work progress (Rasker, Post, and Schraagen 2000), and anticipating others' needs or actions to achieve successful outcomes (Sheppard and Sherman 1998).

Uncertainty is particularly high in geographically distributed groups. Because of delays in remote communication, feedback about others' behaviors is difficult to obtain (Kraut, Egido, and Galegher 1990; Ruhleder and Jordan 1999). With delayed feedback or inaccurate feedback, messages require a few iterations for clarification (Clark and Brennan 1990). Some messages are long, making a response effortful and time-consuming. When important information is lost, it can create the appearance of members acting independently or hiding their need for interdependence (DeSanctis et al. 1999). Hidden interdependence can reduce coordination (Serfaty, Entin, and Johnston 1998), trust in others, and commitment to group goals (Sheppard and Sherman 1998).

In distributed groups, members may need to monitor others' activities to keep informed about the work of the group and what other members of the group are doing (Gambetta 1988). In face-to-face groups, feedback about what others are doing is immediate and can be accomplished passively. Group members, for instance, can observe who attends meetings or participates in hallway conversations about the group's progress (Kraut, Fussell, Brennan, and Siegel, chapter 6, this volume). They can glance over at another person to see if she is working or can hear the sound of a particular machine and know what work is being done (Olson, Teasley, Covi, and Olson, chapter 5, this volume; Gutwin, Roseman, and Greenberg 1996). In contrast, distributed groups can go long periods during which they have no information about their teammates' activities. They may have to rely entirely on the messages that appear on the computer screen to figure out what other members of the work group are doing.

Problems attributed to a lack of information about others' activities have led researchers and designers of computer-supported systems to develop so-called awareness mechanisms in distributed work groups (Dourish and Bellotti 1992; Dourish and Bly 1992; Fussell, Kraut, Lerch, Scherlis, and Cadiz 1998; Gutwin et al. 1996; Steinfield, Jang, and Pfaff 1999). Dourish and Bellotti (1992) define awareness as an *"understanding of the activities of others*, which provides a *context for your own activity"* (107, emphasis in original). Awareness reduces the effort needed to coordinate tasks and resources by providing a context in which to interpret utterances and to anticipate others' actions (Gutwin et al. 1996).

A Study of Team Awareness

The purpose of the study described in this chapter was to better understand how distributed work teams sustain or increase awareness of other group members and how awareness communications are related to members' efforts to coordinate their own work with the work of others. The study looked how team leaders and other members sustain or increase awareness by informing the team members about how the work was progressing, who is doing his or her part, and who is otherwise moving the team toward product completion (Barge 1994). The study also was meant to discover how efforts to sustain awareness and leadership behavior are related to team success.

The study followed geographically distributed student project teams over the course of a project whose product was to be a policy document produced on schedule. Most of these students had never met, and some would never meet. With just thirty-six days to complete the project, the team had to select their members, decide on their topic, determine how the project would be carried out, and then move forward quickly to complete the document.

Creating Group Awareness

It has been claimed that to establish a shared understanding of a task and solve problems, people need to interact continuously (Clark and Brennan 1990, Sheppard and Sherman 1998). Interaction provides cues and information about others' responsiveness and actions that can reduce uncertainty about future events (Schlenker, Helm, and Tedeschi 1973). It allows members to understand the cause-and-effect relationships involved in performing the task (Lindsley, Brass, and Thomas 1995), monitor performance (Rasker et al. 2000), and gain a mutually shared perspective for anticipating and predicting the actions of others (Boland, Maheshwari, Te'eni, Schwartz, and Tenkasi 1992; Klimoski and Mohammed 1994). Interaction to support awareness of others, the task, and the group's progress—in short, group awareness—should lead groups to be more successful (Cannon-Bowers, Salas, and Converse 1993).

Hypothesis 1:   Distributed project teams that communicate to sustain or increase group awareness of one another and their work collaboration will perform better than teams that do not.

Maintaining or increasing group awareness in distributed groups is hard to do. Since awareness is not automatic in the distributed environment, members of a distributed work group have to remember to explicate goals and progress in the work they are doing, to make explicit efforts to request information from others, and alert others to their own activities. This effort adds to the cost of coordination as well as to the potential for cognitive overload (Clark and Brennan 1990, Fussell et al. 1998, Steinfield et al. 1999).

The level of cooperation and effort among team members to maintain these important forms of awareness also will vary considerably (Wageman 2001), as will their technological skills and their infrastructure for doing so (Mankin, Cohen, and Bikson 1996). Because of these variations in need for awareness and motivation to sustain it, groups will vary greatly in their potential and actual use of awareness information (Steinfield et al. 1999). At the outset, they need to communicate frequently to stimulate the desire for, and response to, awareness information.

Hypothesis 2:   The more frequent are the daily interactions of distributed project team members, the better the team will perform.

Task activities in the first half of the project are critical for setting the stage for future interactions and success (Gersick 1989). Habitual routines are established very quickly and early in the group's experience (Gersick and Hackman 1990), and these early task experiences provide individuals with hypotheses about themselves and their ability to succeed (Lindsley et al. 1995).

Hypothesis 3:   Teams that provide and request information to support group awareness early in the project will perform better than teams that do not.

Forms of Group Awareness

Some kinds of awareness may be more important than others (DeSanctis et al. 2000). Designers of collaborative computer systems have attempted to build systems that support important forms of group awareness (Dourish and Bly 1992, Fussell et al. 1998, Gutwin et al. 1996, Steinfeld et al. 1999). These include activity awareness, availability awareness, process awareness, and social awareness.

Activity awareness is knowledge about the project-related activities of other group members, for example, knowing what actions others are doing at any given moment. *Availability awareness* is knowing whether others are available to meet or participate in an activity. *Process awareness* is a sense of where members' tasks fit into the stages of the project, what the next step is, and what needs to be done to move the process along. *Social awareness* is knowledge about the members, and especially about their social situation—what they are doing outside the context of work (Tollmar, Sandor, and Schömer 1996). In this study, communications were stored and categorized as initiations of these four forms of awareness.

Leadership and Awareness

Classic research on leadership isolated two leadership factors, referred to as initiating structure and consideration (Fleishman 1953). *Initiating structure* is the degree to which a leader defines and structures his or her own role and the roles of team members toward the attainment of group goals and results (Yukl 1994). Examples include criticizing poor work, emphasizing the importance of meeting team deadlines, maintaining and enforcing standards of performance, and ensuring that members are working up to capacity. *Consideration* is the degree to which a leader shows concern for others. Examples include behaviors that signal trust, respect, and interest in supporting open communication and participation. Early studies showed that leaders high on initiating structure and consideration were viewed as more effective (Fleishman 1953, Stogdill 1981).

In this study, two types of leadership behavior could be examined to capture the two leadership concepts of initiating structure and consideration. Leaders who initiate task structure in short-term project teams may need to put pressure on group members to focus on the task objectives and complete the project on time (Yukl 1994). We defined *pressure initiations* as occurring when someone (a leader or a member) stressed task objectives and meeting team goals. Effective leaders must also be able to monitor the progress of others and maintain connections with, and awareness of, who is doing their part in order to anticipate problems and integrate members' contributions (Hackman and Morris 1975). In this study, *other awareness* means someone took action to find out what the other members of the team were doing and to include everyone. Effective leaders must be considerate of other members' workload constraints outside the purview of this specific project (e.g., deadlines for a different project).

Hypothesis 4:   Project leaders who initiate pressure to complete the task on time will perform better than leaders who do not.

Hypothesis 5:   Project leaders who assess what group members are doing will perform better than leaders who do not.

Timing of Group Awareness Communications

In distributed teams, at the beginning of their project, effective leaders will need to initiate and model strategies for doing the work and how members should work together. In this way, they promote the interaction patterns necessary for team success (Zacarro, Blari, Peterson, and Zazanis 1995). When leaders set their team on the right track early, they promote the exchange of information that supports group awareness, and the team is more likely to feel confident in their ability to do the work and motivated to work hard on behalf of the team (Kozlowski, Gully, Salas, and Cannon-Bowers 1996).

Hypothesis 6:   Leaders who initiate pressure early in the project will perform better than teams that do not.

Hypothesis 7:   Leaders who assess what group members are doing early in the project will perform better than teams that do not.

Method

Participants
Sixty-six graduate and undergraduate business students in two geographically distant U.S. universities participated in a four-week project using a Web-based computer conferencing system and e-mail to perform their project: writing a short consensus policy document. There were fifteen students (two graduates and thirteen undergraduates) from a northeastern university (NU) and fifty-one students (fifteen graduates and thirty-six undergraduates) from a southwestern university (SU). Students were instructed to select one student from NU on the team and one graduate student as project leader. Thirteen teams consisted of four members with one graduate student and one student from NU; one team ended up with three instead of four members, and one team had two graduate students. Two teams consisted of members from the same university and are not included in this analysis, leaving a total of fifteen teams. Of the fifty-nine students involved, thirty-three were male (56 percent) and sixteen were graduate students (27 percent). Their average age was twenty-three years, and their average grade point average was 3.28. All but six students had a computer and modem at home (90 percent), and most had considerable electronic communication experience. Only one student failed to complete the project. Of the fifteen teams in the analysis, six performed very well (above 90 percent) and nine performed less well (below 90 percent), as evaluated by a group of faculty.

Project Task
The project task was designed to simulate work in short-term distributed work groups. Students had thirty-six days in which to select team members and complete the project, and they were instructed to conduct their discussions as a team elec-

tronically, since not all members could meet face-to-face. The task involved a hybrid form of interdependence (Wageman 2001), where members sometimes worked alone at independent tasks and sometimes worked together as a team.

The project had three stages: (1) forming a team, (2) selecting a policy topic, and (3) researching and writing a five-page policy paper. The teams used a Web-based conferencing system to introduce themselves and select their team members. Students were instructed to change their personal name to include their two-letter school name (SU or NU) so that team composition included one NU student. Similarly, graduate students added a "G" to their name to ensure that one graduate (i.e., project leader) was on the team. Teams had to be selected and announced in the conference within one week. This rule allowed the instructors to ensure that teams satisfied the composition criteria. Once confirmed, project teams then had to negotiate the selection of a project topic and organize themselves to begin the work. How they self-organized was left entirely to the discretion of the team. Teams were expected to announce their topic to the conference by the end of the second week. This deadline gave instructors the opportunity to advise teams about the feasibility of completing their project on time, as well as to request changes to topics that were already chosen by other teams.

Teams were encouraged to use the conferencing system to conduct their work, but were allowed to use e-mail if, as a team, they preferred to do so. All e-mail messages included a copy to one of the instructors. Instructors did not intervene unless they were specifically asked to do so. Due to the asynchronous nature of the medium and the short duration of the project, we stressed the importance of frequent contact with the group and logging on every day if possible.

Project Leaders

Graduate students who served as team leaders were told that their responsibilities were (1) announcing their team members on the Web conferencing system and then later announcing the topic the team chose to research, (2) helping decide how team members would communicate (Web or e-mail), (3) collecting all e-mail messages for archival purposes (if applicable), and (4) managing the team and facilitating the preparation of the final paper. The project leaders could make suggestions for paper topics, help collect information on the Internet, resolve conflicts, offer ways of moving the task forward, help to delegate task responsibilities, and edit papers. Team members were told to direct any questions about what to do and how to do it to the project leader. If project leaders needed advice about managing the team, they could direct their questions to the instructors. All information describing the project and its goals, as well as leader responsibilities and grading requirements, were posted on the class Web page.

Measures

Team members at both universities began and ended the project on the same day, and they were given identical project instructions, requirements, and deadlines. On the first day of the project, all students were ensured of confidentiality before they filled out a prestudy questionnaire to assess demographic information: age, grade point average, gender (male = 0, female = 1), location of school (1 = NU, 0 = SU), whether they had a computer or modem at home (yes = 1, no = 0), and their electronic communication experience ("not much" = 1, "a great deal" = 5), and general attitudes about computers. On the last day of the project, after the paper was completed and turned in, students filled out a poststudy questionnaire to measure attitudes about the process of work, the team dynamics associated with the project, and evaluations of themselves and the other members of their team.

Performance Three instructors graded the project papers separately, then discussed them by telephone, and then awarded a consensus final grade for the paper. All team members received the same grade. Individual grades were calculated for the frequency, number, and quality of e-mail posts; whether students completed all their daily work; and presentations to their respective classrooms. Performance scores were measured by the team's final grade on their joint paper. For the analysis in this chapter, teams whose scores were above 90 percent were coded as high performing and teams whose scores were 90 percent or below were coded as low performing.

Awareness Initiations To measure the amount of team interaction over the course of the project, computer-generated messages for each team were counted for each day, separating out messages from leaders and messages from team members and messages that initiated topics as compared with replies to these messages. A message could contain multiple questions or statements that might be coded as creating, reinforcing, or increasing group awareness. An awareness initiation was defined as new invitations for others involved to respond. Initiations could be questions (e.g., "How was your weekend?") or statements (e.g., "Please send me your comments.") They could be implicit requests for attention (e.g., "I just set up my distribution list. I think it's working.") or explicit requests for information about others ("Are you working today?"). The most important criterion for coding a question or statement as an initiation was that a response had to be possible or plausible. In the analysis presented in this chapter, only leader and member awareness initiations are included, not responses to them. Since multiple responses to one initiation were possible, examining initiations only provides a cleaner analysis of the data.

The coding process used short phrases derived from the team members' own language (Glaser and Strauss 1967). Data were sorted into four categories of group awareness messages (self-awareness, availability awareness, process awareness, and social awareness) and two categories of leader awareness messages (awareness of others and initiating pressure). Examples from the text of the interactions illustrate the definitions. (Names are pseudonyms.)

Self-awareness is information about what the particular team member is doing at any given moment. It sets up an expectation for work and reduces uncertainty about what a team member is doing and why the member may have been absent from recent discussions—for example:

Hello, Sorry about the silence but this past week has been hell. Anyhow I am back and I am investing this entire weekend in my part of the paper. Therefore, you can expect a final product by Sunday as well as a proposal for our suggested policy. Chris.

Availability awareness is information about when team members are available to "meet" through alternate forms of communication (e.g., face-to-face meetings with colocated members, phone calls, on-line chat)—for example:

Hey everyone—I think the early deadline is a good idea. Monday is a bad day for me but I will check in once or twice if at all possible. I should have some time to go over my notes tonight so I hope to have some more concrete suggestions to make tomorrow. If I do run out of time tomorrow, I can commit most of Tuesday to this project.

Process awareness is information about setting up and coordinating the work, deciding who should do what, figuring out what do to next and when the work is due—for example:

We should have the recommendations and conclusion done by Saturday—this gives us a whole day to write the paper and two days to edit. Not much time but definitely doable.

Social awareness is information about team member relationships, supporting team members' efforts, and discussing topics and events unrelated to the topic.

As team members learn about the social lives of participants, what they do when they are not working on the project, or when they hear praise for the work they are doing, it creates the perception that the physical distance between them is not great:

Hi teammateys—Sorry I haven't checked in for a couple days. Camping was way cool. I went up to Madera Canyon with a couple friends of mine and a 10 year old boy. It brought back memories of when I was a kid. Y'know ghost stories around the campfire, slingshots, smores, and the like. Anyway, here I sit again in front of the computer getting doused by tidal waves of low frequency electro-magnetic radiation—pleasant thought eh? I always get cynical upon returning to the rat race from a harmonious respite with mom nature. Remember—You may win the rat race, but you're still a rat!

Leadership–other awareness is information requested about what other team members are doing, where they are, when they can be expected to complete their work, and general consideration of how the team is doing:

OK, I'll be looking for posts/principles from Rick and Matt on Saturday and from Josh on Sunday. If you are having any trouble at all or anticipate any future problems, let me know now rather than later. I can help in any way and take up any slack (if I know in advance). See ya!

Leadership–pressure is initiations of task structure characterized by time imperatives, use of emphasis such as all capitals and exclamation points, and repetition:

Yoshi, how's your part coming along? Isn't it like 10:00 over there by now? I'm just waiting on your part now, so anytime you can send it in the very near future would be greatly appreciated. Thanks.
    Warren
    P. S. Whatever you do, don't wait till tomorrow to send it cuz it'll be too late. I won't have any time to work it into the paper. If I don't get your part in the next couple hours, I'll just do it without your part (although I don't want to cuz I know you've worked hard on the research for your part). But time's running out here.

Analysis and Results

In the analyses that follow, all awareness data were divided into two halves, such that early awareness initiations took place in the first half of the project (days 1–18) and late initiations took place in the second half of the project (days 19–36). Hierarchical regression analyses were conducted on group and leader awareness categories separately to test hypotheses related to team performance.

Preliminary Analysis

Student teams had a choice about whether they preferred to use e-mail or the Web-based conferencing tool. Of the six high-performing teams, two teams used only the Web, two used the Web more than 80 percent of the time, and one team used the Web and e-mail equally. Of the nine low-performing teams, two teams used only e-mail and two used only the Web, three used the Web more than 85 percent of the time, and two used the Web and e-mail about equally. Overall, total messages for each medium revealed no difference between high- and low-performing groups. However, teams that used the Web exchanged more total messages ($M = 86$) than e-mail messages ($M = 23$), $F(1,13) = 8.3$, $p < .05$, and high-performing teams exchanged more Web-based messages ($M = 135$) than did low-performing teams ($M = 54$), $F(1,13) = 10.4$, $p < .01$. Thus, the number of messages posted by team members mattered more than the medium they used to communicate.

Age was positively correlated with grade point average ($r = .48$, $p < .01$) and, because they were graduate students, team leaders were significantly older ($r = .70$, $p < .001$) and had higher GPAs ($r = .76$, $p < .001$) than members, but they had less electronic communication experience ($r = -.42$, $p < .05$). Also, members with less electronic communication experience tended to use more pressure tactics ($r = -.58$, $p < .01$). Since the control variables were unrelated to performance, they were not used in subsequent analyses.

Group Awareness

Table 13.1 presents the results of the hierarchical regression analyses of group awareness initiations on team performance for early and late phases of the project. The first hypothesis, that initiating information exchange to sustain or increase group awareness in distributed collaboration will lead to successful team outcomes, was supported strongly. All awareness measures except process awareness were significant predictors of team performance. Hypothesis 2, that frequent team interactions over the course of the project would lead to successful team outcomes, also was supported. High-performing teams communicated much more frequently than did low-performing teams. The total number of initiations across all coding categories was significantly higher (more frequent) for high-performing teams ($M = 183$) than for low-performing teams ($M = 100$), $F(1,28) = 12.5$, $p < .001$.

Hypothesis 3, that early initiations would predict performance, was partly supported. Table 13.2 and figure 13.1 show that self-awareness was a strong predictor of performance in both the first half ($\beta = .20$, $p < .05$) and second half ($\beta = .40$,

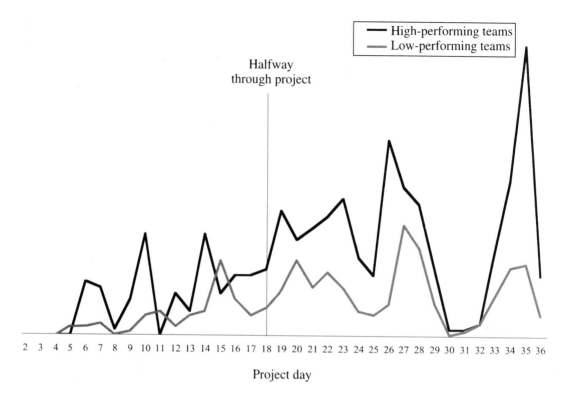

Figure 13.1
Self-awareness initiations in high- and low-performing teams.

$p < .05$) of the project. The results also show the importance of availability in predicting performance early ($\beta = .16$, $p < .05$) and later ($\beta = .43$, $p < .10$) in the project. Social awareness affected performance when it was initiated early in the project ($\beta = .25$, $p < .01$), but not when it was initiated in the second half of the project.

Leadership Initiations
Table 13.2 also presents the results of the hierarchical regression analyses of leadership awareness initiations on team performance for early and late phases of the project. To test hypotheses 4 and 5, leadership awareness initiations by leaders and members were tested separately to determine whether the project leader behaved differently from members. Over the whole project, teams having leaders who initiated pressure ($R^2 = .51$, $p < .01$) and who pursued other awareness ($R^2 = .67$,

$p < .001$) were more successful. Teams having members who initiated pressure and pursued other awareness were not associated with performance.

To test hypotheses 6 and 7, early and late leader initiations were added to the model. Leaders who initiated pressure early ($\beta = .36$, $p < .05$) were associated with higher levels of team performance, thus supporting hypothesis 6. There was evidence that when members initiated messages late in the process to increase awareness of others, the impact on performance was positive ($\beta = .67$, $p < .01$), but if they tried to do so early in the process, there was a negative impact on performance ($\beta = -.47$, $p < .05$). Leaders may have been expected to initiate pressure early, whereas members who did so were disliked or ignored. It seems as though only later in the process was it effective for pressure to be initiated by anyone ($\beta = .35$, $p < .10$).

Hypothesis 7 was also supported. Early initiations of other awareness by the leader was strongly associated with higher levels of team performance ($\beta = .46$, $p < .01$). However, leaders (or any member) who initiated other awareness later in the process had no impact on performance. Possibly pursuing other awareness is effective only when there is time to organize the work. However, the fast-paced nature of the work toward the last half of the project may have prevented members from checking to see how others were doing or they simply gave up on those who had "disappeared."

Discussion

This chapter began with the idea that creating and maintaining group awareness in distributed collaboration is necessary for effective and timely coordination of work in short-term project teams. Although frequently initiating awareness messages to the team is effortful and time-consuming, the result, according to the evidence in this study, is improved team performance. Teams in which members sent messages indicating where they were and what they were doing and messages in which they queried others of their whereabouts, availability, and progress performed better than teams that did not. Teams that interacted frequently were more successful than teams that missed many days on-line (see also Boland et al. 1992; Schunn, Crowley, and Okada, chapter 17, this volume). Figure 13.2 shows the average number of days that went by when no team member sent a message. Low-performing teams were absent significantly more often than were high-performing teams ($F = 8.8$, $p < .01$).

Table 13.1
Descriptive statistics and correlations

Variables	Mean	Standard deviation	1	2	3
Demographic data					
1. Performance	88.73	4.45	1.00		
2. Leader (1 = yes/0 = no)	.50	.51	.00	1.00	
3. Age	24.17	2.65	.00	.70**	1.00
4. Grade point average	3.39	.31	.10	.76**	.48**
5. Modem at home	.91	.24	.22	.12	.18
6. Electronic communications experience	3.72	.63	−.13	−.42*	−.30
Group Awareness Messages					
7. Self-awareness	23.17	18.56	.55**	−.41*	−.24
8. Availability awareness	5.87	9.11	.49**	.01	.19
9. Process awareness	37.67	16.75	.15	.21	.31
10. Social awareness	9.07	7.44	.50**	−.30	−.11
Leader Awareness Messages					
11. Other awareness	5.00	4.28	.37*	.02	.00
12. Initiate pressure	8.30	8.02	.45*	.57**	.55**

Note: Awareness data are totals summed across the thirty-six days of the project.
** $p < .01$. * $p < .05$. † $p < .10$.

The data also showed that early team interactions contributed most to successful team performance. Teams in which members sent information about themselves or inquired after others early performed better than teams in which members did not. In the early days of the project, high-performing team members established successful interaction styles that were continually reinforced (Gersick and Hackman 1990). They put pressure on each other to move quickly, and everyone submitted to that pressure. High-performing teams found out others' schedules, checked up on others' progress, and maintained almost real-time synchronous interaction as the project neared completion. Teams learned enough social information about each other early in the process to know others' preferences, work styles, schedules and habits. This knowledge then could be used to help them become even more effective in working with one another, particularly during the final push to conclude the project.

A process such as the one we observed seems to be iterative. As the level of awareness and peer monitoring in a group increase, the intentions and capabilities of

(Continued)

4	5	6	7	8	9	10	11
1.00							
.39*	1.00						
24.00	.10	1.00					
−.20	.09	−.10	1.00				
.05	.14	.05	.38*	1.00			
.04	−.10	−.33	.49**	.35	1.00		
−.22	.22	−.16	.72**	.64**	.46**	1.00	
.14	.11	−.19	.46*	.62**	.52**	.54**	1.00
.51**	.08	−.58**	.21	.42*	.67**	.33	.50**

the group are uncovered (Powell 1996). Positive, mutually reinforcing cycles of initiations and responses among interdependent team members are critical to the development of collective trust and cooperation (Iacono and Weisband 1997). Members can anticipate future behavior, and when that behavior is viewed positively, trust develops (Jones and George 1998). Understanding the relationship of awareness and trust in distributed work groups may be an important area for future research.

Implications for Leadership

One goal of this study was to understand the role of leadership in distributed work groups. Effective project leaders were expected to initiate task demands and show consideration of others early to set the stage for successful future interaction and performance. The data support this idea. Project leaders contributed to team performance when they initiated pressure and awareness of others. Pressure was

Table 13.2
Hierarchical regression of group and leader awareness messages on team performance

Dependent variable = Team performance	β	R^2	ΔR^2
Group awareness messages			
Self-awareness			
First half (days 1–18)	.23	.20*	
Second half (days 19–36)	.40*	.31*	.11*
Availability awareness			
First half	.08	.16*	
Second half	.43†	.24†	.08†
Process awareness			
First half	.23	.05	
Second half	−.03	.05	.00
Social awareness			
First half	.43*	.25**	
Second half	.17	.27	.02
Leadership awareness messages			
Initiated pressure (leaders only)			
First half	.30	.13*	
Second half	.10	.14	.01
Initiated pressure (members only)			
First half	−.47*	.07	
Second half	.67**	.48**	.41**
Initiated pressure (total group)			
First half	.16	.10†	
Second half	.35†	.20†	.10†
Other awareness (leaders only)			
First half	.39†	.21**	
Second half	.10	.22	.01
Other awareness (members only)			
First half	.45	.14	
Second half	−.34	.25	.11
Other awareness (total group)			
First half	.57**	.32***	
Second half	−.03	.32	.00

Note: The standardized betas presented result when all variables are entered in the equation.
** $p < .01$. * $p < .05$. † $p < .10$.

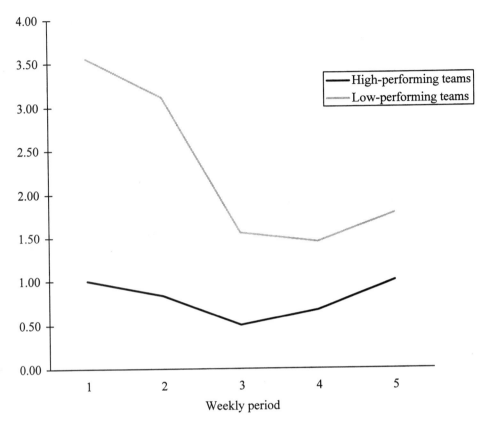

Figure 13.2
Average number of days in which no team member sent a message.

especially effective early in the project. When project leaders began to initiate pressure in the second half of the project, team performance declined.

In this study, all teams had assigned leaders, but assignment as leader is in part a context from which leadership may or may not emerge (Meindl 1993). According to Meindl (1993), "Leadership emerges in the minds of followers" (99). Some teams in this study did not have effective leaders, and this became clear in how team members responded to leader requests. For example, some project leaders initiated awareness in a way that motivated team members to stay in constant touch with each other, whereas others frustrated the members. The data suggest that most project leaders initiated awareness in a positive manner (or the regression results would be different), but in the following two examples, we see two different tones:

DAY14 20:48 Jake [project leader]

Whoa, folks! It's entirely too quiet in here!!! I know this is a broad topic and we're all busy people, but you do realize that this project is due 3 weeks from tomorrow, and with Thanksgiving thrown in there, that gives us less than 2.5 weeks to crank this out!! Of course, needless to say our topic declaration is due manana, and so far there have been precious few helpful contributions to narrow things down.

At the risk of sounding overlord-ish, I can make executive decisions for the group if I have to, to meet deadlines and such, but then we all have to live with the consequences. I want this to be a true group effort and I assume you guys do too, but we all have to contribute.

You know what they say about leaders? You aren't one unless you have followers. Let's remember, the sooner we get this started, the sooner we can finish it! Hope to hear from you soon.

DAY 14 21:03 Eric [a response to Jake]

Sorry Jake your overlordship.

I've been slacking on this the past few days, sorry I will post more tonight . . . a bit later. see you soon.

DAY 14 21:39 Michelle [a second response to Jake]

Greetings gentlemen. I am ready to throw two more cents into this impressive little potluck of topic ideas we seem to have going. I think it's important that we remember that the team assignment was only to develop a policy related to social issue(s). There was no requirement to make revolutionary discoveries or to go "where no <person> has gone before". In this spirit, I propose we develop our own rendition of the FCC guidelines for universal access. After wading through the linked information (thanks again, your overlordship—is that a demotion from Fearless Leader?), I felt that big business could be encouraged to fund a hefty addition to the $2.25 billion set aside for communications development. Please let me know your thoughts.

The next exchange involves Bob, who admonished his team for not making progress (more than halfway through the project), but then offered no suggestions for what to do next. The responses to Bob's message suggest that Bob will not write the parts of the paper and that he has not yet responded to Chad's suggestion five days earlier. The sequence of events also shows a gap in communications of four days.

DAY 15 22:35 Chad

Hello

New York Times has an article about e-mail privacy that I think will be useful. As Bob stated above, I think we should start to formulate our policy principles.

I believe that our policy should:

1) show that a problem exists
2) show that the problem causes harm
3) show that our solution will solve the problem

4) show how the only way to solve the problem is to use our solution

5) Be clear and precise

What do you all think?

DAY 16 13:52 Elaine

Chad:

I agree with your points. Just wanted to add the "organization's viewpoint of email privacy". It can be incorporated into 2), I guess. Also we can "assign authority and responsibility to specific positions/titles" to make the implementation easier.

DAY20 09:57 Bob [project leader's response]

Hey, are you guys working on this or what?

I have a progress report to fill out, and don't feel like a lot of progress is being made.

Seriously, we need to start making some progress toward the paper. I have some ideas I will put in tonight—Any comments or things you want to do? Post here to let me know, I will try and make some assignments and better outline our paper.

DAY 20 10:02 Elaine

I'm not too sure as to what you meant by the 5 items, did you want us to come up with an outline with 5 main points and write out the paper? What do you think of the items we came up with so far? Interesting . . . looks like we're logged on at the same time.

DAY 20 12:22 Ron

Well, based on what Bob gave us as an outline for the paper on privacy, I suggest that of the three of us that are writing this, one of us takes part I, another takes part II, and the last person works on part III and IV. Although this is just one way of doing this, with our time constraints, this is the best way to do it. All of us can work to narrow the five points, but Bob, what do you think of Chad's five? I volunteer to work on Part I—any complaints, changes, ideas?

DAY 20 16:19 Elaine

Oh, I see, so the 5 items are just the guiding principles in Part III, I misread it before.

Team members may not have viewed Jake or Bob as leaders even though they were appointed as such. To evaluate perceptions of leadership across all the teams, leader evaluations were collected from members after students turned in their projects (but before they received their grades). Six questions, based on five-point scales, where 1 = not at all and 5 = almost always, asked members whether leaders: (1) "involved me in problem solving and decision making activities," (2) "motivated and encouraged me," (3) "treated me fairly," (4) "led by example," (5) "demonstrated a definite sense of direction and purpose," and (6) whether they would choose to work with this project leader again (yes/no) (Chronbach alpha = .82).

Members who later received excellent ratings for their projects tended to evaluate their leaders higher ($M = 4.0$) than did members who later received relatively lower ratings for their projects ($M = 3.6$, $F(1,13) = 4.1$, $p < .07$). Leader evaluations were also significantly correlated with the leader's early pressure initiations ($r = .55$, $p < .05$), but not with the leader's initiation of other awareness messages. Possibly a strong focus on the task deadlines early in the process allowed the leader to emerge as such in the minds of team members (Meindl 1993). They were able to develop the interaction patterns necessary to move the team forward quickly and effectively (Zacarro et al. 1995).

Only fifteen teams were involved in this study, and the project requirements may not generalize to other situations. For example, collocated students were asked not to meet face-to-face on the grounds that it was not fair to the distant team member. Certainly, there are distributed teams where some of the members are collocated and where other media are available for communication. Despite these limitations, the findings suggest that some of the distributed work teams were able to conduct their work effectively and on time in spite of their inability to meet face-to-face. But the effort was substantial. The effort required to work successfully may discourage geographically dispersed teams from conducting interdependent work over long periods of time. A comparison of long- and short-term distributed project teams seems a promising area for future research (Druskat and Kayes 2000, Saunders and Ahuja 2000).

Note

This research was supported by a National Science Foundation grant (IIS-9872996). I thank Jonathan Cummings for his help with data analysis and earlier comments on the chapter and Ashley Gilliam and Jonathan Woodard for their help with content coding and preliminary data analyses.

References

Barge, J. K. (1994). *Leadership: Communication skills for organizations and groups.* New York: St. Martin's Press.

Boland, R. J., Maheshwari, A. K., Te'eni, D., Schwartz, D. G., and Tenkasi, R. V. (1992). Sharing perspectives in distributed decision making. In *Proceedings on Computer-Supported Cooperative Work* (306–313). New York: ACM Press.

Cannon-Bowers, J. A., Salas, E., and Converse, S. A. (1993). Shared mental models in expert decision-making teams. In N. J. Castellan, Jr. (ed.), *Current issues in individual and group decision making* (221–246). Hillsdale, NJ: Erlbaum.

Clark, H. H., and Brennan, S. E. (1990). Grounding in communication. In L. B. Resnick, J. M. Levine, and S. D. Teasley (eds.), *Perspectives on social shared cognition* (127–149). Washington, DC: American Psychological Association.

DeSanctis, G., Staudenmayer, N., and Wong, S. (1999). Interdependence in virtual organizations. In C. Cooper and D. M. Rousseau (eds.), *Trends in organizational behavior* (Vol. 6, 81–104). New York: Wiley.

Dourish, P., and Bellotti, V. (1992). Awareness and coordination in shared workspace. In *Proceedings of CSCW'92* (107–114). New York: ACM Press.

Dourish, P., and Bly, S. (1992). Portholes: Supporting awareness in a distributed work group. In *Proceedings of CSCW'92* (541–547). New York: ACM Press.

Druskat, V. U., and Kayes, D. C. (2000). Learning versus performance in short-term project teams. *Small Group Research*, *31*, 328–353.

Fleishman, E. A. (1953). The measurement of leadership attitudes in industry. *Journal of Applied Psychology*, *37*, 153–158.

Fussell, S. R., Kraut, R. E., Lerch, F. J., Scherlis, W. L., and Cadiz, J. J. (1998). Coordination, overload and team performance: Effects of team communication strategies. In *Proceedings of CSCW'98* (275–284). New York: ACM Press.

Gambetta, D. (ed.). (1988). *Trust: Making and breaking cooperative relations*. Oxford: Basil Blackwell.

Gersick, C. J. G. (1989). Marking time: Predictable transitions in task groups. *Academy of Management Journal*, *32*, 274–309.

Gersick, C. J. G., and Hackman, J. R. (1990). Habitual routines in task performing groups. *Organizational Behavior and Human Decision Processes*, *47*, 65–97.

Glaser, B., and Strauss, A. L. (1967). *The discovery of grounded theory*. Chicago: Aldine Publishing Co.

Gutwin, C., Roseman, M., and Greenberg, S. (1996). A usability study of awareness widgets in a shared workspace groupware system. In *Proceedings of CSCW '96* (258–267). New York: ACM Press.

Hackman, J., and Morris, C. (1975). Group tasks, group interaction process, and group performance effectiveness: A review and proposed integration. In L. Berkowitz (ed.), *Advances in experimental social psychology* (Vol. 8, 45–99). New York: Academic Press.

Iacono, S., and Weisband, S. (1997). Developing trust in virtual teams. In *Proceedings of the Thirtieth Hawaii International Conference on Systems Sciences* (412–420). Piscataway, NJ: IEEE.

Jones, G. R., and George, J. M. (1998). The experience and evolution of trust: Implications for cooperation and teamwork. *Academy of Management Review*, *23*, 531–546.

Klimoski, R., and Mohammed, S. (1994). Team mental model: Construct or metaphor? *Journal of Management*, *20*, 403–437.

Kozlowski, S., Gully, S., Salas, E., and Cannon-Bowers, J. (1996). Team leadership and development: Theory, principles, and guidelines for training leaders and teams. In M. M. Beyerlein, D. Johnson, and S. T. Beyerlein (eds.), *Interdisciplinary studies of work teams* (Vol. 3, 253–291). Greenwich, CT: JAI Press.

Kraut, R. E., Egido, C., and Galegher, J. (1990). Patterns of contact and communication in scientific collaboration. In J. Galegher, R. E. Kraut and C. Egido (eds.), *Intellectual teamwork: Social and technological foundations of cooperative work* (149–171). Hillsdale, NJ: Erlbaum.

Kraut, R. E., Fussell, S. R., Brennan, S. E., and Siegel, J. (2002). Understanding effects of proximity on collaboration: Implications for technologies to support remote collaborative work. In P. Hinds and S. Kiesler (eds.), *Distributed work* (137–162). Cambridge, MA: MIT Press.

Lindsley, D. H., Brass, D. J., and Thomas, J. B. (1995). Efficacy-performance spirals: A multilevel perspective. *Academy of Management Review, 20,* 645–678.

Mankin, D., Cohen, S., and Bikson, T. (1996). *Teams and technology: Fulfilling the promise of the new organization.* Boston: Harvard Business School Press.

Meindl, J. R. (1993). Reinventing leadership: A radical, social psychological approach. In J. Keith Murnighan (ed.), *Social psychology in organizations* (89–118). Englewood Cliffs, NJ: Prentice Hall.

Olson, J. S., Teasley, S., Covi, L., and Olson, G. (2002). The (currently) unique advantages of collocated work. In P. Hinds and S. Kiesler (eds.), *Distributed work* (113–135). Cambridge, MA: MIT Press.

Powell, W. W. (1996). Trust-based forms of governance. In R. M. Kramer and T. R. Tyler (eds.), *Trust in organizations: Frontiers of theory and research* (51–67). Thousand Oaks, CA: Sage.

Rasker, P. C., Post, W. M., and Schraagen, J. M. C. (2000). Effects of two types of intrateam feedback on developing a shared mental model in command and control teams. *Ergonomics, 43,* 1167–1189.

Ruhleder, K., and Jordan, B. (1999). Meaning-making across remote sites: How delays in transmission affect interaction. In *Proceedings of the 6th European Conference on CSCW* (411–429). Dordrecht: Kluwer Academic Publishers.

Saunders, C., and Ahuja, M. (2000 August), *Virtual teams: A framework.* Paper presented at the Academy of Management meetings, Toronto, Ontario.

Schlenker, B. R., Helm, B., and Tedeschi, J. T. (1973). The effects of personality and situational variables on behavioral trust. *Journal of Personality and Social Psychology, 25,* 419–427.

Serfaty, D., Entin, E. E., and Johnston, J. H. (1998). Team coordination training. In J. A. Cannon-Bowers and E. Salas (eds.), *Making decisions under stress: Implications for individual and team training* (221–246). Washington, DC: American Psychological Association.

Schunn, C., Crowley, K., and Okada, T. (2002). What makes collaborations across a distance succeed?: The case of the cognitive science community. In P. Hinds and S. Kiesler (eds.), *Distributed work* (407–430). Cambridge, MA: MIT Press.

Sheppard, B. H., and Sherman, D. M. (1998). The grammars of trust: A model and general implications. *Academy of Management Review, 23,* 422–437.

Steinfield, C., Jang, C., and Pfaff, B. (1999). Supporting virtual team collaboration: The TeamSCOPE System. In *Proceedings of GROUP'99* (81–90). New York: ACM Press.

Stogdill, R. M. (1981). *Stogdill's handbook of leadership* (2nd ed.). New York: Free Press.

Tollmar, K., Sandor, O., and Schömer, A. (1996). Supporting social awareness @ work design and experience. In *Proceedings on Computer-Supported Cooperative Work* (298–307). New York: ACM Press.

Wageman, R. (2001). The meaning of interdependence. In M. E. Turner (ed.), *Groups at work: Theory and research* (197–217). Hillside, NJ: Erlbaum.

Yukl, G. (1994). *Leadership in organizations* (3rd ed.). Englewood Cliffs, NJ: Prentice Hall.

Zaccaro, S., Blari, V., Peterson, C., and Zazanis, M. (1995). Collective efficacy. In J. Maddux (ed.), *Self-efficacy, adaptation, and adjustment* (305–328). New York: Plenum.

14

Fostering Intranet Knowledge Sharing: An Integration of Transactive Memory and Public Goods Approaches

Andrea B. Hollingshead, Janet Fulk, and Peter Monge

Intranets—company Web sites designed for internal use—are an important technological innovation in many organizations that can aid in knowledge management, expertise recognition, and communication. This chapter identifies the conditions under which members of work groups are more likely to contribute to the development of intranets and the conditions under which intranets are more likely to result in more efficient and effective knowledge acquisition and dissemination. To that end, two theories developed to examine nontechnological systems are integrated and extended to intranets and computer-based knowledge systems: the theory of transactive memory and the public goods theory of collective action. Transactive memory theory is useful for predicting how organizational members use intranets to acquire, store, and retrieve knowledge. Public goods theory is useful for predicting which, how much, and when members will contribute and retrieve knowledge on intranets.

A key issue for distributed work groups is knowledge management: how distributed group members and their organizational colleagues locate, store, and retrieve the data, information, and knowledge that they need for their individual and collective work (DeSanctis and Monge 1999). *Data* are commonly defined as raw facts out of context, whereas *information* includes context—the people, technology, and other organizational aspects to which the data relate. Knowledge is information combined with experience, insights, beliefs, and lessons learned possessed by people (Nonaka and Takeuchi 1995). For ease of presentation, we use *knowledge sharing* and *knowledge distribution* to refer inclusively to data, information, and knowledge.

Knowledge, compared to data and information, is particularly problematic to transfer across persons because it requires the active and motivated participation of the knowledge holder. Sharing data and information can also be a significant problem in work groups, however, as illustrated by Blau's (1955) classic study of information hoarding within groups of job placement counselors. Gatekeeping, distortion, distillation, and withholding of information are classic organizational challenges that turn what otherwise might be simple information retrieval tasks into information-sharing roadblocks (see Stohl and Redding 1987 for an extensive review). These classic challenges have been met with a variety of nontechnological solutions. In Blau's work, alteration of the reward system to group-level goals and incentives overcame some information hoarding. Ancona (1992) found that teams that interactively sought information and feedback from their environment were better performers than those that focused on sharing existing information within the team. Other nontechnical solutions include institutionalized practices designed to correct at the group and organization level self-serving biases and other flaws in individual human reasoning (Heath, Larrick, and Klayman 1998). These cognitive repairs can be as simple as slogans such as, "Don't confuse brains and a bull market," or as complex as programs that involve communication and interaction with others, such as cross-sectional groupings that observe processes in action to look for flaws.

Increasingly, organizations have expanded on these basic fixes by providing technological support for knowledge sharing, most commonly via intranets, according to a recent survey.[1] Depending on configuration, intranets can support (1) individual activities, such as updating personnel records or changing benefit choices, (2) formal information dissemination, such as company news or policy manuals, (3) pointers to knowledge and knowledge holders, such as experts directories, search engines, and hyperlinks, (4) individual and group data, information, and knowledge sharing, such as document exchange, or jointly maintained repositories, such as project Web sites or so-called knowledge vaults maintained by groups, and (5) group interaction via synchronous or asynchronous methods, such as group discussions, forums, netmeetings, or joint creation and editing of documents (Fulk et al. 2001).

In 1996, two-thirds of Fortune 500 companies had intranets in operation, but as problems arose in locating and determining the accuracy and timeliness of needed information, intranet usage began to plummet (Head 2000). Outside of the practitioner literature, little published theory or research exists about the success or failure of intranets. To begin to address this need in this chapter, we extend two theories developed to examine work groups and decentralized collectives in nontechnological contexts to intranets. The theory of transactive memory (TM; Hollingshead 1998a, Moreland 1999, Wegner 1987) focuses on the optimal level of knowledge distribution within a group and the conditions under which the group may be expected to achieve this state. Public goods theory of collective action (PG; Fulk,

Flanagin, Kalman, Monge, and Ryan 1996, Marwell and Oliver 1993, Olson 1965, Samuelson 1954) focuses on the processes by which individuals can be induced to engage in knowledge sharing in order to achieve a collective outcome—in this case, a transactive memory system. The two theories provide important complements to each other. The next sections review these theories and offer six integrative propositions. Because we are building toward abstract theory, the propositions are domain general (Heath et al. 1998) in that they apply across situations rather than to specific contexts or groups. We end with suggestions for theory, research, and practice.

The Theory of Transactive Memory

TM theory details how people delegate responsibility for managing knowledge in relationships (Hollingshead 1998a, 1998b, Wegner 1987), groups (Moreland 1999), and organizations (Anand, Manz, and Glick 1998). A TM system is a specialized division of labor that develops with respect to the encoding, storage, and retrieval of knowledge from different domains (Wegner 1987, 1995). This division of cognitive labor reduces the amount of information for which each individual is responsible, yet provides all members access to a larger pool of information across knowledge domains. A person who needs information in another's area of expertise can ask the expert instead of spending time and energy learning it. Research has demonstrated that groups that have TM systems perform their tasks and make decisions more effectively than those that do not, because members are better able to identify experts and make better use of expert knowledge (Hollingshead 1998a, 1998b, 1998c, 2000; Liang, Moreland, and Argote 1995; Moreland, Argote, and Krishnan 1996; Wegner, Erber, and Raymond 1991).

People specialize in different knowledge domains based on their relative expertise, skills or experiences, formal assignment (by a manager or based on a job description), or negotiated agreements with other people. Members can learn informally who is the relative expert across knowledge domains through shared experiences and conversations with one another (Hollingshead 1998b, Wegner 1987). For example, the person who knows most about computers in a work group may become the recognized computer expert. Communication often provides the basis for learning about others' expertise, and it is important for coordinating who will learn what (Hollingshead 1998a, 1998b, Moreland and Myaskovsky 2000).

Individuals can also learn what others know or what others should know through more formal means, such as instruction from other people, documents, manuals or other codified reference materials (Hollingshead 2000), or expertise directories. Over time, as individuals learn about one another's relative expertise, they begin to specialize more in their own areas of relative expertise and expect others to do the same (Hollingshead 1998b, 2000, Wegner et al. 1991), and thus, knowledge becomes more distributed and less redundant among individuals in the system.

TM systems are more likely to develop when individuals perceive themselves to be interdependent and when the incentive structure rewards specialization (Hollingshead in press). Research has shown that when people are interdependent, as they are in distributed work groups, they may be more motivated to learn about what others know and what they can contribute to the task (Rusbult and Van Lange 1996). These arguments lead to the following propositions:

Proposition 1:   Given interdependence, individuals who have more interaction with one another have (1) more unique knowledge and less redundancy across individuals and (2) more shared agreement about one another's relative expertise.

Proposition 2:   Given interdependence, individuals who have accurate perceptions about their coworkers' expertise will perform their tasks more efficiently and effectively than those who do not.

Application to Intranets and Distributed Work Groups

A major prerequisite for an effectively functioning transactive memory system is the willingness of people who hold the particular knowledge to make it accessible to others. If someone makes the information available, network effects can quickly make it accessible to many (Shapiro and Varian 1999). Data and information can sometimes be acquired or inferred without the participation of information holders. Consider the wealth of information collected on the Internet by examining patterns of Web site use, often without the knowledge of the user. Specialist information brokers capture and sell information regarding, for example, individual users' interests, political inclinations, and occupation (inferred from the type of Web sites the user visits), economic circumstances (based on patterns of spending and credit card information offered to a single site by unwitting users), and mobility (from travel sales sites). Increasingly companies are using such strategies to track activities by their employees.

Knowledge, however, as Churchman asserted (1971, p. 10, cited in Malnotra 1997), "resides in the user. . . . It is how the user reacts to a collection of information" (10). Without the willing participation of the knowledge holder, knowledge is not accessible. A knowledge holder may choose to translate it into more explicit form through blueprints or manuals, for example, a process that Nonaka and Takeuchi (1995) label *externalization*. Absent such translation, others are dependent on the knowledge holder for the information. Indeed, a major source of power for such persons is an unwillingness to translate such knowledge into formal language, as in Pettigrew's (1973) classic study of the power of technical specialists who refused to codify their knowledge in any manual.

Knowledge that has not been externalized will be difficult to exchange directly over intranets. Whether individuals locate that knowledge will depend not only on their ability to learn about the expertise of coworkers, but also on whether they have informal or formal links to those in the know. Intranets can help individuals to learn about the expertise and knowledge of others in their organization and identify communication links to them through such mechanisms as expert directories, postings of formal job descriptions and responsibilities, search engines for information and expertise, expertise inference systems (capture and analysis of activities such as who got reimbursed for travel to meetings on a particular topic or who participated in which forum), or community-ware, that is, tools to generate visual representations of knowledge and communication networks based on information voluntarily shared by individuals (e.g., I-KNOW; Contractor, Zink, and Chan 1998). We refer to such capabilities as *expertise location mechanisms* and individual access to intranets having such mechanisms as *expertise location access*.

As a result of the availability of expertise location mechanisms, intranets may allow people to locate experts outside their departments and outside their usual communication networks faster and more easily. This may lead to more decentralized communication networks in the organization, which can lead to more effective knowledge sharing in situations when knowledge is distributed across individuals (Rulke and Galaskiewicz 2000). Intranets should also increase network density; that is, individuals will have more direct communication with others in the network. This should result because of individuals' increased knowledge about where information resides. These arguments lead to the following propositions:

Proposition 3:   Compared to individuals without expertise location access, individuals with expertise location access will (1) know more about the knowledge of their coworkers, (2) have more shared agreement about relative expertise, and (3) have more knowledge about expertise outside the division or department.

Proposition 4:   Compared to organizations in which individuals do not have expertise location access, organizations in which individuals do have expertise location access will have (1) more decentralized communication networks, (2) denser communication networks, (3) more effective knowledge sharing, (4) more efficient task performance, and (5) more effective task performance.

A key consideration in whether these benefits accrue is whether people contribute their knowledge and whether others use intranets to access it, as well as the quality of the expert inference system. People who possess unique knowledge or know uniquely where to find it must have the motivation and the time to make their expertise available. In addition, individuals must be motivated to use an intranet for retrieving information about expertise. Public goods theory can be used to predict which, how much, and when members will contribute and retrieve knowledge on intranets in ways that can result in these benefits.

Knowledge, Intranets, and Public Goods Theory
The public goods theory of collective action (Hardin 1982, Marwell and Oliver 1993, Olson 1965, Samuelson 1954) considers how best to induce members of a collective to contribute their resources to the creation and maintenance of a collective resource accessible to all members of the public. The public can be a group, organization, neighborhood, political action group, interorganizational network, community, nation, the globalizing world, or other collective grouping. Two features define a resource as collectively accessible (Barry and Hardin 1982, Head 1972). First, the resource must be *nonexcludable*, in that all members of the collective without exception have the opportunity to benefit from the resource. Second, the resource must be *nonrival*, such that one member's use of the good does not reduce the amount available to others.

A key public goods problem is free riding (Hardin 1968, Olson 1965, Sweeney 1973), where people enjoy the benefits of a collective resource without contributing to its establishment or maintenance. In essence, the nonexcludability feature creates a set of payoffs to each member that discourages contribution; the net effect is to make it "virtually impossible" for decentralized collectives to create such goods spontaneously in the absence of supplemental incentives and organizing forces (Samuelson 1954). Examples of collective resources in the information realm are libraries, databases, bulletin boards, forums, Web sites, and other information repositories, as well as communication networks by which people share data, information, and knowledge (Fulk et al. 1996).

TM systems are collectively produced information and knowledge resources designed to be nonexcludable and nonrival to the relevant public. Intranets offer a capability for identifying and linking people and knowledge in ways that can help to develop and sustain TM systems as collectively shared resources. This capability will be particularly important for distributed work groups, which lack the traditional affordances that proximity provides in support of collaboration. As Kraut, Fussell, Brennan, and Siegel (chapter 6, this volume) elaborate, these affordances include mobility in a common physical environment, audibility within the environment, visibility of other persons, visibility of the environment, and cotemporality. Finholt, Sproull, and Kiesler (chapter 15, this volume) argue from research on expert databases that when communication systems offer information about who knows what, expertise exchange can occur effectively at a distance. Intranets and related communication and information technologies can serve this role if, and only if, members of the collective can be induced to contribute their unique valuable knowledge and participate materially in collective information sharing and communication processes (Connolly and Thorn 1990).

Intranets can support the nonrival and nonexcludable aspects of a TM system. First, every person in the TM system can use an intranet to retrieve knowledge regardless of whether they have contributed to its creation or maintenance. Second, if one person uses an intranet to publish or retrieve information, then it does not diminish the ability of others to do so as well. For transactive memory systems supported by intranets, the classic free-rider problem appears as what has been labeled a "communication dilemma" (Bonacich and Schneider 1992). A communication dilemma exists when a group's or organization's interests demand that people share their unique information, but individuals' own personal interests motivate them to withhold it (Kalman, Monge, Fulk, and Heino 2001b). The interesting issue to explore here is how intranet TM systems can resolve this dilemma and induce members to contribute to the collective.

Monge and associates (1998) applied Marwell and Oliver's (1993) articulation of PG theory to knowledge management. In both instances, individual contribution decisions are based on the value people believe they will receive from the knowledge system minus their perceived costs of participating in it.[2] Value is a function of the current level of collective knowledge available through it: the more collective knowledge available, the more individuals value the system. The current level of collective knowledge available is itself a function of the contributions of knowledge by all of the members of the collective. Costs include the time and energy spent to contribute and retrieve information, assess its veracity, and combat any mistrust of other members with regard to how collectively owned information is used (Fulk et al. 2001).

An illustration of the dynamics of information contribution decisions is the knowledge sharing among members of a distributed design team for a new consumer electronics device. Team members in New York, Amsterdam, and Tokyo have access to an intranet with a project Web site that allows them to post data, information, knowledge, and expertise location information that could be of benefit to other team members. Postings might include technical breakthroughs, roadblocks, information obtained from university contacts made by any of them, and information on people outside the team who have useful information or would be a valuable consultant. This distributed design team has the potential for an effective transactive memory system because different team members have different specialties, levels of experience, external contacts, and types of knowledge. Each team member decides what, if any, of his or her specific knowledge to make available to the rest of the team on the communal Web site.

The value to individuals depends on just how communal that Web site is—how much really useful knowledge other members have made and are continuing to make available through it. The cost to individuals of contributing knowledge is in proportion to the amount the individuals contribute and also depends on how much time and effort it takes to compile it and post it to the Web site. Less tangible costs might include when a person provides a colleague access to a university contact and in doing so incurs personal debt. The latter illustrates that a person might choose to withhold information because it incurs personal costs but provides no direct personal benefits.

Costs and Participation   From the point of view of individuals, the most rational choice to maximize benefit is to minimize costs, since the value component depends on the contributions of others and thus is less readily changeable by any individual. Cost minimization is accomplished by minimizing knowledge contributions, which incur costs. There can be many costs of participating in a communal knowledge system. Physical and social costs associated with the accumulation, transfer, and storage of information include learning how to use the system, compiling information for the system, making the effort required to integrate the knowledge within the knowledge domain, and being available to others (Fulk et al. 1996). Costs for retrieving include the length of time it takes to find the relevant knowledge, the difficulty of using the system, and the potential consequences of retrieving dated or inaccurate information.

Publishing information on an intranet so that it becomes a communal rather than a private possession may also incur political costs. Sharing information that provides a competitive advantage may decrease its utility to the individual who once held it exclusively (Barry and Hardin 1982). Uniquely held knowledge can form the basis of important personal capital to individuals in organizations. Connolly and Thorn (1990) suggest that higher payoffs are associated with withholding rather than contributing information, that is, free riding. Each contribution to shared knowledge benefits everyone else except for the supplier, who already has that information. Thus, people may withhold information that would otherwise enhance the repository on an intranet.

Combating Nonparticipation   Drawing on Kerr (1992), Kalman, Fulk, and Monge (2001a) suggest that there are two ways to solve this nonparticipation problem. A *cooperation contingent transformation* involves the relevant collective (organization or group, for example) applying selective incentives for cooperative behavior. The incentive scheme rewards cooperation or penalizes noncooperation (or both). One type of incentive might be designed to reduce individual costs, such as the provision of support staff for collection, compilation, inputting, and updating knowledge for collective repositories. Systems may also be set up in a tit-for-tat fashion. People provide information such as personal opinions based on expertise and in return are given access to others' opinions on the same issue. The MovieLens movie rating system follows this model. MovieLens (*http:movielens.umn.edu/*) is a collaborative filtering tool through which users provide information and opinions on movies they have viewed. The tool matches users with others who have similar opinions of the movies. Based on this matching, MovieLens provides personalized recommendations for each user, suggesting other movies that they have not yet seen but which are well-liked by others with similar tastes.

A second type of incentive assigns penalties for nonparticipation. For example, police organizations typically require their officers to report certain types of planned events to shared databases, thereby permitting different agencies to coordinate law enforcement actions (such as planned drug busts), with the imposition of heavy penalties for noncompliance. This type of incentive also works on the cost component, in that lower contributions lead to higher costs. A third type of incentive provides direct individual benefits for participation that outweigh the costs involved. Organizations develop rewards for the best and most useful information contributions. This incentive decreases net costs by offering offsetting rewards.

The cooperation-contingent transformation places burdens for monitoring and enforcement at the collective level. Since high-quality information-sharing behavior is not necessarily easy to monitor and identify, this transformation is an imperfect solution. It is particularly problematic for knowledge, which is less visible and separable from the knower than is information.

A second method is the so-called public goods transformation, in which individuals come to place increasing value on the collective resource itself. Increasing individuals' identification with the collective or increasing commitment to an effectively functioning transactive memory system can motivate individuals to contribute their information and knowledge (Kalman et al. 2001a, Staw 1984). Moon and Sproull's study of contributors to the Linux project (chapter 16, this volume) appears to fit this category. A variant occurs when achievement of a collective goal leads to a follow-on benefit for individuals. Employees may increase commitment to knowledge sharing on critical projects in order to get to market first, avoid losing out to competitors, and potentially finding themselves jobless.

With public goods transformations, responsibility for monitoring and regulating performance rests with the individuals, who now have internalized the goals of the collective. In essence, individuals' fates are vested in those of the collective. External monitoring of participation is not required, except perhaps to assist people in coordinating their activities.

Synthesis of Theoretical Perspectives: Integrative Propositions

PG and TM theories can be integrated to pose additional propositions about knowledge sharing and distribution. TM theory predicts that knowledge in a work community will become more specialized and less redundant across people over time. When knowledge is specialized across people, more coordination and communication is required to accomplish complex tasks. Intranets can serve as a mechanism to achieve such coordination and communication, as well as knowledge dissemination. In these cases, individuals should value intranets more. Of course, intranets must also be efficient. The increases in value must be obtained without substantial increases in the costs of locating and securing knowledge in order for the net benefit to increase. In short, when unique knowledge is evenly distributed across members and intranets effectively and efficiently link knowledge holders, then the likelihood that people will publish and retrieve knowledge on intranets increases.

We posit a dynamic, recursive relationship between knowledge specialization and collective knowledge sharing in distributed work groups. As more individuals use knowledge repositories on intranets for publishing and retrieving knowledge, individuals will learn more about the expertise and unique knowledge of other people at distant locations, and they will not need to pay the costs of learning that information on their own. This will lead individuals to develop more specialized and unique areas of relative expertise over time. Kalman and associates (2001a) suggested that the possession of unique knowledge or expertise increases an individual's "information self-efficacy," that is, the belief that one can make a contribution that others will value. Information self-efficacy thus increases the likelihood that individuals will share knowledge through collective stores such as intranets.

This research and theory suggests a recursive cycle. Individuals in work communities that have transactive memory systems and effective intranets will be more likely to publish their knowledge on intranets. In turn, increased publishing will lead individuals to specialize more in areas of relative expertise. Finally, this specialization will contribute to increasing value for the collective knowledge sharing and, at the individual level, reduced costs and higher benefits from participation in the intranet-based collective. Thus, we offer the following propositions:

Proposition 5: Participation in knowledge sharing using intranets is positively related to the degree to which (1) knowledge is distributed across individuals in the work community, (2) individuals perceive their knowledge to be unique, (3) others perceive a person's knowledge to be unique, (4) others retrieve knowledge located on intranets, and (5) other people contribute knowledge to intranets.

Proposition 6: The more members of a collective share knowledge using intranets, the more individuals will specialize in their areas of relative expertise.

Private Benefits, Incentives, and Unexpected Effects

The context in which these processes are embedded can affect knowledge sharing to the degree to which it offers potential contributors other incentives and disincentives. Several of these contextual factors have been investigated in research on group processes and on public goods production. We review several key findings and issues.

Supplemental Incentives   Equally divided group incentives have been shown to lead to high productivity and employee satisfaction (Honeywell-Johnson and Dickinson 1999). This incentive structure may also reinforce individuals' perceptions of their interdependence with their work community, which is likely to be particularly important for distributed work groups (Weisband, chapter 13, this volume). In many organizational situations, however, it is not possible or desirable to offer equal incentives. Research has shown that in situations of unequal incentives, fostering identification with the group can help to even out contributions to some extent by effecting a public goods transformation (Bonacich and Schneider 1992).

Incentives, if not properly designed, can also have unintended effects. Connolly and Thorn (1990) point out that incentives can work against the viability of a database when they reward quantity at the expense of the quality, producing an oversupply of information that may not be useful. This problem may be a function of the difficulty of developing performance criteria and monitoring compliance in the absence of individual commitment.

Group Size, Monitoring, and Efficacy of Contributions   Olson (1965) made the theoretical claim that as group size increases, free riding should increase because the visibility of each contribution decreases. This principle suggests that the number of free riders who use but do not contribute to databases should increase with increases in intranet size (Kraut, Fussell, Brennan, and Siegel, chapter 6, this volume). However, subsequent investigations dispute Olson's group size principle, claiming that visibility need not be related to group size. Interventions to increase visibility of contributions even in large groups can spur participation. In the case of the very large Linux community, visibility came in part from identifying who contributed which pieces of code. For intranets, size may actually be positively related to the visibility of contributions. The larger that intranet communities become, the more persons there are who could potentially view individuals' contributions. Since communal databases allow contributions to be distributed beyond people's immediate communication networks to persons the contributors may not know ahead of time, the potential audience can be quite large. Two features of intranets, if implemented, could help to support such visibility. The first is a mechanism for users to identify who contributed what knowledge. The second is a mechanism to feed back to contributors information on how much their contributions have been used by others. In Kalman, Monge, Fulk, and Heino's (in press) terms, contributors' information self-efficacy will rise, which will lead to greater overall motivation to participate in the collective.

Maintenance Using intranets may lead to negative consequences for everyone when knowledge quality is poor. Inaccurate or dated contributions may affect individuals' perceived costs for retrieving knowledge on intranets, thus diminishing participation. A centralized authority may be needed to provide organization and quality control of intranet knowledge repositories (Samuelson 1954). A prime example is the creation of knowledge domain teams at Ford Motor Company. Each intranet team was responsible for ensuring the usefulness of information in its domain (Austin and Cotteleer 1997).

Implications for Research and Practice

With the trend toward distributed organizational processes has come an increasing awareness of the need to find new ways to identify, deploy, and effectively transfer organizational knowledge throughout the new organizational forms. Recent research by Nextera Enterprises shows that among the most common forms of knowledge management systems are groupware and intranets.[3] To the extent that intranets are used to seek knowledge from others whom individuals did not know ahead of time and to build distributed knowledge resource pools, they can be seen as an ideal complement to network forms of organizing. Can intranets support effective knowledge sharing among specialists working in a distributed environment? One key is to facilitate individual creation and use of the collective resources occasioned by intranets. A second is to develop organizational mechanisms to institute cognitive repairs to naturally flawed human reasoning. The theoretical integration described in this chapter indicates some of the conditions under which intranets and transactive memory systems can recursively influence each other in the service of knowledge sharing. We suggest some further directions for theoretical development and implications for research design. We conclude with practical implications derivable from the theoretical analysis.

Future Directions
Research on collaboration tends to show that people collaborate better with experience and that a successful history of collaboration predicts future success (Schunn, Crowley, and Okada, chapter 17, this volume). Research on communication

technologies in the workplace suggests that with experience, people are better able to communicate and share information using technology (Fulk and Dutton 1984). Clearly, one key consideration in studies of distributed workers is the extent to which these workers have experience working with each other and with the supporting technology.

With time, even unacquainted workers will develop experience, but how do they initially develop the underlying trust to initiate processes of knowledge specialization and coordination toward building effective transactive memory systems? Mannix, Griffth, and Neale (chapter 9, this volume) argue that in distributed work groups with limited history and future prospects of working together, it is difficult to develop trust. They suggest that one possibility is to rely on "swift trust" (Meyerson, Weick, and Kramer 1996), developed by drawing on expectations inherent in roles, specialties, and other forms of category-based information processing. Research reported by Jarvenpaa and Leidner (1999) provides empirical support. In a study of short-term student project groups whose members were globally distributed, culturally diverse, and institutionally separated, the more successful groups were those that developed swift trust. When swift trust leads to success experiences that serve as a basis for more enduring trust, the cycle of successful collaboration may be effectively initiated.

Clearly, temporal issues play a significant role in understanding how knowledge sharing is fostered by using intranets in transactive memory systems. Events and interactions unfold over time and change direction with experience. The interactions of transactive memory systems and intranet knowledge sharing described in this chapter take the form of dynamic, nonlinear, recursive processes in which time and experience are key concerns. The outcomes of a process, once initiated, are not deterministic even if they could be shielded from external influences. Indeed, a central premise is that internal patterns of knowledge sharing and distribution affect the continuing viability of a true public good. Such processes must be studied over time and in relation to themselves. Additional dynamic concerns include how sensitive the systems are to initial conditions, such as whether and when swift trust develops, what types of experiences groups have, and the level of provision of the collective knowledge resource with intranets at the formation of distributed groups. Also, research on use of computer-mediated communication systems shows that over time, mediated groups change their pattern of interaction sufficiently that temporal effects become more important than any effects otherwise assignable to the mediated condition (Walther, chapter 10, this volume).

There may appear to be an underlying assumption in this chapter that the ultimate goal is to get all individuals in groups continually to publish their unique knowledge and retrieve information pertaining to others' knowledge using intranets. This is not the case. Previous research seems to indicate that there needs to be a critical mass of users before shared databases provide benefits to users. However, it may be possible that there is an optimal size and breadth of knowledge for intranets. For example, when intranets contain too much information, searching and tracking down relevant information may become too time-consuming. If the expertise and job categories of too many people are listed, then finding the expert on an intranet may become more cumbersome than simply calling a colleague who may know the answer. And the experts may be so overloaded with requests for information from hitherto unknown persons that they elect to reduce their availability. E-mail has been shown to link more otherwise unacquainted people (Constant, Sproull, and Kiesler 1996; Feldman 1987) and also to increase information load concomitantly. Perhaps information accuracy and timeliness are sacrificed when intranets get too large. Monitoring information and quality control can become much more difficult, request queues can expand substantially, and response times can lengthen (Finholt, Sproull, and Kiesler, chapter 15, this volume).

Today's network organizations are often described as supported by flexible, emergent ties that wax and wane as needed rather than an all-channel network where everyone shares all information with everyone else (Monge and Contractor 2000). Indeed, it is the selectivity and flexibility of the ties that is critical to the effective functioning of these organizations (Fulk 2001). Care must be paid *not* to migrate intranets from this more flexible system where individuals can share information as necessary to one in which sharing is fixed, less selective, and nonemergent. The challenge is to create and maintain transactive memory systems and collective knowledge resources that support differential sharing as task needs require.

This chapter focused on the cognitive aspects related to usage of intranets to support transactive memory systems in distributed work situations. Future research should address affective considerations, such as interpersonal trust in groups linked by transactive memory systems and intranets, confidence in system security, and feelings of threat to privacy linked to technology-based knowledge sharing. We are beginning to learn a great deal about knowledge networks in new organizational forms, but less attention has been paid to noncognitive aspects. For example, does retrieving knowledge from intranets rather than other people affect the nature and quality of interpersonal relationships in groups and in the organization as a whole (see Walther, chapter 10, this volume)? How much do network organizations rely on effective management of interpersonal processes as well? How does trust of others in the organization affect the degree to which individuals contribute their unique information (see Weisband, chapter 13, this volume)? Does relying on intranets for communication and knowledge recursively affect motivation or organizational commitment? These issues are likely to increase in importance in the future as intranets become more commonplace in organizations and as network organizations become the more modal form of organizing.

Practical Implications

Public goods theory suggests some straightforward steps that can foster intranet knowledge sharing. To reduce costs, organizations can provide training in system features and knowledge-seeking strategies. Further, they can offer subsidization of otherwise costly contributions by providing assistance in gathering, compiling, and uploading information to data repositories and in keeping such information up-to-date. Organizations can also provide assistance and training in ways to externalize tacit knowledge, as suggested by Nonaka and Takeuchi (1995). To reduce costs associated with sharing sensitive information using communal repositories, organizations can design systems with options for selective dyadic knowledge exchange. For example, one law enforcement organization added a feature that informed knowledge holders if other users had expressed interest in their knowledge, but did so without informing the knowledge seekers. This feature allowed knowledge holders to identify who was seeking information and make an individual decision as to whether and how much information to release to that person, or to make personal contact to discuss issues with the person, or to do nothing at all (Monge et al. 2000).

Organizations can also develop mechanisms to increase commitment to successful transactive memory systems by providing follow-on rewards for project competition that depend on effective knowledge sharing. For example, a project group may receive a substantial group bonus for completing a project ahead of schedule. To accomplish this, group members must regularly share knowledge and develop an effective communal knowledge base. Rewards are better tied to effective knowledge sharing than to countable inputs devoid of a quality assessment. The key here would be to initiate a process by which individuals could achieve a public goods transformation over time.

The theory proposes that people will contribute more when they value the collective resource and when there is useful knowledge within the system. Organizations can provide maps and statistics that provide on-line real-time views of where knowledge resides, who is contributing, and who is retrieving information on the intranet. This landscape view not only facilitates assessments of value but also provides information on level and types of specialization and on the uniqueness of one's knowledge. Other feedback mechanisms would include notification to a knowledge contributor when another user accesses and uses the contribution and when such information use has had important group- and organization-level impacts. Identification of contributors would increase their visibility and provide recognition. Feedback on how many others are contributing would be useful to individuals in their assessments of value.

Because the early stages of intranet use are critical in gaining the critical mass necessary for the community to become self-sustaining, organizations should focus efforts in the above areas from the very inception of new distributed work groups. The ability to acquire an initial set of effective users in the absence of a real critical mass, at a time when users experience low intrinsic value relative to costs, is paramount. External incentives and motivational programs will be most effective in this initial period. If enough users can be attained beyond critical mass thresholds, the need for external incentives declines significantly.

Finally, given the role that a successful history of collaboration and knowledge sharing has on transactive memory systems, organizations may want to take steps that help positive histories develop quickly for new distributed groups. This might include offering shared training for new groups that involves intranet learning and exercises to build teamwork and develop conflict management skills. Organizations can also initiate teamwork with projects that have a high probability of generating successful collaboration and groupwide trust. Small initial investments in group success provide the potential for large long-term payoffs.

Notes

This research was supported by two grants from the National Science Foundation: Knowledge and Distributed Intelligence Program (IIS-9980109) and Decision Risk and Management Science Program (9602055). Thanks to Pam Hinds, Sara Kiesler, Joe Walther, and Mark Mortensen who provided helpful feedback on earlier drafts of the chapter.
1. See www.knowledgebusiness.com/kmrlframe.html.

2. Formally, the theory states: $b_i = v_i[P(K)] - c_i(k)$. At the individual level, the benefit for publishing knowledge via intranets, b_i, is equal to the value of the knowledge in the network's repositories at its current level of provision (the amount of valuable information available in the knowledge system), $v_i[P(K)]$, minus the costs to the member of making his or her own knowledge available to others via the knowledge system, $c_i(k)$. At the collective level, the function, $P(K)$ shows the provision level of the knowledge repository, P, as a direct function of the total amount of useful knowledge resources available through it, K. K is defined to be the sum of the knowledge made available by each individual (k).

3. www.kknowledgebusiness.com/kmrlframe.html.

References

Anand, V., Manz, C. C., and Glick, W. H. (1998). An organizational memory approach to information management. *Academy of Management Review, 23*, 796–809.

Ancona, D., and Caldwell, D. (1992). Bridging the boundary: External activity and performance in organizational teams. *Administrative Science Quarterly, 37*(4), 634–666.

Austin, R., and Cotteleer, M. (1997). *Ford Motor Company: Maximizing the business value of Web technologies* (Case 9-198-006). Cambridge, MA: Harvard Business School.

Barry, B., and Hardin, R. (eds.). (1982). *Rational man and irrational society.* Beverly Hills, CA: Sage.

Blau, P. (1955). *The dynamics of bureaucracy: A study of interpersonal relations in two government agencies.* Chicago: University of Chicago Press.

Bonacich, P., and Schneider, S. (1992). Communication networks and collective action. In W. B. G. Liebrand, D. M. Messick, and H. A. M. Wilke (eds.), *Social dilemmas: Theoretical issues and research findings* (225–245). New York: Pergamon Press.

Churchman, C. W. (1971). *The design of inquiring systems: Basic concepts of systems and organization.* New York: Basic Books.

Connolly, T., and Thorn, B. K. (1990). Discretionary databases: Theory, data, and implications. In J. Fulk and C. Steinfield (eds.), *Organizations and communication technology* (219–233). Newbury Park, CA: Sage.

Constant, D., Sproull, L., and Kiesler, S. (1996). The kindness of strangers: The usefulness of electronic weak ties for technical advice. *Organization Science, 7*, 119–136.

Contractor, N. S., Zink, D., and Chan, M. (1998). IKNOW: A tool to assist and study the creation, maintenance, and dissolution of knowledge networks. In T. Ishida (ed.), *Community computing and support systems* (201–217). Berlin. Springer-Verlag.

DeSanctis, G. D., and Monge, P. R. (1999). Communication processes for virtual organizations. *Organization Science, 10*, 693–703.

Feldman, M. (1987). Electronic mail and weak ties in organizations. *Office: Technology and People, 3*, 83–101.

Finholt, T. A., Sproull, L., and Kiesler, S. (2002). Outsiders on the inside: Sharing know-how across space and time. In P. Hinds and S. Kiesler (eds.), *Distributed work* (357–379). Cambridge, MA: MIT Press.

Fulk, J. (2001). Global organizational networks: Emergence and future prospects. *Human Relations, 54*, 91–99.

Fulk, J., and Dutton, W. (1984). Videoconferencing as an organizational information system: Assessing the role of electronic meetings. *Systems, Objectives, Solutions, 4*, 105–118.

Fulk, J., Flanagin, A. J., Kalman, M. E., Monge, P. R., and Ryan, T. (1996). Connective and communal public goods in interactive communication systems. *Communication Theory, 6*, 60–87.

Fulk, J., Heino, R., Flanagin, A., Monge, P., Kim, K., Bar, F., and Lin, W. (2001). *Intranet functionality as collective action.* Unpublished manuscript.

Hardin, G. (1968). The tragedy of the commons. *Science, 162*, 1243–1248.

Hardin, R. (1982). *Collective action.* Baltimore, MD: John Hopkins University Press.

Head, J. G. (1972). Public goods: The polar case. In R. M. Bird and J. G. Head (eds.), *Modern fiscal issues: Essays in honour of Carl. S. Shoup* (7–16). Toronto: University of Toronto Press.

Head, A. J. (2000). Demystifying intranet design: Five guidelines for building usable sites. *Online, 24*, 36–42.

Heath, C., Larrick, R. P., and Klayman, J. (1998). Cognitive repairs: How organizational practices can compensate for individual shortcomings. *Research in Organizational Behavior, 20*, 1–38.

Hollingshead, A. B. (1998a). Communication, learning and retrieval in transactive memory systems. *Journal of Experimental Social Psychology, 34*, 423–442.

Hollingshead, A. B. (1998b). Distributed knowledge and transactive processes in groups. In M. A. Neale, E. A. Mannix, and D. H. Gruenfeld (eds.), *Research on managing groups and teams* (Vol. 1, 105–125). Greenwich, CT: JAI Press.

Hollingshead, A. B. (1998c). Retrieval processes in transactive memory systems. *Journal of Personality and Social Psychology, 74*, 659–671.

Hollingshead, A. B. (2000). Perceptions of expertise and transactive memory in work relationships. *Group Processes and Intergroup Relations, 3*, 257–267.

Hollingshead, A. B. (in press). Cognitive interdependence, convergent expectations and the development of transactive memory. *Journal of Personality and Social Psychology.*

Honeywell-Johnson, J. A., and Dickinson, A. M. (1999). Small group incentives: A review of the literature. *Journal of Organizational Behavior Management, 19*, 89–120.

Jarvenpaa, S., and Leidner, D. (1999). Communication and trust in global virtual teams. *Organization Science, 10*, 791–815.

Kalman, M., Fulk, J., and Monge, P. (2001a). *Resolving communication dilemmas: A motivational model for information contribution to discretionary databases.* Unpublished manuscript.

Kalman, M., Monge, P., Fulk, J., and Heino, R. (2001b). *Overcoming communication dilemmas in database-mediated collaboration: A model and empirical test.* Unpublished manuscript.

Kalman, M., Monge, P., Fulk, J., and Heino, R. (in press). Motivations to resolve communication dilemmas by voluntary contributions to a collectively shared database. *Communication Research*.

Kerr, N. L. (1992). Efficacy as a causal and moderating variable in social dilemmas. In W. B. G. Liebrand, D. M. Messick, and H. A. M. Wilke (eds.), *Social dilemmas: Theoretical issues and research findings* (59–80). New York: Pergamon Press.

Kraut, R. E., Fussell, S. R., Brennan, S. E., and Siegel, J. (2002). Understanding effects of proximity on collaboration: Implications for technologies to support remote collaborative work. In P. Hinds and S. Kiesler (eds.), *Distributed work* (137–162). Cambridge, MA: MIT Press.

Liang, D. W., Moreland, R. L., and Argote, L. (1995). Group versus individual training and group performance: The mediating role of transactive memory. *Personality and Social Psychology Bulletin, 21*, 384–393.

Mannix, E. A., Griffith, T., and Neale, M. A. (2002). The phenomenology of conflict in distributed work teams. In P. Hinds and S. Kiesler (eds.), *Distributed work* (213–233). Cambridge, MA: MIT Press.

Marwell, G., and Oliver, P. (1993). *The critical mass in collective action: A micro-social theory*. New York: Cambridge University Press.

Monge, P. R., and Contractor, N. S. (2000). Emergence of communication networks. In L. L. Putnam and F. Jablin (eds.), *The new handbook of organizational communication* (440–502). Thousand Oaks, CA: Sage.

Monge, P. R., and Fulk, J. (1999). Communication technology for global network organizations. In G. D. DeSanctis and J. Fulk (eds.), *Shaping organizational form: Communication, connection, and community* (71–100). Thousand Oaks, CA: Sage.

Monge, P. R., Fulk, J., Kalman, M., Flanagin, A., Parnassa, C., and Rumsey, S. (1998). Production of collective action in alliance-based interorganizational communication and information systems. *Organization Science, 9*, 411–433.

Monge, P., Fulk, J., Parnassa, C., Flanagin, A., Rumsey, S., and Kalman, M. (2000) Cooperative interagency approaches to the illegal drug problem. *International Journal of Police Science and Management, 2*, 229–241.

Moon, J. Y., and Sproull, L. (2002). Essence of distributed work: The case of the Linux kernel. In P. Hinds and S. Kiesler, *Distributed work* (381–404). Cambridge, MA: MIT Press.

Moreland, R. L. (1999). Transactive memory: Learning who knows what in work groups and organizations. In L. Thompson, J. Levine, and D. Messick (eds.), *Shared cognition in organizations: The management of knowledge* (3–31). Mahwah, NJ: Erlbaum.

Moreland, R. L., Argote, L., and Krishnan, T. (1996). Social shared cognition at work: Transactive memory and group performance. In J. L. Nye and A. M. Brower (eds.), *What's social about social cognition? Research on socially shared cognition in small groups* (57–84). Thousand Oaks, CA: Sage.

Moreland, R. L., and Myaskovsky, L. (2000). Exploring the performance benefits of group training: Transactive memory or improved communication? *Organizational Behavior and Human Decision Processes, 82*, 117–133.

Nonaka, I., and Takeuchi, H. (1995). *The knowledge-creating company: How Japanese companies create the dynamics of innovation.* New York: Oxford University Press, 1995.

Olson, M. (1965). *The logic of collective action.* Cambridge, MA: Harvard University Press.

Pettigrew, A. (1973). *The politics of organizational decision-making.* London: Tavistock.

Rulke, D. L., and Galaskiewicz, J. (2000). Distribution of knowledge, group network structure, and group performance. *Management Science, 46,* 612–625.

Rusbult, C. E., and Van Lange, P. A. M. (1996). Interdependence processes. In E. T. Higgins and A. W. Kruglanski (eds.), *Social psychology: Handbook of basic principles* (564–596). New York: Guilford Press.

Samuelson, P. A. (1954). The pure theory of public expenditure. *Review of Economics and Statistics, 36,* 387–390.

Shapiro, C., and Varian, H. (1999). *Information rules: A strategic guide to the network economy.* Boston, MA: Harvard Business School Press.

Schunn, C., Crowley, K., and Okada, T. (2002). What makes collaborations across a distance succeed? The case of the cognitive science community. In P. Hinds and S. Kiesler (eds.), *Distributed work* (407–430). Cambridge, MA: MIT Press.

Staw, B. M. (1984). Organizational behavior: A review and reformulation of the field's outcome variables. *Annual Review of Psychology, 35,* 627–666.

Stohl, C., and Redding, C. (1987). Messages and message exchange processes. In F. Jablin, L. Putnam, K. Roberts, and L. W. Porter (eds.), *Handbook of organizational communication* (451–502), Thousand Oaks, CA: Sage.

Sweeney, J. W. (1973). An experimental investigation of the free-rider problem. *Social Science Research, 2,* 277–292.

Walther, J. B. (2002). Time effects in computer-mediated groups: Past, present, and future. In P. Hinds and S. Kiesler (eds.), *Distributed work* (235–257). Cambridge, MA: MIT Press.

Wegner, D. M. (1987). Transactive memory: A contemporary analysis of the group mind. In B. Mullen and G. R. Goethals (eds.), *Theories of group behavior* (185–208). New York: Springer-Verlag.

Wegner, D. M. (1995). A computer network model of human transactive memory. *Social Cognition, 13,* 319–339.

Wegner, D. M., Erber, R., and Raymond, P. (1991). Transactive memory in close relationships. *Journal of Personality and Social Psychology, 61,* 923–929.

Weisband, S. (2002). Maintaining awareness in distributed team collaboration: Implications for leadership and performance. In P. Hinds and S. Kiesler, *Distributed work* (311–334). Cambridge, MA: MIT Press.

15

Outsiders on the Inside: Sharing Know-How Across Space and Time

Thomas A. Finholt, Lee Sproull, and Sara Kiesler

This study examined how employees of a global corporation sought out technical information from employees distant from them. Data were drawn from the contents and access records of two computer-based employee message archives: the peer archive, which contained questions and answers exchanged over a company-wide electronic mailing list by ordinary employees and the expert archive, which contained questions from employees and answers from designated experts. We predicted that archive accesses by employees would increase with their geographic distance from engineering headquarters and that accesses would increase to the extent that the archive contained know-how information. Content analysis demonstrated that the peer exchanges were more informal and more personal, and were more likely to contain specific references to the company's products, tools, and customers, all indicators of know-how information. Analyses of use showed that workers accessed the peer archive more than they did the expert archive; this difference increased with greater geographic distance from engineering headquarters. The results suggest that know-how archives can be useful in connecting distant employees seeking and providing technical information across space and time.

Organizations are focused on improving access to and use of organizational knowledge—both "know-what" and "know-how" (Brown and Duguid 1998). *Know-what* is explicit rules and principles. *Know-how* is the ability to put know-what into practice. For example, a help line operator may understand general principles of computer operating systems, but this understanding is useful only if it can be deployed to solve a caller's particular problem. Know-what is relatively easily transmitted through books, manuals, or formal instruction and computer-based documents and databases. Know-how, by contrast, is often difficult to transmit in documents and formal instruction because it is embedded in work practices.

Technicians and engineers have always shared know-how in informal face-to-face conversations (Allen 1977, Kusterer 1978, Latour and Woolgar 1986, von Hippel 1994). Face-to-face conversation ties know-how to a particular place because the likelihood of face-to-face interaction diminishes with increased distance (see Kiesler and Cummings, chapter 3, this volume). Face-to-face interaction also typically ties know-how to a particular time because it is usually ephemeral, that is, not recorded and archived for later use.

The dilemma for field engineering is that geographic and temporal distance impose barriers to developing and sharing know-how in face-to-face interaction. Peers or experts with relevant know-how may be located far from the field engineer's customer site. Or they may be physically close, but their potentially helpful conversations may have occurred prior to a point at which they were relevant or needed. To the extent that wider access to know-how represents a strategy for improving field engineering for customer support, organizations must find ways to develop and disseminate know-how that do not depend on geographic or temporal colocation.

In some cases, widespread connectivity to computer networking technology has supported the development and dissemination of know-how across distance. Constant, Sproull, and Kiesler (1996) describe how employees of a global corporation found technical information by posing know-how questions over their corporate computer network to mass mailing lists. Although these were often questions about company products, they were not questions that could be answered by the formal documentation about how things were supposed to work. On average, a question received private e-mail replies from eight people. Only 8 percent of those answering knew the question asker. Yet employees found replies to be very useful, and, in fact, in half the cases, the replies solved the employee's problem.

The broadcast question with private replies can be very useful to the individual questioner, but this mechanism does not spread know-how more broadly. For this reason, organizations may create technology such as bulletin boards or electronic mailing lists (distribution lists) for publishing both questions and answers to anyone who subscribes. Applications of this nature allow many people to read and contribute to both the questions and the replies.

One drawback of e-mail lists for exchanging know-how is that even though they are convenient, people tend to ignore messages that are irrelevant to their immediate concerns. The half-life of a message thread—that is, a question and all replies to it—is typically four days or less (Galegher, Sproull, and Kiesler 1998). Thus, the benefits of information sharing through e-mail lists are most accessible to geographically distant employees who are paying attention when a conversation occurs. Temporally distant employees, that is, those who are not interested in a topic when it is being discussed but who develop an interest in the topic later, may not benefit from electronic mailing lists.

A searchable archive of distribution list e-mail messages or bulletin board posts can extend the benefits of electronic interaction over time and to a broader audience (Ackerman 1994, Ackerman and McDonald 1996). It is technically feasible to archive electronic exchanges of know-how contained in the kinds of exchanges documented by Constant and associates (1996). Every employee who broadcasts a question and receives replies can submit both the question and its replies to an archive, or exchanges can be archived automatically.

Even though it is technically feasible to archive spontaneous exchanges of know-how, it is not clear that reading archived reports of someone else's problem accompanied by suggested solutions will in fact be useful. If archived messages describing problems are couched in idiosyncratic terms, they may not substantially resemble the problem of the person searching the archive. If archived replies suggesting solutions are also idiosyncratic, they may be deemed inapplicable. The original question asker might have engaged in additional clarifying communication with the person who replied, such as a phone call or private e-mail, but someone accessing an archive has much less opportunity to ask follow-up questions of those who provided solutions. Even if archived replies are accompanied by information about the source, such as the source's location, this information could be obsolete by the time it was accessed.

Thus, whereas contemporaneous electronic exchanges plausibly can produce and disseminate know-how across distance, archives of those exchanges might not be useful to people needing know-how across time. Perhaps more useful would be archives of questions sent to officially designated experts, with the experts' replies. These archives would be more authoritative and more generalizable across both distance and time, to the extent that expert respondents focus on universal and enduring principles underlying questions. On the other hand, designated experts, because of their more universal perspective, may provide overly general rules and canonical information rather than pointed stories and advice. Furthermore, the average reply from a designated expert, whose job requires replying to all questions, may be less highly motivated by the wish to provide a quick, helpful answer than the average reply from a peer who chooses to reply to a particular engineer's question (and not to others). Finally, archives containing several coworker replies to each question, even if the average reply is of lower quality than that of the experts' replies, are likely to offer multiple ways of thinking about a problem rather than a single official answer.

These considerations led us to hypothesize that despite the unofficial and voluntary source of its contents, an archive of informal questions and answers by peers would be preferred by field engineers over an archive of experts' answers to questions. Also, because a company's engineering headquarters tends to produce the highest concentration of engineering know-how in one place, we hypothesized that the farther away field engineers are from their company's engineering headquarters, the more they will use an archive of peer exchanges and the more they will prefer it over an archive of expert exchanges.

A Study of Know-How Archives for Field Engineers

In 1988, the first author collected nearly a year's data on field engineers' use of message archives at Tandem Computers, a Fortune 500 computer manufacturing company (since acquired by Compaq Computer) (Finholt 1993). One archive contained questions by field engineers and replies to them by fellow employees in the company; the other archive contained questions by field engineers and answers from designated experts. Here, we describe engineers' use of the archives to understand how people distant in space and time from the original exchange might find such information useful. We note at the outset that these are historical data; computer networks and people's use of them have developed markedly since the 1980s. Nevertheless, although contemporary implementations may use more modern technology, the purpose and function of the Tandem archives are similar to mechanisms widely used today, particularly with regard to worker-to-worker and worker-to-expert exchanges. Furthermore, for its time, the Tandem network and applications were very advanced. For example, 87 percent of Tandem employees across the world had access to the networked archives with an easy-to-use interface. This high proportion of employees connected to the network was unusual in the late 1980s but mirrors current levels of connectivity and use within corporate intranets. Hence, these historical data seem well suited to testing our arguments and hypotheses.

At Tandem, as at other organizations, employees used face-to-face conversations and meetings to develop and exchange know-how. However, opportunities for conversations and meetings were limited by geographic dispersion. Sixty-five percent of Tandem's 10,077-person workforce was distributed over 306 field offices on five continents. The Tandem field engineers installed and supported Tandem products at customer sites all over the world; thus, most field engineers worked at a distance from their engineering colleagues.

Tandem supported a corporate computer network that reached virtually all employees, and management encouraged heavy use of the corporate network for both work-related and personal communication. E-mail and other computer-mediated communication were expected to span barriers of distance and time to improve contact among distributed employees and to speed the flow of information among remote sites. Tandem employees used a class e-mail structure to organize the flow of e-mail. They exchanged electronic messages with each other and with work groups via "first-class mail." They broadcast work-related electronic messages to the entire company via "second-class mail." They broadcast nonwork messages to their local sites or regions via "third-class mail." Each class of mail was delivered into a separate in-box on the employee's computer display, thus providing a simple way of organizing incoming mail.

At Tandem, field engineers used the corporate computer e-mail system to seek and provide work-related information. They could query a broad audience through use of second-class mail or target queries to specific respondents through use of first-class mail. Tandem employees' broadcast question and private reply system described by Constant, Sproull, and Kiesler (1996) was viewed as so useful that in the early 1980s, the field engineering organization began to save these questions and answers into message archives accessible throughout the Tandem corporate computer network. Tandem employees accessed the archives through an archive server with a simple, common interface. The archive server allowed employees to specify a variety of complex searches by combining keywords and data fields. One archive, which we will call the peer archive, contained the technical information exchanges that occurred using second-class electronic mail. Replies in these exchanges came from ordinary members of Tandem's field engineer workforce who voluntarily responded to a broadcast second-class question with information and advice. The peer archive resulted from the practice of saving questions, and the replies to these questions, as public reply files. Reply files were incorporated into the peer archive when a member of the field engineering headquarters staff, seeing an announcement of a public reply file, would retrieve the file using the corporate network and add it to the peer archive. Figure 15.1 shows an example of a reply file stored in the peer archive.

The second archive, which we will call the expert archive, consisted of questions sent in first-class mail from ordinary employees to designated experts at Tandem engineering headquarters. In these exchanges, questioners addressed requests for help to specific computer mailboxes publicized within the organization and

```
Document #: 3538 - Document length:  120 lines - [August, 19xx]
[program v1] to [program v2] CONVERSION

QUESTION
My customer, [university name], is planning to convert
approximately 200 application programs from [program v1] to
[program v2]. They would like to know of other customers'
experience in doing this. Any story, with details, would be
welcome.
                         Many thanks,
                            [Questioner's full name]
-------------------------------------------------------------


*=*=*=*=*=*=*=*=*=*=*=*=*=*=*=*=*=*=*=*=*=*=*=*=*=*=*=*=*=*=*
*=*=*=*=*=*=*=*=*=*=*=*=*=*=*=*=*=*=*=*=*=*=*=*=*=*=*=*=*=*=*
=  COMMENTS from the "TNT" group!     August, 19xx =
=  Please note that the contents of this file have not  =
=  yet been reviewed for technical validity.        =
=                   Tools-N-Technology =
=      ( FOR INTERNAL USE ONLY)            =
*=*=*=*=*=*=*=*=*=*=*=*=*=*=*=*=*=*=*=*=*=*=*=*=*=*=*=*=*=*=*
*=*=*=*=*=*=*=*=*=*=*=*=*=*=*=*=*=*=*=*=*=*=*=*=*=*=*=*=*=*=*

REPLIES

FROM: [Replier1's ID]@HAMBG
Hi [Questioner's first name]!
There exists a utility to convert from [program v1] to [program
v2]. I don't know exactly where it resides but you should check
QUEST-database.
Hope that helps.
Regards
[Replier1's first name]
-------------------------------------------------------------
FROM: [Replier2's ID]@PARIS
[Questioner's first name],
On node \PRUNE you can find files containing usefull
informations for doing convertion from [program v1] to [program
v2] and how to code with [program v2]..
They are on : \PRUNE.$ [program] L. [program] L85.CONVGD
\PRUNE.$ [program].TOMC85. [program] GUIDE
```

Figure 15.1
Question and replies in the peer archive.

```
[Replier2's first name]
--------------------------------------------------------
FROM: [Replier3's ID]@HOLLAND
<Questioner's first name>,
In Holland we started two conversions: <customer's name> had no
real problems - contact <person's ID> <another customer's name>
were advised to stop the conversion, because the compiler had
too many problems, it interfered with the project contact
<person's ID>
success,
<Replier3's full name>
--------------------------------------------------------
FROM: [Replier4's ID]@CSO
[Questioner's nickname]:
There is a good article on [program v2], written by one of the
developers ([author's name]) in the February, 19xx, Systems
Review (Volume 2, Number 1). One section of the article
highlights the differences between the two languages.
[Replier4's first name]
--------------------------------------------------------
FROM: [Replier5's ID]@SILICON
I talked to one of my accounts who has converted to [program
v2]. and about the only change they have made from their
[program v1] programs is to replace computer statements that
used division with explicit divide statements to insure correct
precision in the results.
--------------------------------------------------------
FROM: [Replier6's ID]@STLOUIS
[Questioner's first name],
I'm going thru my second account conversion right now. Here are
some quick notes on the experiences.
1) All of [previously referenced author]'s commentary on the
conversion process is valuable and should be reviewed with the
customer. I believe the location of this info has already been
supplied to you.
2) There has never been a requirement to use the reserved word
conversion program at my accounts. It's comforting to know its
available but I suspect that most customers will not run afoul
of the new reserved words.
3) [program v2] is much more sensitive to numeric field
manipulation. The standard is very specific and rigidly adhered
to in the Tandem implementation. This means that many programs
```

Figure 15.1 (continued)

```
that ran under [program v1] will trap under [program v2],
usually with numeric overflow. Example: My customer had a
program that moved PIC 9(5) to PIC 9(4). Obviously this is bad
practice, but it happens frequently. Under [program v1] the
program continued execution and the invalid results of the move
were later discarded by other program logic. Under [program v2]
a trap #02 reslted. Customers also report occasional divide-by-
zero traps.
4) The Standard specifically states that any key-field
referenced in a program be defined alphanumerically. Consider
the following example: : : SELECT  A-file   ASSIGN TO <disc-
file> ORGANIZATION INDEXED RECORD KEY IS A-File-Key : : FD A-
file    01 A-Record. 02 A-File-Key. 03 Acct-No    PIC 9(6). 03
Jrnl-No PIC 9(6). : : START A-File KEY = Acct-No, GENERIC ....

Under [program v1] this compiles and executes as expected. Under
[program v2] the 'START' statement is rejected by the compiler.
The Standard requires that Acct-No be alphanumeric. According to
at least 1 TPR I've read the compiler will relax this
restriction in a future release, probably C00. You should check
this situation as it may already be dealt with by the recent
EBF.
Hoping this helps ... [Replier6's full name]
```

Figure 15.1 (continued)

corresponding to various Tandem products; designated engineers with special expertise with these products read and replied to these requests. Typically, there was a one-to-one correspondence between experts and mailboxes, although some boxes were read by groups of experts. Each expert filed a copy of the question and his or her reply into the expert archive. About half of the exchanges via second-class mail were archived (Constant, Sproull, and Kiesler 1996). It is unknown what fraction of queries to the designated expert mailboxes were filed in the expert archive. Figure 15.2 shows an example of an exchange stored in the expert archive.

Method

We examined employee log-in statistics over forty-five weeks in 1988 to the peer and expert archives. Employees logged into the archives to search for or read archive content but not to contribute new content. For each log-in, the archive server wrote a record indicating when a log-in occurred, the site from which a log-in was initi-

```
Document #:3 - Document length: 36 lines -26 SEP xx
TRANSFER OF ACU UNITS TO THE SAGE


QUESTION

I have received a question wondering if asynchronous ACU units
which now use 2 async patch panel ports can be transferred to
the [hardware system]. These are implemented with [communication
system] on the async board, and use a special 'Y' cable. Will
the [hardware system] support this?
[Questioner's full name]\world.support [Questioner's first name]
--------------------------------------------------------

REPLY
Following comments by \CASG.CASG.[Expert's ID] on 27 SEP 19xx,
16:21:05

THERE IS NOT, AT PRESENT, ANY SUPPORT FOR ACU's ON THE [hardware
system] ( A NEW LIM WITH THE RS-366 INTERFACE ) HAS BEEN
DESIGNED AND BUILT BY ENGINEERING, BUT IT HAS NOT BEEN PUT INTO
PRODUCTION, AND NO SOFTWARE HAS EVER BEEN WRITTEN TO MAKE USE OF
IT, NOR IS ANY SCHEDULED.

AUTO-ANSWER IS SUPPORTED BY SOME TYPES OF LINES ON THE [hardware
system], E.G. <[line type], BUT NOT ALL.

ONE POSSIBILITY FOR YOUR AUTO-DIAL CAPABILITY MIGHT BE TO USE A
"SMART MODEM" WHICH GETS ITS DIAL DIGITS FROM THE DATA
INTERFACE. THIS WOULD REQUIRE SOME PROGRAMMING EFFORT, AND MIGHT
BE LIMITED TO [line type] AND POSSIBLY [line type]. TO MY
KNOWLEDGE NO ONE HAS DONE THIS TO DATE, THEREFORE I CANNOT
GUARANTEE SUCCESS.

THERE IS NO [communication system] EQUIVALENT SUPPORT USING
[line type] WITH ASYNC POINT TO POINT LINES. THEREFORE, A
PROGRAM WRITTEN WITH [communication system] USING 2 ASYNC PORTS
WILL NOT WORK AND COULD NOT EVEN BE CONVERTED TO CP6100.
[Expert's initials]
```

Figure 15.2
Question and reply in the expert archive.

ated, the commands issued during a log-in session, and the identification numbers of archived messages returned during a log-in session. Archive use was captured at the site level because Tandem's archive logs did not definitively map archive log-ins to identifiable individual users. The risk of ecological fallacy from this approach was mitigated by the finding that at the subset of sites where individual use could be verified, there was low variance across employees in message archive use.

We performed content analyses on a sample of the peer and expert archived reply files stored from 1983 to 1988 by randomly selecting 10 percent of the files stored each month during this period. In months when only one to nine files were stored into an archive, one file was selected at random to ensure a contiguous sample across time. As a result of this strategy 78 (12.0 percent) of the expert files were sampled compared to 465 (10.1 percent) of the peer files. The discrepancy between the expert and peer samples reflected the high number of months when only one to nine files were stored into the expert files. We operationalized know-how through the frequency of three types of critical keywords indicative of know-how: personal experience keywords, referral keywords, and practical knowledge keywords. A text scanning program was written in SNOBOL4+ (Emmer 1985) to process the full text of each sampled reply file automatically to extract content. The program matched content in the reply file with lists of keywords selected as markers of the different content types. The keywords for personal experiences were first-person pronouns and contractions, which indicate an informal style. The keywords for referrals were pointing verbs, such as *call* and *contact*. Keywords for practical knowledge were names of products and references to "customer." The program tabulated the occurrence of keywords per reply file, which were then expressed as rates per thousand words to allow comparison between the peer and expert files, which typically differed dramatically in length.

We used corporate databases to ascertain or calculate the values of control variables used in regression analyses. These included distance in miles of a site from engineering headquarters, median tenure of employees at a site, number of employees at a site, and presence of sales and customer support at a site.

Results

Table 15.1 contains descriptive data showing the nature of the two archives. In December 1988, the peer archive contained 4,582 information exchanges, each with a question and its associated answers. The expert archive contained 651 information exchanges. Consistent with observations of the creation of second-class-mail

Table 15.1
Archive attributes and use over forty-five weeks

	Archive type	
	Peer (*n* = 428)	Expert (*n* = 73)
Archive attributes		
Mean replies per question	7.17 (7.02)***	1.05 (.23)
Mean unique repliers per question	6.57 (6.19)***	1.05 (.23)
Mean unique replier sites per question	5.81 (4.84)***	1.04 (.20)
Archive use		
Number of unique users	1,708	638
Number of archive log-ins	8,450	1,537
Number unique sites from which archives were accessed (*n* = 151)	108	96

*** $p < .01$.

reply files, the average reply file in the peer archive had more replies, more unique repliers, and more unique replier sites than the average reply file in the expert archive.

Preference for Peer Information In support of our hypothesis that archives of coworker exchanges would be preferred to archives of official exchanges with experts, the peer archive was accessed much more frequently than the expert archive. Moreover, the comparisons summarized in table 15.2 show that questions and replies in the average reply file in the peer archive had more personal experience content, more specific referral content, and more practical knowledge content than the average reply file did in the expert archive.

Figures 15.1 and 15.2 illustrate how technical knowledge was conveyed in the peer and expert archives. The peer reply file in figure 15.1 shows first-person description of events: repliers 3, 5, and 6 each mentioned their own experience. By contrast, the expert reply file in figure 15.2 mentioned the experience of a formal subunit, "engineering," rather than referring to the replier's own experience. In the peer reply file, repliers used more informal contracted verb forms (e.g., *it's, don't*) rather than more formal full verb forms (e.g., *it is, do not*). By contrast, in the expert reply file, the replier used more formal full verb forms. Figures 15.1 and 15.2 also illustrate how referral content is conveyed. In the peer reply file, repliers provided several pointers to other employees or to information generated by other

Table 15.2
Mean occurrences (per 1,000 words) of keywords used in content analysis of questions and replies in archives

	Questions		Replies	
Content	Peer ($n = 465$)	Expert ($n = 78$)	Peer ($n = 465$)	Expert ($n = 78$)
Personal experience (number of first-person pronouns, e.g., *I, me*)	14.9 (17.0)	14.5 (18.2)	14.9 (10.7)***	6.5 (9.3)
Informal language (number of contractions, e.g., *can't*)	3.5 (7.6)	3.2 (12.3)	5.1 (5.2)***	1.1 (3.7)
Pointers (number of pointing verbs, e.g., *call, contact*)	0.7 (4.2)***	0.2 (1.0)	2.8 (4.6)***	1.0 (2.8)
References to Tandem products	10.9 (14.3)***	2.4 (10.6)	4.7 (6.3)***	1.9 (4.8)
References to customers (number of uses of *customer*)	6.7 (10.6)***	3.4 (6.9)	2.5 (3.4)***	1.2 (3.3)

*** $p < .01$.

employees. By contrast, the expert offered no such pointers. Finally, in the peer file, replier 6 noted the need for close customer consultation, and replier 3 noted the possibility of variance across customer sites in lines 42 to 46. By contrast, the expert provided no information about customer experience.

Effects of Distance We postulated that as the distance between field sites and Tandem engineering headquarters increased, physical proximity to the heaviest concentration of knowledgeable employees decreased, reducing the opportunity for face-to-face exchange of know-how. Therefore, distance from engineering headquarters should predict accesses to the networked archives, especially to the peer archive. Geographic distance was measured as the distance in statute miles between a site and Tandem engineering headquarters in Cupertino, California.

Table 15.3 summarizes the descriptive statistics for the variables used in our analyses. These analyses included only data from sites with a documented connection to the Tandem computer network. Of the 306 Tandem sites in 1988, 151 had

Table 15.3
Descriptive statistics, network sites ($n = 141$)

Variable	Statistics			
	M	SD	Minimum	Maximum
Distance (miles from engineering headquarters)	2,636.9	2,328.7	0.0	9,182.4
Seniority (median tenure in years)	3.9	1.4	0.8	7.7
Size (number of employees)	63.2	89.2	1.0	553.0
Registered computer accounts (percentage of employees)	93%	19%	0%	100%
Log-ins per employee, peer archive, 45 weeks (1988)	1.6	1.8	0.0	9.0
Log-ins per employee, expert archive, 45 weeks (1988)	0.4	0.3	0.0	1.7

documented connections to the computer network. These 151 sites represented 9,060 employees, or 87 percent of the Tandem workforce. Complete data came from 141 of the 151 sites.

The average Tandem network site was more than 2,000 miles away from engineering headquarters, and only 36 of the 141 Tandem network sites were located within 500 miles of it. These data indicate the high degree of geographic dispersion among Tandem network sites.

Data on log-ins per employee suggest that the computer archives were not frequently used at any site, but the variance and range of the data suggest that the computer archives played a larger role at some sites than others. Specifically, 74 percent of the 141 sites had sales affiliations, and these sites accounted for 85 percent of all log-ins to the peer archive and 83 percent of all log-ins to the expert archive during the forty-five weeks of this study. This pattern reflected the close association between sales and field engineering workers when closing deals and supporting customers.

We examined message archive use in a hierarchical regression against (1) control variables correlated with geographic distance and the dependent variables, such as seniority of employees at a site, size of a site, whether a site was part of the sales organization, and the availability of the computer network at a site; (2) geographic distance; (3) type of archive accessed, that is, peer versus expert; and (4) the interaction of distance and archive type.

A significant proportion of sites recorded no archive use during the period of the study. Therefore, archive use was analyzed using the standard zero, lower-bound Tobit model (Tobin 1958). The Tobit model is an alternative to ordinary least squares (OLS) regression designed for situations where the dependent variable is limited (in this case, it could not assume values less than zero) and a large number of observations are clustered at zero. The concentration at zero violates assumptions for OLS analysis. Simply modeling the probability of a limit or nonlimit value, as a probit model would do, throws away useful information (i.e., collapses all non-limit cases into a single class). The Tobit model, then, is a hybrid of the regression and probit approaches. Under Tobit, models are tested that account for both the effect of independent variables on whether a dependent variable is at limit or non-limit and the effect of independent variables on the dependent variable when above the limit value.

The Tobit regressions tested hypotheses about computer archive use through hierarchical comparison of four theoretical models starting with the control variables alone, then adding distance from engineering headquarters, then adding archive type, and culminating with a term for the interaction between distance and archive type. The full model had the following form:

$$LOGINS\ PER\ EMPLOYEE = \beta_0 + \beta_1 SENIORITY + \beta_2 SIZE + \beta_3 SALES$$
$$FUNCTION + \beta_4 REGISTERED\ ACCOUNTS$$
$$+ \beta_5 DISTANCE + \beta_6 ARCHIVE$$
$$+ \beta_7 DISTANCE*ARCHIVE + e,$$

where *LOGINS PER EMPLOYEE* represented the number of log-ins to the computer archives per employee at a site; *SENIORITY* represented the median o rganizational tenure in years of employees at a site; *SIZE* represented the number of employees at a site; *SALES FUNCTION* indicated affiliation with the sales organization as determined from the corporate directory (1 = employees at the site reported to the sales organization; 0 = no employees at the site reported to the sales organization); *REGISTERED ACCOUNTS* represented the percentage of employees with registered computer accounts at a site; *DISTANCE* represented the distance in miles to Tandem engineering headquarters; *ARCHIVE* indicated the archive type (1 = peer; 0 = expert); and *DISTANCE*ARCHIVE* represented the interaction of distance with archive type.

Table 15.4 summarizes the results of the hierarchical comparison of the theoretical models. The moderated model was the best fit to the data (pseudo $R^2 = .29$, $\beta^2(7) = 112.74$, $p < .01$). Two control variables, seniority and sales function, were

Table 15.4
Regression coefficients (Tobit analysis) predicting mean archive log-ins per employee ($n = 141$)

Variables	Control	Distance only	Distance and archive model	Moderated model
Intercept	−.66	−1.74	−2.32**	−2.01
Registered computer accounts[a]	.13	.15	.14	.14
Seniority	−.33***	−.22**	−.22***	−.22***
Size[b]	.02	.04	.03	.03
Sales function	1.44***	1.25***	1.21***	1.18***
Distance[c]		.16***	.16***	.06
Archive type			1.58***	1.08***
Distance × archive type[d]				.18**
Pseudo R^2	.11***	.14***	.28***	.29**
G of improvement		9.2**	63.1***	5.2***

[a] Registered computer accounts expressed in units of 10^1 percent for interpretative clarity.
[b] Size measured in units of $x^{0.5}$ after recommendation of Weisberg (1985).
[c] Distance expressed in units of 10^3 miles for interpretative clarity.
[d] Distance × Archive expressed in units of 10^3 miles for interpretative clarity.
*** $= p < .01.$ ** $= p < .05.$ * $= p < .10.$

significant: $b_{seniority} = -.22$, $t(274) = -3.91$, $p < .01$; $b_{sales\ function} = 1.18$, $t(274) = 4.65$, $p < .01$, indicating that lower seniority and affiliation with the sales organization led to greater archive use. The coefficient for archive type was significant: $b_{archive\ type} = 1.08$, $t(274) = 7.91$, $p < .01$, confirming that with controls, use of the peer archive exceeded use of the expert archive. Finally, the overall effect of distance lost significance when the interaction was included in the model, but the coefficient for the interaction term was significant: $b_{interaction} = .18$, $t(274) = 2.29$, $p < .05$. This finding supports our hypothesis that accesses to the peer archive would be higher with more distance than accesses to the expert archive. The significant change in the value of the log-likelihood score, represented in the last row of table 15.4 as "G of improvement," also supports the conclusion that there was a differential effect of distance on peer use compared to the expert archive, although the change in the magnitude of the pseudo R^2 was not great. Because it is plausible to expect that the effect of distance is not linear, we reran the analyses using log of distance and using a dichotomous variable for distance (0 = at engineering headquarters; 1 = elsewhere). The pattern of results was the same across all treatments of distance.

Analyses of Alternative Hypotheses

Since the peer files contained more information archived each month, they would also be likely to contain more recent information on any particular topic. It is therefore possible that higher use of the peer archive stemmed from a need for recent information and not a need for contact with distant knowledgeable peers. A preliminary goodness-of-fit test was conducted to assess the effect of timeliness on access to stored reply files in the peer and expert archives. There was disproportionate access to new peer archive reply files relative to old ($\beta^2_{(5,.01)} = 68.4$, $p < .01$), but no similar pattern for access to new and old reply files in the expert archive ($\beta^2_{(4,.05)} = 3.6$, NS). Based on this finding, the age of reply files read at a site was regressed in an OLS model on the key independent variables (remoteness, archive type) and the control variables (seniority, sales function, size, and network access). The sample for this analysis was restricted to sites that used the archive during the study period; therefore, $n = 84$. As with the Tobit regressions, the OLS regressions tested four hierarchical models, culminating in the following full model:

$$AGE\ OF\ REPLY\ FILES = \beta_0 + \beta_1 SENIORITY + \beta_2 SIZE + \beta_3 SALES$$
$$FUNCTION + \beta_4 REGISTERED\ ACCOUNTS$$
$$+ \beta_5 DISTANCE + \beta_6 ARCHIVE$$
$$+ \beta_7 DISTANCE{*}ARCHIVE + e,$$

where *AGE OF REPLY FILES* represented the median age in years of reply files accessed at a site.

The full model was the best fit to the data, but the model did not perform well (adjusted $R^2 = .03$, $F(8, 159) = 1.81$, $p < .10$). The inability to detect consistent and strong relationships between the age of files read, site distance, and archive type suggested that timeliness did not explain the effect of distance in archive use.

A second alternative explanation is that higher use of the peer archive reflected normative use patterns. According to social influence theory, individual choices about use of communication technology reflect patterns of use demonstrated by peers and fellow group members (Fulk and Boyd 1991). Analysts impute social influence through examining variation in use patterns across offices or subunits of organizations (Rice and Aydin 1991). Social influence theory would predict that message archive use will increase as the proportion of employees at a site using archives increases. While the field engineers did spend considerable time alone or in small teams at field sites, they also had assigned home offices where they spent significant time together. Therefore, we explored whether the behavior of others within these offices influenced use of the message archives. We regressed individual archive use, operationalized as the median archive log-ins per archive user at a site, on the independent variables (distance, archive type, and a social influence measure—number of archive users per site) and on the control variables (seniority, sales function, size, and network access). Again, because of censoring on the dependent variable, five theoretical Tobit models were hierarchically compared, culminating in the following full model:

$$INDIVIDUAL\ ARCHIVE\ USAGE = \beta_0 + \beta_1 SENIORITY + \beta_2 SIZE + \beta_3 SALES$$
$$FUNCTION + \beta_4 REGISTERED$$
$$ACCOUNTS + \beta_5 ARCHIVE\ USERS$$
$$+ \beta_6 DISTANCE + \beta_7 ARCHIVE$$
$$+ \beta_8 DISTANCE * ARCHIVE + e,$$

where *INDIVIDUAL ARCHIVE USAGE* represented the median archive logins per archive user at a site.

The main effects model (everything except the interaction term) was the best fit to the data (pseudo $R^2 = .40$, $\beta^2(7) = 87.06$ $p < .01$). In this model, the number of archive users at a site was significant ($b_{\text{archive users}} = .05$ $t(274) = 5.05$, $p < .01$) and important ($B = .35$). But distance also was significant ($b_{\text{distance}} = .18$, $t(274) = 3.02$, $p < .01$) and important ($B = .29$). Therefore, although the number of archive users at a site influenced individual archive use, it did not cancel effects due to distance or archive type.

Discussion

The results from this study support our argument that computer message archives can facilitate dissemination of know-how for a geographically dispersed workforce. Our analyses showed a pronounced preference by engineers for consulting the archive containing informal advice from peers as compared with the archive containing advice from designated experts. This preference increased with greater geographic distance from engineering headquarters, suggesting that the peer archive performed better than the expert archive in offering remote workers an alternative to physical proximity for acquiring know-how. The preference for the peer archive did not seem to be due to a preference for more recent information. It did seem to result partly from a social learning process in which a person was more likely to use any archive if more people in his or her immediate environment also used it.

This study does not tell us exactly what it is about informal e-mail exchanges of questions and replies that are useful when they are archived. It may be partly the specific contents of personal experience, referrals, and practical knowledge. It may be partly the diversity and multiplicity of replies to each question. Note, for example, in figure 15.1 that the questioner asked about the feasibility of converting a program to a more recent version. The repliers were employees in the Netherlands, Germany, France, Missouri, and California, suggesting broad experience with the program within Tandem. Further, the repliers agreed on several points. For instance, repliers 1, 2, and 6 all confirmed the existence of on-line help for the conversion process and that this help was valuable. Repliers 3, 5, and 6 all confirmed that the type of conversion referred to in the question was normal and that others within Tandem had performed such conversions. In this instance, consistency among the replies crudely indexed reliability, and the number of replies roughly validated the original question's significance. The existence of multiple replies did not guarantee that the questioner would find the best solution to the conversion problem, but the multiple replies improved the probability that the questioner would be able to discern the best solution of those shared by the repliers.

Other unmeasured differences might have existed between the two archives we studied and also could account for differential access. For example, engineers might have sent questions to experts mainly when their questions were of a general nature, thinking the experts would not want to be bothered with idiosyncratic local problems. That would lead the experts to reply in kind, leaving the expert archive full of general advice. Another possibility is that the experts archived less diligently than peers did, leaving their archive with advice less valuable to the average engineer. From our previous study of the original exchanges (Constant, Sproull, and Kiesler 1996), we know that employees who used the second-class system announced a reply file in only about half of all cases. Presumably, they announced only the reply files they thought their fellow engineers might find of use.

None of the processes described above undermines our conclusions about the preference for archives of exchanges of know-how among peers. However, other processes might change preferences for archives of know-how exchanges. For example, if all employee questions and answers were automatically archived by machine instead of by humans judging their quality and usefulness, an archive might contain so much useless information that nobody would use it.

Implications

This study did not explore the impact of message archive use on Tandem's productivity or profitability. However, the results do have some bearing on the relationship between information system design and organizational performance.

Hutchins (1995) hypothesizes that the efficiency of key organizational cognitive processes, such as information distribution, can affect an organization's effectiveness. The results of our study suggest that the efficient distribution of know-how can be supported by computer-based information systems. In geographically distributed settings where access to know-how is critical, organizations with information systems that resemble Tandem's employee message archive may outperform organizations with more traditional information systems. A key direction for future work will be a test of Hutchins's hypothesis through comparison of performance gains produced by creating greater access to know-how balanced against the cost of creating this greater access.

Historically, know-how has been viewed as local knowledge about work practice that emerges from specific experiences in particular settings. An unspoken theme of this chapter has been the function of message archives in transforming know-how from information held and circulated among local workers into information held and circulated globally. Transforming local knowledge into global knowledge is probably beneficial under certain circumstances but not others. For example, when workers share a common technology, useful insights about that technology that emerge in a single locality can be generalized to a wider audience. Thus, an engineering workaround developed at one site for a standard product is likely to apply to that product wherever it is used. However, local insights that are tied to cultural and environmental idiosyncrasies may not generalize well. For instance, know-how about a sales approach successful with Tandem's North American customers may be completely inappropriate for Asian customers.

Assuming that an organization can benefit from transforming local knowledge into global knowledge, producing this transformation through the creation of message archives may depend as much on organizational policies regarding information sharing as it does on the design of information systems. If access to mailing lists or the distribution of mailing lists is restricted, workers lose opportunities to request or share help. Similarly, lack of organizational incentives for information sharing may reduce contributions to public data resources (Orlikowski 1992, Markus and Connolly 1990). As a result, potential content for message archives may be diminished. Another important direction for future research is an analysis of how organizational information-handling policies interact with information systems to shape what information is retained by organizations.

In the years since Tandem employees began using archives of technical message exchanges, many useful technical archives have appeared in other settings. Many of them are not located on corporate intranets but rather are found on the Internet.

The open source movement supports many of these archives, which programmers and developers use in seeking to understand and extend open source code or features. These archives more resemble Tandem's peer archive than the expert archive in that most questions have multiple replies from volunteers and there are no organizationally designated formal experts, although some people are acknowledged as more expert than others by the community (Moon and Sproull, Chapter 16, this volume).

Within organizations, the knowledge management community has invested substantial resources in building knowledge repositories—archives of expertise that employees can draw on when they have technical questions (Hansen, Nohria, and Tierney 1999; Henderson, Sussman, and Thomas 1998). These typically do not reflect the question-and-answer structure of the Tandem or open source archives. They do, though, resemble Tandem's expert archive in that "answers" are typically provided or validated by a designated expert rather than coming from multiple volunteers. A big challenge for knowledge managers is getting people to use their repositories. The evidence suggests that employees still prefer asking for help from people, especially when the knowledge to be transferred is complex (Hansen 1999). To the best of our knowledge, none of these endeavors also provides a repository analogous to the Tandem peer archives to give employees the direct choice of accessing know-what organized by experts or know-how voluntarily offered by peers.

An interesting hybrid is the Xerox Eureka system, which is a repository of tips describing how machine service problems have been solved in the field. Tips do not come from designated experts, nor do they report official engineering documentation. They are voluntarily submitted by field service technicians who describe how they solved thorny problems in the field (rather than how the official documentation said they should be solved). Although it does not display the question-and-answer structure of the Tandem employee and open-source archives, the Eureka repository does record know-how voluntarily offered by ordinary employees. Corporate evaluations suggested that Eureka was extensively and productively used by field service personnel in an effort to improve field service distributed over time and space. The system was so heavily accessed that the official corporate product documentation group decided to download all of its official documentation into the system so that technicians would have easy access to it too. Ironically, according to a supervisor of the original (de Kleer 2000), the official know-what was so voluminous that it slowed the system and made it difficult for technicians to find the know-how that had been the system's original rationale. Submission of new tips declined, as did use of the system by field service personnel.

We do not advocate eliminating official documentation. However, a growing body of evidence suggests that corporate officials in charge of officially sanctioned know-what should respect and support systems that encourage peers to share know-how over space and time.

Note

This chapter is based on a doctoral dissertation by the first author (Finholt 1993). The research was supported by a National Science Foundation Graduate Research Fellowship, the System Development Foundation, the Xerox Palo Alto Research Center, and Bellcore. We gratefully acknowledge the cooperation and help of Jimmy Treybig and the rest of the Tandem organization in providing access to their corporate network and archives. In addition, we thank Michael Cohen, Baruch Fischhoff, Mark Kamlet, Gary Olson, Michael O'Leary, Stephanie Teasley, Steve Whittaker, Susan Fussell, and Pamela Hinds for comments on earlier drafts.

References

Ackerman, M. S. (1994). Augmenting the organizational memory: A field study of Answer Garden. In *Proceedings of the ACM Conference on Computer-Supported Cooperative Work 1994* (243–252). New York: ACM Press.

Ackerman, M. S., and McDonald, D. W. (1996). Answer Garden 2: Merging organizational memory with collaborative help. In *Proceedings of the ACM Conference on Computer-Supported Cooperative Work 1996* (97–105). New York: ACM Press.

Allen, T. J. (1977). *Managing the flow of technology.* Cambridge, MA: MIT Press.

Bell, D. G., Bobrow, D. G., Rainamn, O., and Shirley, M. H. (1997). Dynamic documents and situated processes: Building on local knowledge field service. In T. Wakayama, S. Kannapan, C. M. Khoong, S. Navathe, and J. Yates (eds.), *Information and process integration in enterprises: Rethinking documents* (261–276). Norwell, MA: Kluwer.

Brown, J. S., and Duguid, P. (1998). Organizing knowledge. *California Management Review*, 40, 90–111.

Constant, D., Sproull, L., and Kiesler, S. (1996). The kindness of strangers: On the usefulness of weak ties for technical advice. *Organization Science*, 7, 119–135.

de Kleer, J. (2000, May 18–19). Informal remarks presented at the Third Intangibles Conference, Knowledge: Management, Measurement and Organization, Stern School of Business, New York University.

Emmer, M. B. (1985). *SNOBOL4+: The SNOBOL4 language for the personal computer.* Englewood Cliffs, NJ: Prentice Hall.

Finholt, T. A. (1993). Outsiders on the inside: Sharing information through a computer archive. *Dissertation Abstracts International Section A: Humanities and Social Sciences*, 54, 3912.

Fulk, J., and Boyd, B. (1991). Emerging theories of communication. *Journal of Management*, *17*, 407–446.

Galegher, J., Sproull, L., and Kiesler, S. (1998). Legitimacy, authority and community in electronic support groups. *Written Communication*, *15*, 493–530.

Hansen, M. T. (1999). The search-transfer problem: The role of weak ties in sharing knowledge across organization subunits. *Administrative Science Quarterly*, *44*, 82–111.

Hansen, M. T., Nohria, N., and Tierney, T. (1999, March–April). What's your strategy for managing knowledge? *Harvard Business Review*, *77*, 106–116.

Henderson, J. C., Sussman, S. W., and Thomas, J. B. (1998.) Creating and exploiting knowledge for fast-cycle organizational response. In D. J. Ketchen, Jr., *Turnaround research: Past accomplishments and future challenges: Advances in applied business strategy* (Vol. 5, 103–128). Greenwich, CT: JAI Press.

Hutchins, E. (1995). *Cognition in the wild*. Cambridge, MA: MIT Press.

Kiesler, S., and Cummings, J. N. (2002). What do we know about proximity and distance in work groups? A legacy of research. In P. Hinds and S. Kiesler (eds.). *Distributed work* (57–80). Cambridge, MA: MIT Press.

Kusterer, K. C. (1978). *Know-how on the job: The important working knowledge of unskilled workers*. Boulder, CO: Westview Press.

Latour, B., and Woolgar, S. (1986). *Laboratory life: The construction of scientific facts*. Princeton, NJ: Princeton University Press.

Markus, M. L., and Connolly, T. (1990). Why CSCW applications fail: Problems in the adoption of interdependent work tools. In *Proceedings of the Conference on Computer Supported Cooperative Work* (371–380). New York: ACM Press.

Moon, J. Y., and Sproull, L. (2002). Essence of distributed work: The case of the Linux Kernel. In P. Hinds and S. Kiesler (eds.), *Distributed work* (381–404). Cambridge, MA: MIT Press.

Orlikowski, W. J. (1992). Learning from notes: Organizational issues in groupware implementation. In *Proceedings of the ACM Conference on Computer Supported Cooperative Work* (362–369). New York: ACM Press.

Orr, J. E. (1989). Sharing knowledge, celebrating identity: War stories and community memory in a service culture. In D. S. Middleton and D. Edwards (eds.), *Collective remembering: Memory in society* (169–189). Beverly Hills, CA: Sage.

Orr, J. E. (1996). *Talking about machines: An ethnography of a modern job*. Ithaca, NY: ILR Press.

Rice, R. E., and Aydin, C. (1991). Attitudes toward new organizational technology: Network proximity as a mechanism for social information processing. *Administrative Science Quarterly*, *36*, 219–244.

Tobin, J. (1958). Estimation of relationships for limited dependent variables. *Econometrica*, *26*, 24–36.

von Hippel, E. (1994). Sticky information and the locus of problem solving: Implications for innovation. *Management Science*, *40*, 429–439.

Weisberg, J. (1985). *Applied linear regression*, Second edition. New York: John Wiley and Sons.

Box 1
Sense of Presence

Research on the sense of presence is growing more relevant to understanding distributed work. Perhaps objective proximity is not necessary for people to perceive that they are proximate or collocated. Through the use of technology, we might be able to create a sense of presence of others in the group, or virtual presence.

The sense of presence has three facets: social presence (the sense of being with others), control (the sense of interacting in a responsive environment), and personal presence (the sense of immediacy, or "being there"; see Heeter 1992).

The importance of feelings of social presence has been demonstrated often. Sommer (1969) was able to increase the amount of interaction among the residents of a nursing home simply by moving the furniture from rows (which led residents to sit staring into space) to groupings around coffee tables (which greatly increased social interaction). The importance of feelings of control is also well known. The importance of personal presence is less well understood.

The earliest work on technology and sense of presence looked at whether telephone, teletype, and other communication technologies evoked social presence (e.g., Short, Williams, and Christie 1976). Use of the telephone increased subjective social presence over asynchronous forms of communication, such as written messages, but social presence degraded rapidly when more than two people joined the conversation. Video-conferencing has not proved very successful (Dourish and Bly 1992; Fish, Kraut, and Chalfonte 1990). Researchers recently have begun to explore whether so-called immersive environments might evoke a sense of personal and social presence (Blascovich et al., in press). Immersive environments are being explored for use in human services and training, for example, giving speeches to a virtual audience (Slater, Pertaub, and Steed 1999). Whether these environments will bring about a sense of presence when working with members of a distant work group is still unknown.

References

Blascovich, J., Loomis, J., Beall, A. C., and Swinth, K. R. (in press). Immersive virtual environment technology as a methodological tool for social psychology. *Psychological Inquiry*.

Dourish, P., and Bly, S. (1992). Portholes: Supporting awareness in a distributed work group (541–547). *ACM CHI'92 Conference on Human Factors in Computing Systems*. Monterey, CA: ACM Press.

Fish, R. S., Kraut, R., and Chalfonte, B. (1990). The VideoWindow system in informal communication (1–11). *CSCW '90 Proceedings of the Conference on Computer Supported Cooperative Work*. New York: ACM Press.

Heeter, C. (1992). Being there: The subjective experience of presence. *Presence: Teleoperators and virtual environments*, 1, 262–271.

Slater, M., Pertaub, D., and Steed, A. (1999). Public speaking in virtual reality: Facing an audience of avatars. *IEEE Computer Graphics and Applications*, 19, 6–9.

Box 2
Distributed Work Groups and External Task Communication

Research on distributed work has emphasized the (mostly) negative consequences of distance for communication within work groups. What about communication outside of groups? Geographically distributed collaborators may be in a unique position to benefit from, and contribute to, external task communication and extramural work activity. For example, consider a distributed product development team with members in the United States, Europe, and Japan. Being situated in separate parts of the world potentially exposes the group to diverse cultural influences, to various regional adaptations, and to multiple sources of information, such as local customers and employees who are not on the team. External task communication is known to improve performance for collocated teams (Ancona 1990; Ancona and Caldwell 1992). Team performance might benefit even more when distributed members communicate about their work with people outside of the team.

A recent study of distributed work groups sheds light on this possibility (Cummings 2001). Measures of work-related communication and geographic distribution were gathered from 957 members (73%) of 182 work groups in a multinational Fortune 500 telecommunications company. These groups worked together for an average of a year and a half, and completed projects ranging from product development to service improvement. Each team had 4 to 12 members spread across the United States/ Canada (63%), Latin/South America (3%), Europe (15%), Middle East/Africa (5%), India/China (5%), and Japan/Korea/Malaysia (9%). Group members were surveyed about whom they discussed task information with internally and externally as well as whether they talked about planning documents, task requirements, work techniques, project results, and the like. Senior managers rated each work group on dimensions such as teamwork, innovation, and quality.

Work groups whose members communicated about their project work internally and externally were rated as superior performers. Moreover, external task communication about the project predicted even higher performance when work groups were distributed geographically. Thus, talking to people outside of the group about the projects benefited distributed groups even more than collocated groups, and resulted in higher performance for those groups than collocated groups. Distributed groups should be able to capitalize on the diverse environments of their members, but this benefit appears to depend significantly on their degree of external knowledge sharing.

References

Ancona, D. (1990). Outward bound: Strategies for team survival in an organization. *Academy of Management Journal, 33,* 334–365.

Ancona, D., and Caldwell, D. (1992). Bridging the boundary: External activity and performance in organizational teams. *Administrative Science Quarterly, 37,* 634–665.

Cummings, J. (2001). Work groups and knowledge sharing in a global organization. Unpublished dissertation. Carnegie Mellon University.

16

Essence of Distributed Work: The Case of the Linux Kernel

Jae Yun Moon and Lee Sproull

This chapter provides a historical account from three different perspectives of how the Linux operating system kernel was developed. Each focuses on different critical factors in its success at the individual, group, and community levels. The technical and management decisions of Linus Torvalds were critical in laying the groundwork for a collaborative software development project that has lasted almost a decade. The contributions of volunteer programmers distributed worldwide enabled the development of an operating system on a par with proprietary operating systems. The Linux electronic community was the organizing structure that coordinated the efforts of the individual programmers. The chapter concludes by summarizing the factors important in the successful distributed development of the Linux kernel and the implications for organizationally managed distributed work arrangements.

Complex tasks plus a global economy have impelled the creation of many distributed engineering and development groups supported by information and communication technologies. Distributed groups range in duration from weeks to years, they range in size from fewer than ten people to more than a thousand, and they may have members located in two locations or many locations. Distributed engineering and development depends on careful planning, coordination, and supervision. *Careful* does not necessarily imply micromanagement. Contributors who are geographically distant from one another inevitably operate under some degree of autonomy. The management challenge is to ensure that members of geographically distributed engineering and development teams stay focused on shared goals, schedules, and quality. This challenge grows as the number of employees and sites increases. There have been some notable successes in large-scale distributed engineering and development. For example, the Boeing 777 marshaled 4,500 engineers working on three continents (Committee on Advanced Engineering Environments 1999). Nevertheless, successful large-scale distributed engineering and development projects are rare.

That in part explains the business and media fascination with Linux. Linux is a PC-based operating system (OS) that has been produced through a software development effort consisting of more than 3,000 developers and countless other contributors distributed over ninety countries on five continents. It is difficult to provide a precise estimate of the number of programmers who have contributed to it. Published estimates range from several hundred to more than 40,000 (Shankland 1998, Raymond 1999). In its first three and a half years of development (November 1991–July 1995), more than 15,000 people submitted code or comments to the three main Linux related newsgroups and mailing lists. In the next three and a half years, thousands continued to contribute code, and hundreds of thousands of people joined electronic discussions about Linux philosophy, applications, competitors, business models, and so forth. In this chapter, we focus narrowly on people writing code for the operating system kernel.

As of December 1998, more than 8 million users were running Linux on a wide variety of platforms. Linux was estimated to have 17 percent of server operating systems sales in 1998 and was projected to have a compound annual growth rate of 25 percent, two and a half times greater than the rest of the market (Shankland 1998, Berinato 1999). It was widely regarded as being of very high quality and reliability, with a failure rate two to five times lower than that of commercial versions of Unix (Valloppillil 1998). In both 1997 and 1998, Linux won the Info World Product of the Year award for best operating system; in 1997 it won the InfoWorld Best Technical Support award. Such a successful large-scale distributed project would make any organization proud and its shareholders happy.

But the real fascination with Linux stems from the fact that it is *not* an organizational project. No architecture group developed the design; no management team approved the plan, budget, and schedule; no human resource group hired the programmers; no facilities group assigned the office space. Instead, volunteers from all over the world contributed code, documentation, and technical support over the Internet just because they wanted to. This chapter analyzes factors contributing to the Linux kernel story and explores how those factors could be brought into play in formal organizations that are managing distributed work.

A 1971 book about the Cuban missile crisis, *Essence of Decision*, suggested the title and rhetorical structure for this chapter. That book's author, Graham Allison, observed that no single perspective could provide an entirely satisfactory explanation of a complex social phenomenon. Thus, in the book, he told the story of the missile crisis three times, each time from a different explanatory perspective. In this

Table 16.1
Time line of key events

Enabling conditions
1960s: MIT AI Lab, ITS
1969: ARPANET, UNIX (Bell Labs)
1976: Unix-to-Unix copy (UUCP)
1979: Usenet
1984: Gnu's Not Unix
1989: GNU General Public License V.1

Linux kernel development
July and August 1991: Torvalds asked Minix newsgroup for help.
October 1991: Torvalds announces Linux v.0.02. First Linux mailing list.
March 1992: First comp.* hierarchy Linux newsgroup
March 1994: Linux v.1.0. Parallel release structure. Credits File.
February 1996: Maintainers File
June 1996: Linux v.2.0

---

chapter, after a brief description of Linux and its enabling conditions, we tell the Linux kernel story three times. (See table 16.1 for the time line.) First we tell the story from a "great man" perspective, emphasizing the technical and management abilities of Linus Torvalds. We then tell the story a second time from a hacker culture perspective, emphasizing what motivates individual hackers to work on this project. We then tell the story a third time from an electronic community perspective, emphasizing communication forums and role differentiation. We conclude with suggestions for how the factors emphasized in these three perspectives could pertain to distributed work within organizations.

What Is Linux?

An operating system is a computer's central program that oversees resource allocation, program execution, and the control of input, output, file management, and peripheral devices. The kernel is the central module of the operating system—the part of the operating system that loads first, remains in the main memory of the system, and controls memory management, process and task management, and disk management. Common operating systems in use today are Microsoft Windows and Unix-based systems such as Sun Solaris and IBM AIX.

Linux version 1.0, released in March 1994, offered most features of a typical Unix operating system, including multitasking, virtual memory, and TCP/IP networking. It had about 175,000 lines of code. Linux version 2.0, released in June 1996, offered 64-bit processing; symmetric multiprocessing, which allows the simultaneous deployment of several chips in a system; and advanced networking capabilities. It had about 780,000 lines of code. Version 2.1.110, released in July 1998, had about 1.5 million lines of code: 17 percent in architecture-specific code, 54 percent in platform-independent drivers, and 29 percent in core kernel and file systems.

Linux is now much more than an operating system. By July 2000, there were more than 400 Linux user groups in seventy-one countries (Linux User Groups Worldwide, lugww.counter.li.org/). More Linux users meant more interest in applications to run on the operating system. The August 1999 Linux Software Map database lists about 2,500 people who have contributed over 3,500 applications, which range from word processors and mathematical applications to games (Dempsey, Weiss, Jones, and Greenberg 1999). Approximately 300 people have also contributed over 20 megabytes of Linux documentation ranging from information sheets to full-scale manuals.

Anyone can download all Linux files from the Internet for free. Thus, anyone can install a Linux OS, applications, and documentation on his or her PC without going through (or paying) any commercial organization. For people who do not have the time or skill for a do-it-yourself installation, several commercial firms, such as RedHat, Suse, and Caldera, as well as nonprofit organizations such as Debian, sell and support low-cost CD-ROM distribution versions of Linux.

Enabling Conditions: Open Source and Internet

Two enabling factors underlie the Linux development as well as that of similar volunteer distributed software development projects.[1] The first is the social and legal conventions of open source, a means for sharing software code. The second is the information and communications infrastructure of the Internet.

Open sharing of software code was a common practice in the MIT Artificial Intelligence Laboratory in the early 1960s and in similar laboratories at universities such as Stanford and Carnegie Mellon (Levy 1984). Because there were very few computers at that time, people would start a program and leave it available for others using the machine after them to admire and improve upon. By the late 1960s, the scarcity of computers and the growing number of programmers and users led MIT to develop the Incompatible Timesharing System (ITS) for the Digital PDP-10, the large computer in use at the AI Lab. The system had no passwords and gave users the ability to browse both the source code of the system itself, as well as the personal programs and documents created by other users.[2] In essence, the ITS facilitated open sharing of software code.

Also in the late 1960s, a small group of people within AT&T's Bell Laboratories led by Ken Thompson and Dennis Ritchie developed the Unix operating system (Lerner and Tirole 2000, Salus 1994). After Thompson presented the ideas represented in the system at the ACM Symposium on Operating Systems Principles in 1973, Unix began to spread throughout the research and academic community (Salus 1994). AT&T licensed the Unix operating system to academic institutions for a nominal fee and distributed the system in source, but maintained a policy of no official support. Due to the lack of official support, users of the Unix operating system began to share their bug fixes and improvements with one another informally. In 1975, many users met at the first USENIX meeting, designed to bring together various people to share their experiences. In the late 1970s, the Unix user-developers developed a new feature, known as the UUCP (Unix-to-Unix-Copy), that enabled them to exchange files and data over phone lines (Gaffin and Heitkotter 1994). The feature was used to distribute information to the Unix community and led to the beginning of Usenet.[3] In addition to the institutionalization of this open sharing culture, Unix embodied various innovative principles that made the system portable and simple in design.

Advances in computing architecture by the early 1980s saw the demise of the PDP-10 series machines for which MIT's ITS had been developed (Stallman 1998). New machines in the AI Lab were now equipped with proprietary operating systems, which, unlike the ITS, came in binary code wrapped with nondisclosure agreements that forbade sharing with other people. Richard Stallman, who had used ITS at the AI Lab, started the GNU (GNU's Not Unix) project in 1984 to develop a free operating system like ITS to support open sharing and collaboration. However, free access to source code for everyone meant that commercial software developers could exploit the free software to develop proprietary programs. Stallman instituted the Copyleft software license to guarantee sustained easy sharing of code by decreeing that all users of the program have the right to use it, copy it, modify it, and distribute their modifications. Additionally, Copyleft explicitly forbids privatization of derivations from software distributed under Copyleft; derived works must also be distributed under the Copyleft license. The canonical Copyleft license is the GNU General Public License (GPL), which also forbids packaging of proprietary software with GPL-licensed software (Free Software Foundation [FSF] 1991). Copyleft codified the open sharing practices of the early closely knit group of programmers; software distributed under a Copyleft license is known as open source software.

Whereas Copyleft codified the social and legal norms of open sharing,[4] the Internet provided a ubiquitous technology infrastructure that made it easy for programmers to communicate and share their code. While its predecessor, the Advanced Research Projects Agency Network (ARPANET), was a network of research laboratories in academia and industry funded by the U.S. Department of Defense (King, Grinter, and Pickering 1997), the Internet broadened the scope of connectivity through widespread emergence of commercial Internet service providers. It was no longer only the few privileged members of places like the AI Lab at MIT or Bell Labs who could share code and collaborate with others on improving their systems. The standard, robust communication system of the Internet made possible the exchange of both messages and source code among programmers worldwide. People could learn about a project and participate in open discussions about it through Usenet bulletin board discussions and electronic mailing lists. They could also download source code from the Internet and upload their modifications for others to critique and improve. In the early days, the ITS facilitated sharing of code among programmers at the AI Lab; the ARPANET enabled collaboration and open sharing of code among programmers in select geographically dispersed research institutions; and finally the Internet made it possible for people anywhere to share their code and ideas.

Linus Torvalds

In October 1991, Linus Torvalds, a computer science graduate student at the University of Helsinki, announced on the Internet that he had written a "free version of a minix-lookalike for AT-386 computers" and would make it available to anyone who was interested. (See figure 16.1 for Torvalds's announcement message.) Minix was a simplified version of Unix written and maintained largely as a teaching tool by a European computer science professor, Andrew Tanenbaum. It was widely used in computer science courses, even though its license cost $79.95 and restricted its redistribution. As a result of Minix use by computer science students, the professor was bombarded with requests and suggestions for improvement. He was reluctant to implement many of them, however, and some students were frustrated with his unresponsiveness.[5] Torvalds, a frustrated Minix user, noted in his announcement message that all of the code in his operating system was freely available to be copied by others. He also volunteered to add functions written by others if they were also freely distributable. In the next thirty months, Torvalds released ninety additional versions of his OS, culminating on March 14, 1994, with the release of version 1.0.

Torvalds certainly did not set out to create a worldwide distributed OS development project. But he exhibited both technical and management capabilities and decisions without which Linux would not have grown. He makes it easy to build a "great man theory" of the success of Linux. Known as a "damn fine programmer" (Raymond 1999) and an "arch hacker" (Moody 1997), Torvalds's programming skills are widely admired. Even today, up to half the code in key parts of the kernel has been written by Linus (Yamagata 1997). And in the early days, if he did not write the code himself, he edited other peoples' code so heavily "as to be totally unrecognizable" by its original authors (Torvalds 1992, March 8).

Beyond programming skill, Torvalds's chief technical contribution lay in designing a portable, modular architecture for the kernel. Torvalds wrote the initial Linux for his own PC, which had an Intel 386 architecture. By 1993, Linux had been completely rewritten once to run on a Motorola 68K architecture, and it was about to be rewritten yet again to run on a DEC alpha architecture. The prospect of having to maintain a completely separate code base for every new machine architecture was unacceptable to Torvalds. Thus, he redesigned the Linux kernel architecture to have one common code base that could simultaneously support a separate specific tree for any number of different machine architectures (Torvalds 1999b). The architecture greatly improved the Linux kernel portability through establishing systematic modularity. A modular system minimized the need for communication among different components of the kernel and made it possible to write code in parallel on different portions of the kernel (Torvalds 1999a, 1999b). Modularity decreased the total need for coordination and meant that necessary remaining coordination could be deferred.

In creating a worldwide distributed OS development project, Torvalds's management decisions and skills were just as important as his technical ones. Perhaps his most important management decision was establishing in 1994 a parallel release structure for Linux (1994, March 15). Even-numbered releases were reserved for

Date: Sat, 5 Oct 1991 05:41:06 GMT
Reply-To: INFO-MINIX@UDEL.EDU
Sender: INFO-MINIX-ERRORS@PLAINS.NODAK.EDU
Comments: Warning -- original Sender: tag was info-minix-request@UDEL.EDU
From: Linus Benedict Torvalds <torvalds@KLAAVA.HELSINKI.FI>
Subject: Free minix-like kernel sources for 386-AT

Do you pine for the nice days of minix-1.1, when men were men
and wrote their own device drivers? Are you without a nice
project and just dying to cut your teeth on a OS you can try to
modify for your needs? Are you finding it frustrating when
everything works on minix? No more all-nighters to get a nifty
program working? Then this post might be just
for you :-)

As I mentioned a month(?) ago, I'm working on a free version of
a minix-lookalike for AT-386 computers. It has finally reached
the stage where it's even usable (though may not be depending on
what you want),and I am willing to put out the sources for wider
distribution. It is just version 0.02 (+1 (very small) patch
already), but I've successfully run bash/gcc/gnu-make/gnu-
sed/compress etc under it.

Sources for this pet project of mine can be found at
nic.funet.fi (128.214.6.100) in the directory /pub/OS/Linux. The
directory also contains some README-file and a couple of
binaries to work under linux (bash, update and gcc, what more
can you ask for :-). Full kernel source is provided, as no minix
code has been used. Library sources are only partially free, so
that cannot be distributed currently. The system is able to
compile "as-is" and has been known to work. Heh. Sources to the
binaries (bash and gcc) can be found at the same place in
/pub/gnu.

ALERT! WARNING! NOTE! These sources still need minix-386 to be
compiled (and gcc-1.40, possibly 1.37.1, haven't tested), and
you need minix to set it up if you want to run it, so it is not
yet a standalone system for those of you without minix. I'm
working on it. You also need to be something of a hacker to set
it up (?), so for those hoping for an
alternative to minix-386, please ignore me. It is currently
meant for hackers interested in operating systems and 386's with
access to minix.

Figure 16.1
Announcement of Linux v.0.02, October 1991.

```
The system needs an AT-compatible harddisk (IDE is fine) and
EGA/VGA. If you are still interested, please ftp the
README/RELNOTES, and/or mail me for additional info.

I can (well, almost) hear you asking yourselves "why?". Hurd
will be out in a year (or two, or next month, who knows), and
I've already got minix. This is a program for hackers by a
hacker. I've enjouyed doing it, and somebody might enjoy looking
at it and even modifying it for their own needs. It is still
small enough to understand, use and
modify, and I'm looking forward to any comments you might have.

I'm also interested in hearing from anybody who has written any
of the utilities/library functions for minix. If your efforts
are freely distributable (under copyright or even public
domain), I'd like to hear from you, so I can add them to the
system. I'm using Earl Chews estdio right now (thanks for a nice
and working system Earl), and similar works will be very
wellcome. Your (C)'s will of course be left intact. Drop me a
line if you are willing to let me use your code.

  Linus

PS. to PHIL NELSON! I'm unable to get through to you, and keep
getting "forward error - strawberry unknown domain" or
something.
```

Figure 16.1 (continued)

relatively stable systems and focused only on fixing bugs; odd-numbered releases were the development versions on which people could experiment with new features. Once an odd-numbered release series incorporated sufficient new features and became sufficiently stable through bug fixes and patches, it would be renamed and released as the next higher even-numbered release series, and the process would begin again.[6] The parallel release structure allowed Torvalds simultaneously to please two audiences often in conflict with one another. Users who rely on a Linux OS to support their production computing want a stable, reliable system in which new releases introduce only well-tested new functionality, no new bugs, and no backward compatibility problems. Developers, by contrast, want to try out new ideas and get feedback on them as rapidly as possible. The parallel structure offered both relative stability and certainty to users and rapid development and testing to programmers. Table 16.2, which displays the release history of Linux, illustrates the disparate release rate between the two release trees.

Table 16.2
Linux release history

Release series	Date of initial release	Number of release	Time to final release in series (months)	Duration of series (months)
0.01	9/17/91	2	2	2
0.1	12/3/91	85	27	27
1.0	3/13/94	9	1	12
1.1	4/6/94	96	11	11
1.2	3/7/95	13	6	14
1.3	6/12/95	115	12	12
2.0	6/9/96	34	24	32
2.1	9/30/96	141	29	29
2.2	1/26/99	14	9	—
2.3	5/11/99	60	12	—

Note: Versions 2.2.x and 2.3.x were still current as of May 2000.

Despite his position of importance, there is little that is imperious or dictatorial in Torvalds's communication style. Initially he was (appropriately) quite deprecatory about his project—"just a hobby, won't be big and professional like gnu" (Torvalds 1991, August 25). He never orders anyone to do anything, and even his suggestions are mild mannered. Typical suggestions are of the form: "hint, hint, Linus wants to get out of doing it himself;^)" (Torvalds 1995, June 29) or "my personal priority is not that kind of behaviour, so it would be up to somebody else to implement this . . . (hint hint)" (Torvalds 1996, April 16). Yet there is no confusion about who has decision authority in this project. Torvalds manages and announces all releases—all 569 of them up to May 2000. He acts as a filter on all patches and new features—rejecting, accepting, or revising as he chooses. He can single-handedly decide to redo something completely if he wishes. In the early days he personally reviewed every contribution and communicated by personal e-mail with every contributor. As Torvalds says, "[There is] one person who everybody agrees is in charge (me)" (Yamagata 1997).

Hackers

In October 1991, Linus Torvalds announced on the Internet that he had written a "program for hackers by a hacker." (See figure 16.1 for the October 1991 announcement message.) Hackers are people who enjoy "exploring the details of programmable systems and how to stretch their capabilities" and appreciate programming over theorizing (*Jargon Dictionary* 2000). Torvalds encouraged people to look at his program, modify it for their own needs, and send him their code to add to the system. People who had been frustrated with the restricted features of Minix accepted the invitation. By the end of the month, ten people had the system working on their machines (Torvalds 1991, October 31). Some offered to work on different features of the program and began sending contributions.

Within two months of the October 1991 announcement, about thirty people had contributed close to 200 reports of errors and problems in running Linux, contributions of utilities to run under Linux, and drivers and features to add to Linux. When Torvalds released version 0.11 in December 1991, he credited contributions by three people in addition to himself (Torvalds 1991, December 3). In version 0.13, released in February 1992, the majority of patches were written by people other than Torvalds. By July 1995, more than 15,000 people from ninety countries on five continents had contributed comments, bug reports, patches, and features.[7] Why did these people accept the invitation to test and modify Linux?

One motivation for working on the Linux project is that hackers by nature enjoy solving interesting technical problems and building new programs (Raymond 1999). Torvalds labeled himself a hacker and said that he "enjoyed" developing the operating system in his October 1991 message and suggested that "somebody else might enjoy looking at it." (See figure 16.1.) To hackers, who are generally interested in "sexy" and "technically sweet" problems (Raymond 1999, 72), an operating system represents an alluring challenge. Programming an operating system means a hacker has tamed the computer hardware and stretched its functionality. In his October announcement, Torvalds appealed to the hacker's need for such challenges when he asked if they were "without a nice project and just dying to cut [their] teeth on a OS."

People also wrote code to solve particular personal problems. Torvalds himself developed Linux so that he could run a Unix-like operating system on his own PC. In his October announcement, Torvalds noted that Linux was available for anybody "to modify for [their] needs." When people accepted his invitation to try the first Linux release, they wrote their own device drivers to support their choice of hardware and peripherals. For instance, a German programmer using Linux developed the German keyboard driver that was included in the December 1991 release (Thiel

1991). To this day, people work on areas that they know and care about (Raymond 1999). No one tells people what to work on.[8]

Intrinsic pleasure and personal problem solving may be enough to motivate people to write Linux code for their own use, but they do not satisfactorily explain why people contributed that code to a larger effort. People might contribute because they expect others will do so in return (Kollock 1999, Raymond 1999). When Torvalds announced his free operating system, he was also "interested in hearing from anybody who has written any of the utilities/library functions for minix" to add to his system. People posted bug reports hoping others would fix them; people contributed patches expecting that others would post patches to other problems with the system. The Gnu GPL ensured both that their contributions would be made accessible to everyone else and that everyone else's contributions would be accessible to them. This ensured the establishment of a stable generalized exchange system (Kollock 1999) in which people could expect returns to their contributions.

This generalized exchange system, however, could have broken down if everyone waited for someone else to contribute (Kollock 1998). In the Linux case, programmers also contributed because they wanted to be known for writing good code (Raymond 1999). Ackerman and Palen (1996) offer a similar explanation when they suggest that MIT undergraduates contribute to a voluntary on-line help system to develop their reputation as "clueful." An economic explanation suggested that accrued reputation has a positive impact on the programmers' careers (Lerner and Tirole 2000). However, this account fails to explain the motivation of early hackers of the Linux operating system. The potential career opportunities to be gained from building up a reputation as a skilled programmer in the Linux operating system project were not present from the start.

Good code was acknowledged in a variety of ways. The separate management of production and development kernels meant that people contributing good code received rapid positive feedback as their contributions were incorporated in the development kernel in a short period of time. Some programmers left personal signatures within the source code so that others looking at the source code could recognize their work. The GPL ensured that freely contributed code would not be exploited by others. Torvalds also frequently acknowledged the contributions of others. In his original October 1991 announcement message, he credited another programmer for code he had used in the first release ("thanks for a nice and working system Earl ⟨Chews⟩"). In his January 1992 release, he acknowledged the significant contributions of three other programmers (Torvalds 1992, January 9). As the number of contributors grew, it became impossible for Torvalds to acknowledge all those who had contributed code with each release. With the official release of version 1.0 in 1994, Torvalds acknowledged and thanked more than 80 people by name (Torvalds 1994, March 14). Version 1.0 was also the first version to include a credits file that listed the various contributors and their role in developing and maintaining the Linux kernel. The programmers themselves were responsible for requesting to be added to the credits file if they considered themselves to be "worth mentioning" (Torvalds 1993, December 21). In the early days, Torvalds credited programmers personally. The credits file marked a transition to a process in which programmers could credit themselves according to a shared understanding of what constituted creditable contributions.

Whereas reputation as a skilled programmer was the most important motivation for contributing code, it was not the only way of gaining reputation. Credit could also come from significant contributions of documentation and other information useful to developers and users of Linux. In fact, in an early message, Torvalds acknowledged a contributor for compiling the Linux information sheet (Torvalds 1992, January 9) and stated that one did not "need to be a *kernel* developer to be on the credits list" (Torvalds 1993, December 21).

Community

Several months before his October 1991 announcement, Torvalds posted messages to a Usenet group to which he belonged asking the group for help on a project. He asked where to find a particular set of operating system standards, what things group members liked and disliked about Minix, and what features they would want in a free Minix look-alike. (See figure 16.2 for one of these messages.) Torvalds did not create his original project in social isolation. He was a member of an ongoing active community of programmers, electronically organized in a Usenet group, comp.os.minix, with thousands of members.[9] It was to this group that Torvalds turned for advice, suggestions, and code and to which he announced his initial project. It was from this group that early Linux contributors were drawn. And it was out of this group that the first Linux group was created.

Writing code is a solitary activity. Some people may have written Linux code for the joy of it or to solve a personal problem with no thought of contributing to a larger endeavor. But the hackers already described did not upload code to the Internet randomly. Their code was motivated, organized, and aggregated by and through

```
Date:  Sun, 25 Aug 1991 20:57:08 GMT
Reply-To:   INFO-MINIX@UDEL.EDU
Sender: INFO-MINIX-ERRORS@PLAINS.NODAK.EDU
Comments:   Warning -- original Sender: tag was info-minix-
request@UDEL.EDU
From:  Linus Benedict Torvalds <torvalds@KLAAVA.HELSINKI.FI>
Subject:   What would you like to see most in minix?
Hello everybody out there using minix -

I'm doing a (free) operating system (just a hobby, won't be big
and professional like gnu) for 386(486) AT clones. This has been
brewing since april, and is starting to get ready. I'd like any
feedback on things people like/dislike in minix, as my OS
resembles it somewhat (same physical layout of the file-system
(due to practical reasons) among other things).

I've currently ported bash(1.08) and gcc(1.40), and things seem
to work. This implies that I'll get something practical within a
few months, and I'd like to know what features most people would
want. Any suggestions are welcome, but I won't promise I'll
implement them :-)
   Linus (torvalds@kruuna.helsinki.fi)


PS. Yes - it's free of any minix code, and it has a multi-
threaded fs. It is NOT protable (uses 386 task switching etc),
and it probably never will support anything other than AT-
harddisks, as that's all I have :-(.
```

Figure 16.2
Announcement of Torvalds's project, August 1991.

features of the Linux electronic community. Two attributes of this community have been particularly important: its group communication structure and its role structure.[10]

Linux mailing lists and Usenet groups provided a map of the growing and changing Linux territory so that people could know what new code had been written, where to send their code or comments, and where to find information that interested them. The first Linux mailing list, Linux-activists, was created in October 1991, and had about 400 subscribers by January 1992. Today there are more than 700 Linux mailing lists. Comp.os.linux was formed in March 1992, the first of fourteen comp.os.linux.* Usenet groups devoted to Linux formed in the next two years. Beginning in 1994, an additional hierarchy of Linux groups, linux.* was formed, which by 1998 had 369 groups.[11]

The linux-kernel mailing list organizes the behavior of kernel programmers.[12] Feature freezes, code freezes, and new releases are announced on this list. Bug reports are submitted to it. Programmers who want their code to be included in the kernel submit it to this list. Other programmers can then download it, test it within their own environment, suggest changes back to the author, or endorse it.[13] From June 1995 to April 2000, about 13,000 contributors posted almost 175,000 messages to the linux-kernel list. This is how individual behavior is organized into a product with social utility. Coordination of the individual programmers is achieved through the modular structure of the Linux kernel.

The previous two sections might convey the impression that the Linux development project consisted of Linus Torvalds and an undifferentiated band of happy hackers. In fact, the community has developed a differentiated role structure that both reflects and supports its activities. The two most important roles within this community are credited developer and maintainer. Beginning with the v1.0 release in 1994, new releases of the kernel were accompanied by a credits file that publicly acknowledges people who have contributed substantial code to the kernel. The initial credits file listed eighty contributors. By the release of Linux 2.0 in June 1996, there were 190 acknowledged contributors. By July 2000, the list had grown to approximately 350 contributors from over thirty countries worldwide. People who have contributed extensively to the Linux kernel but do not add themselves to the credits file are also recognized by the community.

The maintainer role was first formally acknowledged in February 1996, when the maintainers' file was announced (Cox 1996). The first maintainers' file contained 3 names; today it contains 147 names. Designated maintainers are responsible for particular modules of the kernel. They review linux-kernel mailing list submissions (bug reports, bug fixes, new features) relevant to their modules, build them into larger patches, and submit the larger patches back to the list and to Torvalds directly.[14] Over the years, Torvalds and the community have come to know and trust the technical competence of these maintainers, most of whom still "work on Linux for free and in their spare time" (Linux-kernel mailing list FAQ, www.tux.org/lkml). Indeed, one maintainer, Alan Cox, has complete responsibility for overseeing the stable tree. Torvalds still announces major stable tree releases, but this is a pro forma gesture.[15]

Table 16.3 displays the message contribution profile for the linux-kernel mailing list. Note that approximately 2 percent of the contributors contributed more than 50 percent of the messages, an indicator of the differentiated role structure and

Table 16.3
Message contribution profile

Messages	Number of contributors	Percentage of total contributors	Unique messages contributed	Cumulative message count	Percentage of total (messages)
10 or fewer	10,925	84.07%	27,861	27,861	15.99%
11–100	1,816	13.97	53,186	81,047	30.52
100+	134	1.03	18,999	100,946	10.90
200+	46	0.35	11,334	111,380	6.50
300+	16	0.12	5,563	116,943	3.19
400+	15	0.12	6,608	123,551	3.79
500+	10	0.08	5,483	129,034	3.15
600+	5	0.04	3,266	132,300	1.87
700+	5	0.04	3,750	136,050	2.15
800+	3	0.02	2,490	138,540	1.43
900+	2	0.02	1,837	140,377	1.05
1,000+	18	0.14	33,880	174,257	19.44

Note: The source is the linux-kernel mailing list, June 1995 to April 2000.

contribution profile of the community. Of these 254 contributors, 30 percent are credited developers, and 19 percent are designated maintainers.

Because the linux-kernel mailing list is the central organizing forum for kernel developers and supports a very heavy volume of message traffic, people need a clear understanding of how to contribute to the list. Maintainers of the linux-kernel mailing list FAQ create that understanding. The FAQ is the document that explains the rules of the road for kernel development to newcomers ("How do I make a patch?" "How do I get my patch into the kernel?"). It also reiterates the norms and values of the community ("A line of code is worth a thousand words. If you think of a new feature, implement it first, then post to the list for comments.") In addition to learning through the FAQ, newcomers can learn directly from the more experienced and skilled developers on the list through direct observation and questions posted to the list. Newcomers can develop into skilled Linux kernel programmers through such informal training (Brown and Duguid 1991, Cox 1998). Twelve people maintain the FAQ, all of them credited developers or maintainers. The mailing list, with its thousands of contributors, differentiated role structure, dedicated role incumbents, and rules of the road, is more than just a list. As the FAQ explains, "Remember the list is a community."

Lessons for Organizations

Others have written about lessons from Linux for commercial software development projects (Raymond 1999). Here we consider how factors important in the Linux case might apply more generally to distributed work in and across organizations (Markus, Manville, and Agres 2000). It might seem odd to derive lessons for formal organizations from a self-organizing volunteer activity. After all, the employment contract should ensure that people will fulfill their role obligations and act in the best interest of the organization. Yet, particularly in distributed work, employees must go beyond the letter of their job description to exhibit qualities found in the Linux developers: initiative, persistence, and activism. We suggest that the enabling conditions for Linux (the Internet and open source) usefully support these conditions. We then consider how factors emphasized in each of the three versions of the Linux story (great man and task structure, incentives for contributors, and communities of practice) can facilitate organizational distributed work.

Clearly, easy access to the Internet or its equivalent is a necessary precondition for the kind of distributed work represented by Linux. Developers used the Internet both for easy access to work products (to upload and download files) and easy communication with other developers (to ask and answer questions, have discussions, and share community lore). Both capabilities are surely important, and they are simple. It is noteworthy that despite the technical prowess of Linux developers, they relied on the simplest and oldest of Internet tools: file transfer, e-mail distribution lists, and Usenet discussion groups. Even with today's wider variety of more sophisticated Web-based tools, Linux developers continue to rely on these tools for coordinating their efforts. These tools are simple, they are available worldwide, and they are reliable.

The organizational equivalent of Copyleft is a second precondition for the kind of distributed work represented by Linux. Both the formal and informal reward and incentive systems must reward sharing and discourage hoarding. (See Constant, Kiesler, and Sproull 1996 and Orlikowski 1992 for discussions of incentives for information sharing in organizations.) Moreover, work products should be transparently accessible so that anyone can use and build on good features and anyone can find and fix problems. We do not underestimate the difficulty of creating the equivalent of Copyleft for organizational work products. Failing to do so, however, can hobble distributed work.

Does every successful large-scale distributed project require one great person to be in charge? Clearly this was important in the Linux case. Yet other successful open source development projects have had different leadership models (Fielding 1999, Wall 1999). The capabilities that a singular leader brings to a project—clear locus of decision making, singular vision, consistent voice—are important. But in principle, they can be achieved through a variety of leadership models.

Task decomposition has been an important organizational principle for at least the past forty years (March and Simon 1958). Modularity is an extreme form of task decomposition, one that may be particularly suited to distributed work. Modular task decomposition reduces coordination costs to an irreducible minimum. Moreover, it allows for redundant development, which can increase the probability of timely, high-quality solutions. That is, multiple groups can work on the same module independent of one another. The first (or best) solution is selected for adoption.

Parallel release structures that support both stability and rapid development are not commonly deployed in organizational development projects. More typical are linear structures or phased structures that hand off a project from developers to clients or maintainers. Organizations are typically viewed as having to manage a trade-off between exploration and exploitation (March 1991). Ongoing parallel release structures could generate both more innovation and more continuous improvement.

In the Linux case, people were motivated to work for pleasure and improve their personal work situation. They were motivated to contribute their work to others for the same reasons: for reputational credit and to contribute to the community. Careful attention to motivation and incentive structures are extremely important in distributed work projects. "Careful" need not mean "heavy-handed," however. Encouraging people to sign their work can be a low-cost, high-payoff motivator. Publicly naming contributors can be another. This approach is analogous to one employed in the Xerox system for technical service representatives in which they are encouraged to submit their fixes to machine problems that are not adequately handled by their formal documentation (Bell et al. 1997).

Finally, Linux developers were members of and supported by vigorous electronic communities of practice. Creating and sustaining such communities can importantly contribute to distributed work. Electronic communities require both (simple) computer tools and social tools. We discussed computer tools under enabling conditions. The social tools include differentiated roles and norms. It is not enough to enable electronic communication among people working on a distributed project. In a project of any size, people must understand and take on differentiated electronic roles. These roles, with their corresponding obligations and responsibilities, should be explicitly designated and understood by all. Indeed, one category of community norms is the expectations associated with role behaviors. More generally, norms are the rules of the road for the particular electronic community. Because distributed projects cannot rely on the tacit reinforcements that occur in face-to-face communications, persistent explicit reminders of norms are necessary in the electronic context. (See Sproull and Patterson 2000 for more on this topic.)

The scope of computer-supported distributed work will continue to increase in organizations. The lessons of open source software development are surely not applicable to all distributed work. Indeed one fruitful avenue for further work will be to delineate features of projects for which these lessons are more or less applicable. Still, Linux and its kin will continue to offer fascinating cases of distributed work in their own right and fruitful sources of lessons for organizational distributed work.

Notes

A version of this chapter was presented at the Distributed Work Workshop, Carmel, California, August 2000. A longer version was published in *First Monday*, November 2000 firstmonday.org/issues/issue5_11/moon/index.html). We thank participants in the Electronic Communities seminar at Stern (spring 2000), participants at the NSF Distributed Work Workshop (August 2000), Sara Kiesler, Gloria Mark, Wanda Orlikowski, and Bob Sproull for their valuable comments. We also thank members of the Linux community, in particular John A. Martin and Matti Aarnio, for their help in understanding the community.

1. Other software projects developed by volunteer programmers distributed geographically include the Apache Web server (Fielding 1999), Perl programming language (Wall 1999), GNU Emacs editor (Stallman 1999), the fetchmail e-mail client program (Raymond 1999), and the Tcl/tk scripting language (Ousterhout 1999). A large part of Internet infrastructure also is the product of such collaborations. Sendmail, which enables people to send and receive e-mail, and BIND (Berkeley Internet Name Domain), the technology that makes it possible to navigate Web pages using natural language addresses instead of numbers, are among these (O'Reilly 1999). Several commercial programs adopted an open source collaborative development style. These include but are not limited to Netscape Mozilla, Sun Microsystems Star Office, and Microsoft Virtual Worlds (DuBois 2000, Netscape Press Relations 1998, Virtual Worlds Group 2000).

2. The source code of a software program is a set of instructions that can be understood and modified by programmers. Compiling the source code produces binary code that is executable on the platform for which it was compiled. However, such code is not readily comprehended by people and thus cannot be usefully modified by them.

3. Usenet is a system of interconnected computer networks in which people form newsgroups to discuss topics of common interest. Newsgroups act as a selective broadcasting system: people post to newsgroups, hoping to find interested readers.

4. The enforceability of the GPL has not yet been determined in the courts. However, the GPL as a statement of informal norms and good practices carries power even with companies, which tend to honor the GPL (Powell 2000). The FSF also polices the proper use of software code distributed under GPL license. Detailed exposition of the debate surrounding the legal enforceability of the Copyleft licenses is beyond the scope of this chapter. For a view that GPL is not legally enforceable, see Merges 1997; for an opposing view see Moglen 1999.

5. In response to "most requested features in Minix," replies from the professor included "never." "No. too much hair. Mucks up kernel and MM too much." "Ha, ha" (Tanenbaum 1991).

6. Torvalds did not invent the concept of parallel release series, but he was the first to open his development series to the entire world.

7. We identified the contributors by extracting headers of archived mail and newsgroup messages. Although multiple e-mail addresses were resolved manually, some duplications might have been missed.

8. In the early days, contributors were mostly hackers interested in working on an operating system for fun. Although commercial firms today also develop drivers and products for the Linux system, only 6 percent of maintained kernel modules and drivers (8 of 129) are maintained by people whose job requires it as indicated for Linux version 2.3, released in May 1999. An interview study of developers found that only 10 percent of those interviewed reported that their job in some way involved Linux (Kuwabara 2000, and personal communications).

9. In 1992, there were 43,000 readers of the newsgroup (Tanenbaum 1992). By 1995 that number had fallen to 25,000 (Minix information sheet, www.cs.vu.nl/~ast/minix.html).

10. Other important attributes and practices, which we omit because of space constraints, are norms, boundary maintenance, generational reproduction, and socialization.

11. The first Linux Usenet group was alt.os.linux, which was formed in January 1992 to move the growing Linux discussion off of the Minix group. The number of newsgroups and lists is based on information retrieved on April 25, 2000, from various sources including the Liszt Newsgroups site (www.liszt.com/news) and the Linux Portal Site (www.linuxlinks.com/Newsgroups/Miscellaneous). It is assumed that other Linux-related firms also have forums for discussion, but that these do not take the form of a newsgroup. A search on the Liszt Newsgroup page yielded 143 groups that contained the word *linux* as part of the newsgroup name. A similar search of Liszt listed mailing lists and IRC channels resulted in 128 hits for lists and 192 hits for IRC channels.

12. Prior to the creation of the linux-kernel mailing list, the first Linux kernel mailing list, Linux activists, served this organizing function.

13. Programmers are cautioned not to send code via e-mail directly to Torvalds because he will be unlikely to see it (Linux-kernel mailing list FAQ, www.tux.org/lkml/#s1–14).

14. As Torvalds explained, "What happens is that if I get a patch against something where I'm not the primary developer (against a device driver or a filesystem I have nothing to do

with, for example), I am less likely to react to that patch if it doesn't come from the person who is responsible for that particular piece of code. If I get a networking patch, for example, it's a _lot_ more likely to get a reaction if it is from Alan Cox, and then it usually goes in with no questions asked. Similarly . . . , if it is a patch against the SCSI subsystem, I much prefer to have it from somebody I know works on SCSI (Eric, Drew, Leonard)" (Torvalds 1996, February 19).

15. Red Hat, a Linux distribution firm, funds Cox in addition to other key Linux developers (Shankland 1999). Thus, Cox's role in the Linux community is in large measure subsidized by Red Hat.

References

Ackerman, M. S., and Palen, L. (1996). The Zephyr help instance: Promoting ongoing activity in a CSCW system. In *Proceedings of the ACM Conference on Human Factors in Computing Systems CHI '96* (268–275). New York: ACM Press.

Allison, G. T. (1971). *Essence of decision: Explaining the Cuban missile crisis*. Boston: Little, Brown.

Bell, D. G., Bobrow, D. G., Raiman, O., and Shirley, M. H. (1997). Dynamic documents and situated processes: Building on local knowledge in field service. In T. Wakayama, S. Kannapan, C. M. Khoong, S. Navathe, and J. Yates (eds.), *Information and process integration in enterprises: Rethinking documents* (261–276). Norwell, MA: Kluwer Academic Publishers.

Berinato, S. (1999, April 1). Linux shows 25% annual growth rate. *ZdNet: eWeek*. Available at: www.zdnet.com/zdnn/stories/news/0,4586,1014254,00.html.

Brown, J. S., and Duguid, P. (1991). Organizational learning and communities-of-practice: Toward a unified view of working, learning, and innovation. *Organization Science*, 2, 40–57.

Committee on Advanced Engineering Environments, National Research Council. (1999). *Advanced engineering environments: Achieving the vision, phase 1*. Washington DC: National Academy Press.

Constant, D., Kiesler, S., and Sproull, L. (1996). The kindness of strangers: On the usefulness of weak ties for technical advice. *Organization Science*, 7, 119–135.

Cox, A. (1996, February 21). Maintainers and source submission procedures. Linux kernel source code (v.1.3.68). Available at: ftp://tsx-11.mit.edu/pub/linux.

Cox, A. (1998, October 13). Cathedrals, bazaars and the town council. *Slashdot*. Available at: slashdot.org/features/98/10/13/1423253.shtml.

Dempsey, B. J., Weiss, D., Jones, P., and Greenberg, J. (1999, October 6). *A quantitative profile of a community of open source Linux developers*. Available at: metalab.unc.edu/osrt/develpro.html.

DuBois, G. (2000, July 20). Open-source StarOffice earns early praise. *Zdnet: eWeek*. Available at: www.zdnet.com/eweek/stories/general/0,11011,2605874,00.html.

Fielding, R. T. (1999). Shared leadership in the Apache project. *Communications of the ACM*, 42, 42–43.

Free Software Foundation (1991). *GNU General Public License.* Available at: www.gnu.org/copyleft/gpl.html.

Gaffin, A., and Heitkotter, J. (1994, September). Usenet History. *EFF's extended guide to the Internet: A round trip through global networks, life in cyberspace, and everything . . .* Available at: www.eff.org/papers/eegtti/eeg_toc.html#SEC88.

King, J. L., Grinter, R. E., and Pickering, J. M. (1997). The rise and fall of Netville: The saga of a cyberspace construction boomtown in the great divide. In S. Kiesler (ed.), *Culture of the Internet* (3–34). Hillside, NJ: Erlbaum.

Kollock, P. (1998). Social dilemmas: The anatomy of cooperation. *Annual Review of Sociology, 24,* 183–214.

Kollock, P. (1999). The economies of online cooperation: Gifts and public goods in cyberspace. In M. A. Smith and P. Kollock (eds.), *Communities in cyberspace* (220–239). London: Routledge.

Kuwabara, K. (2000). Linux: A bazaar at the end of chaos. *First Monday, 5* (3). Available at: www.firstmonday.dk/issues/issue5_3/kuwabara/index.html.

Lerner, J., and Tirole, J. (2000, February 25). *The simple economics of open source.* Available at: www.people.hbs.edu/jlerner/simple.pdf.

Levy, S. (1984). *Hackers: Heroes of the computer revolution.* Garden City, NY: Anchor Press/Doubleday.

March, J. G. (1991). Exploration and exploitation in organizational learning. *Organization Science, 2,* 71–87.

March, J. G., and Simon, H. A. (1958). *Organizations.* New York: Wiley.

Markus, M. L., Manville, B., and Agres, C. E. (2000). What makes a virtual organization work? *Sloan Management Review, 42,* 13–26.

Merges, R. P. (1997). The end of friction? Property rights and contract in the "Newtonian" world of on-line commerce. *Berkeley Technology Law Journal, 12*(1). Available at: www.law.berkeley.edu/journals/btlj/articles/12_1/Merges/html/reader.html.

Moglen, E. (1999). Anarchism triumphant: Free software and the death of copyright. *First-Monday, 4* (8). Available at: www.firstmonday.dk/issues/issue4_8/moglen/.

Moody, G. (1997, August). The greatest OS that (n)ever was. *Wired.* Available at: www.wired.com/wired/5.08/linux_pr.html.

Netscape Press Relations (1998, January 22). *Netscape announces plans to make next-generation communicator source code available free on the net.* Available at: www.netscape.com/newsref/pr/newsrelease558.html.

O'Reilly, T. (1999). Lessons from open-source software development. *Communications of the ACM, 42*(4), 32–37.

Orlikowski, W. (1992). Learning from Notes: Organizational issues in groupware implementation. In *Proceedings of the 1992 Computer Supported Cooperative Work,* ACM Digital Library. Available at: www.acm.org/pubs/citations/proceedings/cscw/143457/p362-orlikowski/.

Ousterhout, J. (1999). Free software needs profit. *Communications of the ACM, 42*(4), 44–45.

Powell, D. E. (2000, June 26). Comment: Judgment day for the GPL? *LinuxPlanet*. Available at: www.linuxplanet.com/linuxplanet/reports/2000/1/.

Raymond, E. S. (1999). *The cathedral and the bazaar: Musings on Linux and open source by an accidental revolutionary.* Sebastopol, CA: O'Reilly & Associates.

Salus, P. H. (1994). *A quarter century of UNIX.* Reading, MA: Addison-Wesley.

Shankland, S. (1998, December 16). Linux shipments up 212 percent. *CNET News.com.* Available at: news.cnet.com/category/0–1003–200–336510.html.

Shankland, S. (1999, August 11). Red Hat shares triple in IPO. *CNET News.com.* Available at: www.canada.cnet.com/news/0–1003–200–345929.html.

Sproull, L., and Patterson, J. (2000). *Computer support for local community.* New York: New York University, Center for Information Intensive Organizations.

Stallman, R. (1998). *The GNU project.* Available at: www.gnu.org/gnu/thegnuproject.html.

Stallman, R. (1999). The GNU operating system and the free software movement. In C. DiBona, S. Ockman, and M. Stone (eds.), *Open sources: Voices from the open source revolution* (53–70). Sebastopol, CA: O'Reilly & Associates.

Tanenbaum, A. (1991, February 4). Re: Most requested features in MINIX. *comp.os.minix.* Available at: listserv.nodak.edu/archives/minix-l.html.

Tanenbaum, A. (1992, February 3). Unhappy campers. *comp.os.minix.* Available at: listserv.nodak.edu/archives/minix-l.html.

The Jargon Dictionary. (2000). Available at: info.astrian.net/jargon.

Thiel, W. (1991, November 21). Keyboard.S with German keyboard. *Linux-activists.* Available at: ftp://tsx-11.mit.edu/pub/linus.

Torvalds, L. (1991, August 25). What would you like to see most in minix. *comp.os.minix.* Available at: listserv.nodak.edu/archives/minix-l.html.

Torvalds, L. (1991, October 31). Re: [comp.os.minix] Free minix-like kernel sources for 386-AT. *comp.os.minix.* Available at: listserv.nodak.edu/archives/minix-l.html.

Torvalds, L. (1991, December 3). Last call for diffs for 0.11. *Linux-activists.* Available at: ftp://tsx-11.mit.edu/pub.linux.

Torvalds, L. (1992, January 9). Linux information sheet (non monthly posting). *comp.os.minix.* Available at: listserv.nodak.edu/archives/minix-l.html.

Torvalds, L. (1992, March 8). Linux 0.95. *Linux-activists.* Available at: ftp://tsx-11.mit.edu/pub.linux.

Torvalds, L. (1992, May 5). Re: Writing an OS—questions!!. *Linux-activists.* Available at: www.li.org/linuxhistory.php.

Torvalds, L. (1993, December 21). Re: Credits file. *Linux-activists.* Available at: ftp://tsx-11.mit.edu/pub.linux.

Torvalds, L. (1994, March 14). Linux 1.0—A better UNIX than Windows NT. comp.os.linux.announce. Available at: www.cs.helsinki.fi/u/mjrauhal/linux/cola.html.

Torvalds, L. (1994, March 15). New order. *Linux-activists.* Available at: ftp://tsx-11.mit.edu/pub.linux.

Torvalds, L. (1994, May). Linux code freeze. *Linux journal*. Available at: www2.linuxjournal.com/lj-issues/issue1/2733.html.

Torvalds, L. (1995, June 29). Re: Shared interrupts—PCI. *Linux-kernel*. Available at: www.uwsg.iu.edu/hypermail/linux/kernel/9506/0194.html.

Torvalds, L. (1996, February 19). Re: torvalds@cs.helsinki.fi==/dev/null??? *Linux-kernel*. Available at: www.uwsg.iu.edu/hypermail/linux/kernel/9602/0529.html.

Torvalds, L. (1996, April 16). Re: Unices are created equal, but . . . *Linux-kernel*. Available at: www.uwsg.iu.edu/hypermail/linux/kernel/9604.1/0771.html.

Torvalds, L. (1999a). The Linux edge. *Communications of the ACM, 42*(4), 38–39.

Torvalds, L. (1999b). The Linux edge. In C. DiBona, S. Ockman, and M. Stone (eds.), *Open sources: Voices from the open source revolution* (101–111). Sebastopol, CA: O'Reilly & Associates.

Vallopillil, V. (1998, August 11). *Open source software: A (new?) development methodology*. Available at: www.opensource.org/halloween/halloween1.html.

Virtual Worlds Group. (2000, August 24). *Virtual Worlds Web Site FAQ*. Available at: www.vworlds.org/faq.asp.

Wall, L. (1999). The origin of the camel lot in the breakdown of the bilingual Unix. *Communications of the ACM*, 40–41.

Yamagata, H. (1997, September 30). *The pragmatist of free software: Linus Torvalds interview*. Available at: www.tlug.gr.jp/linus.html.

V

Distributed Scientific Collaborations

Distributed work has many features in common across types of work and organization. However, we see evidence in the previous chapters that if we are to understand distributed work theoretically and practically, we will need to pursue our observations in particular domains. The domain of science is of great interest, not only because it is necessary for this work to become ever more distributed, but also because the organization of the science itself is international.

In this part, we illustrate research on distributed scientific work through two chapters that report studies of scientists. Christian Schunn, Kevin Crowley, and Takeshi Okada in chapter 17 describe a reanalysis of a study they conducted of collaborations in cognitive science. They compared collaborations of coauthors who did at least part of their work while geographically separated with coauthors who worked at the same institution. They observed that the distributed collaborations tended to be more successful than the collocated collaborations. John Walsh and Nancy Maloney, in chapter 18, discovered a similar trend in their data. They surveyed scientists in experimental biology, mathematics, physics, and sociology about their collaborations and found that geographic distance and the use of communication technology were associated with scientific productivity. These chapters raise an important question: whether the observed success of distributed science derived from self-selection (or from unsuccessful collaborators quitting early) or from the nature of the scientific questions, the multidisciplinarity of distributed research, the advantages of using technology, or some other factors. The authors of these chapters pursue these questions in their analyses and use them to discuss the balance of costs and opportunities in distributed science.

17

What Makes Collaborations Across a Distance Succeed? The Case of the Cognitive Science Community

Christian Schunn, Kevin Crowley, and Takeshi Okada

Scientific collaborations increasingly are being conducted at a distance, despite the many factors that make collaboration at a distance difficult. We focus on the discipline of cognitive science because it is young and highly interdisciplinary, thus potentially increasing both the rewards and difficulties of collaboration at a distance. Using questionnaire data from practicing cognitive scientists, we examined the impact of distance on who is likely to collaborate, the success of the collaboration, and the process of collaboration. There were few differences between those collaborating at a distance and locally. Surprisingly, collaborations at a distance were more successful than collaborations conducted locally. Distant collaborations depended crucially on frequent face-to-face contact. We conclude with a discussion of how these results change our understanding of collaboration in general and, in particular, of collaboration at a distance.

Modern scientific collaborations frequently are carried out by researchers who are geographically distributed, in part because necessary resources for the research are often distributed geographically and in part because scientific collaborations continue after collaborators change academic or research institutions. In this chapter, we examine the nature and consequences of scientific collaborations that are collocated or distant. We ask whether they function differently from local collaborations. Understanding how such collaborations function might provide better insight into the nature of collaboration more generally.

There are some recently developing pragmatic reasons to study the differences between local and distant collaborations. With the development of the Internet and various computerized collaboration tools, it is becoming possible to achieve some of the features of face-to-face collaboration from a great distance. These products beg the question of what features of local collaborations are particularly important to duplicate. Certainly, not all features of these collaboration tools are worth the expense, and some features may actually hurt the collaboration process (Vera, Kvan, West, and Lai 1998).

The goal of this chapter is to examine the role of distance in the collaborative process within the domain of cognitive science. We ask if scientists working at a distance differ from those working locally, whether working across a distance changes the collaborative process, and what scientists do to make collaborations across a distance succeed and continue. To answer these questions, we present survey data collected from cognitive scientists at a recent conference.

Three Distinctions among Scientific Collaborations

The way that collaborations function is likely to depend on the needs and relative skills of the collaborators. Three factors are likely to play an important role. First, there is the distinction between peer and apprenticeship collaborations. Peer collaborations are between two researchers at the same professional level (e.g., faculty collaborations, postdoctoral collaborations, graduate student collaborations). By contrast, apprenticeship collaborations are between researchers at different professional levels (faculty–postdoctoral collaborations, faculty–graduate student collaborations, postdoctoral–graduate student collaborations). Apprenticeship collaborations embody an inherent power difference and knowledge difference that can profoundly affect the process of collaboration. However, in many successful scientific apprenticeship collaborations, the collaborators treat one another in some sense as intellectual equals, who each have the authority to challenge each other's thinking. This phenomenon occurs even in otherwise hierarchical societies such as Japan (Schunn, Crowley, and Okada 1998).

Second, there is a distinction between intra- and interdisciplinary collaborations (Dunbar 1995; Schunn et al. 1998; Schunn, Crowley, and Okada in press). For example, Schunn and associates (1998, in press) found important differences in the process, frustrations, and benefits of intradisciplinary and interdisciplinary collaborations. Moreover, different factors predicted which collaborations were successful. Dunbar (1995) found that lab groups in molecular biology were more successful when composed of members with relatively different training backgrounds.

A third important distinction is local versus distant collaborations, where distant collaborations are those that require travel to the primary places of work of each of the collaborators. Distance has been shown to have a large impact on who is likely to collaborate (Allen 1977, Kraut, Egido, and Galegher 1990). One argument is that proximity begets frequent contact, which in turn begets work conversations, which in turn begets collaborative research projects (Kraut et al. 1990). Also many pragmatic factors (time and money) make collaborating across a distance difficult.

Questions about Collaboration at a Distance

Collaboration at a distance among scientists represents a serious challenge to current notions about collaboration. Conventional wisdom is that collaborations on complex projects like those typically found in science require face-to-face interaction. Many social, motivational, and cognitive factors are involved in collaboration on complex tasks that are negatively affected by distance (Kiesler and Cummings, chapter 3, this volume). One wonders why scientists would ever choose to collaborate at a distance and how they ever manage it successfully.

One hypothesis that we explore is that scientists who collaborate at a distance are somehow different from those who collaborate only locally. For example, perhaps collocation is not important for some disciplines or for collaborations that have been ongoing for a long time.

A second hypothesis is that there are no special distinguishing features of scientists who collaborate at a distance, but pragmatic features of the situation could motivate forming a collaboration at a distance. For example, students might seek to finish projects after they have graduated and moved away. Alternatively, collaborations started between colleagues at on institution may continue when one colleague moves away, perhaps because of continued shared funding.

A third hypothesis is that collaborations at a distance can have real advantages that lead to their formation. At the simple physical resource level, scientists at different locations may have access to different equipment or data, an advantage that may cause them to form distant collaborations. More theoretically interesting is the possibility that there is something about the nature of collaborations that is helped by not being collocated. Most research on effects of distance on collaboration suggests that this is not the case (although see Sproull and Kiesler 1991). Yet as we shall demonstrate in this chapter, scientific collaborations at a distance can be distinctly successful.

Whatever the reason for collaboration at a distance, there is also the question of how distance changes the research process. Do scientists collaborate differently when working at a distance? The reduction of physical presence in distance collaborations is likely to affect how researchers exchange information, divide labor, monitor others' progress, deal with frustrations, and so forth.

A final question that we examine is whether scientists need to behave differently in collaborations at a distance. That is, the factors that determine whether the collaboration is successful may or may not differ as a function of distance. If one believes that distance does have many negative influences on the process of the collaboration (as the research literature suggests), then one should expect that collaboration at a distance requires special methods for keeping the collaboration going (e.g., different organizational features, different supporting technologies). Distance also might place differential weighting on the role of social and cognitive factors in collaboration success. For example, local collaborations may depend more heavily on good social interactions and similar research styles. Distant collaborations may depend more heavily on good organization and scheduling. Alternatively, distance may exacerbate conflicting styles.

The Case of Cognitive Science

The field of cognitive science is an interesting domain in which to examine collaborations, and in particular, distant collaborations. First, cognitive science is focused on understanding intelligent behavior from a variety of perspectives and is thus inherently interdisciplinary; it draws primarily on research from cognitive psychology and artificial intelligence, as well as on linguistics, philosophy, neuroscience, education, and anthropology (Collins 1977, Hardcastle 1996, Simon 1980, Simon and Kaplan 1989, Schunn et al. 1998, in press). This interdisciplinarity forces researchers to find collaborators from other disciplines. For example, computer scientists interested in modeling human performance often work with cognitive or developmental psychologists to collect data with which to test their models.

Second, cognitive science is a relatively young field, only twenty-five to forty-five years old, depending on whether one uses the first larger-scale community beginnings in the 1970s or the first academic research projects in the discipline as the official start date in the 1950s (Schunn et al. 1998, Simon and Kaplan 1989). As a young field, comparatively few researchers are trained in cognitive science, and relatively few institutions have large numbers of cognitive scientists in the home disciplines whose perspective or skills might be necessary for a particular research project. Thus, researchers often seek collaborators at distant universities and institutes, even if they might otherwise prefer to work with researchers in their own institution. However, if researchers initiate distant collaborations in cognitive science, they do so primarily because of their need for intellectual resources rather than for physical resources. Unlike particle physics or astronomy in which data are collected and analyzed across distributed locations because there are only a handful of facilities in the world where the appropriate studies can be conducted, the tools of the trade in cognitive science are widely available. Twenty years ago, a lab with an eye tracker or a fast computer may have drawn cognitive scientists from all over the world, but this equipment is no longer exotic and expensive. Currently, some neuropsychological research within cognitive science requires specialized facilities such as functional magnetic resonance imaging, but compared with linear accelerators or a space-based telescope, these machines are cheap and comparatively accessible in medical centers through the world.

Historical Data on Collaboration in Cognitive Science

An interplay of interdisciplinarity and distant collaborations was part of cognitive science from its beginning as a field. One of the earliest and most famous collaborations in cognitive science was that between Allen Newell and Herbert Simon. Through much of the early work, Newell was working at RAND in California and Simon was at the Carnegie Institute of Technology in Pittsburgh (now Carnegie Mellon University). McCorduck (1979) writes: "Their collaboration also included J. C. Shaw, a senior programmer at RAND, though Simon and Cliff Shaw seldom saw or spoke to each other. Newell carried out the middleman's role, mostly by long-distance telephone between Pittsburgh and Santa Monica. 'I thought he was terribly daring, running up those incredible $200-per-month phone bills,' Simon laughs now. 'But, then, Al really taught me how to think big about money'" (139). Thus, we see that significant effort and some technology was required to keep the distant collaboration going. McCorduck notes another interesting fact about the role of distance in this collaboration:

Cliff is a very taciturn guy [Newell says]. One of my dominant recollections is going in and talking with him about some of these problems, and going through a whole session and he wouldn't say a single word, and getting up and leaving. This was when I hardly knew him. It's probably the case that the whole scientific enterprise with the three of us would never have worked out if we were all sitting in one place. Cliff found this way of working, with me located miles away, to be just about the right level of controlled interaction for him to flower. And so I operated both by letter and by telephone—by two and three hour-long conversations a week through this whole period—so in fact the three of us never got together, almost. (144)

Thus, we see distance playing dual roles in this famous collaboration in cognitive science. On the one hand, distance collaborations were a barrier to communication that had to be overcome through effort and expense. On the other hand, distance proved to have some positive consequences for the process of the collaboration.

A Study of Collaboration in Cognitive Science

We used a correlational, retrospective methodology asking scientists to reflect on a particular collaboration that had just produced an intermediate product, a conference publication. We e-mailed authors from a particular yearly meeting of the Cognitive Science Society and asked them a series of questions about the structure and process of their paper. The original goals of the study were to understand the process of collaboration in science and to examine the difference between intra- and interdisciplinary collaborations (Schunn et al. 1998, in press). For this chapter, we have compared local and distant collaborations.

Method

The Annual Meeting of the Cognitive Science Society was first convened in 1979. In 1983, it became peer reviewed. The paper selection criteria have become stricter each year since then. In the past several years, approximately 35 percent of submitted papers were accepted. Over the years, the conference grew steadily in size, stabilizing in the early 1990s at approximately 140 papers and posters (including member abstract posters) and 500 to 600 attendees. The modal number of authors is two, followed by one, and then three authors. Less than 5 percent of papers have more than three authors. Throughout its history, the conference has been a central location for cognitive scientists to meet, network, and exchange findings from their ongoing research.

All authors of multiauthored papers and posters to be presented at the Seventeenth Annual Conference (1995) in Pittsburgh, Pennsylvania, were contacted two months prior to the conference by e-mail. Permission to conduct the interview studies was obtained from the conference organizers in advance of contacting the participants. Ninety-six multiauthor papers and posters had been accepted, 94 for which we had valid e-mail addresses, consisting of 222 total authors. Seventy-five (34 percent) questionnaires were completed and returned, representing at least one author from 56 (60 percent) of the papers.

Three years later, we sent e-mail to the authors of the 1995 conference papers asking them whether the work reported at that conference had been published elsewhere in the form of a book chapter or journal article. It is possible that the authors and reviewers were not able to evaluate the success of interdisciplinary work immediately. We received responses from over 82 percent of our original set of respondents ($n = 34$ local, $n = 12$ distant).

Procedure

The multiple-choice questionnaire we developed was based on exploratory interviews with cognitive scientists and previous questionnaire studies (Okada et al. 1995, Schunn et al. 1995). Three sections of the questionnaire are relevant to the current analyses. The first section assessed the primary backgrounds and professional status (e.g., faculty, graduate student) of the participant and the participant's collaborators. The second section asked participants to estimate how successful they thought the project had been and how likely they were to continue working with their collaborators. The third section asked participants to estimate how often communication had occurred within the collaboration, the means of communication (e.g., face-to-face meetings, e-mail), the mesh or clash of the collaborators' background knowledge and intellectual styles, and the benefits and frustrations of the collaboration. All questions were in multiple-choice format, although additional comments and alternative, additional write-in options were possible for each question.

The unit of analysis for most of the analyses presented is a paper (i.e., a project) rather than a participant. Therefore, we used data from only one author per paper, the highest-ranking person (e.g., first author rather than second author), on the assumption that this person would have the most detailed knowledge of the project. When responses were received from multiple authors of the same paper, their responses were generally quite consistent. Moreover, changing the unit of analysis from paper to respondent did not change any of the results obtained in our analyses.

From the affiliations listed on the papers and posters, we categorized each collaboration as local or distant. Local collaborations ($n = 40$) were all those for which the authors were from the same department or different departments within the same institution. Distant collaborations were all those for which authors were at different institutions within the same city ($n = 2$), in different cities within the same country ($n = 7$), or in different countries ($n = 6$), producing a total of fifteen distant collaborations. When there were more than two authors, we used the locations of the first two authors. However, in data from third and fourth authors, they always had the same local or distant designation as that of the first two authors. This coding scheme does not necessarily reflect where the authors were located while the bulk of the work was completed. However, given that this is a conference submission and that much important work happens at the writing phase of a project, this scheme is likely to be an accurate reflection of where collaborators were for at least part of the project.

For continuous to continuous variable analyses, we used Fisher's *r*-to-*z* and multiple linear regressions. For nominal to continuous variable analyses, we used ANOVAs and MANOVAs. For continuous to nominal and nominal to nominal variable analyses, we used logistic regression.

Results

We first examined whether there were any differences in the types of collaborators and collaborations that occurred across distance. If there were differences in collaborator or collaboration type, then we would need to establish in our analyses whether differences in the process between local and distant collaborations were due to these other structural differences.

Table 17.1 shows the profiles of local and distant collaborations: the mean number of authors, the percentage of papers with any collaborators of different training backgrounds (using categories at the grain size of computer science, psychology, philosophy, linguistics, and other fields), the percentage of papers with all collaborators of equal professional status (at the grain size of undergraduate student, graduate student, postdoctoral, faculty member), the percentage of papers with

Table 17.1
Differences between local and distant collaborations

	Local ($n = 40$)	Distant ($n = 15$)
Mean (SD) number of authors	2.4 (0.7)	2.3 (0.8)
% multidisciplinary	60%	67%
% peer collaborations	18%	33%
% faculty collaborators	42%	60%
% psychology as training background	58%	33%
% recent collaborations (less than or equal to 1 year)	23%	47%

* $p < .05$.

faculty members as collaborators (based on the status level of the author responding to the questionnaire), the percentage of papers with psychology as the primary training background of one of the collaborators, and the percentage of papers in which the collaboration was less than or equal to one year old. A multiple logistic regression predicting collaboration distance (using the six factors listed in table 17.1 as potential predictors) found only one significant predictor and one marginally significant predictor. Distant collaborations involved marginally significantly fewer psychology collaborations ($\chi^2(55) = 2.3$, $p < .15$) and significantly more recent collaborations ($\chi^2(55) = 4.3$, $p < .05$). Both types of collaborations had very similar numbers of authors in the collaborations and a similar frequency of multidisciplinary collaborations. Finally, distant collaborations had slightly (but not significantly) higher proportions of peer collaborations and faculty collaborations.

The relatively high proportion of recently begun collaborations among the distant collaborations suggests that the majority of these collaborations were not primarily local collaborations in which one of the authors had moved recently. Probably the majority of these collaborations had truly been done at a distance. The relatively high proportion of short-term collaborations among the distant collaborations is also consistent with the notion that distant collaborations are difficult and may not be continued as long as local collaborations are continued.

Because there were two significant differences between local and distant collaborations (whether the first author was trained as a psychologist and collaboration length), subsequent analyses included those two factors as control variables.

Success of Collaboration

Before turning to more detailed analyses of structure and process, we will look at some bottom-line measures. Were distant collaborations less successful, reflecting their inherent greater difficulty levels? Figure 17.1 presents a variety of success measures for local and distant collaborations. According to the collaborators, the local and distant collaborations were just as likely to be rated "very successful." However, to our surprise, distant collaborations were more likely to result in a publication three years later. One possible explanation is that perhaps only very good ideas warrant starting a distant collaboration; if sufficient progress is made to produce a conference paper, the odds are better that it will be published as a full paper later. Future research will have to be conducted to examine this possibility further.

Note that rated success and probability of publication is not the same thing. Many factors enter into whether research is considered successful, and publication is only

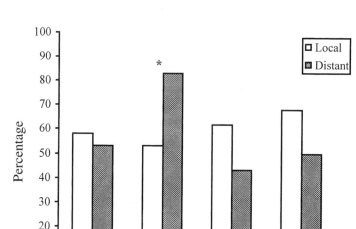

Figure 17.1
Success measures for local and distant collaborations.
Note: Success levels, $n = 54$; probability of publishing the work three years later, $n = 45$; percentage estimated to be very likely to continue working together, $n = 53$; working together three years later, $n = 45$. $^*p < .05$ for the comparison between local and distant.

one of them. Similarly, many factors enter into whether a project is published (e.g., interest of the research community, writing ability of the researchers, importance of publications for one's career). In the case of interdisciplinary work, work that the researchers consider very novel and interesting may turn out to be too novel for the community and hence not publishable. Thus, it is not entirely surprising that we may fail to find an association between rated success and the probability of publication.

Another measure of the success of a collaboration is whether it is continued. Despite the higher probability of publishing the work three years later, respondents in distant collaborations were slightly less likely than respondents in local collaborations to think they would continue the collaboration (and also slightly less likely actually to continue the collaboration three years later). These (small) differences might be attributed to the greater difficulty associated with distant collaborations.

Benefits of Collaboration

There were fourteen benefits of collaboration that respondents regularly listed. Overall, the frequency with which each benefit was selected was similar across local and distant collaborations ($r = .81$). A MANOVA revealed that twelve of the fourteen showed no difference at all (in decreasing frequency of mention): division of labor, different ideas, stimulating, increases enjoyment, challenging, motivating, different styles, different resources, increases the speed of research, similar ideas, helps monitor progress, and supports the research. Two factors were affected by collaboration distance, and these effects did not interact with first author's discipline or collaboration length, the control variables. First, distant collaborators were less likely to mention having similar styles as a benefit of the collaboration (0 percent versus 25 percent in distant and local collaborations, respectively; $F (1,52) = 4.5$, MSE = .14, $p < .05$). Second, distant collaborations were more likely to mention having interaction and discussion as a benefit of collaboration (100 percent versus 72 percent for distant and local collaborations, respectively; $F (1,52) = 5.1$, MSE = .15, $p < .05$). One might imagine that style similarity is not as relevant when the collaborator is far away. Yet when the collaborator does interact, the interaction and discussions are always important, or else there would be little incentive to participate in the collaboration.

Partially as a consistency check, the differences and similarities between local and distant collaborations were examined at a more finely grained level, separating out the various levels of distance between collaborators. In all but one case, the finely grained analyses produced similar results, suggesting that our boundary between local and distant collaborators was appropriately chosen. The one exception was for international collaborations versus intercity collaborations: none of the intercity collaborators listed having different resources as a benefit, whereas two-thirds of the international collaborators listed having different resources as a benefit. Given how widely funding practices, subject pool types, and computational resources differ across countries, this difference is not entirely surprising and is consistent with our own experience in international collaboration.

Frustrations of Collaboration

When asked about frustrations associated with the collaboration, the most common response (just under 40 percent) was to say there were no frustrations. This response may reflect a reluctance to send any negative comments in e-mail about the collaboration. Seven frustrations were mentioned consistently, and their relative frequency was similar across local and distant collaborations ($r = .73$). The frustrations that were mentioned in both types of collaborations were (in decreasing frequency of mention): communication problems, different ideas, slow research process, different styles, personality differences, assignment of credit problems, and motivation problems. A MANOVA revealed that none of the frustrations was mentioned significantly more often in distant collaborations; on average, distance accounted for only 2 percent of the variance in self-reported frustrations. Only one difference approached significance: having different styles was mentioned only in the local collaborations as a frustration.

Communication
Communication attributes of the collaborations were similar across local and distant collaborations. Respondents were just as likely to say they had very similar ideas, had a collaborator who frequently provided alternative hypotheses, had a collaborator with a similar style, felt they had an equal status in the collaboration, used e-mail as a primary collaboration method, and communicated at least several times a week (see figure 17.2).

Two significant differences distinguished the communication in distant and local collaborations. The first was the use of regular research group meetings. Unsurprisingly, local collaborations were much more likely to use research group meetings as a primary communication method, $F (1,53) = 5.8$, $MSE = .23$, $p < .02$. The second difference, equally unsurprising, was the frequency of face–to–face meetings, $F (1,53) = 4.4$, $MSE = 2.4$, $p < .05$. A larger proportion of the distant collaborators met infrequently. Neither of these effects of distance interacted with collaboration length and first author training background, the two factors partially confounded with distance.

Distribution of Work
Respondents were asked to rate what percentage of the work reported in the conference paper was done by them, both overall and on different components of the project: selecting the research questions, selecting a design, providing the resources for the work, collecting the data, analyzing the data, and writing the paper. On all of these dimensions, there was generally an asymmetry in the distribution of work across the authors; first authors tended to do more of the work. The one exception was providing resources for the work, which was slightly more often associated with second and third authors. Note that whereas the sum of these percentages across

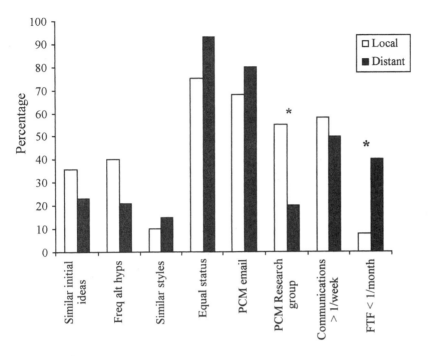

Figure 17.2
Communication attributes of collaborations. *p < .05 for the comparison between local and distant.

authors for a given paper on a given dimension tended to be greater than 100 percent, there was generally good consistency in how the workload was perceived to have been distributed.

Did this authorship-work-asymmetry differ by collaboration type? Generally, the answer is no, with one exception. For data collection, there was a much smaller asymmetry of first and second authors in distant collaborations. In local collaborations, first authors claimed to have done 80 percent of the data collection and second authors only 14 percent. By contrast, in distant collaborations, first authors claimed to have done only 49 percent of the data collection and second authors 28 percent. This effect did not interact with collaboration length and first author training background. It appears that one of the uses of distant collaborations was data collection across multiple locations. When data are collected at one site, there is less need for multiple collaborators to contribute to data collection than when data are collected at multiple sites. The other activities of research are much less location specific by nature, and thus it is not surprising that the other dimensions did not show an effect of collaboration type.

Predicting Success

What factors are important in predicting the success of a collaboration, and do those factors differ between local and distant collaborations? Here we focus on the rated success and estimated probability of continuing to work together because we have the largest number of responses for those variables. We examined which of the eight process features of the collaboration predicted success in local and distant collaborations separately. In predicting rated success for local collaborations, two factors proved important: whether the primary communication method was the research group meeting ($r = .45$, $p < .05$) and the similarity of initial ideas ($r = .50$, $p < .05$). These predictors hold for all the varieties of local collaborations that could be distinguished (there was no interaction with type of collaboration in a multiple regression): psychologists and computer scientists, short-term collaborations and long-term collaborations, and for faculty collaborations and graduate student collaborations.

By contrast, what predicted the rated success of distant collaborations was the frequency of face-to-face meetings ($r = .60$, $p < .05$). To verify that these correlation patterns were indeed different across local versus distant collaboration types, we examined the strength of the correlation with each of these four predictors in the other collaboration type. The correlation strengths were all almost zero in the opposite collaboration type. Thus, the predictors are indeed quite different. Table 17.2 summarizes the results of these regression analyses.

Our analyses do not say that the factors that were not statistically predictive are not important for successful collaborations. We believe instead that in this community, there are generally sufficient levels of the other factors to support successful performance. Further, we have restriction of range because all of these collaborations had obtained a measure of success by having papers accepted at the conference.

What do the correlation patterns imply? First, it appears that the research group meeting is a very important part of the research process for collaborations that can support them (local collaborations) but not for collaborations that cannot support them (distant collaborations). Second, the role of similar ideas is perhaps to avoid important conflict about the details and directions of the project. In distant collaborations, more of the work is distributed (e.g., data collection) and having differ-

Table 17.2
Predicting rated success of local and distant collaborations as a function of process features of these collaborations

Independent variables	Local collaborations			Distant collaborations		
	Beta	SE	p	Beta	SE	p
Intercept	0.60	0.55		−0.37	2.82	
Similarity of initial ideas	0.26	0.17	*	−0.29	0.39	
Frequency alternative hypotheses were proposed	−0.15	0.13		−0.44	0.42	
Similarity of styles	0.0	0.13		0.42	0.43	
Perceived equal status	0.10	0.20		1.01	1.01	
Primary communication is e-mail	−0.18	0.18		0.06	0.63	
Primary communication is research group meetings	0.42	0.19	*	0.09	0.57	
Communication frequency	0.11	0.13		−0.13	0.32	
Face-to-face frequency	−0.07	0.11		0.36	0.16	†
N	39			13		
R^2	.44			.70		

† $p < .10.$ * $p < .05.$

ent initial ideas may be less a source of conflict (even though the distribution of similarity of ideas was the same for local and distant collaborations). Third, it appears that what is most crucial for the success of long-distance collaborations is the feature they are most lacking: face-to-face contact.

For predicting the estimated probability of continuing to work together, one factor proved predictive in distant collaborations: whether the collaboration was felt to involve an equal-status relationship ($r = .52$). By contrast, no factors predicted that outcome in local collaborations (e.g., $r = .07$ for equal status). Schunn and associates (1998) found that interdisciplinary collaborations (but not intradisciplinary collaborations) also required an equal status relationship for the collaborators to want to continue the collaboration. Together these results suggest that collaborations that require extra effort to maintain, such as distant or interdisciplinary collaborations, require the mutual respect that comes with being treated with equal status in order to want to continue the collaboration. By contrast, easier collaborations (local and intradisciplinary collaborations) seem not as sensitive to these social perceptions.

Implications

Our investigation of scientific collaborations in a new interdisciplinary field like cognitive science has provided several insights into the similarities and differences between the structure and process of local and distant collaborations. At their core, the collaboration types are quite similar. That is, it does not appear that there are large differences in who decides to engage in distant collaborations, with the possible exception that psychologists were slightly more likely to do so than researchers from other disciplines. Moreover, there were many similarities in the frequencies of frustrations and benefits and in the types of processes used to coordinate research.

Distance Changing the Process

We did, however, find that distance changed some aspects of the research process. Not surprisingly, distant collaborations involved less use of research group meetings and fewer face-to-face meetings. Distant collaborations also involved a more even sharing of data collection activities across the coauthors, suggesting perhaps that one of the advantages of distant collaborations in this setting is access to a wider variety of data sources. Most important, different factors were important for successful collaborations at a distance. Local collaborations depended on heavy use of research group meetings and similarity of initial ideas. By contrast, distant collaborations depended on having frequent face-to-face meetings.

In a recent study, Epstein (in press) interviewed twenty-one cognitive scientists who had engaged in successful interdisciplinary collaborations (as measured by funding and publications). A few of her findings are of particular relevance here. First, frequent meetings were important. For example, one researcher said that it was important to have students and collaborators present their work to each other regularly. Second, it appeared that the frequency of meetings was especially important at the beginning of a collaboration. For example, many long-term interdisciplinary collaborations start out with a regular weekly meeting. Third, the pragmatics of distant collaborations was an important and difficult hurdle to overcome. Frequent meetings were difficult or impossible. Visiting collaborators was expensive in both money and time and involved significant physical and emotion stress. Similar observations were drawn from interviews of Japanese cognitive scientists who had engaged in successful interdisciplinary collaborations (Okada et al. 1995). The findings of these several studies suggest that regular meetings have both important advantages and disadvantages in distant collaborations.

Distance as a Benefit

Much of the research on distance work and collaborations across a distance has focused on either the negative consequences of distance—on trust between collaborators (Cramton, chapter 8, this volume), shared mental models (De Meyer 1991; Olson Teasley, Covi, and Olson, chapter 5, this volume), shared practice styles (Mark, chapter 11, this volume—remediating those negative consequences, such as, through improved collaboration software (Holtham 1991; Olson and Olson 1991; Hollingshead, Fulk, and Monge, chapter 14, this volume). One of the most surprising findings of our investigations was that there are some positive benefits associated with distance per se. This difference may in part be a selection artifact. That is, researchers may be pickier about projects they work on across a distance as compared with those they work on locally. However, at some level, because we selected only accepted conference papers for a conference with a high rejection rate, the selection artifact should have been reduced.

We argue that there are positive consequences associated with distance. As the example of the Newell, Simon, and Shaw collaboration showed, not all people work well in the same physical space. Azmitia and Crowley (2001) argue that collaboration is best thought of as a rhythm of relatively social and relatively individual moments. It may be that physical proximity is beneficial for the relatively social components and damaging for the relatively individualistic components of collaboration.

Alternatively, it may be that collaboration across a distance provides access to a wider influx of ideas. Researchers at different institutions will attend different talks and are more likely to have nonoverlapping research groups. These differences can provide access to a broader set of expertise and ideas. This access to new ideas also has been examined by Walsh and Maloney (chapter 18, this volume) in their study of scientists. In our own research, which has been primarily a collaboration across a distance, this access to different groups and ideas has been very influential. At the level of theoretical frameworks, it has produced an infusion of both information processing and sociocultural approaches into our work. At the level of research methodologies, it has provided input from numerous research groups into developing instruments (e.g., items in our survey questionnaire). At the level of contextual situativity and practical implications, it has provided models of academic research and work practices across nations (the U.S. and Japanese academic systems) and across fields (applied cognitive science, cognitive psychology, developmental psychology, and education).

Recently, we have partially replicated our finding of slightly greater success associated with distant collaborations. For the 2000 Annual Meeting of the Cognitive Science Society, all submissions (prior to acceptance) were categorized according to number of authors, location of authors (distant versus local), and discipline of authors ($n = 163$). The dependent measure was whether the submissions were accepted at the conference. Overall, only 36 percent of submissions were accepted. Although the difference was not statistically significant, 40 percent of local collaborations versus 48 percent of distant collaborations were accepted. Note that this analysis excludes single-author submissions, which had a substantially lower acceptance rate. Indeed, number of authors proved the best predictor whether a paper would be accepted, suggesting that collaborations are an important part of scientific progress in cognitive science.

Models of Collaboration

What possible models of collaboration processes might underlie the results found here? Two general types of accounts should be distinguished: an individual differences account and a process account. On the one hand, it is possible that different types of people engage in distant collaborations, and this produces a different set of factors that are important not because the collaboration is being conducted at a distance, but because the people themselves are different. On the other hand, it may be that the process of collaboration at a distance is itself different, and this by itself produces a different set of factors that are important. Our data tend to support the process account. There were some differences in background profiles across the local and distant collaborations. However, we examined the influence of those factors and found that they could not account for the differences in which factors were important across local and distant collaborations. We also found some differences in the collaboration process that one might expect, and we have already discussed how those could plausibly lead to the strong influence of the obtained important factors. However, we have not ruled out all possible background differences. For example, we did not gather detailed information about personality types or amount of experience with collaborations generally.

What do our findings tell us about the nature of scientific collaborations generally? They certainly highlight the shared and co-constructed nature of collaborative work. Work is not simply divided among the collaborators and then continued, independently, in parallel. Instead, the success and continuity of the collaboration depend on features of the relationship between the collaborators: that they meet often enough, in the right circumstances, and treat each other as equals. In other words, even if one is interested in the cognitive products of the collaboration, one must still pay careful attention to the social features in order to understand the process and success of collaboration. However, our findings also highlight the potential positive value of distance, and this surprising result must be explored further in future work.

Work at a Distance

Our findings suggest that there may be important advantages of collaboration at a distance, and this has important practical implications for researchers and practitioners who wish to understand work at a distance. First, our findings place in question the general push to create new, expensive technologies that duplicate as many possible features of face-to-face collaboration at a distance (e.g., videoconferencing, shared virtual reality environments). Collaborations at a distance may have their own unique advantages that we may not want to remove through technological changes.

This realization brings us to the second important practical implication of our findings for distance collaboration. In order to decide when to bring in supporting technologies and which technologies to use, we need to know more about why distance might help the collaborative process. Our research has provided the first clues that it might help, but much further research needs to be conducted on why and under which circumstances it might help.

Methodological Caveats

There are many methods that one could use to study scientific collaboration processes, including experiments using undergraduates conducted in the lab (Okada and Simon 1997, Azmitia and Crowley 2001), observations of scientists working on a project (Dunbar 1995, 1997; Trickett, Fu, Schunn, and Trafton, 2000; Trickett, Trafton, and Schunn, 2000), interviews of scientists about their collaborations (Epstein, in press; Okada, Crowley, Schunn, and Miwa 1996; Schunn et al. 1998, in press; Thagard 1994), and historical analyses of famous collaborations (Okada et al. 1995). Each method has its advantages and disadvantages, particularly emphasizing different grain sizes of analysis. Each method contributes to our understanding of scientific collaboration. We were primarily interested in what factors motivated long-distance collaborations and what factors contributed to the success of the collaboration. Therefore, we chose to use a methodology that gave long-term data rather than detailed short-term data. This also motivated our decision to collect data from practicing scientists rather than undergraduates in a lab experiment.

Like every other methodology, our methodology has disadvantages, which should be mentioned here as a caveat to our results. First, we relied heavily on self-report data. When possible, we compared the respondents' answers with publicly available information about them, and in all of those cases it was clear that the respondents were answering those questions accurately. However, there may have been some biases in their responses to some of the more subjective questions.

A second important caveat is that we had a relatively small number of distant collaborations in our sample. It is likely that this relatively small number prevented us from detecting the role of other important factors in the process and success of distant collaborations. At the same time, the advantage of small numbers is that one must focus on the factors with the largest effect size, a good strategy for the first research forays into a new area. Yet the small number also prevented us from exploring further interactions with other distinctions in collaboration type. Within local collaborations, we were able to determine that our patterns held for peer and apprenticeship collaborations, student and faculty collaborations, and computer science and psychology collaborations. Interactions, however, may exist for distant collaborations. For example, an apprenticeship collaboration may require additional structure at a distance that a peer collaboration does not.

Third, it must be acknowledged that we had a potentially narrow range of success in our sample since all projects had been accepted at the conference. It is likely that many other factors play an important role in the successful collaborations but were present in sufficient quantity in all of our respondents' collaborations. So we must qualify our results as being about what differentiates collaborations that have managed to produce at least one work product. However, focusing on collaborations that had all reached a similar threshold ensured that there was some level of equivalence in the phase of research across the various types of collaborations examined.

Fourth, our analyses are entirely correlational, and thus we do not yet know the true causal nature of relationships between our variables, and more important, there were many correlations among our measured variables. Table 17.3 presents the intercorrelations among all the measures that were significantly associated with collaboration distance directly or behaved differently in the local and distant collaboration cases. Luckily, none of the correlations is so large that one should have large worries about mediated correlations.

Table 17.3
Correlations among items differentiating distant and local collaborations

	1	2	3	4	5	6	7	8	9	10	11	12
1. Same location	1.00	-.22	-.30	.07	.14	.28	-.30	.12	-.19	-.12	.31	.28
2. First author psychology	-.22	1.00	.08	-.35	-.28	-.09	-.15	-.31	-.01	.24	.00	-.09
3. Recent collaboration	-.30	.08	1.00	.00	-.15	-.33	-.12	-.15	-.02	.13	-.18	.06
4. Rated success	.07	-.35	.00	1.00	.09	.16	.37	.38	.09	-.19	.29	.32
5. Will continue collaborating	.14	-.28	-.15	.09	1.00	-.02	.04	.02	.09	-.04	.15	.12
6. Benefit same style	.28	-.09	-.33	.16	-.02	1.00	.24	.30	.13	-.22	.03	.17
7. Benefit interact and discuss	-.30	-.15	-.12	.37	.04	.24	1.00	.30	.18	.08	.20	.00
8. Similarity of initial ideas	.12	-.31	-.15	.38	.02	.30	.30	1.00	.04	.02	.27	.02
9. Rated equal status	-.19	-.01	-.02	.09	.09	.13	.18	.04	1.00	-.24	-.12	-.11
10. Primary communication is e-mail	-.12	.24	.13	-.19	-.04	-.22	.08	.02	-.24	1.00	.03	-.35
11. Primary communication is research group	.31	.00	-.18	.29	.15	.03	.20	.27	-.12	.03	1.00	.29
12. Face-to-face frequency	.28	-.09	.06	.32	.12	.17	.00	.02	-.11	-.35	.29	1.00

Note: N varies slightly by item depending on the response rate to each item, with $52 \leq n \leq 55$.

Fifth, we have focused on one particular situation (a new interdisciplinary field), and the generalizability to other situations must be explored further. In particular, the interdisciplinary nature of cognitive science, while perhaps forcing a greater level of distant collaborations, may perversely require even more face-to-face contact. Thus, the dependence on face-to-face meeting frequency may not be as strong in more established monodisciplines.

Note

Work on this project was funded by a grant from the Mitsubishi Bank Foundation. The first author thanks the Department of Psychology at the University of Basel for providing time and support to write this chapter. We also thank Jae Yun Moon, Sara Kiesler, and Pamela Hinds for helpful comments on earlier versions of this chapter.

References

Allen, T. J. (1977). *Managing the flow of technology*. Cambridge, MA: MIT Press.

Azmitia, M. A., and Crowley, K. (2001). The rhythms of scientific thinking: A study of collaboration in an earthquake microworld. In K. Crowley, C. Schunn, and T. Okada (eds.), *Designing for science: Implications from everyday, classroom, and professional settings*. Mahwah, NJ: Erlbaum.

Collins, A. (1977). Why cognitive science. *Cognitive Science, 1,* 1–2.

Cramton, C. D. (2002). Attribution in distributed work groups. In P. Hinds and S. Kiesler (eds.), *Distributed work* (191–212). Cambridge, MA: MIT Press.

De Meyer, A. (1991). Tech talk: How managers are stimulating global RandD communication. *Sloan Management Review, 32,* 49–58.

Dunbar, K. (1995). How scientists really reason: Scientific reasoning in real-world laboratories. In R. J. Sternberg and J. E. Davidson (eds.), *The nature of insight* (365–395). Cambridge, MA: MIT Press.

Dunbar, K. (1997). How scientists think: On-line creativity and conceptual change in science. In T. B. Ward and S. M. Smith (eds.), *Creative thought: An investigation of conceptual structures and processes* (461–493). Washington, DC: American Psychological Association.

Epstein, S. L. (in press). Making interdisciplinary collaboration work. In S. J. Derry and M. A. Gernsbacher (eds.), *Problems and promises of interdisciplinary collaboration: Perspectives from cognitive science*. Mahwah, NJ: Erlbaum.

Hardcastle, V. G. (1996). *How to build a theory in cognitive science*. Albany: State University of New York Press.

Hollingshead, A. B., Fulk, J., and Monge, P. (2002). Fostering intranet knowledge sharing: An integration of transactive memory and public goods approaches. In P. Hinds and S. Kiesler (eds.), *Distributed work* (335–356). Cambridge, MA: MIT Press.

Holtham, C. (1994). Groupware: Its past and future. In P. Lloyd (ed.), *Groupware in the twenty-first century*. Westport, CT: Praeger.

Kiesler, S. and Cummings, J. N. (2002). What do we know about proximity and distance in work groups? A legacy of research. In P. Hinds and S. Kiesler (eds.), *Distributed work* (57–80). Cambridge, MA: MIT Press.

Kraut, R. E., Egido, C., and Galegher, J. (1990). Patterns of contact and communications in scientific research collaboration. In J. Galegher, R. E. Kraut, and C. Egido (eds.), *Intellectual teamwork: Social and technological foundations of cooperative work*. Hillsdale, NJ: Erlbaum.

Mark, G. (2002). Conventions for coordinating electronic distributed work: A longitudinal study of groupware use. In P. Hinds and S. Kiesler (eds.), *Distributed work* (259–282). Cambridge, MA: MIT Press.

McCordock, P. (1979). *Machines who think: A personal inquiry into the history and prospects of artificial intelligence*. New York, NY: W. H. Freeman and Company.

Nardi, B. A., and Whittaker, S. (2002). The place of face-to-face communication in distributed work. In P. Hinds and S. Kiesler (eds.), *Distributed work* (83–110). Cambridge, MA: MIT Press.

Okada, T., Crowley, K., Schunn, C. D., and Miwa, K. (1996, June 20–22). *Collaborative scientific research in Japanese cognitive science: Analyses of questionnaire survey data*. Paper presented at the *1996 Meeting of the Japanese Cognitive Science Society, Kyoto*, Japan.

Okada, T., Schunn, C. D., Crowley, K., Oshima, J., Miwa, K., Aoki, T., and Ishida, Y. (1995). *Collaborative scientific research: Analyses of historical and interview data*. Paper presented at the 1995 Meeting of the Japanese Cognitive Science Society, Tokyo, Japan.

Okada, T., and Simon, H. A. (1997). Collaborative discovery in a scientific domain. *Cognitive Science, 2*, 109–146.

Olson, G. M., and Olson, J. S. (1991). User-centered design of collaborative technology. *Journal of Organizational Computing, 1*, 61–83.

Olson, J. S., Teasley, S., Covi, L., and Olson, G. (2002). The (currently) unique advantages of collocated work. In P. Hinds and S. Kiesler (eds.), *Distributed work* (113–135). Cambridge, MA: MIT Press.

Schunn, C. D., Crowley, K., and Okada, T. (1998). The growth of multidisciplinarity in the Cognitive Science Society. *Cognitive Science, 22*(1), 107–130.

Schunn, C. D., Crowley, K., and Okada, T. (in press). Cognitive science: Interdisciplinarity now and then. In S. J. Derry and M. A. Gernsbacher (eds.), *Problems and promises of interdisciplinary collaboration: Perspectives from cognitive science*. Mahwah, NJ: Erlbaum.

Schunn, C. D., Okada, T., and Crowley, K. (1995). Is cognitive science truly interdisciplinary? The case of interdisciplinary collaborations. In J. D. Moore and J. F. Lehman (eds.), *Proceedings of the 17th Annual Conference of the Cognitive Science Society* (100–105). Mahwah, NJ: Erlbaum.

Simon, H. A. (1980). Cognitive science: The newest science of the artificial. *Cognitive Science, 4*, 33–46.

Simon, H. A., and Kaplan, C. A. (1989). Foundations of cognitive science. In M. I. Posner (ed.), *Foundations of cognitive science*. Cambridge, MA: MIT Press.

Sproull, L., and Kiesler, S. (1991). *Connections: New ways of working in the networked organization.* Cambridge, MA: MIT Press.

Thagard, P. (1994). Collaborative knowledge in science. In A. Ram and K. Eiselt (eds.), *Proceedings of the 16th Annual Conference of the Cognitive Science Society* (990–991). Hillsdale, NJ: Erlbaum.

Trickett, S. B., Fu, W.-T., Schunn, C. D., and Trafton, J. G. (2000). From dipsy-doodles to streaming motions: Changes in representation in the analysis of visual scientific data. In *Proceedings of the 22nd Annual Conference of the Cognitive Science Society.* Mahwah, NJ: Erlbaum.

Trickett, S. B., Trafton, J. G., and Schunn, C. D. (2000). Blobs, dipsy-doodles and other funky things: Framework anomalies in exploratory data analysis. In *Proceedings of the 22nd Annual Conference of the Cognitive Science Society.* Mahwah, NJ: Erlbaum.

Vera, A. H., Kvan, T., West, R. L., and Lai, S. (1998). Expertise, collaboration and bandwidth usability of groupware. In *Proceedings of ACM CHI 98 Conference on Human Factors in Computing Systems* (503–510). New York: ACM Press.

Walsh, J. P., and Maloney, N. G. (2002). Computer network use, collaboration structures, and productivity. In P. Hinds and S. Kiesler (eds.), *Distributed work* (433–458). Cambridge, MA: MIT Press.

"*This is where our trails divide, Luke. You have my E-mail address, right?*"

18

Computer Network Use, Collaboration Structures, and Productivity

John P. Walsh and Nancy G. Maloney

While science has always been a collective enterprise, recent years have seen a substantial increase in scientific collaboration. The widespread adoption by scientists of Internet-related technologies has facilitated this increase in team-based science. Building on previous research on computer network use and on social networks, we suggest this technology may be associated with the changing structure of scientific collaborations and that these changes may affect collaboration productivity. Based on a survey of scientists in four fields (experimental biology, mathematics, physics, and sociology), we analyze the relations between use of e-mail and the structure and outcomes of scientific collaborations. We find that computer network use is associated with more geographically dispersed collaborations, as well as more productive collaborations. In addition, we find that collaborations characterized by intermediate levels of strong ties and fewer interconnections (more structural holes) are more productive.

Faced with the need to solve problems jointly, workers in many fields are joining together with local and distant colleagues to collaborate. How should these collaborations be structured to make them most productive? With the growth of e-mail and related communications tools, are these technologies associated with different ways of organizing collaborations and with more or less productive collaborations? This chapter addresses these questions by examining the relationships among the use of e-mail, collaboration structures, and productivity for a sample of scientists in four fields: experimental biology, mathematics, physics, and sociology. Our findings will help us understand how technology and collaboration structure are associated and how different ways of structuring collaboration affect productivity.

In the same way that biologists use rats, *Drosophila*, and *C. elegans* as model organisms to advance their understanding of animals, we study scientists as model knowledge workers. Scientists must quickly adapt to innovations in their domain and must compete for discoveries, prestige, and resources in a competitive global scientific community. In addition, like many other knowledge workers, scientists are

Table 18.1
Publications with international collaborators, by field, 1981–1997

Field	1981, world	1981–1985, United States	1986, world	1991, world	1991–1995, world	1991–1995, United States	1995, world	1995–1997, United States
Mathematics	9%	11%	13%	17%	19%	19%	N.A.	27%
Physics	9	14	11	16	19	25	N.A.	30
Biology	5	7	7	10	11	13	N.A.	16
Chemistry	9	9	6	9	11	14	N.A.	17
All fields	6	9	8	11	13	16	15%	18

Sources: National Science Board (1993), Appendix Table 5.24; National Science Board (1998), Appendix Table 5.53, National Science Board (2000), Appendix Table 6.60.

increasingly collaborating in their work. The lessons learned from studying the structure and productivity of their collaborations should be broadly applicable in the new economy.

A significant change in the organization of science has been an increase in remote collaboration, particularly in international collaboration. Although science has always been an international activity, in recent years there has been an increased frequency of international collaborations and growth of large collaborations. Table 18.1 shows the increase in the number of international collaborations over a fifteen-year period, by field. The table shows that for all fields, the percentage of papers published with authors from more than one country has nearly doubled. There has been even faster growth in the number of papers from large international collaborations.

Figure 18.1 shows the increase since 1986 in the number of papers with authors from ten or more countries. This figure shows that while the number of international collaboration papers approximately doubled (table 18.1), there was a nine-fold increase in the number of publications by large international collaborations. Thus, we can see that scientific work is increasingly geographically distributed, and often substantially so. This change is likely due to a combination of the increasing scale of scientific problems, changes in funding patterns, and perhaps an overall increase in the number of scientists, as well as the availability of Internet-related technologies (Walsh and Bayma 1996a). The paper that announced the discovery of the top quark listed 398 authors from thirty-four institutions in five countries.

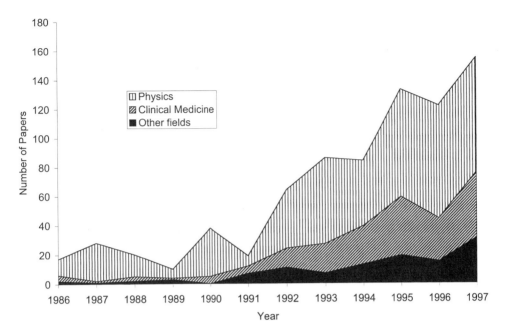

Figure 18.1
Number of papers listing addresses from ten or more countries, 1986–1997.
Source: CHI Research.

The following quotation from a particle physicist points to the role of computer networks in facilitating the very large collaborations that now seem necessary in his field: "Experiments are getting larger. We're trying to understand the nature of matter, the inside of a proton. We need more energy, more money and bigger equipment. There are fewer experiments now, because funds are limited. So, each experiment gets bigger. The size of experiments is growing. It's not a consequence of the nets. But, the nets are a tool that made life easier. It hasn't affected the size of apparatus. But, more people can collaborate effectively now" (Walsh and Bayma 1996a).

A virtue of e-mail and related technologies is that they help overcome some of the interaction barriers that geographic separation creates. This benefit is most noticeable in international collaborations, where cost, time zones, and language all create barriers. Computer networks reduce the need for coworkers to be collocated (Bullen and Bennett 1991, Finholt and Sproull 1990). In one office setting, e-mail and electronic bulletin boards facilitated the formation of geographically dispersed work groups (Finholt and Sproull 1990). Kraut, Galegher, and Egido (1990) observed a relation between use of computer networks and geographic dispersion of collaborations.

Based on prior research, we expect that the availability and use of network technology will be associated with several differences in the structure of scientific collaborations. These differences are likely to be associated with different levels of scientific productivity. In the following sections, we review the prior literature and make predictions about the relationships we expect to observe. We then compare these expectations with data from a survey of scientists in four fields: experimental biology, mathematics, physics, and sociology.

Use of the Internet and Collaboration Structure

Previous research on e-mail and the Internet suggests that the adoption of these technologies can increase the size of work groups, increase the geographic dispersion of groups, and increase the equality of access to information in work organizations (for example, see Sproull and Kiesler 1991, Rice 1994, Wellman et al. 1996). Thus, we expect the use of e-mail among scientists to be associated with changes in the size, geographic dispersion, and heterogeneity of their scientific collaborations and to influence the productivity of these scientific collaborations.

Social Network Size

People cannot simultaneously have relationships with an infinite (or even a very large) number of people (Watts 1999). Marsden (1987) reports that on average, Americans have only three people with whom they "discuss important matters" and that only about 5 percent of the population had more than five such confidants (see also McPherson, Popielarz, and Drobnic 1992). However, the use of network technologies may allow for larger social networks (Hesse, Sproull, Kiesler, and Walsh 1993; Walsh and Bayma 1996a). The overhead of maintaining a mediated relationship may be less than that of maintaining a traditional face-to-face relationship. Further, the overall time available for interaction expands because asynchronicity allows one to be in multiple places at almost the same time and to communicate throughout the day and evening, independent of others' schedules. This argument suggests that larger scientific collaborations become more feasible. The physicist's comments above reflect this idea. Similarly, a sociologist in our survey commented, "I recently finished a complicated piece of research involving a sizable research team, about twenty people. We had only two extended meetings. All the rest was done by e-mail and phone."

Prior surveys of e-mail use among scientists have found a relation between network use and research group size. Cohen (1996) found a significant correlation between e-mail use and coauthoring. According to Bishop (1994), aerospace engineers claim that computer networks have increased the feasibility and size of their collaborations.

When there are more total communication paths in a social network but the population size stays the same, denser networks will result. Also there will be fewer of what Burt (1992) refers to as "structural holes," that is, groups or individuals in the population who are not directly in contact and so must depend on an intermediary contact person (a "bridge") to pass information across the hole. If, on the other hand, use of the Internet leads more people into the community of active researchers (Walsh and Bayma 1996b), then we would expect that the overall density of collaborations (and of the research community as a whole) would decline. Newly added members would likely be peripheral and have relatively fewer contacts with others. In this scenario, there would be more people not in direct contact (structural holes) in a collaboration, providing information benefits (Burt 1992).

Researchers studying social networks have debated the relative advantages of a network with many structural holes (Burt 1992) versus a network that is relatively dense (Coleman 1990). Granovetter (1973) and Burt (1992) argue that networks with many structural holes provide better access to new information because each of the members has unique information and the individual providing the bridge across these holes is particularly well positioned to gain from this diversity of information. Podolny and Baron (1997) and Ahuja (2000) argue that having a denser network is better, as it provides cohesion, trust, and consensus in the face of uncertainty and facilitates knowledge transfer. We test the empirical relationship between e-mail use and the size of collaborations, as well as the relation between e-mail use and structural holes in collaboration networks. We also test the effects of structural holes on scientific productivity (Ahuja 2000).

Geographic Dispersion

Some have argued that the spread of Internet-related technologies has led to a new form of distributed scientific work. Carley and Wendt (1990) call this new form an "extended research group." These are very large, unified, cohesive, and highly cooperative research groups that are geographically dispersed yet coordinated as though they were at one location and under the supervision of a single director. These groups rely heavily on e-mail to coordinate their work activities. Carley and Wendt (1990) point to the Soar group in artificial intelligence research as an example of this new form of working.

Others have used the term *collaboratory* for a similar work arrangement (Lederberg and Uncapher 1989, Finholt and Olson 1997). Collaboratories use computer network technology to provide, without regard to geography, the access to equipment, colleagues, and databases that are traditionally part of the laboratory organization of science. Recent examples of collaboratories include the Upper Atmospheric Research Collaboratory, the Environmental Molecular Sciences Collaboratory, and the Great Lakes Center for Aids Research (see Finholt, in press, for a review of recent studies of collaboratories).

Other large-scale distributed projects include ProjectH, an on-line collaboration of about one hundred researchers in fifteen countries to study computer-mediated communication behavior (Sudweeks and Rafaeli 1996), Common LISP, developed by a nationwide network of computer scientists who communicated almost entirely via e-mail (Orlikowski and Yates 1994), and, more recently, the Linux operating system, which has evolved through the on-line collaboration of thousands of programmers across the globe (Harmon 1999; Moon and Sproull, chapter 16, this volume).

E-mail is critical for these distributed collaborations. As one mathematician commented, "The time difference between the United States and England is such that I finish my day's work and send my collaborator what I've done. He gets it while I'm asleep and his response is waiting for me when I get up. Without e-mail, our collaboration would never have begun and would have been almost impossible to carry out." A biologist wrote: "Time zone problems have been lessened by e-mail but it can be a problem with my Japanese, New Zealand, and Australian collaborators. I have not had any unpleasant experiences yet in any of my collaborations. We share knowledge and reagents openly and credit and include each other appropriately in publications. Very few of these would have gotten very far without e-mail to facilitate the immediate exchange of ideas."

Walsh and Bayma (1996a) find similar effects. According to their respondents, e-mail is fast, cheap, and allows easy transmission of short messages and long documents, all of which make collaborative research with distant colleagues more feasible. Thus, we expect to find a correlation between geographic dispersion of the collaborations and computer network use.

These more dispersed ties are likely to be weaker than local ties, which rely more on face-to-face communication (Allen 1977, Granovetter 1973). Again, like the holes-versus-density argument, there is a debate in the social networks literature on the relative advantages of strong versus weak ties. Granovetter (1973) argues that weak ties are most important for information about job openings and that it is their ability to bridge into distinct social worlds and information spaces that is the key to their efficacy (see also Burt 1992, Podolny and Baron 1997, Sparrowe and Popielarz 2000).

Others argue that strong ties are more critical for effective information flow. For example, Murray and Poolman (1982) suggest that strong ties (scientists whom one knows well) rather than weak ties (scientists whom one barely knows) are the key channels for accessing scientific information. They find that rather than benefiting from a wider net (as is the case in a job search), scientists doing their work benefit most from the person-specific filters to the literature that closer ties can provide. Similarly, Hansen (1999) finds that among R&D units of a firm, weak ties are helpful for information search for simple knowledge, but for complex knowledge, weak ties impede transfer and strong ties facilitate it.

Uzzi (1996) argues that there are advantages of what he and Granovetter term the "embeddedness" of strong ties but strong ties can lead to intellectual inbreeding too. In his study of garment firms, Uzzi found that firms were most successful if they had a mix of one or a few strong ties and many weak ties. He argues that important informational and other benefits flow only across strong ties, yet a network with too many strong ties becomes inbred and also lacks the structural holes that allow leveraging. Supporting this argument, he showed that embeddedness had a curvilinear (inverted-U) relation to firm survival. Uzzi (1999) found a similar result for firms trying to acquire bank financing, where embeddedness had a curvilinear (U-shaped) relation with the cost of financing.

We expect that computer network use is likely to be associated with a greater number of weak ties. E-mail use also may increase the number of strong ties by allowing regular communication with more people, independent of geography, creating or maintaining close relationships with those whom one rarely or never meets face-to-face (Baym 1997). Based on the work of Uzzi (1996, 1999), Hansen (1999), and Murray and Poolman (1982), we expect that strong ties will have a positive, or perhaps curvilinear (inverted-U), relationship to scientific productivity, but that weak ties will have little effect.

Heterogeneity

Prior studies have found that social networks tend to be heavily influenced by proximity, which leads to homogeneity in social networks (Blau 1977, Marsden 1987, Popielarz 1999). Previous research on use of e-mail and similar technologies (Finholt and Sproull 1990, Feldman 1987) suggests this use leads to a reorganization of work groups, increasing substantive overlap and reducing geographic overlap. Work groups using e-mail can be larger and more complex and have more fluid structures than work groups relying mostly on face-to-face communication (Sproull and Kiesler 1991). However, removing geographic constraints could lead to either more or less heterogeneous groups. Van Alstyne and Brynjolfsson (1996) speculate that use of the Internet could lead to a balkanization of science, with researchers using their limited communication time to interact only with those in their specialty (anywhere in the world).

We test whether e-mail use is associated with network heterogeneity and, if so, whether the relation is positive (greater interdisciplinarity) or negative (balkanization). Because diverse networks are likely to provide access to more varied information (Blau 1977, Popielarz 1999), we expect that greater heterogeneity will be associated with higher productivity. However, it is also possible that the difficulty of coordination and consensus development in a diverse group (Rothschild-Whitt 1979, Sirianni 1994) may make more heterogeneous collaborations less productive.

Method

We conducted a survey of scientists in four fields: experimental biology, mathematics, physics, and sociology. We drew a random sample from the professional membership directories for each discipline.[1] This sampling frame provided us with a representative sample of all types of institutions, scientists who do research and those who do not, and those who do and do not use e-mail. The goal was to obtain a large sample representing all levels of the scientific community so as to generalize to the population of working scientists in these fields. This sampling method also provides a random sample of collaborations (with selection probability proportion to size; see Bridges and Villemez 1986).

We sent 889 surveys with stamped return envelopes by postal mail in early March 1998. A cover letter explained the purpose of the survey, stressed the importance of the participant's response, and assured respondents that individual-level responses would be confidential, with results to be published only in aggregate form. We sent a second letter approximately ten days later, reminding the recipient of the importance of a prompt response (and thanking those who had responded for doing so). In early April, a final reminder was mailed to those who had not yet responded. We received 399 responses. The response rate was 51.3 percent of the eligible sample.[2] For the following analyses, we limited our results to the 333 respondents with a Ph.D. or M.D. in order to increase the comparability of answers across respondents.

The eleven-page survey consisted of 191 items measuring demographic information, communication activity, research activity, collaboration, competitiveness of the research field, productivity, and uses and effects of e-mail. Appendix table 18A.1 gives mean, standard deviations, and correlation matrix for our measures. The reported means are weighted so that each field contributes equally to the average, to eliminate variance due to the number of responses from each field.

Measures Used in the Analysis

E-mail   For this analysis, we used one measure of e-mail use: the number of e-mail messages sent per day.[3] We find substantial variance, with a mean of six messages per day, a standard deviation of 5.78, and a range from 0 to 35. Because of the skewness of this variable, we use a log transformation in the analyses.[4]

Collaboration   We have two measures of collaboration. First, we asked if the respondent was currently collaborating. Seventy percent reported they were. In addition, we asked for the number of authors on the respondent's most recent publication. Seventy-seven percent had more than one author on their previous paper. We also used this question as a measure of the size of the collaboration. The average paper had 4.6 authors. We also asked how many collaborators were on their current collaboration project. The average was 6.7 collaborators. We classified as a remote collaboration those with at least one collaborator at an institution different from that of the informant.[5] Fifty-five percent of collaborations included at least one remote collaborator.

We asked those who collaborated a series of questions about their current research group. To measure tie strength, we examined the respondents' relations with each of their collaborators (up to seven) and coded these as strong (a "close" or "very close") or weak ("distant") ties (Ibarra 1998, Marsden 1987, Burt 1992, Podolny and Baron 1997). Our respondents reported an average of 1.65 strong ties and .63 weak ties. To measure structural holes, we examined the strength of ties among the respondents' collaborators, based on the respondents' estimates of their ties with each other (Burt 1992, Podolny and Baron 1997, Ibarra 1998, Sparrowe and Popielarz 2000).

We calculated holes as follows:

$$Holes = 1 - \frac{1}{N(N-1)/2} \left(\sum_{i=1}^{N-1} \sum_{j=i+1}^{N} T_{ij} \right),$$

where N is the number of collaborators (excluding the respondent) and T_{ij} is the tie strength between collaborators i and j (strong = 1; weak = 0). This variable measures the sparseness of the relationship among the collaborators by measuring the number of existing ties divided by the number of possible ties (assuming a symmetric matrix) and subtracting this result from one. Holes can vary from 0 (all collaborators have strong ties with each other) to 1 (none are closely tied to each other). In our sample, the mean of holes is .50 (SD = .33), and the range is from 0 to 1.

To determine heterogeneity of the collaboration, we requested the name of the institution where each team member was located, as well as each individual's field or discipline. We determined institutional heterogeneity based on the first question and field heterogeneity based on the second. To measure heterogeneity, we used the following index (see Blau 1977):

$$Heterogeneity = 1 - \sum p_i^2,$$

where p_i^2 is the fraction of the population belonging to category i. Heterogeneity ranges from 0 (complete homogeneity) to (asymptotically) 1. Thus, we have two measures of heterogeneity: institutional heterogeneity (mean = .39, SD = .28), a measure of geographic dispersion, and field heterogeneity (mean = .34, SD = .28), a measure of balkanization.

Productivity   Although getting a true measure of scientific productivity is highly problematic, prior research on scientific productivity has relied generally on number of publications or number of citations as reasonable proxies (Cole and Cole 1967, Fox 1983, Zuckerman 1988, Long and Fox 1995, Xie and Shauman 1998). Since our focus is on group productivity, we measure the productivity of the collaboration as the number of coauthored papers reported by the respondent (Allison and Stewart 1974, Hesse et al. 1993).[6] Respondents averaged nearly three coauthored publications over the past two years, and 72 percent of all publications were coauthored. Consistent with prior work (Fox 1983, 1992), publication rates were highly skewed. Thirty-five percent of our sample had no coauthored publications in the past two years, and 19 percent account for over half of the total.

Control Variables   In the literature on scientific productivity, several variables consistently predict productivity (Fox 1983, 1992; Zuckerman 1988; Walsh, Kucker, and Maloney 2000). We included these measures in our regression analysis as covariates to control for their influence before testing the relations between e-mail use and collaboration structure, as well as the effects of each on productivity. Table 18A.1 gives the means and standard deviations for these control variables, weighted for field: the number of years since the respondent earned his or her Ph.D. (career age; we also tested years since Ph.D. squared); gender; institution type (Carnegie Research I or not); whether the respondent currently had a funded research project; the number of hours per week spent on research; and organizational citizenship behavior (the extent to which respondents reported putting forth extra effort to benefit their organizations; see Organ 1988, Walsh and Tseng 1998). Also, because of the substantial field-level differences for many of our measures (see Walsh, Kucker, Maloney, and Gabbay 2000), we included dummy variables for field in our regressions as controls (with physics as the excluded category). Table 18A.1 shows that 80 percent of respondents were male, and our sample averaged a career age of almost twenty years. Forty-six percent of respondents had research funding, and respondents spent an average of twenty-six hours a week on their research. Thirty-eight percent of the sample were located at Carnegie Research I institutions. Twenty-nine percent were biologists, 15 percent were mathematicians, 32 percent were sociologists, and 23 percent were physicists.

Results

We begin by discussing the self-reported effects of e-mail on scientists and their work. We then test the relations between e-mail use and the characteristics of the collaboration. Finally, we report regression results predicting the effects of e-mail and collaboration structure on productivity.

Perceived Effects of E-mail

We asked respondents to report their perceptions of the effects of e-mail use on various scientific outcomes.[7] Respondents perceived their use of e-mail as having led to increased contact with scholars and professionals at other institutions (85 percent), information about conferences (78 percent), awareness of scholars and professionals at other institutions (65 percent), productivity (59 percent), awareness of calls for papers (57 percent), and collaboration (57 percent). Smaller increases were indicated for academic prestige (20 percent), graduate student involvement in research (15 percent), and the ability to get grants (9 percent). Apparently graduate education still depends heavily on local contact with advisors. The primary positive effect indicated by the top grouping appears to relate to being in the loop and being connected to a network of scientists and scientific activities, such as conferences and publications (i.e., being included in the "invisible college," Crane 1972).

According to one physicist, "E-mail has greatly increased my interactions and ability to keep up with unpublished information. It has also increased my collaborations." Hesse and associates (1993) noted a similar result in their sample of oceanographers, finding a positive relation between e-mail use and the size of reported professional networks. On the other hand, half our respondents felt that e-mail increased distractions from research (Bishop 1994). As one physicist put it, "E-mail is today's necessity, but also wastes a great deal of time!"

E-mail and Collaborative Work

Using the various indicators of collaboration, we assessed the relationship between e-mail use and the structure of the collaborations. For these analyses, we regressed each collaboration variable separately on (logged) e-mail messages sent per day, adding several controls that are likely to influence collaboration (gender, seniority, institution, and field).[8] Results are reported in table 18.2.

We found two significant effects. First, there was a significant positive relationship between e-mail use and remote collaboration, consistent with our expectations. To get an estimate of the size of this effect, we compare the expected likelihood of being in a remote collaboration for those at the twenty-fifth percentile on e-mail messages sent (two per day) with those at the seventy-fifth percentile (ten e-mails sent per day). We estimate these effects setting the other variables to their means (or modes for qualitative variables). For those sending two messages per day, the expected probability of a remote collaboration is .36. For those sending ten per day, the expected probability is .43, an increase of almost 20 percent.

Table 18.2
Tests of whether scientists' use of e-mail predicts their collaboration structure

Dependent Variable	Log of messages sent	*n*
Number of collaborators	−0.0441 (0.0531)	208
Number of coauthors	0.0481 (0.0531)	258
Structural holes	0.0167 (0.0242)	165
Remote collaboration	0.1899* (0.0964)	285
Institutional heterogeneity	0.0026 (0.0163)	184
Strong ties	0.1478*** (0.0400)	289
Weak ties	0.1586* (0.0706)	289
Field heterogeneity	0.0008 (0.0166)	185

Note: All models control for gender, career age, core institution, and field. Numbers in parentheses indicate standard error.
*** $p < .001$. ** $p < .001$. * $p < .05$.

We also found significant positive effects on both weak and strong ties for messages sent per day. Again, comparing those in the twenty-fifth percentile to those in the seventy-fifth, we calculate a 27 percent increase in strong ties and a 29 percent increase in weak ties. Other factors were not associated with the use of e-mail: collaboration size (number of collaborators and number of coauthors on the most recent publication), structural holes in the collaboration network, institutional heterogeneity (other than captured by the remote collaboration variable), and field heterogeneity (and hence no support for the balkanization hypothesis).

Computer Networks, Collaboration Structures, and Productivity

To test effects of e-mail use and collaboration structure on the productivity of the collaboration, we regressed the number of coauthored publications in 1996 and 1997 against e-mail use and collaboration structure, controlling for other variables expected to affect scientific productivity.[9] Model 1 of table 18.3 reports the effects

Table 18.3
Tests of whether scientists' use of e-mail predict the productivity of their collaborations

	Model 1	Model 2	Model 3	Model 4	Model 5	Model 6	Model 7	Model 8
Log of messages sent per day		0.1192 (0.0764)	0.1354† (0.0788)	0.1464† (0.0784)	−0.0106 (0.1131)	0.0327 (0.0898)	0.0329 (0.0894)	0.0485 (0.1171)
Weak ties			−0.0020 (0.0598)					
Strong ties				0.2347* (0.1076)				0.3225* (0.1639)
Strong ties squared				−0.0415* (0.0184)				−0.0496* (0.0234)
Structural holes					0.6190* (0.2958)			0.5743* (0.2907)
Field heterogeneity						−0.4628 (0.3415)		
Institution heterogeneity							0.5210 (0.3473)	
Years since Ph.D.	0.0512* (0.0218)	0.0516* (0.0219)	0.0490* (0.0221)	0.0471* (0.0219)	0.0382 (0.0322)	0.0497 (0.0312)	0.0510 (0.0312)	0.0312 (0.0323)
Years since Ph.D. squared	−0.0011* (0.0005)	−0.0010* (0.0005)	−0.0010* (0.0005)	−0.0009† (0.0005)	−0.0010 (0.0007)	−0.0014* (0.0007)	−0.0014* (0.0007)	−0.0009 (0.0007)
Research funding	0.2863† (0.1614)	0.2380 (0.1626)	0.2657 (0.1651)	0.2666 (0.1642)	0.0940 (0.2101)	0.2324 (0.2088)	0.1930 (0.2077)	0.2302 (0.2170)

Time spent on research	0.0092† (0.0048)	0.0085† (0.0048)	0.0083† (0.0048)	0.0080† (0.0048)	0.0024 (0.0062)	0.0066 (0.0061)	0.0049 (0.0059)	0.0029 (0.0061)
Number of authors on most recent publication	-0.0162 (0.0146)	-0.0160 (0.0145)	-0.0160 (0.0145)	-0.0114 (0.0148)	-0.0245 (0.0173)	-0.0204 (0.0175)	-0.0223 (0.0176)	-0.0203 (0.0173)
Male	0.3511† (0.1985)	0.3522† (0.1972)	0.3403† (0.2009)	0.3991* (0.1980)	0.3303 (0.2410)	0.5616* (0.2320)	0.5181* (0.2313)	0.3662 (0.2400)
Core institution	0.2091 (0.1631)	0.1753 (0.1614)	0.1467 (0.1666)	0.1370 (0.1652)	0.0031 (0.1986)	0.1703 (0.1991)	0.1460 (0.1945)	-0.0895 (0.2017)
Organizational citizenship	0.0920 (0.0921)	0.0632 (0.0962)	0.0526 (0.0969)	0.0319 (0.0965)	0.0321 (0.1176)	0.0528 (0.1179)	0.0128 (0.1157)	-0.0216 (0.1183)
Biology	-0.1415 (0.2090)	-0.0651 (0.2116)	-0.0767 (0.2121)	-0.0541 (0.2144)	-0.2204 (0.2378)	-0.1754 (0.2442)	-0.2207 (0.2404)	-0.1896 (0.2379)
Mathematics	-0.4573† (0.2569)	-0.4919† (0.2590)	-0.4900† (0.2628)	-0.4521† (0.2668)	-0.9757* (0.4052)	-1.0308** (0.3489)	-0.9538** (0.3479)	-1.0558** (0.4004)
Sociology	-0.5559* (0.2263)	-0.5450* (0.2240)	-0.5420* (0.2266)	-0.5365* (0.2281)	-0.7802** (0.2750)	-0.5987* (0.2694)	-0.6099* (0.2697)	-0.7699** (0.2715)
Chi square	205.88	206.76	207.66	208.02	110.88	123.65	133.27	116.58
Degrees of freedom	194	189	187	186	110	125	125	107
Value/df	1.06	1.09	1.11	1.12	1.01	0.99	1.07	1.09

Note: Numbers in parentheses indicate standard error.
** $p < .01$. * $p < .05$. † $p < .10$.

of the control variables. As expected, time spent on research and research funding were significant predictors of productivity. Years since Ph.D. had a curvilinear (inverted-U) relationship, with productivity increasing as a scientist gained experience and then eventually leveling off and then declining.

Model 2 added the measure of e-mail use, the log of messages sent per day. The effect on collaboration productivity is positive though not statistically significant ($p = .12$). Models 3 to 7 then added, singly, measures of collaboration network structure. Weak ties (model 3) had no direct effect. Strong ties (model 4) had a curvilinear (inverted-U) effect, with the main effect being positive and the quadratic being negative. This implies that a moderate number of strong ties are most productive. (It is unproductive to feel close to nobody in your collaboration or to feel close to all of your collaborators.) Structural holes (model 5) had a positive effect on collaboration productivity, implying that productivity is impaired by overly dense network ties among collaborators (e.g., everyone knows well and feels close to everyone else, and everyone talks to everyone else). Neither field nor institutional heterogeneity (models 6 and 7) had a significant effect on collaboration productivity. Putting the previous significant effects together, model 8 tested the effects of strong ties (and strong ties squared), structural holes, and e-mail use on collaboration productivity. Strong ties had an inverted-U effect and structural holes had a positive effect (each net of the other). For structural holes, a shift from the twenty-fifth percentile (.30) to the seventy-fifth percentile (.71) was associated with a 27 percent increase in collaboration publications ($\exp[.41 * .5743] = 1.27$). For strong ties, the effect was even stronger, with a shift from the twenty-fifth percentile (0) to the seventy-fifth percentile (3) producing nearly a 70 percent increase in collaboration productivity ($\exp[3 * .3225 - 9 * .0496] = 1.68$). Thus, while structural holes are important, as Burt (1992) suggests, strong ties are even more important, as Uzzi (1996, 1999), Hansen (1999), and Murray and Poolman (1982) reported.

The results of model 8 suggest that collaborations with some strong ties and with structural holes provide the best efficiency or mix of access to new information and the ability to transfer that information effectively (Murray and Poolman 1982, Hansen 1999). Too many strong ties may lead to redundancy or isolation from external influence and less effective collaboration. The inflection point (beyond which the costs outweigh the benefits) is 3.25 strong ties in our data, with the net effect turning negative at about 6.5 strong ties. In model 8, e-mail use, after controlling for collaboration structure (strong ties and structural holes), had no independent effect on collaboration productivity. Across all the models, the effects of e-mail use were generally positive (though not always statistically significant, particularly when we included structural holes in the models).

Conclusion

Prior work suggests that the adoption of e-mail and related technologies into a work organization may lead to a restructuring of the social ties in the work group and that this restructuring may produce beneficial outcomes, particularly increased productivity. This study used the case of e-mail use among scientists to see if there is an association between use of e-mail and differences in the network structure of scientific collaboration. Respondents report that e-mail increases their contact with other scholars and their access to information, as well as their productivity and their collaboration. We found that e-mail use had a positive relation with geographic dispersion of collaborations, though not with the size of collaborations. There was also a positive relation with the number of strong ties and weak ties. There was no overall effect on structural holes, perhaps due to the offsetting effects of building more ties among scientists and expanding the number of active researchers (see Walsh and Bayma 1996a). We found no evidence that e-mail led to balkanization (working only with people like yourself) or that it was associated with greater multidisciplinarity of collaborations.

We found that the relation between e-mail use and the productivity of collaborations (multiauthored papers) was generally positive, though it was not significant statistically when we controlled for the social structure of the collaboration. The number of strong ties in the collaboration have an inverted-U relation with productivity, and structural holes had a positive relationship, consistent with earlier work on the effects of social network embeddedness on performance (Uzzi 1996, 1999, Podolny and Baron 1998). Thus, collaborations with a moderately high number of strong ties and many structural holes were most productive. We interpret these results as showing that collaborations were likely to benefit from the members' knowing different pieces of useful information, so that there would be little redundancy in each person's contribution, and from the ability to communicate freely with at least some of their colleagues through their strong ties with them. A pattern of relationships with mixed strong and weak ties was likely to produce the most effective collaborations, according to our results.

This research has several important limitations that must be kept in mind. In particular, because we used cross-sectional survey data, we are unable to determine causality or even be sure of the direction of the relations reported. We do have some evidence suggesting that e-mail is having effects, as our respondents report that e-mail had positive effects on their collaborations and productivity. An additional limitation is that we do not have a direct measure of the whole collaboration's productivity and use the coauthored papers of the respondent as a proxy.

Similarly, for other measures of the characteristics of the group, we have only one informant. This is a larger problem for some measures than for others. For example, there is probably high (though not perfect) agreement on the institution and field of all the members of the research group, and so our informant information is probably fairly accurate (but see Mortensen and Hinds, chapter 11, this volume) on the problems of getting agreement on even the membership of the group. On the other hand, while on average our measure of using e-mail to contact collaborators should converge on the population score (since our measure is a random sample of the collaborations and of the e-mail use in that collaboration), there will be additional error due to sampling, which should depress the effects observed. Measures of tie strength and structural holes should have similar shortcomings.

Finally, while we might want a more expanded measure of computer network use that incorporates such activities as Web browsing, file transfer, remote access to databases, on-line meetings, and so on, our simpler measure of e-mail use is perhaps more applicable across a wide range of disciplines and institutions and is likely to be correlated with more sophisticated uses of computer networks. In addition, it is interesting to see the effects of e-mail because of its wide availability and potential to facilitate communication in a research group. Further study of more sophisticated groupware technologies is needed to see how the characteristics of the technology might affect the relationships observed. Additional work is needed to see how developments in communication technologies affect the relationships we observed and how they affect other types of knowledge worker collaborations.

Finally, as a personal footnote, this collaboration experienced firsthand the effects of both local and remote collaboration when the first author temporarily relocated to Japan. The collaboration continued through frequent e-mail, attachments, and remote log-in into a shared computer account that contained the data and analysis files. While this e-mail did not create the opportunity for a distant collaboration, it was instrumental to the process, as is seen in the number of messages exchanged.

From September 20, 2000, to February 5, 2001, we recorded 150 e-mail messages compared with 35 for the same period one year earlier. (The latter number points to the importance of e-mail, even when face-to-face is available.) But the increased number of messages did not cure all the ills of the remote collaboration. As the biologist noted earlier, the time difference of fifteen hours was problematic in that the turnaround time meant a significant lag in progress. However, given the alternatives (express mail, postal mail, fax), e-mail was much more timely, required far less effort, and was less expensive. Still, progress was impeded by the time difference. This difference became evident on the lucky (but rare) occasions when we were both on-line at the same time. Nearly synchronous communication afforded us the opportunity to deal with issues more expeditiously.

Another positive of e-mail was having a written record of the exchange. This record was particularly helpful when communicating complex ideas, in that each of us could review the documents at length at a later time and did not need to rely on sketchy notes or memory. The junior author, a graduate student, particularly appreciated these notes. However, she also occasionally had to turn to locally available faculty to get answers to questions that she would normally ask the senior author. As we noted earlier, our respondents did not think e-mail was effective in increasing graduate student involvement in research, suggesting that graduate education may rely more on local contact. Remote work mediated by e-mail can be difficult if the tasks are tightly coupled (as the task of training new researchers often is). On the other hand, without e-mail, such collaboration is almost unimaginable.

Appendix

Table 18A.1
Correlation matrix of variables used in the analyses

Variable	Mean	SD	Min	Max	(1)	(2)	(3)	(4)	(5)	(6)	(7)
(1) Number of coauthored publications	2.92	3.60	0.00	21.00	1.00						
(2) % of publications that are coauthored	0.70	0.40	0.00	1.50	0.44***	1.00					
(3) Messages sent/day	6.04	5.60	0.00	35.00	0.09	0.00	1.00				
(4) Log of messages sent	1.29	1.39	−4.64	3.56	0.08	0.05	0.67***	1.00			
(5) Collaborate (yes/no)	0.70	0.46	0.00	1.00	0.20**	0.11†	0.07	0.11†	1.00		
(6) Number of coauthors	4.47	8.85	1.00	81.00	0.02	0.07	0.02	0.03	0.07	1.00	
(7) Number of papers with more than 1 author	0.77	0.42	0.00	1.00	0.29***	0.54***	0.01	0.03	0.23***	0.21***	1.00
(8) Number of collaborators	6.46	16.07	1.00	220.00	0.10	0.03	0.06	0.05	na	0.28***	0.06
(9) Remote collaboration	0.55	0.50	0.00	1.00	0.24***	0.07	0.09	0.10†	0.73***	0.03	0.15*
(10) Strong ties	1.65	1.97	0.00	7.00	0.22***	0.03	0.12*	0.13	0.56***	0.03	0.21***
(11) Weak ties	0.64	1.21	0.00	6.00	0.11†	0.01	0.05	0.07	0.35***	0.03	0.09
(12) Structural holes	0.50	0.34	0.00	1.00	0.16*	0.03	0.10	0.02	na	0.07	0.13
(13) Institutional heterogeneity	0.39	0.28	0.00	0.84	0.14†	0.03	0.07	0.00	0.10	0.10	0.04
(14) Field heterogeneity	0.35	0.28	0.00	0.82	0.01	0.04	0.01	0.01	0.09	0.10	0.05
(15) Male	0.78	0.42	0.00	1.00	0.11†	0.03	0.02	0.06	0.07	0.01	0.04
(16) Years since Ph.D.	19.27	12.97	0.00	65.00	0.14*	0.04	0.11†	0.23***	0.07	0.05	0.07
(17) Research funding	0.46	0.50	0.00	1.00	0.29***	0.13*	0.10†	0.18*	0.40***	0.06	0.23***
(18) Time spent on research/week	25.78	18.64	0.00	100.00	0.24***	0.07	0.08	0.12*	0.32***	0.01	0.23***
(19) Organizational citizenship behavior	0.00	0.89	−1.80	1.20	0.09	0.02	0.28***	0.22***	0.14*	0.03	0.03
(20) Core institution	0.39	0.49	0.00	1.00	0.07	0.02	0.09	0.13*	0.15**	0.02	0.07

*** $p < .001$. ** $p < .01$. * $p < .05$. † $p < .10$.

(8)	(9)	(10)	(11)	(12)	(13)	(14)	(15)	(16)	(17)	(18)	(19)	(20)
1.00												
0.05	1.00											
0.18**	0.48***	1.00										
0.32***	0.34***	0.18**	1.00									
0.04	0.14†	0.00	0.21*	1.00								
0.08	0.76***	0.12†	0.07	0.14†	1.00							
0.08	0.02	0.06	0.15*	0.04	0.03	1.00						
0.06	0.03	0.00	0.12*	0.09	0.07	0.07	1.00					
0.00	0.03	0.12*	0.06	0.17*	0.18*	0.01	0.33***	1.00				
0.15*	0.39***	0.36***	0.27***	0.05	0.13†	0.10	0.02	0.10†	1.00			
0.09	0.28***	0.34***	0.27***	0.19*	0.02	0.12	0.05	0.01	0.38***	1.00		
0.08	0.10	0.17**	0.00	0.09	0.10	0.06	0.11	0.07	0.11†	0.12†	1.00	
0.05	0.14*	0.11†	0.13*	0.10	0.04	0.01	0.09	0.10†	0.21***	0.20***	0.23***	1.00

Notes

We thank Sara Kiesler, Pamela Hinds, Pam Popielarz, Shaul Gabbay, Bonnie Nardi, and members of the NSF Computation and Social Systems Workshop on Distributed Work for their comments on earlier drafts of this chapter. We also thank Stephanie Kucker for her work on the data collection and analysis. This research was supported in part by the UIC Campus Research Board, Office of Social Science Research and Center for Human Resource Management. The first author also thanks the Hitotsubashi University Institute of Innovation Research for support during the writing stage of the project.

1. The membership directories were those of the Federation of American Societies of Experimental Biology (Biochemical and Molecular Biology and Cell Biology divisions), American Mathematical Society, American Physical Society, and American Sociological Association.

2. Our sample is skewed somewhat toward those who use e-mail (74 percent of respondents versus 65 percent of nonrespondents report an e-mail address, χ^2 (1 d.f.) = 8.14, $p < .01$), and those at nonresearch institutions (41 percent of respondents are in Carnegie Research I institutions versus 51 percent of nonrespondents, χ^2 (1 d.f.) = 7.48, $p < .01$). The data also slightly underrepresent women, with females representing 21 percent of our sample, as compared to 27 percent of the employed scientists in 1997 (National Science Board 2000).

3. Hesse and associates (1993) report that self-reported e-mail messages per day were correlated .50 ($p < .0001$) with actual usage data drawn from a three-month period. A parallel analysis using likelihood of using e-mail to contact collaborators produced qualitatively similar results.

4. We recoded zero to 0.01 before taking the log.

5. For those who do not collaborate, REMOTE is coded as missing.

6. Coauthored papers were highly correlated with total papers published ($r = .82$, $p < .0001$; $r = .71$ for the logged values, $p < .0001$) and slightly negatively correlated with solo authored papers ($r = -.04$, n.s.; $-.24$ for the logged values, $p < .0001$). Time spent on collaboration may limit time available for solo research, or possibly, researchers prefer either solo or collaborative research. Allison and Stewart (1974) report a correlation of .94 between self-reported papers and productivity based on data from *Chemical Abstracts*. Cole and Cole (1967) report that papers published (from archival sources) and their measure of citations are correlated .72. We compared our self-report measure of productivity with publications listed in the Web of Science (the on-line version of the Science Citation Index and the Social Science Citation Index). The Web of Science improves over the print version of the citation indexes because it tracks all the authors on a paper, not just the first author. We selected a random subsample of 81 of our respondents, stratified by field. For this subsample, we coded publications from 1996 and 1997 and citations during 1998 and 1999 to publications from 1996 and 1997 in the Web of Science. The distribution is highly skewed. Citations and publications from the Web of Science are correlated .77 ($p < .0001$); the logged values (to correct for skewness) are correlated .85 ($p < .0001$). Publications from the Web of Science and self-reported papers are correlated .75 ($p < .0001$); the logged values are correlated .68 ($p < .0001$). The correlation between citations and self-report publications is .64 ($p < .0001$), .64 for the logged values ($p < .0001$).

7. The item was: "As a result of your use of email, how have the following changed for you?" Answer categories were a five-point scale with -2 = large decrease, 0 = no change, and $+2$ = large increase.

8. We used ordinary least squares, logistic, Poisson, or negative binomial regression models as appropriate.

9. Because our dependent variable, number of coauthored publications, is a count (discrete, nonnegative) variable rather than a normal variable, OLS regression will produce biased results. We used negative binomial models to adjust for overdispersion in the data (Barron 1992; Guo 1996).

References

Ahuja, G. (2000). Collaboration networks, structural holes and innovation. *Administrative Science Quarterly, 45,* 425–455.

Allen, T. J. (1977). *Managing the flow of technology.* Cambridge, MA: MIT Press.

Allison, P., and Stewart, J. (1974). Productivity differences among scientists: Evidence for accumulative advantage. *American Sociological Review, 39,* 596–606.

Barron, D. N. (1992). The analysis of count data. *Sociological Methodology, 22,* 179–220.

Baym, N. K. (1997). Interpreting soap operas and creating community. In S. Kiesler (ed.), *Culture of the Internet* (103–120). Mahwah, NJ: Erlbaum.

Bishop, A. P. (1994). The role of computer networks in aerospace engineering. *Library Trends, 42,* 694–729.

Blau, P. (1977). *Inequality and heterogeneity.* New York: Free Press.

Bridges, W. P., and Villemez, W. J. (1986). Informal hiring and income in the labor market. *American Sociological Review, 51,* 574–582.

Bruce, H. (1994). Internet services and academic work. *Internet Research, 4,* 24–34.

Bullen, C., and Bennett, J. (1991). Groupware in practice. In C. Dunlop and R. Kling (eds.), *Computerization and controversy* (357–387). Boston: Academic Press.

Burt, R. S. (1992). *Structural holes.* Cambridge, MA: Harvard University Press.

Carley, K., and Wendt, K. (1990). Electronic mail and scientific communication. *Knowledge: Creation, Diffusion, Utilization, 12,* 406–440.

Cohen, J. (1996). Computer mediated communication and publication productivity among faculty. *Internet Research, 6,* 41–63.

Cole, S., and Cole, J. R. (1967). Scientific output and recognition. *American Sociological Review, 32,* 377–390.

Coleman, J. (1990). *Foundations of social theory.* Cambridge, MA: Harvard University Press.

Crane, D. (1972). *Invisible colleges.* Chicago: Chicago University Press.

Feldman, M. S. (1987). Electronic mail and weak ties in organizations. *Office Technology, People, 3,* 83–101.

Finholt, T. A. (in press). Collaboratories. In *Annual Review of Information Science and Technology.*

Finholt, T., and Olson G. (1997). From laboratories to collaboratories. *Psychological Science,* 8, 28–36.

Finholt, T. A., and Sproull, L. (1990). Electronic groups at work. *Organizational Science, 1,* 41–64.

Fox, M. F. (1983). Publication productivity among scientists. *Social Studies of Science, 1,* 285–305.

Fox, M. F. (1992). Research productivity and the environmental context. In T. G. Whiston and R. L. Geiger (eds.), *Research and higher education* (103–111). Buckingham, U.K.: SRHE and Open University Press.

Granovetter, M. (1973). The strength of weak ties. *American Journal of Sociology, 78,* 1360–1380.

Granovetter, M. (1985). Economic action and social structure. *American Journal of Sociology, 91,* 481–510.

Guo, G. (1996). Negative multinomial regression models for clustered event counts. *Sociological Methodology, 26,* 113–132.

Hansen, M. T. (1999). The search-transfer problem. *Administrative Science Quarterly, 44,* 82–111.

Harmon, A. (1999, February 21). The rebel code. *New York Times.*

Hesse, B. W., Sproull, L. S., Kiesler, S., and Walsh, J. P. (1993). Returns to science. *Communications of the ACM, 36,* 90–101.

Ibarra, H. (1998). *Network assessment exercise: MBA version.* Harvard Business School Press Reprint Number 9-497-002.

Kraut, R. E., Egido, C., and Galegher, J. (1990). Patterns of contact and communication in scientific research collaboration. In J. Galegher, R. E. Kraut, and C. Egido (eds.), *Intellectual teamwork* (149–171). Hillsdale, NJ: Erlbaum.

Lederberg, J., and Uncapher, K. (1989). *Towards a national collaboratory.* Washington, DC: National Science Foundation, Directorate for Computer and Information Science.

Long, J., and Fox, M. (1995). Scientific careers. *Annual Review of Sociology, 21,* 45–71.

Marsden, P. V. (1987). Core discussion networks among Americans. *American Sociological Review, 52,* 122–131.

McPherson, M., Popielarz, P., and Drobnic, S. (1992). Social networks and organizational dynamics. *American Sociological Review, 57,* 153–170.

Mortensen, M., and Hinds, P. (2002). Fuzzy boundaries: Membership dissensus in distributed and collocated teams. In P. Hinds and S. Kiesler (eds.), *Distributed work* (283–308). Cambridge, MA: MIT Press.

Moon, J. Y., and Sproull, L. (2002). Essence of distributed work: The case of the Linux kernel. In P. Hinds and S. Kiesler (eds.), *Distributed work* (381–404). Cambridge, MA: MIT Press.

Murray, S. O., and Poolman, R. C. (1982). Strong ties and scientific literature. *Social Networks, 4*, 225–232.

National Science Board. (1993). *Science and engineering indicators—1993*. Washington, DC: Government Printing Office.

National Science Board. (1998). *Science and engineering indicators—1998*. Washington, DC: Government Printing Office.

National Science Board. (2000). *Science and engineering indicators—2000*. Available at: www.nsf.gov.

Organ, D. W. (1988). *Organizational citizenship behavior*. Lexington, MA: Lexington Books.

Orlikowski, W. J., and Yates, J. (1994). Genre repertoire. *Administrative Science Quarterly, 39*, 541–574.

Podolny, J. M., and Baron, J. N. (1997). Resources and relationships: Social networks in the workplace. *American Sociological Review, 62*, 673–693.

Popielarz, P. A. (1999). (In)voluntary association—A multilevel analysis of gender segregation in voluntary organizations. *Gender and Society, 13*, 234–250.

Rice, R. E. (1994). Network analysis and computer-mediated communication systems. In S. Wasserman and J. Galaskiewicz (eds.), *Advances in social network analysis* (167–203). Thousand Oaks, CA: Sage.

Rothschild-Whitt, J. (1979). The collectivist organization. *American Sociological Review, 44*, 509–527.

Sirianni, C. (1994). Learning pluralism. In F. Fischer and C. Sirianni (eds.), *Organization and bureaucracy*. Philadelphia: Temple University Press.

Sparrowe, R. T., and Popielarz, P. (2000). *Weak ties and structural holes: The effects of network structure on careers*. Unpublished manuscript, University of Illinois at Chicago.

Sproull, L., and Kiesler, S. (1991). *Connections*. Cambridge, MA: MIT Press.

Sudweeks, F., and Rafaeli, S. (1996). How do you get a hundred strangers to agree? In T. M. Harrison and T. Stephen (eds.), *Computer networking and scholarly communication in the twenty-first-century university* (115–136). Albany: State University of New York Press.

Uzzi, B. (1996). The sources and consequences of embeddedness for the economic performance of organizations. *American Sociological Review, 61*, 674–698.

Uzzi, B. (1999). Embeddedness in the making of financial capital: How social relations and networks benefit firms seeking financing. *American Sociological Review, 64*, 481–505.

Van Alstyne, M., and Brynjolfsson, E. (1996). Could the Internet balkanize science? *Science, 274*, 1479–1480.

Walsh, J. P., and Bayma, T. (1996a). The virtual college. *Information Society, 12*, 343–363.

Walsh, J. P., and Bayma, T. (1996b). Computer networks and scientific work. *Social Studies of Science, 26*, 661–703.

Walsh, J. P., Kucker, S., and Maloney, N. G. (2000). *Scientific communication, new technology and inequality*. Unpublished manuscript, University of Illinois at Chicago.

Walsh, J. P., Kucker, S., Maloney, N., and Gabbay, S. (2000). Connecting minds: CMC and scientific work. *Journal of the American Society for Information Science, 51*, 1295–1305.

Walsh, J. P., and Tseng S. F. (1998). Active effort at work. *Work and Occupations, 25*, 74–96.

Watts, D. J. (1999). Networks, dynamics, and the small-world phenomenon. *American Journal of Sociology, 105*, 493–527.

Wellman, B., Salaff, J., Dimitrova, D., Garton, L., Gulia, M., and Haythornthwaite, C. (1996). Computer networks as social networks. *Annual Review of Sociology, 22*, 213–238.

Xie, Y., and Shauman, K. (1998). Sex differences in research productivity: New evidence about an old puzzle. *American Sociological Review, 63*, 847–870.

Zuckerman, H. (1988). The sociology of science. In N. Smelser (ed.), *Handbook of sociology*. Newbury Park, CA: Sage.

Contributors

David J. Armstrong (David.Armstrong@personneldecisions.com) is a senior consultant in organizational solutions with Personnel Decisions International. Specializing in organizational collaboration, executive teamwork, virtual organizations, and strategic global account teams, he leads projects in human capital strategy and metrics, customer relationship management, and strategic account management.

Susan E. Brennan (susan.brennan@sunysb.edu) is an associate professor of psychology, cognitive area, at the State University of New York at Stony Brook. Her research interests include spontaneous speech, referring and repair in conversation, coordination of individuals' mental states and perspectives in conversation, multimedia communication, and natural language and speech interfaces.

Paul Cole (pcole@highwired-inc.com) is vice president of research and product strategy at HighWired.com, a company providing e-learning and communication technology to high schools. His research focuses on the adoption and impact of educational and collaborative technology.

Lisa Covi (covi@scils.rutgers.edu) is an assistant professor at the School of Communication, Information and Library Studies at Rutgers University. She earned her Ph.D. in information and computer science from the University of California–Irvine and worked for two years on corporate collaboration as a postdoctoral research fellow at the Collaboratory for Research on Electronic Work at the University of Michigan's School of Information.

Catherine Durnell Cramton (CatherineCramton@som.gmu.edu) is an associate professor in the School of Management at George Mason University. Her research explores contemporary issues of collaboration and leadership, including distributed work, interorganizational collaboration, project team leadership, and the impact of technology on collaboration.

Kevin Crowley (crowleyk@pitt.edu) is an assistant professor and research scientist at the Learning Research and Development Center at the University of Pittsburgh. His research focuses on the development and practice of scientific thinking in everyday, classroom, and professional settings.

Jonathon N. Cummings (jnc@cs.cmu.edu) is a postdoctoral fellow in the Human Computer Interaction Institute at Carnegie Mellon University. He studies communication processes and the use of technology among individuals, groups, and organizations. In his dissertation, he examined knowledge sharing within work groups, focusing on the role that external social networks play in distributed, cross-functional teams.

Thomas A. Finholt (finholt@umich.edu) is the director of the Collaboratory for Research on Electronic Work and an assistant research scientist at the University of Michigan's School of Information. His current research focuses on the design and impact of collaboratories, or virtual settings for scientific and engineering work.

Robert L. Frost (rfrost@umich.edu) is a visiting associate professor in the School of Information at the University of Michigan. Trained as a modern French social historian, his work now focuses on the invention of users and the cultural meaning of artifacts in the process of innovation.

Janet Fulk (fulk@usc.edu) is a professor of communications in the Annenberg School for Communication and a professor of management and organization in the Marshall School of Business, University of Southern California. Her interests include knowledge management, coevolution of technology and social systems, strategic uses of information technology, network organizational forms, and strategic alliances.

Susan Fussell (susan.fussell@cmu.edu) is a system scientist in the Human Computer Interaction Institute, Carnegie Mellon University. She conducts research on face-to-face and computer-mediated communication, electronic groups, and shared mental models in work teams.

Terri L. Griffith (tgriffit@scu.edu) is a professor of management at Santa Clara University. Her research focuses on technology in organizations, especially virtual teams. She recently coedited the book, *Research on Managing Groups and Teams: Technology*.

Pamela J. Hinds (phinds@stanford.edu) is an assistant professor in management science and engineering at Stanford University. Her research investigates the effects of technology on group dynamics and on the way work is coordinated. She also studies information sharing across distance, disciplinary boundaries, and levels of expertise.

Andrea B. Hollingshead (hollings@uiuc.edu) is an associate professor of psychology and speech communication at the University of Illinois at Urbana-Champaign. Her research investigates transactive memory, knowledge management, and information processing in groups and organizations. She also studies the impacts of technology and the Internet on group collaboration.

Sara Kiesler (kiesler@cs.cmu.edu) is a professor of human computer interaction in the School of Computer Science, Carnegie Mellon University. She conducts research on the social and organizational effects of technological change, electronic groups and communication, and interaction with agents, robots, and other computer-based objects.

John Leslie King (jlking@umich.edu) is dean and a professor in the School of Information at the University of Michigan. His research concerns the coevolution of institutional and technological artifacts. He was professor of information and computer science and management at the University of California, Irvine, from 1980 to 1999.

Robert Kraut (robert.kraut@cmu.edu) is Herbert Simon Professor of Human Computer Interaction in the School of Computer Science, Carnegie Mellon University. His research is on the design of technology for small group work and the impact of computing for individuals and organization.

Nancy G. Maloney (nmalon1@uic.edu) is working on her Ph.D. in sociology at the University of Illinois at Chicago. Her primary research interest is social organization, with a focus on social networks. Other interests include technology and the sociology of health and medicine.

Elizabeth Mannix (eam33@cornell.edu) is an associate professor of organizational behavior at the Johnson Graduate School of Management, Cornell University. Her research activities include negotiation, teams, and power and influence. She is coeditor of the book series Research on Managing Groups and Teams.

Gloria Mark (gmark@ics.uci.edu) is an assistant professor in information and computer Science at the University of California, Irvine. Her research area is computer-supported collaborative work, and she is interested in evaluation and requirements analysis of collaborative technologies. Her primary focus is on virtual collocation.

Peter Monge (Monge@usc.edu) is a professor communication at the Annenberg School for Communication and professor of management and organizations (by courtesy) in the Marshall School of Business, University of Southern California. His research focuses on organizational communication networks, collaborative information systems, globalization and communication processes, and research methods.

Jae Yun Moon (jmoon@stern.nyu.edu) is a doctoral candidate at the Stern School of Business, New York University. Her research interests include electronic communities and knowledge management, and consumer behavior in electronic commerce.

Mark Mortensen (mmorten@stanford.edu) is a doctoral candidate in the department of management science and engineering at Stanford University. His research focuses on the impact of technology use in organizations, especially the effects of technology and technological mediation on team dynamics.

Bonnie A. Nardi (bonnie_nardi@agilent.com) is an anthropologist in the Bioscience Information Solutions Department at Agilent Laboratories. She studies the work practices of molecular biologists. She is the author of *A Small Matter of Programming: Perspectives on End User Computing, Context and Consciousness: Activity Theory and Human Computer Interaction*, and *Information Ecologies: Using Technology with Heart* (with Vicki O'Day).

Margaret A. Neale (Neale_Margaret@gsb.stanford.edu) is the John G. McCoy–Banc One Corporation Professor of Organizations and Dispute Resolution at Stanford University. Her research interests include bargaining and negotiation, distributed work groups, and team composition, learning, and performance. She is coauthor of three books and coeditor of a research series, Research on Managing in Groups and Teams.

Takeshi Okada (j46006a@nucc.cc.nagoya-u.ac.jp) is an associate professor of psychology at Nagoya University, Japan. He is a cognitive psychologist who studies scientific discovery and artistic creation.

Michael O'Leary (michael.oleary@sloan.mit.edu) is a doctoral candidate at MIT's Sloan School of Management. His research focuses on geographically dispersed work, especially in a team context. He is interested in the intersection of team performance, working relationships, and the social and behavioral aspects of information technology use. He previously worked as a management consultant and public policy analyst.

Gary M. Olson (gmo@umich.edu) is the Paul M. Fitts Professor of Human-Computer Interaction and associate dean for research at the School of Information at the University of Michigan, as well as a professor of psychology. He has over 100 publications in computer-supported cooperative work, human-computer interaction, and psychology. He is active in the CHI conferences and serves on a number of editorial boards, including HCI.

Judith S. Olson (jsolson@umich.edu) is the Richard W. Pew Professor of Human-Computer Interaction in the School of Information, a professor of computer and information systems in the Business School, and a professor of psychology at the University of Michigan. She has over seventy publications, spanning computer-supported cooperative work, human-computer interaction, and psychology. She has been active in the CHI conferences and serves on a number of editorial boards, including HCI.

Wanda J. Orlikowski (wanda@mit.edu) is the Eaton-Peabody Chair of Communication Sciences and an associate professor of information technologies and organization studies at the MIT Sloan School of Management. She is exploring the organizational and technological aspects of working virtually. She serves as a senior editor for *Organization Science*.

Erika Bill Peter (Erika.Bill@personneldecisions.com) is an associate consultant with Personnel Decisions International. She holds a degree in Applied Work and Organizational Psychology from HAP Zurich in Switzerland. Her interests are focused on international team dynamics, cultural diversity, on-line collaboration, and learning.

Christian Schunn (schunn@pitt.edu) is an assistant professor of psychology at the University of Pittsburgh Learning Research and Development Center. He is a cognitive scientist who studies scientific discovery at the individual and group levels. He held a previous faculty appointment at George Mason University.

Jane Siegel (j.siegel@cs.cmu.edu) is senior systems scientist in the Human Computer Interaction Institute at Carnegie Mellon University. Her interests include evaluation methods and behavioral aspects of computer-supported cooperative work. She is conducting field evaluations of collaborative on-site wearable computer systems and studying the design of technologies to support remote collaboration.

Lee Sproull (lsproull@stern.nyu.edu) is the Leonard N. Stern School Professor of Business at the Stern School of Business, New York University. She has held previous faculty appointments at Boston University and Carnegie Mellon University. Her current research focuses on the dynamics and consequences of electronic groups and communities.

Stephanie Teasley (steasley@umich.edu) is an assistant research Scientist at the Collaboratory for Research on Electronic Work at the University of Michigan's School of Information. Her work has focused recently on collaboration in corporate work groups and scientific communities. She serves as the collaboratory director for the Great Lakes Center for AIDS Research.

John P. Walsh (jwalsh@uic.edu) is an associate professor of sociology at the University of Illinois at Chicago. His current research is on industrial R&D in the United States and Japan, including the impact of patents and patent policy on innovation and the relations between universities and industrial research.

Joseph B. Walther (walthj@rpi.edu) is an associate professor with appointments in communication, social psychology, and information technology at Rensselaer Polytechnic Institute. His research focuses on theoretical and applied issues relating to relational dynamics of computer-mediated communication in professional, social, personal, and educational settings.

Suzanne Weisband (weisband@bpa.arizona.edu) is an associate professor of management information systems at the University of Arizona. Her research investigates multidisciplinary collaboration and the social processes of electronic groups.

Steve Whittaker (stevew@research.att.com) is senior research scientist at ATT Labs–Research. His interests include the theory, design, and use of systems to support computer-mediated communication (CMC), including video, shared workspaces, and lightweight communications applications. His more recent work has addressed e-mail, Lotus Notes, speech-as-data and voice mail, with a view to generating general principles for CMC.

JoAnne Yates (jyates@mit.edu) is Sloan Distinguished Professor of Management at MIT Sloan School of Management. She studies change over time in historical and contemporary communication and information systems in organizations. She is the author of *Control Through Communication* and coeditor of *IT and Organizational Transformation: History, Rhetoric, and Practice.*

Index